The Ethnographic Character of Romans

The Ethnographic Character of Romans

The Dichotomies of Law-Faith and Jew-Gentile in Light
of Greco-Roman and Hellenistic Jewish Ethnography

Susann M. Liubinskas

☙PICKWICK *Publications* • Eugene, Oregon

THE ETHNOGRAPHIC CHARACTER OF ROMANS
The Dichotomies of Law-Faith and Jew-Gentile in Light of Greco-Roman and Hellenistic Jewish Ethnography

Copyright © 2019 Susann M. Liubinskas. All rights reserved. Except for brief quotations in critical publications or reviews, no part of this book may be reproduced in any manner without prior written permission from the publisher. Write: Permissions, Wipf and Stock Publishers, 199 W. 8th Ave., Suite 3, Eugene, OR 97401.

Pickwick Publications
An Imprint of Wipf and Stock Publishers
199 W. 8th Ave., Suite 3
Eugene, OR 97401

www.wipfandstock.com

PAPERBACK ISBN: 978-1-5326-5212-7
HARDCOVER ISBN: 978-1-5326-5213-4
EBOOK ISBN: 978-1-5326-5214-1

Cataloguing-in-Publication data:

Names: Liubinskas, Susann M., author.

Title: The ethnographic character of Romans : the dichotomies of law-faith and Jew-Gentile in light of Greco-Roman and Hellenistic Jewish ethnography / by Susann M. Liubinskas.

Description: Eugene, OR: Pickwick Publications, 2019 | Includes bibliographical references.

Identifiers: ISBN 978-1-5326-5212-7 (paperback) | ISBN 978-1-5326-5213-4 (hardcover) | ISBN 978-1-5326-5214-1 (ebook)

Subjects: LCSH: Ethnology in the Bible. | Bible. Romans—Criticism, interpretation, etc.

Classification: LCC BS2665.52 L38 2019 (print) | LCC BS2665.52 (ebook)

Manufactured in the U.S.A.   01/31/19

Contents

Acknowledgments | viii

Abbreviations | ix

CHAPTER ONE
Introduction | 1

1.1 Purpose of This Study | 2
1.2 Previous Studies: The Three Dichotomies and the Genre of Romans | 3
1.3 Lacunae in the Study of the Three Dichotomies in Romans | 18
1.4 Bridging the Gaps: The Ethnographic Characteristics of Romans | 21
1.5 Outline of the Argument | 23
1.6 Assumptions and Terminology | 25

CHAPTER TWO
**Greco-Roman Ethnography & Ethnic Discourse:
The Creation and Legitimization of Social Identity** | 28

2.1 The New Age of Roman Rule: The Greco-Roman *Historie Humaine* and Indigenous Ethnographic Responses | 30
2.2 Ethnic Discourse: Constructing Ethnic-Racial Identity | 49
2.3 Ethnic Identity and Social Identity Theory | 61
2.4 Conclusion | 67

CONTENTS

CHAPTER THREE

Paul as Ethnographer: Writing with an Ethnographic Purpose as a Reliable Interpreter of Tradition | 69

3.1 Redefining the Occasion of Romans | 70
3.2 Set Apart for the Gospel: Establishing the Credentials of an Ethnographer | 96
3.3 Conclusion | 99

CHAPTER FOUR

The Historical Legitimacy of the Christ Movement (Part I): Law and Faith: Establishing Points of Continuity and Discontinuity between God's People in the Past and the Present (Rom 1–5) | 101

4.1 Israel's Past Reinterpreted in Light of the Unfolding Eschatological Present: To the Jew First and also the Greek (Rom 1–3) | 102
4.2 Israel's Etiological Accounts Reinterpreted in Light of the Unfolding Eschatological Present: Abraham and Christ, Divinely Instituted Founding Figures (Rom 4–5) | 134
4.3 Conclusion | 151

CHAPTER FIVE

The Historical Legitimacy of the Christ Movement (Part II): Establishing a Positive Identity (Rom 6–8 and 9–11): Children of God Apart from the Law | 153

5.1 Constructing a Favorable In-group Bias: Living Righteously Apart from the Law (Rom 6–8) | 154
5.2 Identity and Out-group Comparison: The Place of Israel in the Eschatological Present (Rom 9–11) | 187
5.3 Conclusion | 216

CHAPTER SIX

The Historical Legitimacy of the Christ Movement (Part III): The Manner of Life of the New People of God (Rom 12:1—13:14 and 14:1—15:6): Spirit-Wrought Allocentric Identity and a Transformed Ethos | 219

6.1 Constructing an Allocentric Identity: Renewed Mind, Living Sacrifice, and a Transformed View of Self in Relation to the Other (Rom 12:1—13:14) | 222

6.2 Intracommunal Allocentric Identity in Action: Mutual Acceptance, Nested Ethnic Identities, and Communal Worship Practices (Rom 14:1—15:13) | 242

6.3 Conclusion | 263

CHAPTER SEVEN

Conclusion | 268

7.1 A Summary of Reading the Dichotomies of Law-Faith and Jew-Gentile in Light of Ancient Greco-Roman and Hellenistic Jewish Ethnography and Social Identity Theory | 270

7.2 Implications for Further Study | 294

7.3 Suggestions for Contemporary Application | 296

7.4 Conclusion | 299

Bibliography | 301

Acknowledgments

This monograph is a slightly revised version of my dissertation completed at Asbury Theological Seminary under the supervision of Ben Witherington III, who has been a constant source of inspiration and encouragement. I am grateful not only for his expertise as a scholar and mentor, but also for his friendship. I have benefitted greatly from his example of how a professor can demand academic excellence without ever losing sight of the fact that, at their heart, teaching and mentoring are an art.

I would also like to thank the other members of my committee for their assistance in bringing this project to its completion. I am grateful to Dr. Craig S. Keener for his willingness both to read and comment on my work. I am also grateful to my examiner, Dr. Aaron Kuecker, not only for his scholarship on Spirit-wrought, allocentric identity, upon which this project depends, but also for his careful and perceptive comments and questions that helped me to clarify and strengthen my own thoughts and arguments.

Special thanks go to my OT colleague and dear friend, Deb Endean. I treasure our long, candid discussions about anything and everything. I would also like to thank Pickwick Publications for the opportunity to publish my work.

My deepest thanks go to my family. I am grateful for my sons, Nick and Alex, who keep me smiling. I am most grateful for the steadfast support of my husband, Tauras, whose love, encouragement, and humor hearten me. My mutual partner in life, he took on the lion's share of family responsibilities, freely sacrificing his time and energy, so that I could pursue my research. He is a man who understands the true meaning of loving his wife, as Christ loved the church. I dedicate this work to him.

Abbreviations

DPL   *Dictionary of Paul and His Letters.* Edited by Gerald F. Hawthorne and Ralph P. Martin. Downers Grove, IL: InterVarsity, 1993.

LCL   Loeb Classical Library

TDNT   *Theological Dictionary of the New Testament.* 10 vols. Edited by Gerhard Kittel and Gerhard Friedrich. Translated by Geoffrey W. Bromiley. Grand Rapids: Eerdmans, 1964–1976.

WUNT   Wissenschaftliche Untersuchungen zum Neuen Testament

CHAPTER ONE

Introduction

When it comes to Paul's letter to the Romans, it is fair to say that three interrelated dichotomies have by and large defined the course of scholarship on this epistle. First, there is the question of how to resolve the tension created by the apostle's juxtaposition of the law and faith.[1] This lack of resolution has, in turn, spawned a centuries-long debate over the respective roles of grace and works in salvation and the relationship between Judaism and Christianity. Scholarly consensus has proven to be elusive with respect to all three. This is no less true today, despite the fact that many of the assumptions underlying the traditional resolution of these polarities have been successfully challenged in recent decades.[2]

These developments have had a profound effect on the interpretation of perhaps the most challenging and intriguing of the Pauline Letters. Most, if not all, scholars, irrespective of where they stand with regard to the three dichotomies and the many other issues surrounding the interpretation of this epistle, agree that, among other things, Paul is intent on addressing the polarization among members of the Christ movement in Rome resulting from varying degrees of attachment to Judaism.[3] In other words, there is the general acknowledgment that the issue of the law and its relationship to faith is itself intertwined with and embedded within the larger matter of the relationship between first-century Judaism and emerging Christianity as a sociohistorical phenomenon. However, despite the recognition that Paul's theologizing occurs within a particular and concrete social matrix, the issue of how the key motifs, represented in the three dichotomies, are related and the nature of the role that each plays in Paul's arguments, remain hotly contested issues.

---

1. Paul uses the term νόμος with several different nuances. I will use the designation "(the) law" and, unless there is a specific context under discussion that clearly indicates otherwise, I will take it as referring to the Mosaic law.

2. For instance, the notion that Romans is a compendium of Paul's theology has for the most part given way to the recognition that it is an ad hoc document written to a specific audience facing specific issues and problems. Simultaneously, there has been a significant shift in the portrayal of Paul from dogmatic, Christian theologian, to pastoral, Jewish apostle actively engaged in the praxis of mission.

3. Donfried, "Introduction 1991," xlvix–lxxii.

1.1 Purpose of This Study

In this study, I maintain that the controversy surrounding the three dichotomies and their relationship to the issue of gentile inclusion is largely due to a failure to adequately define the purpose and genre of Romans. This has led to various bifurcations between its theological and sociological elements, such that the law-faith dichotomy, which underlies the other two, is misconstrued as referring to two incompatible paths of salvation. In other words, when the law-faith dichotomy is considered within the larger context of Paul's ethnic discourse, its primary function as the means by which Paul draws lines of continuity and discontinuity between the Christ movement and its Jewish roots comes to light. Since the purpose and genre of Romans and the meaning of the three dichotomies are linked, I will demonstrate three interrelated points.

First, I will show that Paul's main, although not sole, purpose in writing is not to heal ethnic divisions among its members, but rather to encourage the Christian community in Rome to continue in faithful obedience to the gospel in the face of general, social persecution by the larger nonbelieving community within which they live and with which they necessarily have contact. The call to unity/reconciliation reflects this guiding purpose and, as such, is secondary. Once the purpose of Romans is redefined as such, its primary function as an ethnographic apology directed to beleaguered insiders becomes apparent.

Thus, in the second place, I will argue that this epistle evidences many of the characteristics of Greco-Roman and Jewish ethnography, particularly as this genre was employed for the apologetic purpose of legitimizing a marginalized people group in order to create a positive social identity. In other words, I will demonstrate that Paul, like his contemporaries, harnesses the apologetic power of this genre in order to fortify the members of his group (in this case, members of the Christ movement) in their effort to maintain their distinctiveness vis-à-vis the larger sociocultural matrix within which they are embedded, and which is exerting pressure upon them to conform to its cultural, ethical, and social norms. Like his contemporaries, the apostle argues for the historical legitimacy of his group and the legitimacy of its laws, customs, and way of life, so as to create a favorable self-evaluation, thereby increasing the probability of continued group affiliation among its members.

Third, reading Romans as ancient ethnography not only brings into focus the organic links between the various parts of the letter, but also brings to light the coherence of its theological and sociological aspects. As a consequence, the meaning of and relationship between the three dichotomies is clarified. As I will show, Paul utilizes the law-faith dichotomy, *not* to describe two paths of salvation, but to redefine the chosen people of God, in the new age, as ethnically inclusive. In this way, working within the framework of a present, unfolding eschatological reality, the apostle maintains the new movement's rootedness in its venerable, Jewish past, thus proving its historical legitimacy; the primacy of Israel and the Jewish people, thus clarifying

INTRODUCTION

the relationship between Judaism and the new movement; and the presence of ethnic diversity within a distinctive people group unified by an allocentric, Spirit-wrought identity, thus establishing both the legitimacy of the movement's customs and way of life and the embodied, ethnic character of this life.[4]

1.2 Previous Studies: The Three Dichotomies and the Genre of Romans

1.2.1 The Law-Faith Dichotomy & Its Siblings

1.2.1.1 *Traditional View*

By and large, contemporary scholars writing in the traditional vein concur that the notion that the Judaism of Paul's time was unequivocally a legalistic religion of works-righteousness can no longer be maintained on historical grounds. However, although writers in the traditional vein have reframed their questions to reflect this shift in scholarship, they nevertheless continue to maintain that salvation is by grace alone, exclusive of any and all works of the law, and that at least some strands of first-century Judaism were legalistic, with Paul reacting against these in his letter to the Romans.[5] Accordingly, Paul's theology is interpreted as mainly antithetical to Judaism.

This interpretation, however, results in an enigmatic Paul radically severed from his Jewish roots, since neither the Jewishness of Paul's thought nor the points of continuity between the new movement and Judaism are explored in any meaningful way.[6] There is little textual evidence that indicates that Paul challenges Judaism per

---

4. I am borrowing the term "allocentric" from Aaron Kuecker, who defines this type of identity as "characterized by or denoting interest centered in persons other than oneself." Moreover, "allocentric" describes an identity that can express in-group love and out-group love simultaneously. According to Kuecker, such an identity is possible only by virtue of the Spirit's work within the believing community. This new identity is created by means of "dual identity transformation," whereby incoming members receive a new, Spirit-created social identity, while current members are called upon to "re-conceptualize their own social identity to reflect the reconfigured constitution of their in-group." This new social identity does not negate ethnic identity, since only ethnocentrism is prohibited (Kuecker, *Spirit and the 'Other'*, 18n83, 19).

5. For example, D. A. Carson writes, "Despite all the diversity which enriches Intertestamental Judaism, . . . With the partial exception of the Dead Sea Scrolls, legalism is on the rise, and with it merit theology" (Carson, *Divine Sovereignty & Human Responsibility*, 120). Similarly, Timo Laato concludes that Paul is criticizing Judaism for the self-righteous boasting that arises from the erroneous belief that the righteous Jew cooperated in salvation by doing the works of the law (Laato, *Paul and Judaism*, 209–10, 213). Likewise, Timo Eskola concludes that first-century Judaism manifests a synergistic soteriology, resulting in synergistic nomism (Eskola, *Theodicy and Predestination*, 2, 307–10, 312).

6. For example, Eskola's effort to place Paul in some continuity with his Jewish heritage falters due to the fact that it is contradictory. He states that the apostle's theology is closely connected with both the OT and first-century Jewish theology. However, he then argues that Paul teaches a radical anthropology, theology of predestination, and interpretation of the law and works of the law. One wonders what connection remains between Paul and his Jewish roots other than the fact that both he and Judaism address the question of theodicy, albeit in radically different ways (Eskola, *Theodicy and Predestination*, 308–9).

se, and/or that he targets a specific Jewish teaching(s). Evidence from the apostle's extant letters indicates that his invectives against Jews were specifically directed either toward judaizers who maintained that gentile Christians must become Jews in order to belong to the Christ community (e.g., Gal 6:12–16) or at nonbelieving Jews who were persecuting the community (e.g., 1 Thess 2:14–16). That is, Paul's condemnation of fellow Jews is specifically directed against individuals who actively opposed or hindered his mission to the gentiles,[7] whether this opposition came from inside or outside of the believing community.[8] Similarly, there is little evidence indicating that Paul thought that certain strands of Judaism were legalistic and made these the target of his polemic. Such readings rest on the presupposition that the law versus faith dichotomy signifies specific doctrine in the Jewish religion that the Christian Paul now finds reprehensible.[9] In turn, this conclusion appears to be based on a presupposed theological framework that necessitates reading the contrast between faith and the law in Romans as Paul's claim that faith in Christ obviates human obedience. In other words, traditional interpretations of the law-faith/grace-works dichotomies raise the issue of reading later theological presuppositions into the Pauline texts.

Moreover, traditional interpretations of the law-faith dichotomy have given rise to the dubious notion that the difference between Judaism and Christianity ultimately resides in the fact that the former is limited by the particularities of ethnicity, while the latter represents a universal, transcendent religion that escapes the very particularities that render Judaism inferior to it.[10] However, the notion that Christianity has always been and continues to be a nonethnic, supra-cultural phenomenon is overly simplistic and simply begs the question of continuing Jewish ethnic identity within the Christ movement. Moreover, to define Jews as embodied, ethnic people and then argue that it is this embodied existence that is "too exclusive and limited for God's purposes,"[11] is similarly facile. In addition, the perpetuation of the idea of a nonethnic or universal Christianity more often than not opens the door to the imposition of the dominant, Anglo-Saxon, Western view of Christianity and Christian identity (albeit touted as

---

7. Stowers, *Rereading of Romans*, 178.

8. Although it is clear that Paul disagreed with his judaizing Christian colleagues, this does not entail the corollary that he considered Judaism to be purely a religion of works-righteousness, and that he believed that what distinguished Christianity from Judaism was that it was a religion of faith apart from works.

9. The theological complexity of Second Temple Judaism warrants caution in simply assuming that even if Paul was aiming to demolish some form of Jewish legalism, then this necessarily means that works have no place in his conception of Christian salvation.

10. For example, Marvin C. Pate maintains that the pre-Christian Saul identified wisdom with the law and shared Judaism's particularist perspective. The Christian Paul, by way of contrast, severed wisdom from the law, as evidenced in his wisdom Christology and negative statements concerning the Torah, replacing nomism and particularism with fideism and universalism (Pate, *Reverse of the Curse*, 170, 190, 324).

11. Hodge, *If Sons, Then Heirs*, 8.

nonethnic or supra-cultural) on minority people groups, which has had and, in some cases, continue to have a deleterious effect on Christian mission and evangelism.

In sum, traditional reading of the law-faith dichotomy in Romans continue to define Judaism and the Christ movement as embodying two alternative paths of salvation, with emphasis placed on the theological aspects of the letter, often to the detriment of its sociological elements. Despite acknowledgment that the letter expresses the apostle's concern with ethnic diversity in Christ, traditional interpretations preclude any meaningful exploration of the possibility that this dichotomy plays a different, equally important role in the apostle's attempts to either define some continuing, historical and/or theological relationship between Judaism and the new movement, or to explain how ethnic diversity is maintained in the context of in-Christ unity.

1.2.1.2 *The New Perspective on Paul*

Broadly speaking, these writers argue that the antithesis between Paul and the Judaism of his day is not a real one on the grounds that Paul's teaching about the law and grace is congruent with first-century Jewish soteriology, whereby obedience to the law is viewed as the appropriate human response to salvation given as a gift through the covenant.[12] Thus, willful or heinous disobedience to the covenant would result in exclusion from salvation. By the same token, all Jews who are maintained in the covenant by obedience, atonement, and God's mercy belong to the group which will be saved. Accordingly, Israel's election and ultimate salvation are by God's mercy, rather than human achievement, and are best described as constituting covenantal nomism.[13] In addition, according to these interpreters, the answer to the question of how covenantal nomism works in relation to Paul and his understanding of the law rests on the premise that the apostle's perspective can be correctly understood only in relation to the larger issue of gentile inclusion.

However, although the work of these scholars goes far in resolving some of the perceived tension between the law-faith dichotomy in Romans and those passages which seem to make, at least, some aspects of salvation dependent on works, the meaning of this dichotomy continues to be understood as describing two paths of salvation, although in a more subtle way than that evident among traditional scholars. For example, according to E. P. Sanders, Paul denies that the Jewish covenant can be effective for salvation, since, simply put, Judaism is not Christianity.[14] Accordingly, Paul's pattern of religion falls outside the purview of covenantal nomism,[15] suggesting that, for Sanders,

---

12. Sanders, *Paul and Palestinian Judaism*, 419–20, 422.
13. Sanders, *Paul and Palestinian Judaism*, 422. Similarly, Wright, *New Testament*, 334.
14. Sanders, *Paul and Palestinian Judaism*, 551–52.
15. Morna D. Hooker argues that Paul's pattern of religion accords with that of Judaism. Judaism understood obedience as the proper response of Israel to the covenant, with final judgment dependent on works of obedience. Similarly, Paul assumes that salvation under the new covenant evokes

the law-faith dichotomy represents two dispensations, which, in effect, prescribe two alternative paths of salvation; a view corresponding closely to that of interpreters writing in the traditional vein, whom he purports to critique. Moreover, this interpretation obfuscates the issue of the meaning of and relationship between faith and works of the law.[16] In addition, upon closer inspection, a stark contrast between Judaism and Christianity is entailed by Sanders's schema, since it posits a post-Damascus Paul who no longer sees anything of value in Judaism. Yet, this picture does not accord with much of what the apostle has to say regarding his own heritage and people; the Jewish framework within which he appears to work; his reliance on Jewish scripture; and his recognition of Christ as the messiah promised to the Jews.

Parting ways with Sanders on these grounds, James D. G. Dunn places Paul along with ancient Judaism under the rubric of covenantal nomism, arguing that the apostle's primary complaint against Judaism was its proclivity to use the law as a means of maintaining Israel's separateness from the nations.[17] By defining works of the law as referring specifically to Jewish identity markers and by positing that Paul separated initial from final justification (Rom 4:4–5), Dunn is able to maintain that Paul teaches that obedience is required of believers, including fulfillment of the law, but excluding those works that discriminate and separate.[18] Similarly, N. T. Wright emphasizes the primacy of symbolic identity markers for Second Temple Judaism and takes works of the law as referring to Jewish identity markers.[19]

Thus, unlike both traditional interpreters and Sanders, both Dunn and Wright see some degree of continuity between Paul and Judaism via the ethical elements of the Torah, which stripped of ethnic markers, is, thus, seen as applicable to both Jewish and gentile believers. Although this interpretation of works of the law is arguably more nuanced than that provided by more traditional readings, the premise that the main purpose of the law-faith dichotomy is to establish gentile inclusion and soteriological equality results in the continuing practice of reading it as a description of two alternative paths of salvation. Thus, the law, which, in actuality, means works of the law, describes the way of the unbelieving Jew, who observes the Torah in its entirety,

---

answering obedience by those who profess Christ. Accordingly, the final judgment of believers is according to works of obedience to the law of Christ: "It is not the 'pattern of religion,' then, that separates Paul from Judaism, but the pieces which make up the pattern" (Hooker, *From Adam to Christ*, 156–57, 160).

16. Sanders concludes that the purpose of the final judgment is only to reward good behavior and to punish bad behavior, but in a way that does not affect eternal destiny. For those outside the covenant, eternal destiny is dependent on deeds; that is, God punishes the wicked for their deeds, and by contrast he bestows mercy on the righteous (Sanders, *Paul and Palestinian Judaism*, 517–18, 551–52). However, according to the pattern described by Sanders, if human obedience in some degree is a requirement for remaining in Christ, then faith apart from works of obedience is insufficient for salvation.

17. Dunn, *New Perspective on Paul*, 8–13, 16, 52–53.

18. Dunn, *New Perspective on Paul*, 49–51, 72, 75–77.

19. Wright, *New Testament*, 336.

while faith describes the path taken by Jewish and gentile believers in Christ, who observe the ethical elements of the law.

However, this formulation of the law and works of the law has been critiqued on the grounds that it has no exegetical basis.[20] This position also assumes that Paul maintains the continuing validity of the Mosaic covenant (sans ethnic boundary markers) in the new age of the Spirit; a position that has also been challenged.[21] Moreover, by maintaining that the apostle's critique of the law is limited to those parts which are concerned with defining and maintaining Jewish ethnic identity markers, these interpreters, seemingly unwittingly, succumb to the same temptation as their more traditional peers in pitting Judaism against Christianity, irrespective of their acknowledgment of Paul's Jewish identity.[22] Implicitly, Christianity is superior precisely because it transcends the particularity of Jewish ethnicity.

In sum, although these scholars place much needed emphasis on the social and ethnic matrix within which Paul develops his arguments, the all too familiar portrait of Judaism as exclusive, limited by its ethnic identity, surfaces in contrast to its nonethnic counterpart. Gentile inclusion is accomplished at the expense of ongoing Jewish ethnic identity among believing Jews. Thus, in addition to the fact that this position effectively ignores Paul's critique of the law in its entirety, and not just its ethnic boundary markers, especially its temporary, limited role in God's dealings with humanity, it also contributes to the myth of Pauline Christianity as a nonethnic, supra-cultural, disembodied phenomenon.

1.2.1.3 *Beyond the New Perspective on Paul*

The key characteristic which defines this approach from both traditional and New Perspective readings is a depiction of Paul as the upholder of ethnic identities in Christ.[23] Although their approaches to the issue of identity in Paul and the methodologies they employ in the analysis of the relevant texts differ, these scholars contend that Christianity never existed as a nonethnic, supra-cultural phenomenon. Although

---

20. Cranfield, "'Works of the Law,'" 89–101. Dunn points out that although the phrase "works of the law" refers to the Torah in its entirety, it is those works by which Judaism distinguished itself that trigger Paul's formulation of justification by faith alone (Dunn, *New Perspective on Paul*, 23–28).

21. E.g., Witherington and Hyatt, *Paul's Letter to the Romans*, 214–15.

22. For Dunn, it is precisely those ethnic markers which distinguish the Jewish people as a nation from their non-Jewish neighbors that Paul renders as presently obsolete in Christ (Dunn, *Theology of Paul the Apostle*, 119).

23. Tucker, *"Remain In Your Calling,"* 8–9. Other defining characteristics include: a rejection of the universal/particular (ethnic) dichotomy; an understanding of justification in terms of gentile inclusion, rather than in terms of humanity in general; and an insistence that there is no implicit critique of the law, Israel, or Judaism in Paul. Although the scholars in this group follow a similar broad mode of approach to Paul and his writings, and seek to move beyond the interpretations offered by Sanders, Dunn, and Wright, their positions on particular matters, such as soteriology and soteriological categories and their relationship to Jews and gentiles, differ.

writers in this group agree that the universal-particular dichotomy with reference to Paul and the early Christ movement is a false one, there is disagreement as to the type of identity that Paul set about forming both among his converts and the communities of followers in Rome. These approaches may be divided into two general categories: those which argue that Paul sought to form a supraordinate Christian identity within which previous identities continue but in a relativized way; and those which conclude that Paul's conception of Christian identity is essentially that of two ethnic identities that exist in parallel in Christ, apart from a supraordinate "third" identity.

1.2.1.3a Supraordinate Identity: Philip F. Esler and William S. Campbell

Taking chapters 14–15 as one of the key reasons for Paul's sending his letter to the Roman believers, Philip F. Esler maintains that there were at least some Christ followers in Rome who were actively seeking to subvert what Paul thought was essential to in-Christ identity.[24] In response, Paul engages in a process of "recategorization" whereby he redefines the situation of conflict so that "members of subgroups antagonistic to one another are subsumed into a larger single, superordinate category."[25]

At its basis, in-Christ identity, according to the author, consists of being righteous, a status established by Christ (Rom 3:21–26 and Rom 5) and accessed through baptism (6:1–10), and, as such, transcends ethnic division. With respect to the law, Esler maintains that, according to Paul, it was "not strong enough for the dirty job God gave it."[26] The issue of how ethnic difference is embodied within theological unity is left unexamined. Similarly, the precise meaning and role of the law-faith dichotomy in Paul's discourse on gentile inclusion remains unexplored.

By way of contrast, William S. Campbell does not use the term "supraordinate" to describe Pauline identity formation. Yet, his notion of two types of in-Christ sub-identities, Jew and gentile, in a nested hierarchy of identities where faith in Christ is the primary identity marker accomplishes the same result.[27] According to Campbell's assessment, Christian identity, whether gentile or Jewish, has a decisively Jewish flavor, albeit, more so, in the case of the latter than in the former. This decidedly Jewish-like, Christian identity is an identity defined by Christ and grounded in him. However, "to be united with Christ is not to be fused with Christ." Consequently, "particularity is retained but transformed through the relationship."[28] In other words, there is both a specific Jewish-Christ identity and a particular gentile-Christ identity. However, both

---

24. Esler, *Conflict and Identity in Romans*, 29, 340.
25. Esler, *Conflict and Identity in Romans*, 29, 340.
26. Esler, *Conflict and Identity in Romans*, 362.
27. Campbell, *Paul and the Creation*, 157.
28. Campbell, *Paul and the Creation*, 156.

INTRODUCTION

of these ethnic groups are part of a larger group, the in-Christ group, which in a sense transcends and, thereby, encompasses both.

Campbell maintains that Paul's theology is best described as a theology of transformation, whereby the past, including the cultural identity of individual believers is not obliterated and replaced by a culture-free Christian identity, but is reshaped by virtue of their being in-Christ. In this way, "Christ-identity can pervade all cultures," "transforming them but not imperialistically obliterating everything," so that Christian faith remains in some sense continuous with "previously existing patterns of life."[29]

According to Campbell, faith in Christ is the primary marker of Christian identity. This ultimately comes down to faith as belief, since it stands apart from any distinct praxis which would distinguish it in any real sense from Jewish praxis. This is pointedly expressed in the author's contention that Paul is a paradigm for Jewish in-Christ identity but not for gentile in-Christ identity.[30] In other words, Campbell maintains ethnic differences in full while insisting on unity only at the cognitive level. Moreover, like Esler, the meaning and role of the law-faith dichotomy in Paul's discourse on gentile inclusion is left unexamined.

1.2.1.3B In-Christ Identity as Particular: Caroline Johnson Hodge, Joshua D. Garroway, and J. Brian Tucker

Caroline Johnson Hodge maintains that in-Christ identity is inherently and particularly Jewish. Paul never makes the case that Jewish Christians must give-up any portion of their ethnic or religious identity. By way of contrast, Greeks or gentiles must give-up everything that is central to their identity. In other words, "Jews are marked by ethnic continuity and Greeks by ethnic disruption."[31] Jews and gentiles in Christ are related by virtue of the fact that they both manifest the faithfulness of their ancestor, Abraham.[32] According to the author, Paul assumes that Jews who are not teachers of gentiles would continue to be faithful to the law, while gentiles, although affiliated with Israel and sharing some Jewish characteristics, would remain separate by avoiding circumcision.[33] Accordingly, being in-Christ is a hybrid identity for gentiles only, since being in-Christ "is already a Jewish identity."[34] Consequently, Paul's rhetorical

---

29. Campbell, *Paul and the Creation*, 14.
30. Campbell, *Paul and the Creation*, 156.
31. Hodge, *If Sons, Then Heirs*, 140–41.
32. Hodge, *If Sons, Then Heirs*, 80–84.
33. Hodge, *If Sons, Then Heirs*, 117–18, 123, 133–34.
34. Hodge, *If Sons, Then Heirs*, 150.

task in his letter to the Romans is to provide an explanation for his gentile audience of how their new composite identity works.[35]

Unlike Campbell, and to some extent Esler, the author places some emphasis on the role of the Spirit in the creation of gentile in-Christ identity. However, her discussion does not extend beyond the Spirit's role in creating new kinship among gentile believers, which implies that Jewish followers of Christ are exempt from the work of the Spirit, presumably because they already belong to God's family. In addition, Hodge's analysis includes a relatively longer discussion, in contrast to the two studies mentioned above, of the role that the law-faith dichotomy plays within the context of Paul's larger ethnographical concerns. However, Hodge's insistence that in-Christ identity is already a Jewish identity implies that the status of being in Christ has no effect on Jewish believers, at least not in terms of their identity and related praxis. They simply continue as *believing* Jews, although what that would look like is unclear. For that matter, it is also unclear in what sense gentiles in-Christ retain a gentile identity. Rather, gentile unity with Christ, wrought by the Spirit, appears to result in an essentially Jewish identity. Apart from remaining uncircumcised, gentiles apparently have Jewish characteristics and behave like Jews. Thus, although the author maintains that God shapes these newly adopted gentiles after the image of Christ,[36] that image is essentially Jewish, rather than Christlike.

Ultimately, for Hodge, as for Campbell, it is faith in Christ which differentiates both Jewish and gentile Christ followers from their nonbelieving counterparts.[37] Yet, although the author insists that faith understood as mental assent is a modern notion,[38] the fact that the identity and praxis of Jewish believers is not affected by their incorporation into Christ, suggests that there are no specific and/or unique character traits and resulting behaviors accompanying this belief; neither for Jewish nor for gentile believers who simply mirror the traits and behaviors of their ethnic counter-parts. Essentially, Johnson Hodge's interpretation resolves into the view of faith prevalent among traditional exegetes. Her analysis of the law-faith dichotomy, with its emphasis on a static status, appears to further support this conclusion.

Conceding that Paul does in fact use ancient kinship discourse to construct an ethnic, Abrahamic identity for gentile converts, Joshua D. Garroway pushes Hodge's insight further by arguing that, for Paul, faith in Christ transforms gentiles into "authentically ethnic Jews."[39] This is possible because the death and resurrection of Christ profoundly altered the way that the identity of Israel was to be construed. With the in-breaking of the eschatological age the ethnic markers of patriarchal descent, cir-

---

35. Hodge, *If Sons, Then Heirs*, 118.
36. Hodge, *If Sons, Then Heirs*, 111–13.
37. Since the author assumes that Romans is addressed solely to gentiles, her stance regarding Jewish believers is implicit.
38. Hodge, *If Sons, Then Heirs*, 82–83.
39. Garroway, *Paul's Gentile-Jews*, 4–5.

INTRODUCTION

cumcision, and law observance could now be achieved only through Christ.⁴⁰ Thus, Paul "refashions" his understanding of Judaism "in contradistinction to competing understandings of Judaism," in order to properly integrate the death and resurrection of Jesus Christ as the decisive event.⁴¹ This means, that for the apostle, the "circumcision received by gentiles [from Christ] is no less real or authentic" than circumcision in the flesh by human hands, much like gentile "physical descent from the patriarchs is no less genuine than an empirically verifiable pedigree."⁴²

Garroway concludes that Paul's representation of Jewishness produces a category of liminal identity, a non-Jewish Jew.⁴³ This hybrid, in-between identity lacks a definitive label since it can only be described in terms of the dichotomy it resists.⁴⁴ Thus, a term such as gentile-Jew "signifies those persons who are Jews but not quite Jews, gentiles but not quite gentiles."⁴⁵ In other words, "gentiles remain a peculiar sort of Israelite."⁴⁶ Accordingly, the theory of hybridity explains the seemingly contradictory statements Paul makes regarding circumcision and the status of his gentile converts.⁴⁷

However, even if one grants the validity and explanatory power of the hybrid theory of discourse, the author's exegesis of the Pauline texts appears to rest on two assumptions that lie outside of the theory itself. First, the author maintains that Paul's intent at the Jerusalem Council (Acts 15) was not to defend the idea that gentiles did not need to become Jews in order to be part of the Christ movement, but rather to defend his view that in the wake of Christ, circumcision was to be performed by the risen Lord and not by humans.⁴⁸ The second assumption flows from the first, it is the "imperceptible removal of the foreskin wrought by Christ" that makes one circumcised (Rom 2:25).⁴⁹

Although it is likely that the early followers of Christ experienced some degree of liminality with respect to their new identity as Christ-followers, Garroway fails to consider both Paul's metaphorical use of language and the rhetorical context within which ethnic terms, such as circumcision, occur. In other words, the theory of

40. Garroway, *Paul's Gentile-Jews*,5, 57–58, 164.
41. Garroway, *Paul's Gentile-Jews*, 163.
42. Garroway, *Paul's Gentile-Jews*, 166.
43. Garroway, *Paul's Gentile-Jews*, 8–9.
44. Garroway, *Paul's Gentile-Jews*, 8, 55.
45. Garroway, *Paul's Gentile-Jews*, 55.
46. Garroway, *Paul's Gentile-Jews*, 157.
47. Garroway, *Paul's Gentile-Jews*, 47–48, 63–64, 67.
48. Garroway, *Paul's Gentile-Jews*, 60–61.

49. Garroway, *Paul's Gentile-Jews,* 60–61. However, to state that an imperceptible mark made by spiritual means is a replicate of a physical mark is to essentially say that a spiritual mark is in some sense physical. Conversely, a physical mark is not physical because it is manifested physically, but because of some other unstated reason. This suggests that Paul not only redefines the term "Jew," but also the terms "spiritual" and "physical" in such a way that he is able to equate them. Yet, there is no evidence that he does so. Nor is there any evidence that Paul believed that gentiles were to be circumcised, by any means, in order to become Christ followers.

11

hybridity may help to explain *why* Paul referred to his gentile audiences in seemingly contradictory terms. However, it does not explain the meaning of ethnically charged terms and categories as these appear in particular contexts throughout his letters, wherein the apostle negotiates and articulates in-Christ identity. Yet, it is precisely in these particular contexts, and not in an assumed superstructure equating physical and spiritual circumcision superimposed on the text, that Paul formulates and reveals his understanding of this identity and its relation to both the law and to Christ.

In his work, *"Remain in Your Calling": Paul and the Continuation of Social Identities in 1 Corinthians*, J. Brian Tucker challenges the universalistic approach of Esler on the grounds that it necessarily implies the relegation of ethnic identity. This problem, he notes, is particularly acute for Jewish identity, as even Esler himself admits.[50] Accordingly, Tucker argues that Paul's approach to ethnic identity is particularistic. That is, rather than seeking to obliterate existing social and ethnic identities, the apostle draws from these in order to form geographically and situationally specific, diverse and valid expressions of Christ movement identity. Moreover, this approach is open-ethnic in the sense that the extent of the continuation of various identities remains an open question and is situationally determined within the context of Paul's mission to the communities which he establishes and oversees.[51]

Accordingly, with respect to his gentile converts, Paul saw his mission "as bicultural mediator," mediating "between at least two shared macro-identities: social identification with Judaism through its scriptures and Roman imperial ideology."[52] Tucker maintains that the state of being in-Christ "intersects" existing gentile identities "in a transforming process to produce micro-identities that are negotiated in the intercultural communication between Israel's symbolic universe, Roman imperial ideology, and local knowledge."[53] By supplying the community with this alternate, eschatological vision of reality, Paul guides his converts in patterning their lives according to Christ, thus preventing conformation to the world and its value systems.[54]

With respect to the apostle's Jewish converts, Tucker, like Hodge, implies that Jewish in-Christ identity does not need to undergo this process of transformation, presumably because it is already firmly rooted in Israel's symbolic universe which, in turn, is in complete continuity with Christ. Moreover, Tucker's proposition that transformation of gentile identity consists solely of a cognitive change, ignores the prominent role that Paul accords the Spirit in accomplishing this change. Similarly, although the author grapples with the question of the continuing validity of the law

---

50. Tucker, *"Remain in Your Calling,"* 6. Although Tucker explores the intricacies of Paul's strategy of identity formation in 1 Corinthians, several key points emerge from his analysis of the text that have some bearing on Romans.

51. Tucker, *"Remain in Your Calling,"* 227–28.

52. Tucker, *"Remain in Your Calling,"* 105, 117.

53. Tucker, *"Remain in Your Calling,"* 105, 119.

54. Tucker, *"Remain in Your Calling,"* 225.

in the new age, faith remains at the level of cognitive assent to a theological belief. Implicitly, the law-faith dichotomy is interpreted as the apostle's explication of two alternative paths of salvation. Like Dunn, he assumes the continued validity of the law, for Paul, in the new age, albeit interpreted in different ways for gentile (lenient) and Jew (observed in its entirety), respectively.[55]

In sum, for writers in this group, continuity between Judaism and the new movement occurs via the continued validity of the law, at least to some degree, with faith, defined, by and large, as a cognitive belief, differentiating believing Jews and gentiles from their nonbelieving counterparts. What is clear is that Jews and gentiles in-Christ retain their ethnic particularity, to some degree. What is unclear is both how this community united in Christ is distinguished from nonbelieving communities, apart from some cognitive change and/or adjustment in worldview, and how the transformative unity of Jew and gentile in this community is achieved. The latter is particularly pressing, given the intractable nature of interethnic conflict throughout human history.[56] This historical and social reality suggests that much more is needed to achieve ethnic unity than a change simply in one's perception of the world; something Paul is acutely aware of and addresses in Romans, even though his interpreters often fail to see it.

1.2.2 The Issue of Genre: Romans as *Logos Protreptikos*

Attempts to categorize Romans as a specific epistolary type, e.g., ambassadorial letter, letter of friendship or self-recommendation, have proven to be unhelpful since these categories tend to be very general and as such cannot account for the complex argumentation found therein.[57] The most plausible proposal put forth to date has been to read Romans as an example of *logos protreptikos*.

1.2.2.1 David E. Aune

David E. Aune argues that Rom 1:16—15:13 is a *logos protreptikos* in an epistolary frame (1:1–15; 15:14—16:27), wherein Paul writes a speech of exhortation in order to convince and/or remind the Roman Christians of the truth of his version of the gospel and to define and encourage the particular lifestyle and commitment consistent with it. Thus, Romans is protreptic in the sense that Paul is arguing for his version of Christianity over competing schools of Christian thought, much like what is seen in

---

55. Tucker, "*Remain in Your Calling*," 103–5, 112, 114, 123, 128–29. The author argues that Paul distinguishes between Pharisaic *halakhot* and the more lenient *halakhah* based on the paradigmatic model of Christ, who ate with sinners but remained Torah-observant. This lenient *halakhah* is embodied in "Christ's law," which gentiles are to keep. Agreeing with Campbell, Tucker maintains that Paul was a less-than-perfect model for gentile believers in that he maintained a way of life that would not have been appropriate for them.

56. Kuecker, *Spirit and the 'Other,'* 19.

57. Aune, "Romans as a *Logos Protreptikos*," 91–121.

philosophical protreptic writings, whereby the writer uses both encouragement and rebuke in an effort to bring a person to the truth.[58]

In terms of genre analysis, Aune's approach is commendable for its ability to relate the structure of philosophical λόγοι προτρεπτικοί to the general structure of Romans.[59] However, this strength proves to be an achilles heel in relation to Rom 9–11, which the author sees as "a kind of excursus or digression," presumably because it does not fit into the tri-partite structure of ancient protreptic.[60] Moreover, with respect to the content of Romans, Aune describes the genre as exclusively exoteric, aimed at conversion of the outsider.[61] Aside from the fact that it is unclear in what sense Paul's Christian audience was composed of outsiders, or persons in need of evangelization, there is no textual evidence that the apostle believes that his audience is following some sort of sub-standard or alternate gospel. Nor is there any evidence that Paul believes that their present lifestyle, generally speaking, does not comport with the expectations of the gospel. Rather, he commends them for their faith (Rom 1:8). Finally, it is equally unclear what these so-called competing schools of Christian thought are and what Paul's relation to them is.

1.2.2.2 *Anthony J. Guerra*

Aune's analysis was further refined and developed by Anthony J. Guerra, who critiques Aune for his indecisiveness over the question of audience and purpose of Romans. According to the latter, it is this ambivalence that hinders the former's argument for reading the letter as an example of protreptic, particularly with respect to Rom 9–11.[62] According to Guerra, Paul's most pressing concern in Rom 1–8 as well as much of 9–11 is both to defend his gospel against Jewish criticism by the judaizing Christians in his mixed audience and to promote and encourage respect between Jewish and gentile Christians. It is only by presenting himself and the content of his gospel as acceptable, that the apostle can be hopeful about receiving help for his mission to Spain.[63]

In support of these conclusions, Guerra forges a link between second-century Christian apologetic literature and Greco-Roman philosophical protreptic. Christian apologetic writings, according to the author, are primarily positive appeals, not defenses, to win converts to the Christian movement. In this sense, they fulfill the same

---

58. Aune, "Romans as a *Logos Protreptikos*," 91–92.
59. Aune, "Romans as a *Logos Protreptikos*," 101, 114–19.
60. Aune, "Romans as a *Logos Protreptikos*," 118. Aune's suggestion that the coherence of Rom 9–11, and the fact that it does not seem to flow directly from the argument in Rom 5:1—8:39 warrants the conclusion that this section is best interpreted as a delayed answer to an earlier objection to Paul's gospel, presupposes that Romans follows a tripartite structure.
61. Aune, "Romans as a *Logos Protreptikos*," 95.
62. Guerra, *Romans and the Apologetic Tradition*, 11.
63. Guerra, *Romans and the Apologetic Tradition*, 31, 34, 41–42.

function as philosophical protreptic.⁶⁴ Moreover, since second-century Christian protreptic evidences the closest parallels to the structure, content, and function of the letter, the motifs common to this type of apologetic literature may be applied to an analysis of the content of Romans.⁶⁵

In this sense, Guerra's analysis has more explanatory power than Aune's, since the method of motif analysis lends itself nicely to a detailed exegesis of the content of the letter. However, it is precisely on these grounds that Guerra's work falters, since there is no evidence that judaizing tendencies were at play in Rome when Paul penned his letter. In addition, the author's analysis assumes a radical discontinuity between Judaism and Christianity. In relation to Rom 1–3, he writes, "Paul pursues the protreptic task of criticizing alternate world views (Jewish and gentile) and affirming the superiority of a preferred perspective (the gospel)."⁶⁶

To the extent that protreptic discourse necessarily engages in criticism of alternative world views and life styles, this would seem to preclude its ability to adequately explain either the continuity between Judaism and Christianity that Paul advocates (e.g., Rom 1:2), or the kinship language that the apostle uses in relating various ethnic groups in-Christ (e.g., Rom 8:14–17), or the seemingly wide latitude that he gives for expressions of difference in the worship practices of the community (e.g., Rom 14:2–8). In other words, this genre does not readily lend itself to explaining the subtle and complex ethnic discourse which runs throughout the text and appears in most of the major argumentative sections.

Thus, although elements of the genre of ancient philosophical protreptic are evident in Romans, for example, the diatribe style and the use of philosophical language, it is unclear whether the epistle may legitimately be classified as a protreptic, in the full sense of the term. Moreover, it is not entirely clear that Paul's intent was to present Christianity as a philosophy, as later Christian apologists did. Rather, the apostle's emphasis is on the gospel as the fulfillment of scriptural promise (e.g., Rom 1:2); an emphasis which is underscored by his use of Scripture at major points in his argument (e.g., 3:4; 3:10–18; 4:7–8) and his recourse to biblical figures (4:1–22; 5:12–14). Although Paul draws on philosophical terms and categories, these are couched within a larger matrix of Jewish motifs, symbols, and language drawn from its own sacred writings. In this regard, it is revealing that Aune distinguishes Rom 9–11 from the other sections of the letter by virtue of the fact that it consists of approximately thirty references to the OT.⁶⁷

---

64. Guerra, *Romans and the Apologetic Tradition*, ix.
65. Guerra, *Romans and the Apologetic Tradition*, 7, 13–21.
66. Guerra, *Romans and the Apologetic Tradition*, 176.
67. Aune, "Romas as a *Logos Protreptikos*," 118–19. In addition, Aune admits that in Romans Paul uses and combines genres and forms in unique ways.

1.2.2.3 Mixed Forms, Genre Fluidity, and Christian Adaptation: Northrop Frye

The above discussion highlights several issues related to determining the literary character of Romans. First, it is not unusual to find mixed forms in writings from this period.[68] This makes determination of a text's genre difficult, given that, in order to do so, one must determine the degree of material present from any given genre(s) that is needed to push the work, as a whole, from one genre to another.[69] In such cases, it is helpful to determine the host genre or that which makes the regular incorporation of the other forms possible.[70] However, this endeavor raises issues of its own.

Genres were fluid in antiquity, thus resisting neat categorization. What made a genre recognizable was not so much a set of conventions unique to it but rather a specific clustering of certain individual conventions shared with other genres.[71] This specific, discernible pattern of clustering allowed ancient audiences to recognize particular genres, even in cases where these were not the subject of extensive treatment in treatises and/or when the writer did not state explicitly what sort of work he or she was composing.[72] Yet, there is no direct correlation between the fact that ancients were able to discern particular genre patterns and the ability of modern-day scholars to correctly categorize these works, since modern categories are not always clearly distinguished in ancient terminology.[73]

With regard to the NT documents, the problem of genre identification is further complicated by the fact that these texts are distinctly Christian. That is to say, their content is unique and quite distinct from that of their Greco-Roman generic counterparts.[74] Paul's letters not only display a broad stylistic range, but also employ a variety of literary conventions, including contemporary rhetorical forms, early Christian hymnic material and confessional formulas, in addition to numerous appeals to OT authority, making these letters richer than either the brief private letters or the more developed letter essays of their contemporaries.[75] Even Aune admits, despite his belief that the body of Romans stands as an example of ancient philosophical protreptic, it "is not precisely similar to other surviving examples of the λόγος προτρεπτικός" not only because "of the

---

68. Sterling, *Historiography & Self-Definition*, 15, 16n73. For example, a genre that is primarily epic may also have elements that are present in romance and pastoral works.

69. Sterling, *Historiography & Self-Definition*, 15–16.

70. Sterling, *Historiography & Self-Definition*, 15–16.

71. Tobin, *Paul's Rhetoric in Its Contexts*, 90.

72. Tobin, *Paul's Rhetoric in Its Contexts*, 90.

73. Skinner, *Invention of Greek Ethnography*, 31.

74. Dunn, "Romans, Letter," 838–50. Although a good case has been made for viewing the Gospels (aside from Luke) as belonging to the genre of ancient *bios*, and Luke-Acts as an example of ancient historiography, much of the debate over the literary character of the NT letters, including Romans, has been inconclusive.

75. O'Brien, "Letters, Letter Form," 550–53.

inherent flexibility of the genre, but also because Paul has Christianized it by adapting it as a means of persuading people of the truth of the gospel."[76]

Consequently, some scholars have suggested that although it is clear that Paul employed contemporary literary conventions, the form he constructed in his letters, including Romans, is unique in both character and content.[77] Given this, attempts to classify the epistle as belonging to one or another contemporary genre are pointless, since they will necessarily be inconclusive. One the one hand, there is some truth in the above observation. Paul wrote letters, not treatises, whether philosophical, apologetic, or otherwise. His letters, as noted above, are singular with respect to their length, richness, and complexity. Even if we grant that Romans, like Paul's other letters, is best understood as a written speech/lecture, it is nevertheless distinct from a philosophical lecture aimed at attracting potential adherents, particularly in light of Paul's stated purpose for writing, as it was noted above. On the other hand, an understanding of the literary conventions Paul did use is necessary for correct interpretation. As a form of meaningful communication, these letters would have necessarily been composed according to contemporary conventions and traditions. Furthermore, as potentially effective means of communication they would have been written according to the cluster of conventions that best suited the apostle's reason for addressing his audience. In other words, one would expect an effective communicator, like Paul, to choose the genre most appropriate for the particular communicative task in view.

This being said, caution must be exercised in both identifying what constitutes a particular ancient genre and determining which of these has the closest affinity with Romans. The operative term, in this case, is affinity. In this regard, Northrop Frye, who has attempted to move beyond traditional genre criticism with its paradigmatic orientation and taxonomic end, provides some insight, writing that the purpose of genre identification "is not so much to classify as to clarify such traditions and affinities, thereby bringing out a large number of literary relationships that would not be noticed as long as there were no context established for them."[78]

Frye's reassessment is particularly helpful for evaluating the issue of the genre of Romans. It is safe to say, for the reasons noted above, that Paul never sat down with the intent to compose an ethnography, an apologetic treatise, or a λόγος προτρεπτικός, for that matter, as these forms were understood by his ancient contemporaries. The notion that the distinctively Christian content of the apostle's message can simply be poured into a particular generic structure without either altering that external structure and/or the internal content assumes the absence of a dialectical relationship between form and content. Content determines form as much as form determines content. Thus, at best, it can be said that Paul's letter to the Romans evidences certain affinities with particular ancient genres, while also exhibiting dissimilarities. However, it is also safe

---

76. Aune, "Romas as a *Logos Protreptikos*," 119.
77. E.g., Dunn, "Romans, Letter," 841.
78. Frye, *Anatomy of Criticism*, 247–48 cited in Sterling, *Historiography & Self-Definition*, 16.

to say that Paul had a reason(s) for writing each letter he composed and that this purpose(s) may be reasonably determined from the text itself.[79] Like any good writer/orator, Paul would have carefully chosen the literary conventions of his day best suited for conveying this particular message to this particular audience. In this sense, it is reasonable to assume that Romans has certain continuity with discrete genres existing at that time. The question then becomes which of these may be considered the host genre, not in the sense of providing a category into which Romans may be neatly inserted but in the sense that it exhibits the most points of continuity, in terms of motifs and type of discourse, with the epistle.

1.3 Lacunae in the Study of the Three Dichotomies in Romans

Both the New Perspective on Paul and scholars exploring Pauline formulations of Christian identity in the vein of Beyond the New Perspective have made many advances in disclosing the unexamined assumptions undergirding traditional readings of Paul and his letter to the Romans.[80] However, several issues remain; all of them entangled with the larger issue of genre:

1. Although there is a consensus that Romans deals with both the respective roles of the law and faith in light of Christ and the relationship between Jews and gentiles in Christ, the role that the law-faith dichotomy plays in Paul's ethnic discourse aimed at the formation of in-Christ identity remains, by and large, unexamined. As a consequence, the purpose of the law-faith dichotomy continues to be understood as Paul's way of referring either to two alternative paths of salvation and/or religious systems. This suggests that, despite the recognition that Romans deals concretely with the issue of gentile inclusion, interpreters nevertheless maintain that justification by faith alone is the apostle's central point from which all of his arguments move. In other words, Romans continues to be read as a kind of manifesto on Pauline soteriology, in spite of assertions to the contrary. However, if we grant both that Paul's theologizing occurs within a specific historical and sociological context and that the issue of Jewish and gentile unity and identity in Christ is a central concern in Romans, then we must also consider the specific role that Paul's law-faith discourse plays in the construction of identity, particularly in light of the fact that Romans is replete with ethnic discourse that is tightly linked with its theological elements.

    Hodge's insight regarding Paul's ironic use of from the law/from faith language is a step in this direction. However, her premise that Paul is writing only

---

79. I will argue in chapter 3 of this work that sufficient attention needs to be paid both to Paul's own stated intent and to the language of suffering, affliction, and hope that runs through the letter in discerning the purpose of Romans.

80. This study presupposes that Paul's view of the law is coherent despite the lack of scholarly consensus as to what the apostle actually thought about the role of the law in the new movement.

INTRODUCTION

to gentiles and that he is not addressing universal human sinfulness,[81] precludes adequate examination of texts which point to the provisional nature of the law as a whole (e.g., Rom 7:1–6) and thus, its irrelevance, at least in some degree, for in-Christ identity. Similarly, her work on Paul's aggregative and oppositional ethnic discourse and his use of kinship language brings to light some of the ethnographic aspects present in Romans, raising the question of whether the letter, as a whole, might represent an example of early Christian ethnography, an issue the author does not explore, bringing us to the following point.

2. Scholarship on Paul's formation of in-Christ identity in Romans, with its emphasis on the sociological mechanisms underlying Jew-gentile unity in Christ, provides a rightful corrective to the tendency to overly distance the apostle and his converts from their Jewish roots. However, the task of securely anchoring the Pauline Christ movement to Judaism has proceeded without consideration of the letter's generic framework. Moreover, the perceived need to firmly establish that Paul upheld ethnic diversity in unity has led to a selective focus on certain portions of the letter without adequate consideration of how these sections relate to the larger whole. As a result, transformation, if discussed, is understood in merely cognitive terms, with Jewish believers remaining largely exempt from the process. However, the fact that these same scholars concede that Paul is actively engaged in forming some sort of distinct in-Christ identity, itself suggests that he conceives of both continuity and discontinuity between the Christ movement and the Judaism of his day. In other words, the apostle's understanding of the relationship between Jewish and gentile identity, and, for that matter, law and faith, is more nuanced, and, I argue, more Spirit-centered than the studies examined above imply.

Moreover, Paul's insistence that the one God is God of both Jews and gentiles (Rom 3:29–30) and his appeal to believers to welcome one another, in all of their ethnoracial particularity, on the grounds that Christ has welcomed both Jew and all manner of gentile (15:7–12), suggests that this in-Christ identity is neither Jewish nor non-Jewish, yet is, at the same time, able to embrace both in a way that ensures ongoing subgroup particularity. Put differently, Pauline in-Christ identity is, in this sense, supraordinate, as Esler points out, and Campbell intimates. However, the apostle's christology and related pneumatology indicate that the formation of this identity involves the transformation of *all* believers, such that they are enabled to accept the ethnoracial other, in a way that preserves subgroup saliency within a unified group self-identity. In short, the identity that the apostle constructs for his Roman audience is the product of a profound spiritual transformation, with equally profound social implications, and, as such, is not simply the result of either social re-categorization or a change in worldview.

---

81. Hodge, *If Sons, Then Heirs*, 11, 45.

Furthermore, that Paul portrays Christ as welcoming all of humanity, in all of its ethnoracial particularity, suggests that ongoing subgroup saliency, both Jewish and all manner non-Jewish, is necessitated by the gospel.

Thus, the question of how Paul constructs in-Christ identity in Romans must be considered within the eschatological framework that structures both the apostle's theological and ethnic discourse in the letter. This also means that this in-Christ identity can only be understood within the context of what the apostle says regarding the role of the Spirit in the new age and how he conceives of this in relation to the Jewish past. The fact that he makes copious recourse to Jewish Scripture suggests that he is deliberately working within an assumed narrative, which he believes is basic to the lived reality of his audience. This means that an adequate understanding of an ethnically diverse in-Christ identity must provide an explanation for: how and why Paul reworks this basic Jewish narrative in the way he does; how does the law-faith dichotomy fit into this and what bearing does it have in the construction of in-Christ identity; and, finally, how does the new age of the Spirit make a difference in the concrete, embodied life of an ethnically diverse community composed of Jew and gentile united in Christ. In other words, the issue of identity can only be understood within the larger framework of the letter's purpose and structure. This leads us to the next point.

3. The general consensus that Paul is addressing the respective roles of the law and faith in light of the Christ event, the relationship between Jews and gentiles in Christ, and in-Christ identity, raises the question of whether there existed at that time a literary mode concerned with the construction and legitimization of social identity which might shed light on both the textual integrity of Paul's argumentation and his purpose for writing to the Romans. In turn, a clearer understanding of both the generic characteristics of the letter and its purpose would shed greater light on the meaning of the three, related, dichotomies. A fruitful reexamination of these perceived polarities is not likely to emerge apart from such an integrative framework. Apart from a major generic shift, the interpretational battle-line will continue to be drawn over the validity of traditional interpretations.

What is clear is that although some studies account for the textual data in a more comprehensive manner than others, none of the proposals on offer, including Romans as *logos protreptikos*, adequately addresses, in an integrative way, every aspect of this complex, richly textured document. Moreover, although some of the ethnographic elements present in Romans and have been brought to light by Hodge, a study of Romans as an example of apologetic ethnography remains to be done. Similarly, an examination of Paul's kinship discourse within the larger context of his ethnic discourse as it is found throughout the letter would shed greater light on both how the apostle constructs kinship relationships between Jewish and gentile believers and how he conceives ethnic particularity in in-Christ unity. That continuing subgroup saliency is of concern to him, particularly as this is expressed in the desire to achieve reconciliation between the weak and the strong, is incontrovertible. What often goes unnoticed is that Paul's ethnic and kinship discourse, as he applies it both in relation to Christ and believers and among believers themselves, demonstrates that he understood continuing ethnoracial identity as necessary in light of the new eschatological situation in Christ.

Once the purpose of Romans is redefined to include the textual evidence pointing to suffering, general, social oppression and adversity, it becomes clear why Paul chooses to write his letter within an ethnographic framework common in his time. By the same token, an examination of the ethnographic characteristics of Romans brings together its ethnic/kinship language and theological discourse in a meaningful way that shifts focus away from viewing the letter as Paul's manifesto on justification/inclusion of gentiles by faith. Although both the New Perspective and its critics have shed considerable light on certain aspects of Romans, what is needed is a generic framework which makes sense of all its pieces.

1.4 Bridging the Gaps: The Ethnographic Characteristics of Romans

Greco-Roman ethnography, including its indigenous versions, provides a framework for the interpretation of Paul's letter to the Romans, allowing us to place the various pieces of the puzzle, the letter's theology, ethnic and kinship language, and its sociological elements into a meaningful whole. Put differently, the multifaceted nature of this literary genre provides a central interpretational point where the main purpose of the letter and the meaning of the law-faith dichotomy and its siblings intersect, whereby each element is illumined by and illumines the others. Prior scholarship has concerned itself primarily with defining Pauline justification and what that means in terms of the law and in-Christ identity. Yet, because this task was carried out without the benefit of an organizing structure the results have been piecemeal at best. Similarly, by examining Paul's ethnic discourse within the context of how ethnicity and kinship were perceived and constructed in the first century, it becomes apparent that the Judaism-Christ movement dichotomy, along with its implications for in-Christ identity, traces its roots to the same ancestor.

The genre of ancient ethnography expanded and evolved during the Imperial period in an effort to legitimate the continuing presence and place of diverse ethnic identities in the quickly expanding hegemony of the Roman Empire. Ancient writers, representative of this style of literature, were intent on fashioning and relating the story of their own group in an effort to offer a self-definition of that group over and against, yet valid with respect to, the Empire and Roman identity. In an analogous way, Paul refashions and relates Israel's story to reflect the eschatological reality of Christ's coming and the concomitant events of gentile inclusion and the empowerment and transformation by the Spirit of both ethnic groups. Just as these ancient apologetic ethnographers forged a social identity for their respective groups able to meet the challenges of a new era, so Paul refashions Jewish identity in light of the dawning of a new age such that worship of Israel's God is transformed in both how it is done, in the Lord/Spirit, and by whom, both Israel and the nations.

For Paul, the law-faith dichotomy is central to his in-Christ identity forming discourse that rethinks and refashions, not simply affirms, Jewish ethnic identity while simultaneously allowing for the incorporation of refashioned non-Jewish ethnic identities into the people of God. Moreover, the apostle's identity forming discourse directly reflects the historical reality of Christ's coming and the profound transformation of believers' identity resulting from this event. Paul does this within the context of his larger project of exhorting the communities of Christ followers in Rome to persevere in faithful obedience to the gospel message by creating a positive in-Christ identity that legitimates ethnically diverse Christ followers as the people of God.

It is specifically by means of the law-faith dichotomy that Paul revisions Israel's story in order to redefine Jewish identity, so that it is both continuous and discontinuous with that of historic Israel. Simultaneously, this redefinition allows for both the inclusion of the nations and the formation of an in-Christ identity that is both continuous and discontinuous with Jewish identity. It is in the interstice of discontinuity, where the old and the new meet, that a unique in-Christ identity emerges that is rooted in historic Israel and, yet, represents something new. This rootedness in an ancient religion gives in-Christ identity its validity, since despite its relative newness, it is fundamentally an identity with traceable mythic origins, and as such, legitimate. Moreover, it is the incorporation/adoption of both Jews and gentiles into the family of God, specifically through unity with Christ, in his death and resurrection, that both signals and describes a new identity that embraces and, as such, affirms distinct ethnic identities. For Paul continuing subgroup saliency, Jew and all manner of gentile, within the people of God is necessary for the very reason that Christ is the answer to humanity's (in all of its ethnoracial particularity) alienation from its Creator. Christ, in his faithfulness to God's redemptive plan and purposes, stands as the nexus between past and present, the old, Jewish law and the eschatological outpouring of the Spirit, Israel in its particularity and all the nations in their universality. This eschatological reality has concrete sociological implications in that, for Paul, the allocentric, Spirit-wrought identity of the believing community is patterned on the Christ who has presently welcomed all into the people of God (15:7–12).

In addition, for Paul, this new in-Christ social identity is expected to inform the believing community's ethical choices and, thus, produce an ethos distinct from both the nonbelieving Jewish community and that of the broader Greco-Roman culture.[82]

---

82. Here I am drawing on Tucker's notion of "identity salience in-Christ." The author utilizes this concept to describe Paul's method of leading his audience to make the ethical choices proper for a

INTRODUCTION

This Spirit-wrought, allocentric identity, that makes the living out of the community's ethos possible, in turn, provides legitimization, in ethnographic terms, for the Christ movement's laws, customs, and way of life.

1.5 Outline of the Argument

This study is composed of seven chapters. In an effort to adequately grasp the complexity of the letter, I have divided the letter into three parts (discussed below) and will limit myself to a detailed examination of certain portions of the text that are particularly relevant for my thesis. The law-faith dichotomy is part and parcel of a tangled mass of arguments associated with the purpose and genre of Romans. Accordingly, chapters 2 and 3 will be concerned with establishing the context necessary for an analysis of the ethnographic characteristics of Romans.

In chapter 2, I will explore the important role that ancient apologetic ethnography played in fashioning group self-definition, particularly in cases where the legitimacy of a group and/or its continued existence was seen as being threatened by the dominant or majority culture and the sociopolitical powers supporting it. This will include a brief survey of contemporary and near-contemporary Greco-Roman and Jewish texts that describe responses to the other in the face of threatened identity. In addition, I will utilize relevant tools and concepts from social identity theory and from modern sociological theories of ethnicity where necessary in an effort to clearly define the complex concept of identity as it is manifested in ancient texts. Having outlined this methodology, I will then apply it to the examination of Paul's double task of exhortation and in-Christ identity formation in Romans, beginning with the apostle's ethnographic purpose.

Chapter 3 will demonstrate that Paul's main purpose (although, not his sole reason) in writing this letter is to construct a positive group identity for the believers in Rome, so as to strengthen them in persevering in faithful obedience to the message of the gospel in the face of general social hostility from nonbelieving gentile and Jewish communities. Accordingly, Rom 1:8–17 and relevant sections from chapters 15–17 will be examined in some detail in order to lend further textual support for the argument that Paul writes his letter to the Romans in response to this state of affairs. Having established that the epistle represents the apostle's attempt to establish the legitimacy of the new movement, thus, strengthening group affiliation, in the face of various, external social pressures, I will show that, given this purpose and given the prevalence of ethnic discourse and ethnographical elements, this letter may best be interpreted against the background of Greco-Roman apologetic ethnography.

---

community of Christ-followers. In sum, the apostle points out and reprimands those behaviors which he sees as intolerable and commends those that are congruent with in-Christ identity, thereby creating a distinct community ethos (Tucker, "*Remain in Your Calling*," 47–48, 54–55).

Since a writer's purpose and his or her choice of genre are intimately related and mutually determinative, chapters 4–6 will involve the detailed exegesis of relevant portions of the text of Romans that both demonstrate the ethnographic character of the letter and substantiate the claim that it is best interpreted within the framework of ancient ethnography. More specifically, chapter 4 will address Rom 1–5, reading it in light of the history of origins found in ancient ethnographical literature. I will demonstrate that Paul uses the law-faith dichotomy to establish both continuity and discontinuity between Judaism and the early Christ movement and, accordingly, between the divinely instituted founding figures of each movement, Abraham and Christ. For Paul, faith, defined as active trust (not simply, cognitive assent to his universal lordship) in the God of Israel as evidenced in a life of obedience to him, is the point of continuity, while the provisional nature of the Jewish law makes it the locus of discontinuity.

Chapters 5 and 6 build on the previous chapter. In chapter 5, I will analyze the sections of Romans that deal with the issue of divine filiation, both past and present, and the related question of Israel's historic validity as the people (sons and daughters) of God. Accordingly, I will examine relevant sections of Rom 8 and Rom 9–11. As we will see, the law-faith dichotomy not only continues to play a role in the apostle's identity discourse but also serves to establish the priority, both temporally and hierarchically, of the Jewish people in the new age of the Spirit. The analysis of the role of the Spirit both in forming kinship ties and in creating a Spirit-wrought self-identity presented in chapter 5 will be further expanded in chapter 6, where I will examine Paul's articulation of the manner and lifestyle (a major building-block of ethnographic texts) of the people whom he identifies as heirs with Christ. The focus in this chapter will be on relevant sections from Rom 7 and 12, with particular attention paid to Rom 14:1—15:6 as a specific example of how an allocentric, Spirit-wrought, Christ identity is manifested in the ethnically diverse community of believers where the law continues to have saliency as a source of criteria defining inter-group ethnoracial identity for its Jewish members.

My argument as a whole will demonstrate that Paul's use of the law-faith dichotomy is part of his effort to establish the Christ movement as a historically legitimate movement with both ancient roots in Israel's revered past and with divinely mandated customs, laws, and way of life. Paul's ethnography to the Romans is meant to provide the beleaguered community with the encouragement they need to continue in faithful obedience to the gospel in a social environment hostile to both them and the gospel message. In other words, I will demonstrate that Paul, like other indigenous ethnographers of his time, sought to provide an apology for his people, directed specifically to them.

Chapter 7 will conclude this study, offering a summary of my findings as an affirmation of my thesis. In addition, I will discuss the implications of this study for

INTRODUCTION

the three dichotomies. Finally, I will suggest several areas for further research and contemporary application.

1.6 Assumptions and Terminology

1.6.1 Integrity and Audience of the Letter

First, for the purposes of this study, I am assuming that Romans is a unified literary work composed of sixteen chapters. Although, some scholars have argued that Rom 16 is not a part of Paul's original letter, I find the arguments for the original integrity of chapters 1–16 more compelling.[83]

A second area of contention concerns Paul's audience. Recently, some scholars have challenged the consensus view that the apostle wrote to both Jews and gentiles on the grounds that the encoded audience; that is, the audience reconstructed from the letter itself, suggests that the letter targets gentiles exclusively, irrespective of whether or not Jewish believers were physically present in Rome.[84]

I do not find the notion of an encoded audience particularly helpful, since it is more than likely that at least some of the believers in Rome were Jews and would, as a matter of fact, have heard the letter read. If Paul was well aware that Jews were present, as Rom 16:3 and 16:7 clearly indicate, it defies common sense to think that they were meant to ignore his missive, especially, given that such a directive is neither expressly stated nor implied.[85] Moreover, the notion of an encoded audience appears to support a particular interpretation that rests on a presupposition of an exclusively gentile audience. The textual evidence rallied in support of an exclusively gentile audience is not as cut and dry as it first appears. For example, Rom 11:13 may well refer to the immediate context and not to the letter as a whole.[86] In addition, although Paul did regard his mission to the gentiles as central to his apostolic duty to address gentile believers with reference to Judaism, this special calling also made it important that he explain to Jewish believers the place of the law in relation to the believing community.

Thus, in light of the above, it best to presume that Paul is addressing a mixed audience of Jewish and gentile believers. However, it is difficult to assess the

---

83. See Donfried, "Short Note on Romans 16," 44–52, for a brief, helpful summary of the various arguments and objections. Also, Lampe, "Roman Christians of Romans 16," 216–30. See Witherington and Hyatt, *Paul's Letter to the Romans*, 375–77, for a discussion of the text-critical issues associated with Rom 16.

84. Das, "Gentile-Encoded Audience of Romans," 29–46. Also, Hodge, *If Sons, Then Heirs*, 9–10, 46–47.

85. As Peter Lampe points out, Paul calls three persons in 16:3–16 "my kindred": Andronicus, Junia, and Herodion (Lampe, "Roman Christians of Romans 16," 224–25). Moreover, Aquila and Priscilla (Rom 16:3) are referred to as Jews in Acts 18:2. It is also possible, although not certain, that Mary (Rom 16:6) and those from the household of Aristobulus, were of Jewish origin (Tellbe, *Paul between Synagogue and State*, 159–60).

86. Watson, "Law in Romans," 93–107.

proportion of Jews to gentiles from the text itself. Moreover, the relative power of these two groups is not easily discerned.[87]

1.6.2 Hearer Competency

The issue of hearer competency invariably arises in relation to Paul's copious use of scripture in Romans and the related notion that he is working with a basically Jewish narrative arising from this tradition. First, the view that most members of Paul's audience(s) would have lacked the necessary competence to grasp and appreciate his frequent scriptural quotations and more allusive evocations of the same is unfounded. As J. Ross Wagner has pointed out, such a view is often supported by the widely held reconstruction of the history of the Roman churches, which maintains that the supposed expulsion of all Jews under Claudius in 49 CE resulted in gentile-only assemblies that had little or no access to or interest in the Jewish scriptures. However, the historical evidence neither conclusively supports the idea that gentile believers far out-numbered Jewish believers in Rome, nor that all gentile believers were uniformly and basically illiterate with regard to the Jewish scriptures.[88]

For one, the fact that Romans is full of OT citations, allusions, and echoes itself strongly suggests that Paul believed exactly the opposite—that his audience would be able to follow his argument, numerous subtle and not so subtle scriptural references and all. In fact, the rhetorical efficacy of the missive rests on that assumption. Although it is possible that the apostle seriously misjudged the scriptural literacy of his hearers, it is unlikely that a movement with Jewish roots would not seek to instill a more than passing knowledge of its sacred scriptures in its converts. As discussed in more detail in chapter 3, Paul's audience consists of mature believers who more than likely heard these texts read and expounded on numerous occasions during worship. Moreover, the singing of psalms, hymns, and spiritual songs (Eph 5:19) based on these sacred texts would have facilitated worshipers' scriptural literacy.

Second, there is no reason to assume either that Paul's audience was exposed to only one hearing of the letter or that all members of the audience heard it in the same way and understood it to the same degree.[89] Rather, it is more plausible to imagine that such a complex document, which offered its audience an ethnography to boot, would have been subjected to multiple public readings in the course of study and debate necessary for the apostolic teaching contained therein to be adequately interpreted and assimilated by the Roman communities.[90] This suggests that believers less familiar with Israel's sacred texts and the narratives derived from them would have been instructed by those more versed in such matters, including the letter's carrier who would have

---

87. Here, I am in agreement with Mikael Tellbe (Tellbe, *Paul between Synagogue and State*, 160).
88. Wagner, *Heralds of the Good News*, 33–34.
89. Wagner, *Heralds of the Good News*, 36–39.
90. Wagner, *Heralds of the Good News*, 36–39.

had the authority to interpret the letter's content and teach it to others. Moreover, the experience of multiple readings implies that a grasp of both the subtleties of Paul's argument and the complex interconnectedness of its pieces is not limited to modern exegetes who have the luxury of rereading passages multiple times.

1.6.3 Terminology: Ἰουδαῖοι τὰ ἔθνη, and Χριστιανός

In this work, the term, "Ἰουδαῖοι," is translated as "Jew," since "Judaean" places to much emphasis on geographic location to the detriment of other aspects of identity. There is no inherent reason that the term "Jew" cannot connote an attachment, symbolic or real, to the Judaean homeland and the temple while simultaneously allowing other aspects of ethnicity, especially religious practices and customs, to remain in view.

With respect to the second term, the common scholarly practice of interpreting "Greeks" as a synonym for ἔθνη is highly problematic, since the latter did not denote an actual social entity in the ancient world and would not have been recognized as an ethnic self-designation of a particular people group.[91] Rather, it was developed and used by Jews to represent a conglomeration of all non-Jewish ethnic groups.[92] Thus, it is best translated as "gentiles."

Finally, when it comes to the designation "Christian," the near absence of this term in the NT suggests that these communities did not refer to themselves as Christians, although outsiders may have. However, if interpreters remain aware of the fact that the term "Christian" often carries associations related to the later church, then extra care can be taken to avoid anachronisms when using it in reference to the NT communities. In other words, the designation "Christian" may be correctly applied without neglecting its origin as an outsider term. That said, I will refrain from using the term when dealing directly with the Pauline texts themselves for the simple reason that Paul never uses it.

---

91. Stanley, "Ethnic Context of Paul's Letters," 177–202.

92. Stanley, "Ethnic Context of Paul's Letters," 189. Those whom the Jews identified as "gentiles" would have referred to themselves as Greeks, Romans, Syrians, Cretans, etc. The term and its meaning appears to be adopted from the OT where it is used in reference to neighboring non-Jewish people groups against which the biblical writers defined Israel (Hodge, *If Sons, Then Heirs*, 55).

CHAPTER TWO

Greco-Roman Ethnography & Ethnic Discourse: The Creation and Legitimization of Social Identity

THE IDEA THAT RIGID boundaries exist between historiography, ethnography, mythology, and other categories of ancient prose has been challenged by recent advances in classicist scholarship. These developments have in turn revealed the broad and comprehensive scope of many late Hellenistic texts traditionally classified as belonging to one or another genre. As a result, the genre category conventionally labeled as ethnography has been expanded to include these comprehensive works, which display carefully arranged historical-ethnographical-geographical-mythological elements aimed at accomplishing a specific rhetorical purpose; that is, to either legitimize hegemonic rule, in the case of Greece and Rome, or preserve the continuing place and relevance of a subject people group within the existing hegemony. This has resulted in a reassessment of ancient ethnography's purpose. As all-encompassing, composite works, replete with historical, ethnographical, mythological, and geographical components that are interwoven in complex ways, these texts do more than provide descriptions of either people groups, including their mythic origins and customs, or places, and the political and military events associated with those places. Concerned as they are with re-evaluating and reinterpreting the known world in the face of first, Greek and then, Roman conquest and imperialism, these texts speak to the place and position of various people groups within and without the vast network of the new world brought about by hegemonic rule. As such, they necessarily speak to issues of identity and the legitimization of that identity vis-à-vis the imperial order.[1] Moreover, these writings are examples of how ethnic discourse was utilized by ancient authors for apologetic purposes; that is, to either correct views of the self by outsiders, strengthen insider self-identity, or both.

This reassessment of traditional, modern genre classification of ancient texts has yielded several findings of importance for understanding Romans. As I will argue in the chapters that follow, Paul draws from this reserve of literary texts a variety of motifs and strategies as he fashions a document that is at the same time unique in its own

---

1. Examples of such works include: Polybius, *History* (second century BCE); Strabo, *History* and *Geography* (late first century BCE); and Diodorus Siculus, *Library* (late first century BCE). Strabo's *History* is lost, but his *Geography* has survived in its entirety.

right. He does this in order to establish for his Roman audience a consciousness of their distinctiveness as a communal entity and their particular role in history. At the same time, he demonstrates how this community, with its associated practices and social arrangements, is grounded in the past and how, as a people group living in a new age, it is to construct present meaning from revered traditions.[2] By means of this process of self-definition Paul seeks to strengthen the Roman believers in their resolve to remain faithful as an ethnically diverse people, united in Christ, in a world largely hostile to the community's beliefs and practices. In a broad sense, his purpose is similar to that of his contemporaries. However, unlike his Greco-Roman contemporaries, Paul's historical framework is provided by Scripture and his account of the origin and direction of the Christ community emphasizes its rootedness in a divine plan and purpose that has all of creation in view. Moreover, according to the apostle, this divine plan and purpose has been fully revealed and confirmed in and through the work of Christ, wherein lies the believing community's hope and its legitimization.

The task in this chapter is to examine the characteristic features of these contemporary and near-contemporary Greco-Roman works in order to determine the motifs, strategies, and discourse common to them. My primary focus will be on those texts written during the period of Roman expansion and imperialism, particularly Strabo's *Geography* and Dionysius of Halicarnassus's *Roman Antiquities*. However, I will make recourse to earlier texts written in response to Greek imperialism under Alexander, since these texts served as models for later ethnography. In this regard, Herodotus's *Histories* is especially important, since this text is seen by many classicists as providing not only a model for all of these later all-encompassing works but also a template for reinterpreting a world transformed by global change.[3] Paul works within a largely Jewish worldview, as evidenced by the numerous scriptural quotations and allusions that pepper his letter to the Romans. Thus, the works of Jewish authors, writing in an effort to relate the story of their own people to the larger world of foreign rule and to offer a self-definition of their group in response to that provided by gentile outsiders (apologetic or native ethnography), are especially salient and will also be examined. In this regard, Josephus's *Jewish Antiquities* and *Against Apion* are singularly representative of Jewish-Hellenistic ethnographical works that utilized a scriptural frame of reference in an effort to define and legitimate the place and standing of the Jews within the Roman Empire after the Jewish revolt.

Although the *Geography*, the *Roman Antiquities*, the *Jewish Antiquities*, and *Against Apion* will be of primary focus in this work, I will also make some use of Homer's *Iliad* and *Odyssey*, and Virgil's *Aeneid*, primarily for the purpose of illustrating the flexibility of the genre of ethnography. In addition, at certain points in the discussion, I will make recourse to several indigenous ethnographers, who wrote prior to the first century CE, since it may be safely assumed that these earlier insider apologetic texts

---

2. Wilson, "Urban Legends," 77–99.
3. Clarke, *Between Geography and History*, 69.

had some influence on later writers. Because these texts have not come down to us in intact form, I will be relying on Gregory E. Sterling's in-depth analysis and reconstruction of the existing fragments. The reader is encouraged to consult his work for further study of these earlier indigenous, ethnographic works.

In addition, it is important to note that, although the genre of *Jewish Antiquities* is debated, this work shares the same framework governing the ethnographical writings of Berossus and Manethon (discussed below) in that each, as a member of a misrepresented subgroup, undertakes the task of setting out the story of his own people for the Hellenistic world, utilizing native sources as the historical/mythological frame of reference.[4] Furthermore, the scope of Josephus's work is broad and comprehensive (*Ant.* 1.13; 20.259–61). In it, he reinterprets his people's past in light of their present situation for the purpose of establishing their antiquity in an effort to gain respect and standing within the Empire, while simultaneously strengthening insider identity (*Ant.* 1.5, 9). Moreover, Josephus ascribes an apologetic role to the *Antiquities* in the repeated references back to it in *Against Apion*.[5] As part of this purpose, he Hellenizes his native tradition (i.e., Hebrew Scripture), in both language and in substance, in order to render it intelligible to Greek speakers (*Ant.* 1.5).[6] Similarly, Josephus's later work, *Against Apion* evidences features characteristic of ethnographical texts. The author argues for the antiquity of the Jewish nation, challenges the Greek claim to supreme antiquity, and provides a defense of the lawgiver, Moses, and his code (*Ag. Ap.* 2.151–178). As such, it is a rejoinder to outsiders bent on discrediting the Jewish people, their origins, and their laws.[7] As Josephus puts it, he writes to convict the detractors of deliberate falsehood, correct the ignorance of others, and to instruct all desirous of the truth regarding his people (*Ag. Ap.* 1.1–4).

2.1 The New Age of Roman Rule: The Greco-Roman *Historie Humaine* and Indigenous Ethnographic Responses

2.1.1 General Character of These Texts

As noted above, literary constructions of the new world in the wake of Greek and Roman conquest and expansion are characterized by their broad and comprehensive scope. This suggests that the conventional definition of Greco-Roman ethnography as "the self-conscious prose study of non-Greek people"[8] is misleading in the sense that it

---

4. Sterling, *Historiography & Self-Definition*, 228–29.
5. Sterling, *Historiography & Self-Definition*, 263, 298–308.
6. Sterling, *Historiography & Self-Definition*, 282, 297, 308.
7. Sterling, *Historiography & Self-Definition*, 298.
8. Skinner, *Invention of Greek Ethnography*, 3. Although the Romans also composed ethnographical texts, the Greeks, especially Hecataeus of Miletus and Herodotus, are considered to be the inventors of ethnography.

excludes the larger context of this type of study; that is, its historical and geographical imbeddedness and rhetorical purpose. Similarly, the label, ethnography, is somewhat of a misnomer, since it implicitly detaches the author's description of various people groups from his or her larger historical and rhetorical concerns. In so far as human life in all its ethnic diversity takes place in the matrices of time and space, ancient ethnography necessarily intersects with history/mythology and geography.[9] Accordingly, the category Greco-Roman or indigenous ethnography is better viewed as encompassing a wide array of texts that tell the story of a particular people(s) (content) in an attempt to define and legitimize that people(s) (function).[10] This suggests two things in relation to this group of texts.

First, the literary form noted above, the *historie humaine*, could just as well be labeled ethnography or geography of humanity, since in these works history is intertwined with descriptions of foreign lands and peoples. In other words, since the purpose of these works was to interpret the past in relation to the present or, put differently, the relationship of the various alien cultures, all with their own past, to the ruling power, it is difficult, if not impossible, to separate the historical from the geographical and ethnographical elements. Although there were Greek works specifically identifying the people and locality under discussion,[11] the type of ethnographical writing evidenced in these so-called stand-alone ethnographic treatises is utilized by authors conventionally labeled as either ancient historians and/or geographers, or even epic poets, for that matter.[12] For instance, the influence of Homer, who authored the first periegetic composition, on later authors writing in the *historie humaine* tradition cannot be overemphasized.[13] Strabo begins his *Geography* with an extended tribute to Homer, whom he describes as the inventor of geography, who surpassed all men by going "to the uttermost bounds of the inhabited world, encompassing the whole of it in his description" (*Geogr.* 1.1.1–3). In addition, he identifies Homer as a philosopher and reliable historian (*Geogr.* 1.2.1–40). Moreover, it is Homer whom Strabo cites most often in his own work, explicitly and repeatedly setting the former as the key precedent for what he is attempting to do.[14] Polybius does the same, although less insistently, suggesting that he perceived the past literary tradition embodied in the Homeric epics as providing the most suitable framework within which to construct the present Roman world.[15]

9. Clarke, *Between Geography and History*, 20.

10. Sterling, *Historiography & Self-Definition*, 18.

11. Fornara, *Nature of History*, 12. Examples of such texts include: Hecataeus of Abdera, *Aegyptiaca* (305–302 BCE); Megasthenes, *Indika* (third century BCE); Berossus, *Babyloniaca* (third century BCE). These works will be discussed below.

12. Dillery, "Greek Sacred History," 505–26.

13. Clarke, *Between Geography and History*, 334.

14. Galinsky, "Virgil's *Aeneid* and Ovid's *Metamorphoses*," 340–58; Clarke, *Between Geography and History*, 75–76.

15. Clarke, *Between Geography and History*, 334–35.

A similar example is found in Virgil's epic, the *Aeneid*, a combination of the *Iliad* and the *Odyssey*, which was written in response to the new age of Roman rule and shaped by the new order of the Augustan οἰκουμένη. As such, it provides an excellent case in point of genre fluidity with respect to ancient ethnographical interests.[16] The *Aeneid* is a foundation myth and thus, functions as an etiological account of the Roman Empire, tying it to the legends of Troy. Foundation accounts are ethnographic in that they provide a description of the origin and founding of a people group, in a specific place, at a specific time, as orchestrated by the gods. Evidence of the divine orchestration of founding events serves to legitimize the group under consideration.

Thus, the conventional definition of ethnography as descriptive prose that relates the regional history and local wonders of foreign lands and recounts the customs, laws, and religion of the alien peoples populating them is overly simplistic, since it excludes forms of literature or written discourse that does not follow this generic structure. Works, such as the *Iliad* and the *Odyssey*, appear to have been considered *historie humaine* by the ancient authors who utilized them in composing their own oeuvres. Moreover, even in those prose works that are recognized as stand-alone ethnological treatises, there is considerable fluidity in terms of their structure. For example, in Hecataeus of Abdera's *Aegyptiaca*, all the standard ethnographical elements (land, history, local wonders, and laws, which includes the customs and religion, of a people) are present. However, the importance of geography is diminished by moving it from first position to second. Religion is moved to first position under the description of Egyptian laws and customs, and instead of a simple account of its related cult and practices, the author provides a developed theology viewed through the lens of Greek philosophy (Diodorus, *Library* 1; 21.1; 26.1; 43.6; 69.7; 86.2; 96.2).[17] By way of contrast, Berossus in his *Babyloniaca* emphasizes the history of the Babylonian people, thereby decreasing the significance of land, laws and customs, and local wonders, emphasizing the noble and illustrious heritage of the Babylonians (*Babyloniaca* frags. 2–22).[18] Similarly, Josephus consistently deemphasizes the land theology of his source, the Jewish scriptural text, by omitting covenant scenes, reinterpreting other covenant scenes in order to emphasize the greatness of Israel's numbers, and presenting land acquisition in the form of predictions rather than divine promises. For example, in his rendition of Numbers 22:35, Josephus has Balaam state that the Jews will acquire the land to which God has sent them. Yet, the earth and the sea will

---

16. Galinsky, "Virgil's *Aeneid* and Ovid's *Metamorphoses*," 348–49.

17. Sterling, *Historiography & Self-Definition*, 70–73, 110, 114. The *Aegyptiaca* has not come down to us. However, a version of it exists in Diodorus Siculus, in the first book of his *Historical Library* (Bar-Kochva, *Image of the Jews*, 95, 109–19). Bar-Kochva takes a position similar to Sterling's, arguing that Hecataeus rearranges the standard ethnographic elements to suit his rhetorical purposes.

18. Berossus was the first indigenous ethnographer to present a native perspective. However, the *Babyloniaca* has not come down to us in its entirety. See, Sterling, *Historiography & Self-Definition*, 104–17, for a reconstruction of the text based on the extant fragments and a discussion of its contents.

be filled with their fame and the world in each land will be supplied with residents from the Jewish race (*Ant.* 4.115).[19]

Thus, ethnography, as understood by the ancients themselves, is ill-suited to modern definitions and analytical frameworks. Rather, the antique understanding of this genre was much broader in terms of both structure and function. Not only could an ethnographical work take on a variety of literary forms, but also the various ethnographical elements could be arranged and emphasized according to the author's compositional purpose. This brings us to the second, related point. Ancient ethnography, whatever form it took, be it narrative, epic, prose, poetry, etc., was concerned with far more than simple description. The flexibility of both form and content was largely due to the fact that these works served a variety of purposes. Although many were aimed at preserving a Helleno-centric view of the world, grafting barbarian groups (including the Romans) into Greek myths of origin, these texts also satisfied various political and apologetic agendas.[20] For example, assimilation of Roman history to the Greek past and, especially, to the events related in the Homeric epics was a major preoccupation of writers such as Dionysius and Livy who wrote on early Rome.[21] The ready-made Trojan heritage provided by the Greeks supplied Rome with a respectable genealogy and heroic past that was highly symbolic of its present greatness,[22] thereby legitimizing its self-identity as the sole and rightful world power.[23] Ethnography used for apologetic purposes is evidenced in the work of Manethon and Berossus. Of Egyptian and Babylonian descent respectively, these priests offered indigenous corrections of their respective peoples in response to Greek ethnographic portrayals. Using their native records as proof of their antiquity, they argued that the Greeks were their heirs and debtors, thereby claiming cultural and ethnic superiority (Berossus, frag. 1.4; Manethon, frags. 3a and 4).[24] Likewise, Josephus in all probability deemphasizes the role of the land in Jewish ethnic identity in his *Antiquities* due to his affiliation with and dedication to both the diaspora and his homeland and his desire to avoid the revolutionary implications of Davidic messianism, which would do little to advance his apologetic purposes.[25]

19. Sterling, *Historiography & Self-Definition*, 292.
20. Sterling, *Historiography & Self-Definition*, 101.
21. Clarke, *Between Geography and History*, 321.
22. Donlan, "Foundation Legends of Rome," 109–14.

23. Similarly, Hecataeus of Abdera in his *Aegyptiaca* demonstrates how ethnography could be used for political purposes. A court writer in Egypt, making his point against rival Hellenistic kingdoms, Hecataeus interpreted his Egyptian sources through a Greek lens in order to demonstrate to the Greeks in Egypt that the Ptolemaic kingdom was the ideal state (Sterling, *Historiography & Self-Definition*, 70–91).

24. Sterling, *Historiography & Self-Definition*, 103–36. Similarly, Bezalel Bar-Kochva surveys a gamut of Greek ethnography on the Jews and argues persuasively that Greek attitudes toward Jews were extremely complex and dependent on many variables related to the individual authors, including the various aims that motivated their writing (Bar-Kochva, *Image of the Jews*).

25. Sterling, *Historiography & Self-Definition*, 292.

In sum, rather than being merely descriptive, these writings are highly rhetorical, aimed at a specific audience for a specific purpose. In other words, their authors saw "knowledge of foreign peoples and practices and places as inextricably bound up with understanding the course of human events" and "the construction of identities."[26] Yet, despite fluidity in terms of structure and/or literary form there are motifs common to these texts that both capture the worldview that they share and explain the overlap in content among works that on the surface appear to be quite different. Several of these motifs, as will be demonstrated in the following chapters, are of particular relevance to Romans.

2.1.2 Key Motifs

Greco-Roman and indigenous ethnography are sufficiently similar to warrant examining them together with respect to significant literary topics or themes. Greco-Roman authors, who moved among the circles of the intellectual and political elite, interpreted the new world order resulting from military conquest and expansion in light of the beneficent rule provided by its conquerers, with an eye toward legitimizing their power and authority. Conversely, writers such Hecataeus of Abdera, Megasthenes, Berossus, Manethon, and Josephus, who represented, in one way or another, the various subgroups comprising the new world order, sought to interpret for their new rulers the foreign peoples and cultures which now belonged to them,[27] with an eye toward legitimizing the subgroup's place and standing within it. Despite this difference in perspective, an outsider looking in, in the case of the former, or an insider looking out, in the latter case, all of these texts embrace the Herodotean model of the *historie humaine*. Although indigenous authors sought to correct or improve on this traditional, Greco-Roman model by privileging native sources, they nevertheless continued to work within its conventions.[28] The fact that they wrote in Greek and

---

26. Skinner, *Invention of Greek Ethnography*, 248.

27. Clarke, *Between Geography and History*, 70. Hecataeus of Abdera (c. 320–290 BCE), a Greek who lived in the East, argued that only the Egyptian people were capable of defining themselves. Similarly, Megasthenes (c. 351–281 BCE), a Greek philosopher and diplomat to India, argues for both the supreme antiquity of Indian culture and its identity as a society ruled by philosophers, heightening India's image in the eyes of the Greek world. Berossus (c. 350 BCE), a Babylonian and contemporary of Megasthenes, combines his use of native cuneiform sources with a criticism of Greek sources, arguing that civilization was first given to the Babylonians, not the Greeks. Menathon, an Egyptian and younger contemporary of Berossus, uses native royal records to prove Egypt's antiquity, making the Greek people and their culture heirs and debtors to his own. Similarly, Josephus (c. 37–100 CE) utilizes Jewish Scripture to insist on the antiquity of the Jewish people (Sterling, *Historiography & Self-Definition*, 70, 101, 104, 111, 115–16, 118–23, 133, 262–63).

28. Clarke, *Between Geography and History*, 68, 70; Sterling, *Historiography & Self-Definition*, 110–13. The latter argues that indigenous writings veered sufficiently away from the Greek model so as to create a new genre of apologetic historiography. I am not convinced that there is a significant enough of a shift in function between Greco-Roman ethnography and that of indigenous authors to warrant the conclusion that the writings of the latter constituted an entirely new genre. In both cases,

presented, to one extent or another, their material in Greek dress, while following the general pattern of ethnography, attests to their affinity with their Greco-Roman counterparts, who in turn sought to define them from their own perspective.[29] Moreover, like their Greco-Roman counterparts, these writers assumed the existence of a universal new world order and sought to redefine their own group within the context of this new age. Thus, although indigenous authors were concerned with providing an account of their group's identity that stood in contrast to that provided by Greek and Roman outsiders, they were equally concerned with defining their respective groups in a manner relevant to the present world order.

Nevertheless, the difference in perspectives (insider or outsider, with respect to the dominant power) and frames of reference (Greek or indigenous) does affect how the motifs are expressed in each of the two groups of texts. Thus, for the sake of clarity, the first five motifs addressed below will be examined mainly, and, in the case of the first two, solely, from the Greco-Roman perspective. The sixth motif is especially prominent in indigenous ethnographical works, although not absent from Greco-Roman texts, and will be discussed mainly in relation to these texts. As we will see, the first two motifs come into play in relation to the sixth in indigenous/apologetic ethnography, giving them a distinct expression in these texts.

2.1.2.1 *A Universal Perspective of the World United by a Revered, Traditional, Greek Past Interpreted and Reformulated by the Present New Age*

A major preoccupation of Greco-Roman ethnographers was tracing the origins of the various people groups comprising the Roman Empire and recounting earliest city-foundations in an effort to account for how they came to be in their present state, as either ruler, in the case of Rome, or subject.[30] For all intents and purposes, expanding Roman hegemony had ushered in a new age, characterized by a formerly politically, culturally, and economically diverse world unified under Roman rule,

---

the authors are concerned with legitimizing and defining a people, utilizing similar ethnic discourse (discussed below) to achieve their goal. The difference, rather, seems to lie in perspective, which then determines the sources and/or frame of reference that are utilized. The Greco-Roman accounts were also apologetic insofar as their aim was to legitimate, in the eyes of both insiders and outsiders, the identity of the ruling power in question as the true and rightful world power. In addition, although Sterling refers to this type of writing as apologetic historiography proper, he nevertheless maintains that its basis is ethnography and that it "represents a synthesis of native texts placed together within the general pattern of ethnography" (Sterling, *Historiography & Self-Definition*, 133). If this is the case, then how does it differ from Greco-Roman ethnography, aside from a difference in the sources used? Moreover, the category "apologetic historiography" implies that ethnography and historiography operated as distinct genres in this time period —a view that has been successfully challenged by classicists. Thus, I prefer to see these writings as representing indigenous or apologetic ethnography in line with my use of the descriptor Greco-Roman ethnography.

29. Stering, *Historiography & Self-Definition*, 110–13.
30. Clarke, *Between Geography and History*, 278.

that required both explanation and legitimization. For the ancients, the oldest was the best and, in regard to human origins, the Greeks held the prize, at least in the eyes of the Romans. Although the East would beg to differ, as far as the West was concerned, it was the Greeks who provided both a pre-history and an account of human origins suitable for explaining the Empire's present greatness.[31] Relying on Hellenization rather than Latinization to unite the empire,[32] Rome's willing embrace of Greek culture was the result of many factors, two of which are important for understanding ethnographical constructions in this period. For one, Roman intellectuals, moving at the center of the new world power, embraced the ancient, thus superior, heritage of Greek mythology and the Greek literary forms and style that allowed them to connect these heroes and demi-gods to their own history and tradition. For another, Greek intellectuals such as Strabo, who moved among these same circles of the Roman elite, formulated their re-evaluations of the Roman world against the backdrop of previous periods of expansion, particularly Alexander's imperialism, in essence embracing the Herodotean model, including its Greek frame of reference, refashioning it, in order to apply it to Rome.[33]

Accordingly, these etiological accounts invariably involve figures from the Greek mythical past, particularly demigods and heroes. For example, Virgil takes Aeneas, a figure from Homer's *Iliad*, and the various tales of his wanderings, including his association with the foundation of Rome, and refashions these Greek accounts into an epic that ties the Roman people and the Empire to the Trojan legends (*Aen.* 1.1–7). Similarly, Strabo attributes the foundation of the city of Rome to Romulus and Remus and alternatively to Evander and Heracles (*Geogr.* 5.3.2–3). However, in both instances, the authors are careful to relate the changes taking place over time, so that the past, including the mythical past, is important precisely because it accounts for the present state of affairs.[34]

---

31. Donlan, "Foundation Legends of Rome," 113. An excellent example of this Western preoccupation with all things Greek is provided by Virgil, who sets the story of the *Aeneid* at the time of the fall of Troy, yet retains the cultural discourse of the Augustan "household" (Galinsky, "Virgil's *Aeneid* and Ovid's *Metamorphoses*," 346–47).

32. Lightstone, "Roman Diaspora Judaism," 346–77.

33. Clarke, *Between Geography and History*, 312–13.

34. Clarke, *Between Geography and History*, 278. The rigid distinction between myth and history in modern scholarship on ancient historiography is anachronistic. For ancient writers, although the mythic heroes lived and acted in a time undefinable by human chronology (pre-history), they nevertheless were historically credible figures, since the mythic past was seen as being continuous with the present (Edmunds, "Introduction," 1–20; Brillante, "History and the Historical Interpretation," 91–138 and Doty, *Mythography*, 4, 8). Carl Brillante points out that myths did not enjoy unconditional acceptance. The alternative was between mythical stories that appeared more or less credible based on whether or not they seemed distorted (an unacceptable variant), or were from another group's tradition (Brillante, "History and the Historical Interpretation," 93). For example, Strabo, in his critique of writers who maintain that Dionysus and Heracles were the founders of two cities in India, does not dispute the veracity of Dionysus and Heracles as historical figures. Rather, he argues that the foundation stories themselves are fabrications (*Geogr.* 15.1.8–9).

Thus, Virgil's epic in essence legitimates the Julio-Claudian line as the descendants of the Trojan son of the goddess, Venus/Diana. Similarly, Strabo chronicles individual cities, places, and peoples each with its own pre-existing regional account. However, he uses as sources only those local accounts written within a Greek frame of reference, disregarding those utilizing a coherent but different frame of reference (i.e., countries of the Fertile Crescent).[35] In the case of the latter, foundation accounts are not provided, with the emphasis falling on the present order of things. Moreover, he links all these diverse regions and peoples (including countries of the Fertile Crescent) into a coherent whole, not by linking them together, but via their own individual links to Rome.[36] What emerges is a picture of a great, tiered wheel (with the tiers representing relative distance from the center) with Rome as its hub. It is telling that Strabo conceptualizes India as being timeless, given that it had not yet been conquered by Rome, while other non-Roman areas are presented as unprofitable and undesirable for conquest (*Geogr.* 4.5.3–4; 15.1.1–26).[37]

Thus, the new age of Roman rule derives its own meaning from the past while simultaneously reinterpreting it. It is important to note that this universal perspective involves not only a temporal aspect but also a spacial facet.[38] As to just how universal this spacial perspective is, Strabo writes that the geographer needs only to take into account the inhabited world, the οἰκουμένη (*Geogr.* 2.5.34); that is, those portions of the earth that are populated by humans who by virtue of their place in the οἰκουμένη are related to Rome and the *pater orbis*. The inhabited world thus finds its spacial limits in relation to the scope of Roman power. For Strabo, "after the initial period of coherence under the heroes of Troy and their global wanderings, the world did not lend itself to universal history again until the Romans reunited it."[39] This brings us to a second, related motif.

2.1.2.2 A Universal Perspective of Humanity Whereby Diverse People Groups are Amalgamated While Retaining Their Distinctiveness Via the Ruling Power of the New Age

This significant theme of the fusion of peoples is evident in the *Aeneid* where Aeneas, the Trojan, is given an Italian ancestor, Dardanus (*Aen.* 3.167; 7.207) and is habituated to the Italian lifestyle by a Greek, the mythic Evander, who inhabits the future site of Rome long before the time of Romulus and Remus (*Aen.* Book 8).[40] By

---

35. Clarke, *Between Geography and History*, 278, 314–28.
36. Clarke, *Between Geography and History*, 314–28.
37. Clarke, *Between Geography and History*, 326–27.
38. Galinsky, "Virgil's *Aeneid* and Ovid's *Metamorphoses*," 353.
39. Clarke, *Between Geography and History*, 330–31.
40. Galinsky, "Virgil's *Aeneid* and Ovid's *Metamorphoses*," 346–47, 349. Karl Galinsky points out that the Trojans could be considered as either Greeks or Asiatics. However, Asia had been censured by

means of this Romanized founder of Trojan-Italian-divine descent, Rome is linked to a glorious Greek mythic past, including its pantheon. Moreover, Virgil's Aeneas embodies Roman attitudes and values, without any diminishment of his Trojan heritage. The fact that Rome's noblest families eagerly continued to lay claim to Trojan descent at the time of Augustus, attests to the powerful claim that the past provided by the Greeks had on present day Roman conceptions of the self.[41] Like Aeneas, they conceived of themselves as both Trojan and Roman, with an ancestry that also linked them to the gods.

This idea of synthesis without loss of distinction also finds expression in another central theme that runs through the epic. According to Virgil, Rome is qualified to be the master of the οἰκουμένη precisely because it espouses an ecumenical culture.[42] Put differently, Roman attitudes and virtues are for all people, regardless of such particulars as ethnic descent. This notion of Romanness as something that ideally can be achieved by any person so desiring, rather than something solely determined by biological inheritance (i.e., attributed), finds expression in several different ways as will be discussed below in relation to ethnic discourse. What is important to note here is that being Roman is in some sense equated with being human, thereby resulting in a universalization of the human condition.

This motif is also utilized by Strabo, although in a different and less explicit manner. For Strabo, the world is constructed with a periphery and a primary center,[43] under the governance of providence. In this conceptional framework, nature or providence works to make all things converge to the center of the whole, forming a sphere around it (*Geogr.* 17.1.35–36).[44] Similarly, since the forces of fate and history are themselves governed by providence, they work, like the atoms in the realm of physics, to draw everything to the center of the universe and the world.[45] This idea finds concrete expression in Strabo's final survey of the empire, wherein he depicts it as spreading in concentric circles at the capital, from Rome to Italy, and to areas beyond, suggesting that temporally and spatially everything moves toward this city-center (*Geogr.* 17.3.24).[46] That this philosophical-geographical view of the world is further bound-up with Strabo's political and economic view is evidenced by the picture that emerges as the reader moves through the various descriptions of the people and places in the text. What comes into view is a panoramic scene depicting

---

Octavian in the decade before Virgil wrote his epic, since it was the habitat of his rival, Mark Antony, and his consort, Cleopatra of Egypt. Thus, it was necessary for Aeneas to be de-Asianized. Similarly, Dido, a refugee from the east, like Aeneas, is portrayed as possessing Roman virtues.

41. Galinsky, "Virgil's *Aeneid* and Ovid's *Metamorphoses*," 346–47.

42. Galinsky, "Virgil's *Aeneid* and Ovid's *Metamorphoses*," 346–47.

43. Clarke, *Between Geography and History*, 210.

44. Strabo considered himself a Stoic philosopher and his work a philosophy (*Geogr.* 1.1.1, 22–23).

45. Clarke, *Between Geography and History*, 216.

46. Clarke, *Between Geography and History*, 216–17.

a constant stream of human, material, and intellectual resources toward the center of the world, Rome.⁴⁷ As noted above, Strabo achieves worldwide unity not by linking the diverse regions and peoples addressed in the main body of the work to each other but rather to the capital. All of this suggests not only that Rome and the Roman people, represented by the *pater orbis*, are providentially ordained to be the center of the universe, but also that all of humanity finds its ultimate expression, identity, and meaning under the aegis of Roman rule.

2.1.2.3 *A Loose Chronology and the Use of Broad Mythological Indicators of Time*

As noted above, an important aim of these works, broadly speaking, is to interpret the present state of affairs in light of the remote past. This remote past involved a time frame that could not be measured by human generations or other human chronologies.⁴⁸ The point of narrating such traditions, set in so to speak "timeless time," was not to recount the past systematically but rather to safeguard the memory of events worthy of being remembered for the very reason that they performed an important social function in the present.⁴⁹

In Strabo, the Trojan war, the heroic age, the mythical return of the Heracleidae, along with the battle of Actium are used to indicate time (*Geogr.* 8.5.5; 8.6.15; 8.7.5; 10.5.8; 13.4.5; 15.3.2).⁵⁰ In addition to these fairly crude chronological markers, other vague temporal indicators (e.g. τὸ παλαιόν or πάλαι; νῦν or νυνί; πρότερον μέν; νῦν δέ; ὕστερον) are common (e.g., *Geogr.* 4.1.11; 4.6.10; 6.1.6; 6.2.1), suggesting that precise time is irrelevant.⁵¹ This is borne out by the theme of the succession of empires or individual rulers over a region used to indicate the passage of time, where few details are given concerning the dates involved (e.g., *Geogr.* 11.3.5; 12.4.6). A similar pattern is evident in Herodotus's history of the Egyptian kings which also does not include any dates (*Hist.* 2.99–146). Moreover, Strabo regularly, but for no apparent reason, abandons chronological sequence when describing events (e.g., *Geogr.* 12.8.16).⁵²

Similarly, Berossus of Babylon, utilizing a non-Greek frame of reference, begins his history at the time of the great flood and interweaves his dynastic succession with the Babylonian creation story (frag. 680).⁵³ Aside from the flood story to which the ethnographer gives a specific date, there appears to be, from what can be discerned from the

---

47. Clarke, *Between Geography and History*, 219–20, 223. Clarke notes the following passages as examples of the movement of people groups to Rome: 4.3.2; 10.5.3; 14.1.26; 15.1.73; 17.1.54.
48. Edmunds, "Introduction," 13.
49. Brillante, "History and the Historical Interpretation," 99.
50. Clarke, *Between Geography and History*, 252–54.
51. Clarke, *Between Geography and History*, 255–56.
52. Clarke, *Between Geography and History*, 256–59.
53. Clarke, *Between Geography and History*, 323–24.

fragments, a lack of precise dating of the other major historical events in his chronology.[54] A similar use of native over Greek sources is evident among Hellenistic Jewish writers. Like his Babylonian counterpart, Demetrius utilizes biblical chronological markers to indicate time (frag. 722).[55] Although he provides dates for as many of the events, as hints in the scriptural text allowed, he also identifies and sets forth major events into which all other events are subsumed. As a result, key events and persons in the history of the Jewish people become the major chronological markers in his account.[56]

A comparable method of marking the passage of time is evident in the *Antiquities*. For example, the chronological summary found at the end of Josephus's account of the Babylonian exile, consists of key events in the life of Israel (*Ant.* 10.147–48). Although, he provides precise figures for the span of years occurring between these major events, the focus of his narrative remains on key figures in the biblical narrative, which function as epicenters for his own account.[57] In addition, and analogous to Strabo's chronological method, Josephus rearranges the order of biblical events for his own narrative purposes and brings data in from various places in order to fill gaps and to deal with inconsistencies in the text. Furthermore, he omits a number of biblical episodes, apparently out of concern that they might tarnish the image of the Israel of the past, on occasion retelling potentially unseemly stories in an effort to put his ancestors in a better light.[58]

This lack of attention to precise chronological detail and order suggests that all of these authors were primarily concerned with preserving the traditions associated with key figures and events important for a community's present self-understanding, rather than with presenting a comprehensive account of a region and its people in precise chronological sequence. These persons and occurrences were worthy of remembrance because they spoke of moments of foundation and transformation in the present life of a community.[59] Thus, the emphasis is placed on origins, change, the current state of affairs, and the explanation of the precise relationship that presently exists between the old and the new.

---

54. Clarke, *Between Geography and History*, 323–24.

55. Clarke, *Between Geography and History*, 322.

56. Sterling, *Historiography & Self-Definition*, 160–61, 165–66. These events are: Adam; the flood; the call of Abraham; the entrance into Egypt; the fall of Samaria, followed by Jerusalem; and the reign of Philopator.

57. Sterling, *Historiography & Self-Definition*, 295.

58. Sterling, *Historiography & Self-Definition*, 290, 292.

59. Clarke, *Between Geography and History*, 260.

2.1.2.4 *The Divine Ordering of Human Affairs Without the Negation of Parallel Human Causation*

In one form or another, there is evidence of either super-human or supra-human participation in the major developments related in these texts. In both Homer and Virgil, the role of the pantheon in orchestrating the principle events surrounding the major characters is direct and dramatic. For example, Juno's love for Carthage and her animosity toward the Trojan people underlies the human-divine drama surrounding Aeneas (e.g., *Aen.* 1.8–33, 125–41, 225–96). Similarly, in the Homeric epics, the gods are portrayed as dramatically entering into human affairs, not only orchestrating key events, but also choosing sides (e.g., *Od.* 1.15–20, 45–70; *Il.* 1.44–47, 206–9). Although the role of the divine is less direct and dramatic in nonepic, ethnographic texts, in view of the important role that foundation myths play, the preeminent role that superhuman or semi-divine founders have in the establishment of a city, place, or people group is likewise guaranteed. In these stories, the founder functions as a locus of divine activity that determines the necessity and course of founding a new community.[60] For example, Strabo relates that Massilia was founded by the Phocaeans who followed an oracle given by Ephesian Artemis (*Geogr.* 4.1.4).

In addition to the importance of divine sanction in foundation accounts, whether in the form of oracles, visions, and/or dreams given to founding figures, some texts make an appeal to a larger, guiding force. As noted above, in Strabo's *Geographies*, providence works to ensure that history reaches its climax in the new age of Roman rule. Similarly, although Herodotus provides few examples of events attributed to individually named gods, references to the divine (τὸ θεῖον), the gods (θεοί), or god (θεός) are numerous in the *Histories*, creating the impression of a singular, divine force operating indirectly in human history.[61] This divine agency reveals future events through dreams and oracles that require interpretation and involves lesser divinities who come into contact with humans through dreams and apparitions (e.g., *Hist.* 1.46–48; 1.209; 3.30; 7.12; 8.38–39).[62] Herodotus interprets unusual coincidences of events as evidence of their divine ordering (e.g., 9.100–1), in addition to including more direct and unambiguous divine interventions in his accounts (e.g., 7.12, 14, 17–18; 8.37–39).[63] However, in neither Strabo nor Herodotus does supernatural causation render human agency inoperative or replace empirical cause and effect. Rather, as in Greek thinking in general, these are seen as parallel sets of causation.[64]

With respect to Hellenistic Jewish ethnographers, Josephus's work provides a good example of one way that indigenous ethnographers may have conceptualized

---

60. Wilson, "Urban Legends," 81–82.
61. Niskanen, *Human and the Divine*, 93.
62. Niskanen, *Human and the Divine*, 93–96, 100.
63. Niskanen, *Human and the Divine*, 99.
64. Niskanen, *Human and the Divine*, 102–3.

the role of the divine or providence in human affairs. The central role that providence, πρόνοια, plays in binding together all of the material in the *Antiquities* is acknowledged by the majority of scholars of the literature of this period.[65] Josephus's scathing critique of the Epicureans who exclude providence from human life and declare that God has no thought for human affairs (*Ant.* 10.277–79; also, *Ag. Ap.* 2.180–81) is clear evidence that he strongly believed otherwise. For Josephus, providence, in the sense of God's care, is conditional, in that he attends to those who pursue virtue (*Ant.* 1.346; 4.185; 11.169; 18.309); that is, those who observe his laws.[66] He first makes this point in the *proem* where he states that the main lesson to be learned from this work is that those who conform to the will of God prosper, while those who depart from strict observance of his laws face irretrievable disasters (*Ant.* 1.14); a point he repeatedly makes throughout the narrative (e.g., 1.20, 23, 72; 6.307; 7.93; 17.60; 19.16).[67] The majority of the recipients of this divine care are Israel in the past and its illustrious heroes, who serve as *exempla* for those willing to learn from this account of the Jewish people (e.g., *Ant.* 1.46; 3.38; 4.114; 5.107; 7.95; 10.214; 11.169; 13.80; 14.391; 18.197; 20.18).[68] Given this statement, together with the claim that his purpose is to inform the Greek-speaking world about the Jewish people, suggests that, for Josephus, the God of the Jews and his laws are for all people. His providential care and judgment extends over all of humanity, with the truth of this claim specifically evidenced in his dealings with Israel past and present.

2.1.2.5 *Causal Links Established between Different Sets of Ethnographic Information, so that One Section Explains Elements Found in Another*

Given the apologetic or rhetorical nature of these texts, ethnographers generally not only omitted insignificant and unreliable information (i.e., information not useful to their aims), but also sought to explain customs and laws as a reaction to or a result of events related in the account of origins.[69] In addition, or alternatively, customs were explained as the result of certain geographical or climatic conditions. While, in yet other cases, individual customs received their own unique causal explanation (e.g., Diodorus, *Library* 1.27.1; 1.86; 1.89.1–2).[70]

For instance, according to Herodotus, the political state of the Persian people is a result of their customs and behavior, which are in turn directly related to their physical

---

65. Sterling, *Historiography & Self-Definition*, 295.
66. Sterling, *Historiography & Self-Definition*, 296.
67. Sterling, *Historiography & Self-Definition*, 296.
68. Four postexilic Jewish figures and three gentiles also make the list, the latter three for demonstrating sympathy, in one way or another, with the Jewish people. The three gentiles are: Alexander of Syria (*Ant.* 13.80), Petronius (*Ant.* 18.309), and Izates (*Ant.* 20.18, 91) (Sterling, *Historiography & Self-Definition*, 296).
69. Bar-Kochva, *Image of the Jews*, 96–97.
70. Bar-Kochva, *Image of the Jews*, 97.

environment (*Hist.* 9.122). Likewise, he attributes the contrary nature of Egyptian laws and customs to Egypt's peculiar climate (*Hist.* 2.35–36). Similarly, for Strabo, Rome's centrality is premised on its temperate and habitable climate (*Geogr.* 17.2.1–2). He also attributes Rome's success to the excellence of its form of government, especially its foresight in giving imperial rule to "one man, as to a father," beginning with Augustus Caesar (*Geogr.* 6.4.2). Strabo's writings also provide an example of a case where the account of origins serves as an explanation of a present-day people's customs and laws. According to the Stoic, the ancestors of the Judaeans were Egyptians who were led by one of the Egyptian priests, Moses, to Judaea in protest of the Egyptian practice of worshiping the divine being with images resembling created beings. As Strabo relates, although Moses's immediate successors pursued the same course, superstitious and tyrannical persons were subsequently appointed to the priesthood, giving rise to the present day superstitious practices associated with the Jews (*Geogr.* 16.2.34–37).[71]

As the last example suggests, these causal connections and explanations do not always accurately reflect the reality of the people described, influenced as they are by Greek historical tradition and typical ways of thinking and, in some cases, by the inventiveness of the author.[72] For instance, according to Josephus, the laws and associated customs of present day Jews are not only ancient (*Ag. Ap.* 2.151–54) but also have a divine source (*Ant.* 3.89–90, 93–94), having been transmitted through the Scriptures to the Jewish people (*Ant.* 3.280, 286, 322; 4.302), who are "the most law-abiding of all the nations" (*Ag. Ap.* 2.150). Like Strabo, Josephus's account of origins serves as an explanation of his people's customs and laws. However, in Josephus's case, there is no gradual decline of Judaism in the sense that its laws devolved from their original content and purpose. Rather, they are "engraved" on the "souls" of the Jewish people (*Ag. Ap.* 2.178) in their original form (*Ag. Ap.* 2.183); so that they live under a theocratic constitution that cannot be improved in any way (*Ag. Ap.* 2.184–85).

In sum, as a consequence of Greco-Roman ignorance of native accounts, whether deliberate or unintentional, the imperial vision of a coherent, unified world existed alongside ethnic stereotypes and misinformation regarding various people groups in the literature from this period. The misrepresented subjects could do one of two things: they could simply accept or ignore them; or they could attempt to correct outside perceptions of their group by redefining themselves within the context of the new world order. Some, as we have seen, chose the latter. This brings us to a sixth motif. This theme is especially prominent in indigenous ethnographic works, although

---

71. Strabo's account is less a foundation story than it is a moralizing tale of people led astray by subsequent bad government and superstition (Clarke, *Between Geography and History*, 279n76). The majority of scholars believe that Strabo uses Posidonius, a fellow Stoic philosopher and ethnographer, as a source (*Geogr.* 16.2.43). For Posidonius, the idea of decline was central (Bloch, "Posidonian Thoughts," 284–94.

72. Bar-Kochva, *Image of the Jews*, 97, 100–3. Another example is provided by Hecataeus, who attributes present-day Jewish hostility to strangers as a result of past expulsion from Egypt.

not absent in Greco-Roman texts, and is aimed at correcting the misperceptions and distorted accounts provided by outsiders.

2.1.2.6 *Proof of Both the Historical Legitimacy of the People-Group and of Their Divinely Sanctioned/Mandated Customs and Laws*

In the ethnographical tradition, a given people group was identified by its geographic location, customs and laws, including and especially religion, and, to some extent language; although, the ubiquity of the Greek language made the last element in the list a less salient feature.[73] More importantly, a particular people group's civic and religious laws were deemed legitimate as long as they were given by either a divine or a divinely inspired lawgiver to a people with licit historical claims.[74] As Strabo puts it, the ability for a people group, whether Greek or barbarian, to live together in harmony as a state is premised on the existence of common mandates which make possible a life lived in common. Such harmony is especially evidenced by the existence of a honored and revered cult center or holy place for common worship. Consequently, it is those laws which come from the gods that are to be held in greater honor and veneration (*Geogr.* 16.2.38). In other words, a group's authenticity as a people was dependent on divine constitution through the mediation of the divinely appointed lawgiver who bestowed both the citizenship and the religion which bound the group together as a coherent social, cultural, and political unit. These gods were inevitably Greek.[75] Likewise, the lawgivers were either Greek or could claim Greek ancestry.

Thus, Greco-Roman foundation accounts, such as those seen in Strabo and Herodotus, emphasize Greek superhuman archetypes and the role of the divine in both the establishment of a people group and the social arrangements and religious observances stemming from these divinely orchestrated inaugural events, including and especially the institution of the cults of the patron deities. Moreover, by grafting people groups, including barbarian groups, into Greek mythical lines of descent, these

---

73. For example, in the case of the Jews, the temple, and especially the law, came to be the central symbols of Jewish identity in the period from 300 BCE–70 CE. Since the Hebrew language was closely associated with these two central symbols, and given that diaspora Jews usually spoke the languages of the regions in which they lived, it came to have a certain symbolic force. (Schwartz, "Language," 3–47). With respect to geographic location, it was sufficient for diaspora groups to claim a specific homeland.

74. Olster, "Classical Ethnography and Early Christianity," 15.

75. Although regional gods often went by foreign names, Greco-Roman ethnographers often drew parallels between the Greek gods and the gods of various ethnic groups. Strabo, for instance, points out the common relationship between the rites exhibited in the worship of Dionysius among the Greeks and those among the Phrygians in the worship of the Mother of gods, Rhea, despite the fact that they happened to call her by different names (*Geogr.* 10.3.10–13). Similarly, Herodotus maintains that the Arabians, Assyrians, and Persians all worship Aphrodite, although she is called by different names by these groups, while in the Scythian tongue, Hestia is called Tabiti and Zeus, Papaeus (*Hist.* 1.130; 4.59).

ethnographers ensured both the historical legitimacy of these groups themselves and the legitimacy of their customs and laws.

Conversely, groups deemed to be either spurious or as standing outside of the new world order were simply denied such ancestry. For example, Strabo vehemently denies the fanciful speculations of certain writers who claimed that Dionysus and Heracles were the founders and ancestors of two cities in India and their respective tribes (*Geogr.* 15.1.8–9). India was not a part of the Roman Empire. Recall that according to the Stoic, Moses was a legitimate lawgiver, whose divinely given mandates were subsequently lost under tyrannical rule (*Geogr.* 16.2.39). Consequently, although he concedes that present day Jews continue to engage in common worship, Strabo nevertheless implies that they are spurious followers of Moses and thus, a spurious people. Moreover, a spurious people is expected to have nothing less than spurious laws and customs, which Strabo refers to as "superstitions."

Accordingly, polemical attacks on a given group were aimed at discrediting either the lawgiver and/or the historical legitimacy of his or her followers.[76] However, in instances where Greco-Roman writers expressed distaste toward the Jews, or any other group, for the peculiarity of their laws and customs, this did not amount to denial of that group's legitimacy.[77] Such accusations of inferiority did not necessarily need to be refuted as long as the historical legitimacy of the group and its customs and laws could be established, suggesting that for ancients, the "new" could potentially be deemed "good." The real issue was the legitimacy of any given group's ancestral roots.[78] Vilification of a particular group was achieved by destroying these roots. For example, Apion makes the double claim that the ancestors of the Jews were in fact Egyptians, who were expelled from Egypt on account of their contagious diseases (*Ag. Ap.* 2.8) and that their lawgiver, Moses, was a charlatan and impostor (*Ag. Ap.* 2.145). Josephus counters by establishing the antiquity of the Jewish race and its purity (*Ag. Ap.* 1.1), pointing out the absurdity of the legends about leprosy and Egyptian ancestry (*Ant.* 2.265–66), and establishing Moses's legitimacy as lawgiver (*Ant.* 2.205–6, 230–31, 238–55, 255–57, 286; 4.329–30; also, *Ag. Ap.* 2.154, 157–58, 162–67).

In general, indigenous, apologetic, ethnographical works, such as the *Antiquities* and *Against Apion*, made use of the first two motifs in providing legitimization for their respective people groups and their laws and customs. They did this by assuming a bi-polar stance or hermeneutic, wherein through the glorification of their indigenous past they provided an apology to Hellenism, while simultaneously Hellenizing,

---

76. Olster, "Classical Ethnography and Early Christianity," 15.

77. Olster, "Classical Ethnography and Early Christianity," 15.

78. Olster, "Classical Ethnography and Early Christianity," 15, 26–28, 27n37. Later examples include Celsus's attack on Christians, which centers on accusing Christ of perverting and plagiarizing Jewish customs. Hence, Christianity lacks both ethnic and historical legitimacy since its founder lacks such legitimacy. Aristides, in his *Epistle to Diognetus*, defends Christianity on ethnographical grounds, arguing that its progenitor and lawgiver is God himself, while believers are a new race created through adoption by Christ.

to various degrees, their own traditions so as to engage meaningfully with the larger Greco-Roman world.[79] The tension resulting from this double hermeneutical stance was solved by claiming that the Greeks, and implicitly the Romans, were in reality their groups' heirs and debtors.[80] Although it is more than likely that many, if not most, Greco-Roman outsiders would not have accepted these indigenous versions of reality, they nevertheless served as necessary reminders to insiders of their own ancient heritage and traditions and as such were an important means of reassuring nondominant groups of their historical legitimacy as a people. However, these authors often did not hesitate to establish a variety of links between their own founding ancestors and other people groups. Thus, on the one hand, like their Greco-Roman counterparts, they maintained a universal perspective of the world and its people. On the other hand, their distinct frame of reference necessitated that they cast this universal perspective to reflect their role as the actual founders of human culture and civilization.

Undoubtedly, Josephus stands at the peak of this tradition, consistently recasting key biblical figures into categories of the Hellenistic world.[81] Thus, Abraham is portrayed not only as the father of the Jews but also as the instructor of the Egyptians, who taught them arithmetic and astronomy, which they in turn passed on to the Greeks (*Ant.* 1.158–59; 166–68).[82] Similarly, Adam becomes a figure of universal importance.[83] According to Josephus, his descendant, Seth, produced virtuous progeny, who also discovered the science of astronomy (*Ant.* 1.70–71). From this progeny came Noah, whose sons were the ancestors of all the people groups of the earth. Accordingly, the Greeks cannot be humanity's primal ancestors. Rather, when the Greeks rose to power, they embellished "the nations with names which they

---

79. Sterling, *Historiography & Self-Definition*, 297.

80. Sterling, *Historiography & Self-Definition*, 297. For example, the Hellenistic Jewish writer Artapanos writes that Abraham taught astronomy to Pharaoh, portrays Joseph as both a great land reformer and the discoverer of measures, and presents Moses as the founder of Egyptian civilization (Sterling, *Historiography & Self-Definition*, 175–76, 184, 204, 216–19). Pseudo-Eupolemus's work evidences a distinct universal perspective. For instance, Abraham is consistently presented in relation to foreigners, Greek and Babylonian gods are consistently identified with biblical characters, and the new Greco-Roman culture with its traditions is assimilated into the biblical account and cast into a subordinate role. Eupolemos also freely supplements and alters the biblical text, although, unlike Artapanos and, to some extent, Pseudo-Eupolemus, there is no evidence of the use of non-Jewish sources. He presents Moses as the first wise man and lawgiver, who first gave the alphabet to the Jews, who then transmitted it to the Phoenicians, from whence it finally came down to the Greeks. Hence, Moses is affirmed as the first benefactor of civilization, a claim that the author further supports with elaborate chronological computations.

81. Sterling, *Historiography & Self-Definition*, 295.

82. In this way, Josephus insures that the Jewish people are the only ones who can lay legitimate claim to being the first to unlock the secrets of the heavens. Sterling points out that astronomy was one area of knowledge that was hotly contested among the Babylonian, Egyptian, and Greek ethnographers. All of these people groups were eager to lay claim that their ancestors were the first to discover it. Artapanos was the first Jew to claim that Abraham was the first astronomer (Sterling, *Historiography & Self-Definition*, 177–78). Josephus simply follows suit.

83. Feldman, *Studies in Josephus' Rewritten Bible*, 16.

could understand and" imposed "on them forms of government, as though they were descended from themselves" (*Ant.* 1.120–47). However, despite this insistence that the world as a whole and its diverse peoples are to be understood within the framework of the Jewish scriptural tradition, Josephus keeps an eye on the present order of things. For example, his depiction of humanity's decline after creation stands squarely within the Greco-Roman classical tradition of the Golden Age and its subsequent decline (*Ant.* 1.60–62; 72–73).[84] Providence, which, as noted above, plays a significant role in the *Antiquities*, does not completely escape Hellenization. In a passage dealing with Ahab's death (1 Kgs 22:36) Josephus relates that this story demonstrates the power of fate and shows that even with prophetic foreknowledge, it is impossible to escape it (8.418–20). Essentially a "paraphrase of the Bible within a Greek framework," Josephus's work simultaneously answers critics of the Jews and instills in Jews a sense of pride in their traditions.[85]

2.1.2.7 *The Author's Establishment of His/Her Credentials as an Ethnographer*

The motif of travel in Greco-Roman ethnography played a significant role in establishing both the writer's credentials as an ethnographer and the veracity of his or her account.[86] The task of ethnography involved more than simply relating facts and information about the diverse peoples and places comprising the new world order, since the requirement of autopsy mandated some degree of personal, experiential knowledge of these distant places and the people occupying them. In addition to establishing credibility and veracity, the theme of travel also held a symbolic place in ancient rhetoric and literature. Beginning with the Homeric epics, on through Herodotus, and up into the first-century ethnographers, the extent of a given ethnographer's personal, experiential knowledge of the world functioned as a metaphor for the extent of his or her wisdom.[87]

Thus, Strabo takes great pains to establish himself as an ethnographer both intellectually and experientially. He begins by insisting that the science of geography lies exclusively within the purview of the philosopher, who alone possess learning that is broad enough for the task (*Geogr.* 1.1.1, 11–13, 16, 19).[88] Moreover, the philosopher

---

84. Feldman, *Studies in Josephus' Rewritten Bible*, 11–13.

85. Feldman, *Studies in Josephus' Rewritten Bible*, 1, 570.

86. John Elsner points out that the traveler's tale, the ethnographic account of wonders from the boundaries of the known world, has its roots in Herodotean autopsy, which was appealed to in order to bolster the authority of the text (Elsner, "Hagiographic Geography," 22–37).

87. Elsner, "Hagiographic Geography," 31.

88. That Strabo considers himself a philosopher is indicated by his reference to "our Zeno" (1.2.34); a reference that is further reinforced in book seven, where he confesses himself a Stoic (7.3.4). Moreover, he describes his treatise as a serious work, worthy of a philosopher, and useful to the educated person capable of virtue and practical wisdom (1.1.22–23).

who undertakes such a task must follow in the footsteps of its founder, Homer, and go to the uttermost boundaries of the inhabited world (1.1.2, 16). Accordingly, Strabo describes himself as a person who has travelled much (2.5.11) and makes reference to personal witness of events in specific places throughout the span of the text (e.g., 6.2.6), describing the routes taken to these places (e.g., 2.5.12; 10.5.3). Although his reliance on the accounts of others is clear (2.5.11), it is equally clear that he considered himself a great traveller and intended for his audience to perceive him as such.

The credibility of native ethnographers, preoccupied as they were with the task of providing a self-definition for their own respective subgroups that was both reputable and meaningful within the context of the new world order, was rooted in the authority they had as accurate and reliable interpreters of their own traditions.[89] For example, Josephus, born into one of the priestly lines, with a pedigree tracing his ancestry back to several high priests and noteworthy Hasmoneans (*Life* 1–6), unequivocally states that this illustrious ancestry and his own status as a priest more than qualifies him as an authoritative translator of the sacred texts of the Jews (*Ag. Ap.* 1.53–54; *Ant.* 1.5, 16.84). His excellent achievements in Jewish education and learning (*Ant.* 20.263; *Ag. Ap.* 1.54; *Life* 7–8) ensure that his treatise contains the full story of the Jewish people in accurate detail (*Ant.* 20.261–62), since as one credited with having exact knowledge of the law and the ability to interpret the meaning of the Scriptures, he may in turn be credited with having wisdom (*Ant.* 20.264–65). Josephus also notes his mastery of Greek grammar and literature (*Ant.* 20.263); knowledge and skills which make him particularly suited to the task of writing an ethnography of his people that would be meaningful and understandable to the larger Greco-Roman world.

In addition to these explicit statements regarding his credibility as an ethnographer there is some textual evidence that suggests that Josephus also perceived himself to be a prophet. At the fall of Jotapata, Josephus records that while hiding in a cave from the Roman forces, he came to the recognition of God's election of the Romans and his own prophetic role in the ensuing events, interpreting his subsequent surrender to the Romans as obedience to God's call to the prophetic office (*J.W.* 3.340–408).[90] Moreover, although Josephus does not explicitly identify himself with the prophet Jeremiah, his references to the prophet in the *Antiquities* suggest that he saw himself as of the same ilk.[91] This is borne out in the *Jewish Wars* where Josephus, upon appearing before the walls of Jerusalem, urges surrender (5.391–93).[92] According to Josephus, the human authors of Scripture were Moses and the prophets (*Ag.*

---

89. Similarly, Hecataeus of Abdera castigates Herodotus for placing his own investigations before native, Egyptian sources, arguing that outsiders cannot accurately define who the Egyptians are or what their history is (Diodorus, *Library,* 1.69.7, as quoted in Sterling, *Historiography & Self-Definition*, 69–70).

90. Sterling, *Historiography & Self-Definition*, 235–36.

91. Sterling, *Historiography & Self-Definition*, 237n58.

92. Sterling, *Historiography & Self-Definition*, 237.

Ap. 1.37, 40). However, since the succession of prophets had not remained unbroken (*Ag. Ap.* 1.41), it is the life of his people under the new age of Roman rule that must be interpreted in light of the revered, sacred tradition of the Jews.[93]

2.2 Ethnic Discourse: Constructing Ethnic-Racial Identity

What emerges from the above survey of texts and motifs is the crucial role that ancestry plays in the process of self-definition. For authors of indigenous ethnography, the prototypical ancestor of the subgroup functions primarily as the legitimizing factor of both the group itself and its laws and customs. In the case of Greco-Roman ethnography, the grafting of non-Greek peoples into Greek ancestral lines of descent functions both as a universalizing factor, uniting diverse groups of people under one pedigree and, in the case of Rome, as a legitimating factor, providing a past equal to the ruling power's present image and status.[94] However, Greek ancestry did not necessarily equate to being Greek. According to ancient thinking, Romans remained ethnically Roman despite their ancestral ties to Greek heroes, demi-gods, and deities, and Greeks, like other ethnic groups, could also identify themselves as Roman. Moreover, one's status as a Roman was not necessarily determined by ancestry or birth, since Romanness, like Greekness, was also understood and described in ascriptive terms.

Thus, what underlies the ethnographical motifs discussed above is a complex understanding of ethnicity-race and ancestry-kinship that is reflected in an equally complex system of discourse. As I will discuss below, ethnicity-race and kinship are best envisaged as social constructions. As such, they are malleable constructs, open to being shaped and formed through a variety of cultural mechanisms, including literary discourse.[95] The social embeddedness of ancient conceptions of peoplehood made these constructs particularly useful to writers writing with an apologetic intent; that is, to those seeking to either correct views of a given people group by outsiders, strengthen insider identity, or both. Kinship and ethnicity constructs are well-suited to arguments for group self-definition because while "they present themselves as natural and fixed, they are also open to negotiation and reworking," making them "effective tools" for both defining group membership and shaping group self-understanding.[96]

---

93. Sterling, *Historiography & Self-Definition*, 238.

94. This universalization is also evident in Josephus, who claims universal human descent from the sons of Noah. Although, for this Hellenistic Jewish author, Moses, and to some extent Abraham, functions as the quintessential ancestor of the Jews.

95. Joseph E. Skinner argues that Greek and non-Greek identities in antiquity were formulated and negotiated through diverse media and genre, including art, poetry, song, prose, amulets, coinage, epithets, etc. Thus, interest in the manners and customs of foreign peoples can be found across a wide range of subliterary, iconographic, and material evidence, both Greek and non-Greek alike (Skinner, *Invention of Greek Ethnography*).

96. Hodge, *If Sons, Then Heirs*, 17.

Consequently, in order to understand these texts, we must understand the seemingly paradoxical way that both ethnicity-race and the claim that often accompanied such assertions, kinship-ancestry, were conceived and constructed in antiquity. However, as an essential part of this task, it is necessary to determine what is meant by the terms "ethnicity," "race," and "identity," especially as they are used in relation to ancient societies and cultures. As will be discussed below, race and ethnicity often carry contemporary connotations of immutability and determinism that are anachronistic when applied to the ancient sources. Similarly, although the concept of identity is in many ways an anachronism, it has explanatory potential when used as a heuristic tool in relation to ancient texts. Social or group identity is a trans-historical, trans-cultural, human phenomenon. And although the ancients did not articulate their answer to the question, "Who are we?," in the language and mode of modern sociopsychological categories, the sources indicate that it was a question of central importance to them. This being said, modern articulations of the dynamics of social and, in particular, ethnoracial identity formation similarly provide a useful heuristic aid in understanding the power that discourse had in shaping and forming group identity in antiquity.

2.2.1 Ethnoracial Criteria in Antiquity

2.2.1.1 Ethnoracial Terminology

It is important to note at the outset that race and ethnicity are modern concepts.[97] The terms "race" or "ethnic-group" do not have a one-to-one counterpart in antiquity. Rather, the ancients employed a variety of terms for denoting "peoplehood" or "people group," including: γένος; ἔθνος; λαός; πολιτεία (Greek); *genus* and *natio* (Latin).[98] Moreover, there was considerable variety in what constituted an ethnoracial group in antiquity. In both ancient Greece and imperial Rome, birth relations were achieved more often than not through ritual and not solely by biology, and genealogies were often putative and not necessarily genetic.[99] In addition, the terms themselves had a range of meanings and applications.[100] For instance, γένος and ἔθνος are often used interchangeably in the ancient sources, and although they

---

97. Many classicist scholars view ethnicity, but not race, as a viable analytic category for interpreting the Hellenistic and Roman imperial periods (Buell, *Why This New Race*, 17–18). This is because "ethnicity" is a term that was coined in the mid-twentieth century to provide scholars with an alternative to biologically or genetically based understandings of race that were invoked in support of racist agendas. However, the idea that ethnicity can be perceived as mutable, and thereby nonracist, while race can only be perceived as immutable, and thereby deterministic and racist, does not hold up. Biological or natural definitions of race are the product of a particular Western scientific paradigm, while ethnicity often has biological connotations. Thus, I will use the two terms interchangeably to translate the words used in antiquity to denote the idea of peoplehood or people group.

98. Buell, "Race and Universalism," 433.

99. Hodge, *If Sons, Then Heirs*, 27–28.

100. Buell, "Rethinking the Relevance of Race," 456–57, n. 20.

appear to have been the preferred terms in the Roman imperial period to refer to ethnoracial groupings, they were just as easily applied to the inhabitants of single *polis*, a group we would tend to label as citizens, and even to a larger population inhabiting several cities.[101] Similarly, although γένος could refer to a family group, it could also be applied to a category of any size that recognized its members to be enlisted by birth, either putatively or biologically, or ritually.[102]

However, whether or not the terms "ethnic-group" and "race" when used in reference to antique classifications are truly analogous with modern reference, ancients did use what can best be called ethnic or racial categories to describe themselves and others.[103] Thus, regardless of how these terms are translated, as "race," "ethnic-group," "people group," "kind," etc., their use would have been understood by an ancient audience as signaling a group classification based on such things as: shared ancestors; common worship, gods, laws, rites of inheritance, ritual practices, and ways of life; and commonly held teachings and knowledge.[104]

2.2.1.2 Roman Humanitas, Greek Paideia, and Civic Identity

Based on the objectively observable attributes listed above, what constituted an ethnic group in antiquity appears to be relatively straightforward. Yet, a comprehensive survey of the ancient texts yields a more complex and nuanced picture. Herodotus (*Hist.* 8.144.2) is commonly cited by scholars as identifying an important cluster of conventions defining Greek ethnicity both in his time and long after. These are: a common purpose (avenging the burning of Greek temples by the Persians); shared blood/ancestry; a common language; shared sanctuaries of the gods and sacrifices; and similar ways of life or customs. However, although these criteria were invoked in various combinations and with different emphases in ancient definitions of Greekness after Herodotus, the evidence indicates that they were neither essential to Greek ethnicity, nor the only criteria used. In some texts, climate is deemed a more significant factor in defining a γένος or ἔθνος.[105] In other works, the presence or absence of virtuous

---

101. Buell, "Rethinking the Relevance of Race," 456–57.

102. Hall, *Ethnic Identity in Greek Antiquity*, 34–35. Also, Buell, "Rethinking the Relevance of Race," 456–57 n. 20. Hodge points out that both Greek and Roman sources indicate that birth did not automatically grant membership into the household. Rather, a child had to be ritually admitted into the family by the father. In Rome, adoption created a kinship tie between parents and children parallel to that created by birth, with some texts emphasizing the double kinship of adoptees. There is evidence that adoption was also known among the Greeks and the Jews (Hodge, *If Sons, Then Heirs*, 26–31).

103. Lieu, *Christian Identity*, 16. Some have argued that the concept of race is a peculiarly modern concept. However, the condition for using the concept of race is dependent on the rough idea that people who share a putative common ancestry, and/or customs and laws, and/or way of life, resemble each other and form a distinctive category of people (Kamtekar, "Distinction Without a Difference?," 1–13).

104. Buell, *Why This New Race*, 2.

105. Buell, *Why This New Race*, 37–38.

conduct determines one's γένος. This range of possible criteria extends also into the Roman imperial period,[106] so that any given list of conventions simply provides a glimpse of one plane of a composite, multifaceted construct.

Moreover, although the term γένος is etymologically linked to descent, and genealogical appeals appear across a wide range of texts, claims of kinship or common ancestry are not a necessary feature of ethnicity-race. Consequently, neither are genealogical claims a sufficient indicator of ethnic discourse.[107] For instance, relatively little emphasis was placed on shared ancestry or language in defining Romanness in the imperial period. Rather, weight was given to such criteria as education, observance of Roman laws, morality, piety, citizenship, and the keeping of traditions.[108] Similarly, Greekness could be achieved through *paideia*. Although classical *paideia* was never actually accessible to all persons, it nevertheless presupposed some fluidity in the development of character. Ideally, by means of this educational process, male persons could become citizens who embodied what it meant to be Greek. Accordingly, human difference could be defined in terms of the relative success or failure in achieving the qualities of Greekness. In this sense, *paideia* universalized Greek ethnicity by making it something that could in principle be attained by anyone who desired to do so.[109] Such thinking is evident in the self-appellation "Hellenes," which encompassed members from a variety of people groups, functioning as a unifying term on a number of political and cultural levels.[110] The Roman concept of *humanitas* functioned in a similar way. Essentially defining what it meant to be Roman, it was characterized by the notion that elite male persons best embodied it, while simultaneously maintaining that all persons could attain to its criteria, if they so desired.[111]

The idea that Romanness and Greekness could be achieved, meant that civic identity and ethnicity-race, during the imperial period, were interrelated, causally connected, and interdependent.[112] A case in point is Plutarch, a Greek elite who purports to write authoritatively on Rome and Roman culture for other Greeks. The lack of clarity as to how Romans are to be located in the traditional Greek-barbarian dichotomy in his *Roman Questions* suggests Plutarch's position as an outsider with regard to the Roman people. Yet, the breadth and depth of his knowledge of Rome and the assertion of authority to write about it places him squarely within that ethnoracial group. This suggests that he identified himself as possessing two, legitimate

---

106. Buell, *Why This New Race*, 38.
107. Buell, *Why This New Race*, 40.
108. Buell, *Why This New Race*, 40.
109. Buell, "Race and Universalism," 438. Buell notes that intersecting identity categories such as gender and status functioned to distinguish those who could attain to full Greekness through *paideia*.
110. Lieu, *Christian Identity*, 241.
111. Buell, "Race and Universalism," 462.
112. Buell, "Race and Universalism," 440. Aldo, Buell, "Rethinking the Relevance of Race," 459–60. Although Romanness maintains its civic ties to a particular city, it takes on universal connotations through the practices of empire.

ethnoracial identities.¹¹³ In similar fashion, nested or overlapping ethnic identities also allowed groups to emphasize one ethnoracial identity over another in response to changing political circumstances.¹¹⁴ For instance, the eleven regions of Italy, artificially constructed by Augustus on the basis of a purported mythology of descent, allowed for the unification of ethnoracially heterogenous population under the concept of *tota Italia*. However, in practice, and depending on the particular social or historical context, local populations could choose and did choose to either identify themselves as Roman or distance themselves from Rome by referring to themselves by either their local or regional ethnonym.¹¹⁵

The overlap between civic and ethnoracial identity is also evident in Jewish writings from this period. For example, both Philo and Josephus explicitly label Judaism a *politeia* and write of non-Jews becoming citizens of the Jewish community by adopting its institutions and conventions (e.g., Josephus, *Ant.* 12.142, 15.253; Philo, *Spec. Laws* 1.9.51).¹¹⁶ Similarly, in rabbinic legal discourse on slavery, as in Roman, political and ethnoracial categories were perceived as mutually constituting. Both the rabbis and Roman jurists maintained that the state of enslavement resulted in the effacement of the enslaved individual's past history, social connections and ethnic affiliations, in essence, rendering the slave a nonperson. However, in both instances, this state of denigrated nonpersonhood simultaneously held the potential for transformation. That is, through the legal process of manumission a slave could become a Jewish or Roman citizen, attaining either a Roman or Jewish identity by submitting to Roman or Jewish laws.¹¹⁷

This suggests that we should not be too insistent on separating ethnicity-race from civic identity in antiquity. The same holds true for the categories of religious and racial-ethnic identity. Rather, ethnicity-race, citizenship, and religion were interrelated and interdependent, providing ethnographers with great flexibility in establishing a variety of links between the various people groups comprising the empire. The notion of civic and religious identity as mutually constituting is evidenced by both Philo and Josephus. For both of these authors incorporation into the Jewish *politeia* likewise signifies membership in a particular religious community with its own unique set of practices and beliefs.

2.2.1.3 *The Centrality of Shared Customs and Beliefs*

The key role that shared customs, including common religious beliefs, practices, and modes of worship, played in defining ethnoracial identity is especially evident in

---

113. Preston, "Roman Questions, Greek Answers," 86–119.
114. E.g., Marshall, "Constructing the Self," 49–63.
115. Laurence, "Territory, Ethnonyms and Geography," 95–110.
116. Cohen, *Beginnings of Jewishness*, 126.
117. Dohrmann, "Manumission and Transformation," 51–65.

outsider texts which deal with what constitutes membership in the Jewish race. For instance, although Cassius Dio describes Jews in terms of geographical reference and origins, he notes that this ethnic-racial term is applicable also to other nations who followed Jewish customs, so that the race is even found among the Romans (*Hist. Rom.* 37.17.8).[118] For this writer, anyone devoted to Jewish ways is appropriately called a Jew (37.17.1).[119] Similarly, writing in the first century, Ptolemy explained the difference between Idumeans and Jews in the following way. Jews are those by nature from the the beginning. However, Idumeans, originally not Jews but Phoenicians and Syrians, when defeated by the Jews and compelled to be circumcised and to be counted in the nation and to practice the same customs were called Jews.[120] The Romans also understood that the observance of Jewish laws was an essential part of what constituted being a Jew.[121] Thus, in 49–48 BCE, proconsul Lucius Lentulus, in the context of granting privileges to Roman citizens in Ephesus who were Jews, defined Jews as "those who have and observe Jewish sacred things" (*Ant.* 14.228; 234).

Thus, at least in the eyes of outsiders, Jewishness expressed itself primarily via the observance of practices.[122] This also appears to have been the case for Jews themselves, although the evidence is not unambiguous and there is little in insider texts from this period that points to the use of the term "Jew" with converts.[123] However, contemporary epitaphs suggest that converts to Judaism declared themselves as Jews.[124] Although converts were counted as affiliates of the synagogue and participated in

118. Lieu, *Christian Identity*, 241.

119. Cohen, *Beginnings of Jewishness*, 60.

120. Lieu, *Christian Identity*, 241.

121. Cohen, *Beginnings of Jewishness*, 58.

122. Cohen, *Beginnings of Jewishness*, 28. 39, 40–41, 59. Circumcision functioned as a marker of Jewish ethnicity-race in certain times and places. For Jews, it became the primary marker of Jewish identity in the Maccabean period. Although the association between Jewishness and circumcision is made by a number of Latin writers from this period, some of these authors who mention or discuss Jews do not make this association. Circumcision was also practiced among the Egyptians (Strabo, *Geogr.* 17.2.5), which may be the reason why it did not function as the primary marker of Jewish identity in the eyes of some outsiders. However, it is clear that those who admired and followed Jewish practices, whether or not this included circumcision, were regarded as Jews in the full sense of the term by Roman satirists (Stanley, "Ethnic Context of Paul's Letters," 192).

123. Lieu, *Christian Identity*, 242. It is not clear whether later rabbinic debates about the status of converts within the Jewish community should be read back into earlier texts. These later debates indicate that at least some rabbis saw a difference between accepting the religion of the Jews and becoming a full member of the ethnic community (Stanley, "Ethnic Context of Paul's Letters," 192n36).

124. Lieu, *Christian Identity*, 243. Conversion to Judaism entailed three elements: practice of the law; exclusive devotion to God of Israel; and integration into the Jewish community (Jdt 14:10), with some authors explicitly mentioning only one or two of the three (Philo, *Virt.* 20.102–21.108, 34.182, 39.210–12 and *Spec. Laws* 1.9.51–55, 4.34.178; Josephus, *Life* 113, 149; Bar 41:1–5, 42:4–5). Moreover, although Greek-speaking Jews of the Second Temple period and Hebrew-Aramaic-speaking Jews after 70 CE debated the meaning of circumcision and its place in the conversion process, as far as it is known, no Jewish community accepted male proselytes who were not circumcised (Cohen, *Beginnings of Jewishness*, 157–58).

sacred meals, the label "proselyte" remained attached to them, suggesting their distinctiveness from pedigreed members of the community (e.g., Josephus, *Ag. Ap.* 2.210; Philo, *Moses* 1.147; *Yevamot* 47b).[125] However, the label "proselyte" may simply indicate that such persons were seen as having a dual ethnic identity. That is, they were viewed as being both Jewish *and* Greek/Roman/Syrian, etc. This is highly probable given the fluidity of ancient criteria of race-ethnicity, the selective recourse to kinship and ancestry in particular rhetorical contexts, and the nested nature of ethnoracial identity in antiquity. Thus, it cannot be assumed that affiliation with the Jewish community was simply a matter of adopting a new religion and did not involve a change in ethnic-racial identity. Such persons could have multiple ethnic identities that could be activated or ignored according to the social context.[126]

2.2.1.4 *Shared Religion and Ethnoracial Identity*

This brings us to an observation of particular salience to the analysis of ethnic discourse in ancient ethnographic texts, including Romans. Generally speaking, ethnoracial identity was often deemed to be produced and indicated by religious practices.[127] More specifically, discourse of religion and ethnicity was used to establish a variety of relationships between people groups. In some cases it functioned to mark differences between the people group in question and other groups, so as to produce a collective ethnoracial/civic identity for a group in a diaspora situation. Conversely, it could be used to forge connections between distinctive groups or to enable ethnoracial transformation, as in the case of Jewish proselytes.[128] Moreover, the appearance of similar worship practices across different groups could function to either make claims for ethnoracial ties between diverse people groups or to make appeals to religious customs less important for assertions of ethnic-racial difference.[129]

Moreover, in these texts the connection between who one is and who one worships is interwoven with other criteria for defining membership in an ethnoracial group, including appeals to kinship and ancestry. For example Achior, the leader of the

---

125. Cohen, *Beginnings of Jewishness*, 159–62.

126. Christopher D. Stanley makes a similar point (Stanley, "Ethnic Context of Paul's Letters," 192n37).

127. Buell, "Rethinking the Relevance of Race," 451. For instance, Roman vitriol against Druids suggests that, in some instances, complete religious transformation is necessary for becoming Roman (Buell, *Why This New Race*, 44). The acceptance or rejection of a particular cult was another important mechanism for clarifying what counted as Roman (Buell, "Rethinking the Relevance of Race," 460). The Romans also reconstructed a range of Greek and Etruscan cults, rituals, and rites to bring them under the umbrella of Roman religion (Gruen, *Rethinking the Other in Antiquity*, 348–57). In this way, Rome was able to incorporate the aspects of foreign cultures that they found desirable, while maintaining a clear sense of Roman identity by defining Roman styles of worship (Orlin, "Urban Religion in the Middle," 58–70.

128. Buell, *Why This New Race*, 41.

129. Buell, "Race and Universalism," 430n30.

Ammonites, describes the Israelites as descendants of the Chaldeans, who abandoned the ways of their ancestors to worship the God of Heaven (Jdt 5:6–8). Although there is a clear reference to genealogy, the worship of the same god(s) is foregrounded as that which establishes ethnoracial identity. Thus, when the Chaldeans (referring to Abram in Gen 12) change their religious allegiances and practices, they cease to be Chaldeans and become a new *ethnos*.[130] Similarly, when Achior himself becomes a member of the Israelite community by swearing allegiance to the God of Israel and accepting circumcision, his new identity as an Israelite becomes a hereditary trait for his descendants as they are also counted members of Israel (Jdt 14:10).[131] What is important to keep in mind is that, during this period, religious and civic identity were constructed, defined, and positioned, with respect to each other, in a variety of ways, as ancient ethnographers went about the task of delineating the lines of ethnoracial sameness and difference among the various peoples comprising the new world order.

2.2.1.5 *Ethnic Criteria and the Rhetoric of Identity Construction*

The above discussion highlights the fact that the criteria used in defining what constituted an ethnic-racial group in antiquity were highly flexible. Although shared ancestry was a common criterion of ethnoracial classification, it was not the sole or even definitive one. The criterion of common ancestry, like the criteria of shared civic and religious affiliation, is more often than not interwoven, in these texts, with other salient criteria to form either a backdrop or a foreground for the other criteria, depending on the author's rhetorical purposes. It is likely, for example, that Herodotus framed his particular definition of Greek ethnicity to address intra-Hellenic tensions, specifically the possibility of Athenian dominance, by emphasizing Hellenic unity in the wake of the Persian Wars.[132] This may be contrasted to how Greekness is later defined in the Roman imperial period where it is negotiated in relation to Roman ethnicity, serving as both a model and a foil for definitions of Romanness.[133] In this case, Greek ethnic-racial identity was used either to buttress the claims of Rome's present greatness in light of its questionable past or to assert its superiority over all other subordinate people groups, including the group which it admired most and whose cultural norms it sought to assimilate. Whatever the author's particular aim in such cases, the definition of Greek race-ethnicity which emerged differed from that offered by Herodotus, given its specific rhetorical, historical, and social context.

Thus, the ancients perceived the category of ethnicity-race as fluid, even though crossing such a boundary was also seen as acquiring a permanent identity.[134] This

---

130. Buell, *Why This New Race*, 43.
131. Buell, *Why This New Race*, 44.
132. Buell, *Why This New Race*, 39.
133. Buell, *Why This New Race*, 39.
134. Buell, "Rethinking the Relevance of Race," 451, 459; Buell, *Why This New Race*, 45.

seemingly paradoxical understanding of human sameness and difference was possible due to the nature of ethnoracial categories as social constructs. However, this did not mean that this identity was void of any meaningful ethnoracial content.[135] For example, although *paideia* and *humanitas* resulted in the universalization of Greekness and Romanness, this did not equate to a leveling of ethnic difference. One strategy used by ancient Latin authors to differentiate elite Greeks from elite Romans was to position Greek culture as the first stage of *humanitas* and to claim that the Romans were the legitimate bearers of this process, whereas Greeks have become degenerate.[136] In this way, Roman ethnoracial identity was given respectable roots while it simultaneously surpassed the very heritage that gave it legitimacy.[137] Similarly, universalizing arguments that preserved Greekness as the apex of humanity simultaneously claimed that *paideia* and philosophy were quintessentially Greek and embodied by the Greek few.[138] In other words, ethnic identities were ranked hierarchically in antiquity and any given group could do this to communicate competing ideals regarding its own identity.[139]

In sum, if ethnoracial categories are discursively produced as well as socially and historically contingent, then the terms of their production are contingent not fixed, which suggests that the rhetoric of race-ethnicity in any given text must be investigated in order to establish both how the author defines these categories and how they are used to further the writer's argumentative aims.[140] In addition, the proper interpretation of any given construction of ethnoracial identity is dependent on the understanding that ancient notions of ethnicity-race have a double character.

2.2.2 Fluidity and Fixidity in the Construction of Ethnoracial Identity

The flexibility with which ethnic criteria were utilized in defining ethnicity-race might suggest that this category was completely fluid in antiquity. However, as the concepts of Greek *paideia* and Roman *humanitas* illustrate, ethnic fixity in the form of ancestral descent could be invoked by authors in cases where there was the perceived necessity

---

135. Some scholars argue that the shift over time of definitions of what constitutes a particular ethnicity in antiquity represents a shift from an ethnic to a cultural or religious (in the case of Jewish ethnicity) understanding (e.g., Cohen, *Beginnings of Jewishness*, 132–34, 137–38). However, such a conclusion follows only if one assumes that the meaning of ethnicity inheres solely in fixed criteria such as claims of common descent (Buell, *Why This New Race*, 45). Thus, it is more correct to say that terms such as "Jew," "Greek," and "Roman" remained culturally intelligible as ethnicities up to and into the Roman imperial period, but that what was understood to constitute each group as such changed over time (Buell, "Rethinking the Relevance of Race," 469), with any given author reflecting the intellectual and cultural milieu of the period within which he or she wrote.

136. Buell, "Race and Universalism," 462–63.

137. Buell, "Rethinking the Relevance of Race," 469–70.

138. Buell, "Race and Universalism," 464–65.

139. Buell, "Rethinking the Relevance of Race," 469.

140. Buell, "Race and Universalism," 439, 441n32.

to establish the superiority of a particular ethnoracial group. Accordingly, many classicists and ancient historians argue that ancient notions of ethnicity-race shared a double character: fixity and fluidity, with a spectrum running between these two poles.[141] Thus, a given writer could appeal to genealogical claims or lineages, either putative or biological, essences, or nature to support assertions of ethnic identity as fixed or ascribed.[142] By the same token, ethnoracial identity might also be constructed through appeals to malleability. In this case, achievement, not merely ascription, can be foregrounded, so that ethnicity is portrayed as attainable through common purpose, common language or education (*paideia*), way of life, or religious practices.[143] What is important to realize is that ancient definitions of ethnicity-race do not necessarily occupy one of the extreme ends of the ascribed/achieved or fixed/fluid spectrum. Rather they evidence some combination of appeal to both poles.[144]

2.2.2.1 *Dionysius of Halicarnassus,* Roman Antiquities

The *Roman Antiquities* provides an excellent case in point. In this ethnographic work, Dionysius of Halicarnassus sets out to put to rest issues regarding Rome's questionable past by proving that the Romans are the descendants of Greeks and not of base barbarians as commonly thought (*Ant. rom.* 1.5.1). Accordingly, he transforms each barbarian γένος affiliated with Roman history into a Greek one and cites further evidence of Roman Greekness in its customs, temples, images of gods, and worship practices (*Ant. rom.* 1.9–70; 1.21.1–2), with the ritual practices involved in Greek sacrifice providing the most convincing evidence of the Roman people's true ancestry.[145] The shifting saliency of ancestry is also illustrated in Dionysius's claim that Greeks could become barbarians by forgetting their Greek heritage, neither speaking the language, nor observing Greek customs, nor acknowledging ancestral gods and laws (*Ant. rom.* 1.89.4).[146] Thus, although descent is a salient feature for Dionysius's construal of ethnicity-race in the case of the Roman people, it does not play as important a role as customs and religious practices, particularly with respect to defining Greeks. As a Greek writing under Roman patronage it is noteworthy that Dionysius applies the totalizing categories of Greek and barbarian to the ancestors of the Romans, recasting the Romans as insiders, so that they can now be defined over and against all barbarians

---

141. Buell, "Race and Universalism," 438.
142. Buell, *Why This New Race*, 40–41.
143. Buell, "Race and Universalism," 438.
144. Buell, *Why This New Race*, 41.
145. Hodge, *If Sons, Then Heirs*, 34–35. Dionysius was a Greek rhetorician who came to Rome in 30 BCE and allied himself with the Roman aristocracy and the intellectual and cultural elites who were beginning to embrace Greek culture in response to Augustus's campaign to promote the image of Rome as a legitimate and glorious ruling power. Augustus himself welcomed the cultural hegemony of the Greeks, making it his own.
146. Hodge, *If Sons, Then Heirs*, 35–36.

(now defined as all non-Greeks *and* non-Romans) comprising the world.¹⁴⁷ In effect, he creates both a new ethnic identity for the Romans and a bond of kinship between Greeks and Romans.¹⁴⁸

2.2.2.2 *Oppositional and Aggregative Discourse*

The *Roman Antiquities* also provides a clear illustration of two discursive strategies for defining and constructing ethnicity-race in antiquity that Jonathan Hall identifies and labels as "oppositional" and "aggregative."¹⁴⁹ Oppositional strategies most commonly utilize racial classifications that divide humanity into comprehensive parts. The binary divisions Greek and barbarian, Jew and gentile, and in the case of Dionysius, a semi-tri-partite division, Greek-Roman and barbarian are examples. These strategies function primarily as a means of asserting a people group's self-identity. In these instances, the binary (or semi-tertiary) pair works to negate the collective other, while simultaneously asserting the self by selecting particular, distinguishing boundary markers while purposefully ignoring similarities among different people groups.¹⁵⁰ For instance, the common stereotype of barbarian peoples as characterized by tyranny and a lack of social institutions, the pursuit of luxury and immorality, and the display of sexual degeneracy, serves as the mirror opposite of the social structures and virtues claimed by the Greeks and their successors for themselves.¹⁵¹ This is held to be true despite the fact that not all non-Greek people exhibited these vices, while some Greeks did.

Alternatively, aggregative discursive strategies affirmed inclusivity, allowing for the establishment of connections primarily by positing common genealogies.¹⁵² In these instances, the comprehensive categories of humanity, noted above, when harnessed for aggregative purposes, serve universalizing rhetorical goals.¹⁵³ Claims to common ancestry "provided a means for tying the new to the old, and the other to the familiar."¹⁵⁴ However, it is important to note that people groups linked by means

---

147. Hodge, *If Sons, Then Heirs*, 36.
148. Hodge, *If Sons, Then Heirs*, 36.
149. Hall, *Ethnic Identity in Greek Antiquity*, 47.
150. Lieu, *Christian Identity*, 270–71.
151. Lieu, *Christian Identity*, 272.

152. Hall, *Ethnic Identity in Greek Antiquity*, 47–51. In this regard, see Erich S. Gruen. He argues that although the ancients could accentuate the differences between themselves and foreign groups, they could also visualize themselves as part of a broader cultural heritage. Gruen challenges the traditional scholarly understanding of the construction of Greek identity pioneered by Edith Hall in her highly influential work, *Inventing the Barbarian: Greek Self-Definition through Tragedy*. Edith Hall argues that the concept of Panhellenism and its corollary of all non-Greeks as a collective genus, "the barbarian," were the products of the Athenian ideology which buttressed Greek alliance against the Persians (Gruen, *Rethinking the Other in Antiquity*).

153. Buell, "Race and Universalism," 445.
154. Hodge, *If Sons, Then Heirs*, 36.

of aggregative discourse, nevertheless remain distinct people with their own history, law, and customs.[155] Thus, for Dionysius, Romans were Romans, not Greeks, despite their Greek ancestry. This amalgamation of diverse ethnic groups without the loss of distinction was possible due to the double-natured, seemingly paradoxical character of kinship or ancestry as it was perceived in antiquity.

In ancient, as in modern thinking, the notion of kinship embraces, on the one hand, the idea of a transfer of traits from ancestors to descendants accomplished through biological processes that are seen as natural.[156] Accordingly, inherited traits are perceived as immutable or infallible givens. Since ancients believed that status, personality, character, intellect, and emotional make-up were passed along ancestral lines along with physical characteristics, conceptions of shared blood could be used to legitimate certain patterns of social relationships and identities.[157] However, like ethnicity, kinship constructions, while seen as natural and fixed, were simultaneously malleable, dependent on the specific context and interests involved. For example, elite Athenian families would publish their genealogies, highlighting particular politically appropriate ancestors, in order to legitimate and/or promote their current status, only to adjust these genealogies by including other ancestors who may not have appeared in the previous version when the political climate changed.[158] Thus, although the status of a family was seen as guaranteed by blood, that blood relationship was open to negotiation and change.[159]

Moreover, although kinship was often formulated in terms of biological relationship, it was just as often established by other criteria, such as shared language, territory, religion, customs, and/or laws.[160] As in ethnoracial constructs, which criteria were emphasized and how they were interwoven was a product of the aims of the individual or group proposing the construct. What is important to realize in this regard is that the construction of convincing, authoritative kinship relationships is dependent on the essentialist assertions inherent to the concept of kinship. Without the belief that kinship depends on blood or seed the purported ancestral identity of any given individual or group would lack any real substance.[161] Thus, it is precisely because the Romans share the same blood that runs through the veins of their Greek compatriots that they are no longer accounted as barbarians. However, by simultaneously emphasizing that the Romans possess their own unique bonds of kinship through a shared history, laws, and customs, their integrity as a distinct people is insured. Similarly, Plutarch in his portrait of Alexander has the conquerer announce that all good people

155. Hodge, *If Sons, Then Heirs*, 36.
156. Hodge, *If Sons, Then Heirs*, 20.
157. Hodge, *If Sons, Then Heirs*, 20.
158. Hodge, *If Sons, Then Heirs*, 16.
159. Hodge, *If Sons, Then Heirs*, 16.
160. Hodge, *If Sons, Then Heirs*, 16.
161. Hodge, *If Sons, Then Heirs*, 22.

should be regarded as kin (συγγενεῖς) and all the wicked as foreigners (ἀλλοφύλους) (*Alex. fort.* 329C–D). Describing these totalizing categories (the virtuous and the non-virtuous) in kinship terms serves to naturalize them, while simultaneously preserving the hegemonic position of Greek identity.[162]

In sum, ancient constructions of kinship and ethnicity may seem contrived to modern persons. One need only note the dominant scholarly construction of earliest Christianity as a movement transcending the ethnic particularity of Judaism as a case in point. The influence of this paradigm reflects a particular outworking of the modern tendency to view ethnoracial difference as inherited and immutable. Although affiliation with the believing community was voluntary in the sense that membership was open to all persons, this did not necessarily differentiate it from other religions of the period, nor did it mean that believers did not see themselves as constituting a distinct people group in ethnoracial terms, much like other, similar groups in antiquity who shared common beliefs and worship practices.[163] Moreover, anthropologists and social scientists have recently challenged the essentialist conception of race and ethnicity, arguing that ethnoracial categories are best seen as social constructs. What this suggests is that, although the ancients did not have access to the models and data available to scholars today, they were nevertheless cognizant of the dynamic, context-dependent nature of this means of categorizing human sameness and difference.

2.3 Ethnic Identity and Social Identity Theory

The term "identity" has a variety of meanings dependent on the particular field of scholarship within which it is used.[164] Regardless of which school of thought is adopted, the fact remains that identity is an anachronism when it comes to first-century

---

162. Hodge, *If Sons, Then Heirs*, 39.

163. In this regard, see Buell's work. The author critiques the dominant scholarly construction of early Christianity that maintains that early Christians perceived their religion as transcending ethnoracial differences, arguing that early Christians viewed themselves as an ethnoracial group, defined becoming a Christian in terms of changing one's race, and developed universal claims that all ought to join the Christian people. She reads the early Christian texts as examples of rhetorical practices that define Christianness in and through claims of peoplehood, referring to these specific rhetorical practices as "ethnic reasoning" (Buell, "Race and Universalism," 429–31; also Buell, "Rethinking the Relevance of Race," and Buell, *Why This New Race*). However, unlike Paul, the early Christian apologists presented Christianity as offering an alternative ethnoracial identity for both Jewish and non-Jewish people groups. This raises the issue of the continuation of ethnoracial particularity within the believing community. As we will see, Paul envisions the continuation of ethnoracial diversity within in-Christ unity. It is possible that the view of ethnoracial identity espoused by the early Christian apologists may have opened the door to the modern scholarly construct of Christianity as universal and as superior to the particularity of Judaism. Unfortunately, the vision of a universal peoplehood, without any meaningful retention of ethnic particularity, more often than not resolves into a "universality" that in reality is simply an expression of the dominant/majority group's ethnoracial identity.

164. That is, philosophers speak of the essence of the "self," psychologists define identity within a psychoanalytic framework, and social identity theorists view the "self" in terms of changing roles or group affiliations that individuals take on throughout life.

Greco-Roman and Jewish texts. Yet, as the previous sections demonstrate, the ancients were keenly interested in identity, particularly ethnic-racial identity, despite the fact that they neither used the term nor attempted to delineate the explanatory psychological and social mechanisms and models lying behind it. Since social identity theory attempts to understand and explain the effects of group membership on human identity, it can function as a useful heuristic tool in bringing to light the social dynamics underlying ancient conceptions of group identity, of which, ethnic identity is the most basic. These dynamics are not easily observed by postmodern individualists, who do not come from collectivist cultures; cultures, such as those found in both ancient ethnographic works and in the biblical texts.[165]

2.3.1 Defining Identity and Ethnic Identity

Since there is a gamut of specialized understandings of identity on offer, a rudimentary, working definition that, although simple, nevertheless both captures the term's basic meaning and is equally applicable in both modern and ancient contexts, is in order. Fundamentally, identity involves ideas of sameness and difference, continuity over time, a certain degree or sense of homogeneity, and a recognition of such by both self and others.[166] Essential to this understanding is the notion that without some sense of continuity, there is no identity. The relationship between who we are and the past (history) we tell is a reciprocal one in that the sense of sameness over time and space is sustained by remembering one's history, while what is remembered is contingent upon the identity one assumes.[167] Thus, identity not only involves some idea of stability, as evidenced by the concern with origins prevalent among ancient writers, but also requires the means whereby continuity can be maintained in the context of change, as evidenced by the variety of ways Greco-Roman and indigenous ethnographers negotiated the vicissitudes that accompanied Greek and then Roman imperial expansion. Moreover, as noted above, while ancient discourse on identity has at its core the idea of stability, it simultaneously recognizes that, in practice, identities are dynamic and subject to change.[168]

Thus far, I have been speaking of identity in a broad sense. However, our concern is with ethnicity or ethnoracial identity, which necessarily entails group identity. It is at this point that social identity theory provides some valuable insights.[169] Social identity,

---

165. Kuecker, *Spirit and the 'Other,'* 25–26.
166. Lieu, *Christian Identity*, 12.
167. Lieu, *Christian Identity*, 62.
168. Lieu, *Christian Identity*, 14.

169. Social identity theory is a construct of social psychology and is used by its practitioners in the effort to understand and explain the mechanisms underlying the dynamic relationship between group membership and the creation and formation of identity. It was developed by Henri Tajfel in the early 1970s. See, Kuecker, *Spirit and the 'Other,'* 26n4.

of which ethnoracial identity is an important aspect, is defined as "that part of of the individual's self-concept which derives from their knowledge of their membership in a social group (or groups) together with the value and emotional significance attached to that membership. Some of these group memberships are more salient than others; and some may vary in salience in time and as a function of a variety of social situations."[170] In addition, what distinguishes ethnic identity from other forms of social identity is its orientation toward a reference group (real or imagined) that posits a common origin or history for its members. In other words, ethnicity-race is experienced as a kinship phenomenon, whether biological, putative, or both, that allows such groups to think in terms of family resemblances.[171] Thus, an individual's most basic social identity, his or her terminal identity, is ethnicity-race. Since it answers the question, "Who are my people?" it orients all other social identities.[172] Moreover, since ethnic identities are not necessarily exclusive, an individual may claim multiple ethnoracial identities.[173] Accordingly, given the key role that social identity plays in forming personal identity, it is only to be expected that ancient collectivist cultures would be intensely interested in and preoccupied with ethnoracial categorization. The fact that these classifications more often than not involved a number of other key social categories, such as religious and civic/national identity (as discussed above), makes this fascination with human sameness and difference all the more understandable.

2.3.2 The Formation of Ethnic Identity

2.3.2.1 Social Categorization and Stereotypes

According to social identity theory, the answer to the question "Who am I?" is answered by locating oneself (or another person) within a system of social categories. That is, individuals define themselves (and others) by systematically including themselves within some categories, and excluding themselves from other related social categories.[174] Thus, social identity construction necessarily occurs vis-à-vis the other. Thus, one is a Greek, rather than a Jew, an Egyptian, or a Syrian, whereby Greekness is defined over and against other alien attributes that are deemed both salient and characteristic of non-Greek people groups. In specific social situations, for example, where the attributes of a Jewish social identity become salient an individual who has received a classical, Greek education, speaks the Greek language fluently, and moves easily within Greek economic, political, and social circles will

---

170. Tajfel, "Introduction," 1–11. Also, Tajfel, *Human Groups and Social Categories*, 255.
171. Stanley, "Ethnic Context of Paul's Letters," 179, 179n5.
172. Kuecker, *Spirit and the 'Other,'* 29.
173. Stanley, "Ethnic Context of Paul's Letters," 179.
174. Turner, "Towards a Cognitive Redefinition," 15–40, and Tajfel, *Human Groups and Social Categories*, 258.

foreground his or her education in and practice of the Torah and grasp of Aramaic and Hebrew in order to define him or herself as a member of the Jewish community and to be perceived by others as such. Conversely, in situations where a Greek identity becomes salient, such an individual will bring to fore those attributes which define one as a Greek. This is the case even if this person may identify him or herself as primarily Jewish. This ability to nest ethnoracial identities and arrange them hierarchically is itself premised on the common practice of stereotyping, which, as we have seen, is prevalent in ancient ethnographical texts.

The practice of stereotyping, according to social identity theorists, is essential to the construction of a social identity. The process of systematic inclusion and exclusion from social categories mentioned above is referred to as social categorization. Categorization, or the segmenting of humanity into groups, provides both necessary order to an individual's world and a point of identification.[175] Moreover, this process necessarily involves a set of descriptive, evaluative or normative criteria which characterize what members of the same group are perceived to have in common and how they differ from nonmembers.[176] Hence, the need for stereotypes. At the most fundamental level, individuals stereotype themselves and others in terms of the most basic common or critical attributes that are perceived as defining the ethnoracial category to which they and others belong.[177] As such, stereotypes, which may or may not be accompanied by prejudice, introduce simplicity and order into a complex world of random variation among the individuals comprising any given people group. They serve this function either by changing imprecise differences between groups into clearly defined ones or by creating new differences where none existed before.[178] Consequently, stereotyping tends toward simplification and is accompanied by the tendency both to exaggerate the differences between individuals falling into distinct ethnoracial groups and to minimize these differences within particular groups themselves.[179] In other words, stereotypes operate to reduce judged differences between individuals within an ethnic group, both by insiders themselves and by those outside of the group.[180] Finally, such

---

175. Brown and Ross, "Battle for Acceptance," 155–78.

176. Turner, "Towards a Cognitive Redefinition," 26. It is important to note that members can disagree about what criteria determine ethnoracial membership. Like all forms of social identity, ethnic-racial identity may be contested. In severe cases, this can lead to sectarian tendencies (Stanley, "Ethnic Context of Paul's Letters," 181).

177. Turner, "Towards a Cognitive Redefinition," 26. Henri Tajfel points out that it is clear that the content of various stereotypes has its origins in cultural traditions, which may or may not be related to overgeneralized common experience, past or present, and arise from a process of categorization (Tajfel, *Human Groups and Social Categories,* 132).

178. Tajfel, *Human Groups and Social Categories,* 132.

179. Turner, "Towards a Cognitive Redefinition," 28.

180. Tajfel, *Human Groups and Social Categories,* 121.

stereotypes become socially operative and useful when they are shared by large numbers of people both within and without the particular groups in question.[181]

This final point highlights the significance of social categorization as a heuristic tool for grasping the rhetorical power inherent in stereotyping. In effect, ancient ethnographers, whether defining their own indigenous group in relation to the larger world or establishing the current world power as the legitimate ruling authority, relied on stereotyping to delineate the boundaries of their group of interest. The attributes or critical dimensions that they selected in order to accomplish this task would have necessarily become part and parcel of the ethnic discourse of the day, regardless of whether they used existing stereotypes, modified them to some degree or another, or even created new ones.[182] Moreover, while a number of stereotypes might have existed regarding a particular people group, which one was used and when would naturally have varied according to the context. In some cases, new forms would have arisen on an ad hoc basis as a particular writer or speaker selectively affirmed, denied, or glossed over a variety of stock characteristics associated with a specific ethnoracial group, including his or her own.[183] Whatever the particular aim(s) of the author, and given the prominent role that stereotyping played in social categorization and the construction of a social identity, it was imperative for any group to present a favorable, self-evaluative stereotype, whether the goal was to strengthen insider group identity, preserve or heighten the status of the group within the larger social context, or both.

2.3.2.2 *Positive Intragroup Stereotyping*

Hence, social categorization also explains the pressing need among ancient writers to establish a positive identity for the ethnoracial groups for which they were advocating. Social identity theorists point out that intragroup stereotyping is strongly biased towards a favorable self-evaluation. This means that positive characteristics are more likely than negative characteristics to be perceived as in-group attributes and are more likely to be assigned by group members to themselves when membership in a particular ethnoracial group is salient.[184] This is understandable, given that persons evaluate themselves in terms of their social memberships. However, social categories do not exist in a vacuum and are subject to constant evaluation through comparisons with other similar social categories on relevant value dimensions.[185] Thus, in cases where the in-group is seen to lack positive distinctiveness, there will be a tendency for members to either leave the group, if possible, and seek membership in a higher status

---

181. Tajfel, *Human Groups and Social Categories,* 145.
182. Skinner, *Invention of Greek Ethnography,* 117–18.
183. Skinner, *Invention of Greek Ethnography,* 117–18.
184. Turner, "Towards a Cognitive Redefinition," 30.
185. Turner, "Towards a Cognitive Redefinition," 34.

group, if this is possible, or dissociate themselves from it psychologically.[186] In cases where leaving the social group is not possible, members will seek to adopt creative and or competitive strategies to restore the group's positive distinctiveness.[187]

2.3.2.3 Intragroup Insecurity

As the above suggests, an intensified affiliation with a group is only possible when the group is perceived as capable of supplying some satisfactory aspects of an individual's social identity.[188] Where such satisfaction is lacking, a decrease in affiliation with or even alienation from the group is inevitable.[189] This underscores the dynamic nature of social identity and provides a framework for understanding why the ancient ethnographers set about constructing a favorable identity for their respective groups in the way that they did.

Social change is inevitable, which means that changes in how an individual relates him or herself to his or her group(s) are also inevitable. These changes are described in social identity theory by the notion of insecurity, which arises in stratified situations whenever there is a change in the status quo, due to either some instability in the positions of the various groups within the social system or because the status and power in one of the groups are perceived as illegitimately acquired.[190] This would have been particularly true in the case of both Greek and Roman hegemonic expansion, as has already been discussed. Regardless of the exact causal factor involved, the consequences of an insecure identity are the same—a renewed search for positive distinctiveness among the group(s) involved.

This search may take two different forms: direct competition among groups on the existing criteria of comparison or a redefinition or alteration of these criteria.[191] The first type of search is manifested as in-group favoritism along the mutually agreed upon comparative standards.[192] As discussed above, ancient ethnographers aimed to establish both the antiquity and divine origin of their respective people groups in an effort to secure the much sought after title as the founders of human civilization. The second strategy, called "social creativity" can itself take two forms. It may involve comparing the in-group to the out-group according to some new standard(s), especially in cases where the existing criterion/criteria hold little potential for distinctiveness, or it may involve the reinterpretation of existing characteristics, so that what was

---

186. Turner, "Towards a Cognitive Redefinition," 34.
187. Turner, "Towards a Cognitive Redefinition," 34.
188. Tajfel, *Human Groups and Social Categories,* 140.
189. Tajfel, *Human Groups and Social Categories,* 37.
190. Brown and Ross, "Battle for Acceptance," 157.
191. Brown and Ross, "Battle for Acceptance," 157.
192. Brown and Ross, "Battle for Acceptance," 157.

once deemed unfavorable is now seen favorably.[193] The success of these two strategies in achieving an adequate social identity involves two interrelated stages. First is the positive evaluation by the in-group of its newly created characteristics. Second is the acceptance by the out-group(s) of this evaluation.[194] This last point highlights the social nature of group identity, which depends upon three things. First, it presupposes the existence in the society or culture at large of a common background of myths, images, perspectives and interpretations concerning the social system and its organization. This provides the context for the second phase of construction, which involves the points of convergence and divergence, within this common social/cultural background, of the perspectives adopted by the various subgroups within the social system, who differ from each other due to their particular location within it. The third phase consists of the choices made by individuals between the perspectives (and, consequently, social groups) which are available to them.[195] Thus, it was imperative for ancient ethnographers to securely establish the place of their respective groups within the larger context of the Roman Empire in order to shape the attitudes and behaviors of members in a way that would intensify their affiliation with their own people group in a social context characterized by tremendous diversity and change. This was particularly true for groups such as the Jews and members of the in-Christ movement who faced the double threats of assimilation and persecution.

2.4 Conclusion

Ethnographic texts were concerned with far more than providing a description of foreign peoples and their lands. Flexible in both form and content, such works satisfied a variety of political and apologetic agendas, including relating the story of a people for the purpose of defining and legitimizing them within the vast network of a new world order. As such, they were highly rhetorical and the ethnic-racial discourse present within them reflects that character. Ethnicity-race, including the notion of kinship upon which this construction rests, although often presented as natural and fixed through appeals to common ancestry and shared blood, was equally open to negotiation and reworking through the selective choice of varying ethnoracial criteria and attributes. The social embeddedness of ancient conceptions

---

193. Brown and Ross, "Battle for Acceptance," 157. In theory, these two strategies are equally available to both dominant and subordinate groups. However, in practice the first is more characteristic of high-status groups, given that it is easier for them to defend an existing superiority than for a low-status group to reverse it. Low-status groups have more to gain by finding new sorts of comparisons and hence will be likely to use the second strategy. In this regard, it is interesting that indigenous writers sought to compare their ethnoracial groups on the same dimensions as Greco-Roman writers seeking to legitimate Roman power and rule. Yet many of these writers were either Greek and/or moved comfortably among Greco-Roman political and social circles. In either case, they were members of the elite, and thus would most likely not have viewed themselves as members of a low-status group.

194. Brown and Ross, "Battle for Acceptance," 157.

195. Tajfel, *Human Groups and Social Categories,* 226.

of peoplehood made these constructs particularly useful to writers writing with an apologetic intent. Consequently, in order to understand these texts, we must not only understand how ethnic identity was defined and constructed in antiquity, but also how the rhetoric of ethnicity-race and kinship is specifically used in any given work in light of the author's larger purpose(s) in writing. Moreover, since these texts necessarily deal with group identity formation, their interpretation is greatly aided by a grasp of the categories used by social identity theorists in analyzing and explaining the social dynamics underlying ethnoracial identity formation. The latter is essential for modern interpretations that do justice to both the ideological and the sociological elements of these works.

This is no less true of Paul's letter to the Romans. Both the letter itself and the larger sociohistorical-political context suggest that the primary purpose for the apostle's writing to the believers in Rome is to strengthen and encourage them to continued faithful obedience to the gospel. By proclaiming the gospel of hope, Paul presents his Roman audience with a positive communal self-identity that legitimates their standing vis-à-vis the broader culture so as to strengthen and encourage them to continued faithful obedience to its message. By portraying the believing community as a distinct people group related by the shared worship of the one, true God, a common way of life, and shared ancestry, Paul joins the ranks of contemporary Greco-Roman and Hellenistic Jewish ethnographers in telling the story of a particular people in an attempt to situate and legitimate that people within the context of a new age.

Thus, in order to properly interpret this letter, one must not only consider its ethnographic nature, but also its ethnic discourse, paying close attention to both the ethnic criteria Paul chooses and how he utilizes these descriptors within the context of his larger aims for writing. As will be argued in the remaining chapters of this work, careful attention to the ethnographic character of Romans, when used in conjunction with the theoretical grid provided by social identity theory, provides a more robust interpretation of the letter as a whole by shifting the interpretational focus away from the overly narrow preoccupation with Pauline justification and the related issue of gentile inclusion. Since the value of any method, or its proof, can be judged only from the results it yields, the task in the following chapters will be to examine the text of Romans for evidence of its purpose and of points of continuity, in terms of motifs and type of discourse, with ancient Greco-Roman and Jewish ethnography. I will demonstrate that not only is such continuity evident, but also that reading Romans as ancient ethnography best accounts for both its structure and content. Put differently, the proof or value of such a reading is established when its explanatory power as an interpretive framework is established. As I will show, this reading sheds light not only on the textual integrity of Paul's argumentation, but also on the related dichotomies of law-faith (works-grace) and Judaism-Christianity that have vexed scholars of this epistle.

CHAPTER THREE

Paul as an Ethnographer: Writing with an Ethnographic Purpose as a Reliable Interpreter of Tradition

AS DISCUSSED IN THE previous chapter, the purpose, broadly stated, of both Greco-Roman and indigenous ethnography is to tell the story of a particular people in order to define and legitimize that people within the larger context of a universal new world order. Although indigenous authors privileged native sources in constructing their foundation accounts, they, like their Greco-Roman counterparts, sought to redefine their own group within the context of a new age brought about by imperial expansion and consolidation. Moreover, as already noted, the legitimacy of these retellings and redefinitions was closely tied to the intellectual and experiential credentials of the ethnographers themselves. In the case of indigenous writers, it was imperative that they establish their credibility as accurate and reliable interpreters of their own traditions.

This suggests two things in relation to the ethnographical character of Romans. First, given that the choice of genre is directly related to the author's purpose, one would expect to find textual evidence that points to a situation in Rome that might plausibly compel the apostle to write an apology, aimed at insiders, with the purpose of strengthening the Roman believers' communal identity. Second, and similarly, one would expect to find evidence in the text of Paul substantiating his credentials as a reputable ethnographer of the people of God in the new age of the Spirit, inaugurated by the life, death, and resurrection of Christ. That the presence of such evidence would only strengthen the case for the ethnographic character of Romans, necessitates another look at the contentious issue of the letter's occasion and purpose. As far as I am aware, the idea that Paul wrote with an ancient ethnographer's purpose has yet to be considered.

Thus, the goal of this chapter is to demonstrate that Paul, as a credible ethnographer, wrote for the purpose of promoting the new movement's rightful standing as a distinct entity, standing in some relation to Judaism, among the heterogenous people groups comprising the known world of the first century.[1] I will argue that the pervasive theme of hope and encouragement and its negative counterpart, the theme

---

1. The contours of this relationship are examined in the following chapters of this work.

of suffering and persecution, provide an important clue to the letter's occasion. That is, I will show that the Christ followers in Rome were facing communal ostracism and general social persecution perpetrated by nonbelieving friends, neighbors, business associates, and family, including nonbelieving Jews. It is this historical reality which Paul seeks to address by exercising his apostolic authority and duty in proclaiming the gospel of hope. He does this in order to present the believers in Rome with a positive communal self-identity that legitimates the standing of the Christ movement vis-à-vis the broader culture, so as to strengthen and encourage believers to continued faithful obedience to its message. This initial foray into the letter's ethnographic purpose and Paul's credentials as an ethnographer provides the substructure undergirding the ethnographic framework composed of the more specific and discrete ethnographic motifs and strands of ethnic discourse woven throughout the text to be discussed in the chapters that follow.

3.1 Redefining the Occasion of Romans

3.1.1 Historical-Sociopolitical Context

There is no evidence that persecution of members of the Christ movement was sanctioned by the empire during the time Paul penned his letter to the Romans. That state sanctioned persecution did not occur before 64 CE has tended to obscure the fact that persecution, instigated by members of one's family and/or larger community, coming in the form of gossip, slander, and/or ostracism is no less real and painful than government sanctioned oppression.[2] Hostility aimed at destroying personal honor and reputation would have been particularly harmful in an agonistic society highly dependent on social relationships and networks of benefaction for economic and psychological survival and well-being. This is no less true for those who inhabited the city of Rome. Such attacks would have seriously undermined an individual's position within the social networks that made life in the capital possible.

For instance, although gentile believers might have maintained various of their former social networks, they would have had, nevertheless, to renounce their former pagan way of life as a whole. This would have meant relinquishing aspects of their previous social and civic practices, traditions, and habits that were tied to the worship of pagan gods. It is more than likely that some, if not most, experienced at least some opposition from the larger nonbelieving community, including family members, in the hope that such pressure would result in full re-assimilation to Greco-Roman values and traditions, which included the practice of and participation in appropriate religious rituals and celebrations. Void of temple and cult the new movement would have attracted attention as a strange religion, incompatible with traditional Greco-Roman conventions and, thus, posing a danger to peace and security. Moreover, even

---

2. Carolyn Osiek makes a similar point (Osiek, "Romans 'Down the Pike,'" 149–61.

if believers were granted some refuge under the sheltering wing of Judaism, Judaism's status as protected was itself precarious, since Jewish rights were continually renegotiated and renewed by the Roman authorities on an ad hoc basis.[3] On occasion, Jews became the target of local harassment and sporadic persecution by inhabitants of the larger communities within which they lived. In the case of natural disasters, for example, it was assumed that the gods had not been fittingly honored and groups who were known for not worshiping the gods of the *polis* were seen as naturally to blame (e.g., Acts 19:21–41).[4] Moreover, this intimidation need not have attracted the attention of the Roman authorities in order to be rightly considered as persecution. As long as Jewish and gentile believers were viewed as a sect of Judaism they too would have experienced localized persecution in cases where there was the belief that the god(s) had been dishonored in some way.

Similarly, in the case of Jewish believers and former gentile proselytes and sympathizers, it is highly that these members of the Christ movement experienced some level of hostility and/or ostracism from nonbelieving Jewish family members (in the case of Jewish believers) and the larger nonbelieving Jewish community of which they had formerly been a part. It is difficult to conceive that the worship of a crucified messianic pretender as the God of Israel would simply be accepted as one more acceptable permutation of Judaism[5] and not provoke the ire of Jewish religious teachers and authorities. The evidence from Acts suggests otherwise (e.g., Acts 8:1–3, 9:1–2). This in turn suggests that Jewish believers and former gentile proselytes and sympathizers, who wished to attend the local synagogue, would have needed to keep their beliefs concerning Jesus of Nazareth to themselves. Yet, given this, it is not clear why they would continue to attend synagogue, since believers were meeting in their own venues (e.g., Rom 16:5), a practice which allowed them to worship the God of Israel in light of the risen Christ. Moreover, there is no evidence indicating that Christians were

---

3. That is, Judaism's status was not a legal given, but rather something that was negotiated and renegotiated through time. The civic status of diaspora Jews emerged primarily from ad hoc confirmations of a series of city laws mainly relating to conflicts between Jews and Greek citizens that later became part of the Roman *corpus iuris* as an expression of policy. In other words, there did not exist a formal and legal edict or document that defined the legal status of all Jews in the diaspora. Rather the Roman authorities responded to whatever political situations happened to arise (Tellbe, *Paul between Synagogue and State*, 35, 55, 57). Nevertheless, since the empire was generally willing to support Jewish rights when problems arose, Roman policy created a political and social norm throughout the empire that had some legal value. This meant that there was some geographical and chronological consistency in Rome's stance toward the Jews (Rutgers, "Roman Policy towards the Jews," 93–116).

4. Harland, "Declining *Polis*?," 21–49. Almost every city chose a particular deity as benefactor to whom proper honor was due. Acts 19:21–41 realistically portrays the relation between a civic community and its god(s), whereby any threat to that relationship was considered a serious offense. Also, Tellbe, *Paul between Synagogue and State*, 27.

5. The contentious issue of when (and if) the earliest church began to worship Jesus as God cannot be discussed here. I am of the opinion that Larry Hurtado has presented the most compelling case on this point to date. That is, such worship can and should be attributed to the very earliest Christian communities (Hurtado, *Lord Jesus Christ*).

meeting in synagogues. Rather, all of the evidence suggests that they met in private homes. Similarly, with respect to Romans specifically, Andrew Das aptly notes that speculation regarding believers "meeting in the context of synagogue gatherings is to posit a situation to which Paul never refers and which is therefore unlikely."[6] Accordingly, the house church would have functioned as a *replacement* for the synagogue, rather than an alternative or additional venue for traditional Jewish worship in the synagogue.[7] The creation of this alternate worshiping community would have only served to increase the tension between nonbelieving Jews and their believing counterparts, despite the fact that some members of this alternative community continued to keep certain aspects of the Jewish law.

As already mentioned, Jews and members of the Christ movement would have had to maintain their place within the social networks comprising the *polis*, despite their rejection of polytheistic cultic life. For all practical purposes, they could not completely reject all participation in the social, economic and cultural features of civic life if they hoped to survive.[8] The resulting tension would have been difficult to bear. Hostile pressure, the desire for economic and social advancement, the need for maintaining particular social affiliations, and the pull of prior religious participation were all reasons for apostasy.[9] Pressure on Jews to join in pagan worship is indicated by Josephus who writes of the persistent problem of assimilation and apostasy (*Ant.* 12.125–26, 16.58–59; *Ag. Ap.* 2.123, 2.66).[10] Similarly, Philo describes apostate Jews who not only abandon Jewish practice but also embrace pagan worship (*Spec.* 1.316; also *Praem.* 162).[11] Assimilation also appears to have been a threat faced by believers (e.g., Heb 6:4–8).

The pull to assimilate to the broader Greco-Roman culture was not the only temptation experienced by both Jewish and gentile believers. Hostile pressure by nonbelieving Jews may have resulted in some members of the Christ movement assimilating or re-assimilating to Judaism. Although Judaism appears to have been despised among the cultural elite, there is evidence that its moral precepts appealed to at least some non-Jews in Rome (Ovid, *Ars. am.* 1.75–80, 413–16; Lucan *Phars.* 2.592–93; Epictetus *Dissert.* 1.11.12–13, 1.22.4, 2.9.12–19).[12] Gentile believers experiencing hostile, social pressure might find Judaism appealing in that, unlike the new movement, it had ancient roots and at least some standing in the Roman state, precarious as that

---

6. Das, "Gentile-Encoded Audience of Romans," 39.

7. Accordingly, I disagree with both Mark Nanos's and Francis Watson's reconstruction of the Roman situation, which involves believers as being in some degree or another attached to the synagogue (Nanos, *Mystery of Romans*; Watson, *Paul, Judaism, and the Gentiles*).

8. Harland, "Declining *Polis*?," 49.

9. Wilson, "Rivalry and Defection," 51–71.

10. Wilson, "Rivalry and Defection," 57.

11. Wilson, "Rivalry and Defection," 57–59.

12. Tellbe, *Paul between Synagogue and State*, 62.

standing may have been. The need to be affiliated with a religion that had ancient and, therefore, reputable roots would have been pressing for gentile believers who would have had to disassociate themselves both from pagan, ancestral religious practices and from family members who continued to engage in those practices. Given that these believers lived in an agonistic culture built upon participation in viable, life-supporting social networks, the Jewish community, protected as it was, would have provided some sense of identity and belonging.

Complicating matters even further, there is evidence that suggests that first-century Jewish communities in the diaspora, including Rome, sought to distance themselves from believer communities, in an effort to secure their own rights and status in the empire. In other words, the need to prevent Roman association between Judaism and a religion that potentially might be viewed as politically subversive would have been pressing. The evidence from Acts indicates that the Christ movement during its early decades was largely indistinguishable from Judaism when viewed from the outside by the Roman authorities (Acts 18:12–17, 23–29; 25:18–21).[13] However, the picture that emerges on the local level when the relationship between Judaism and the new movement is viewed from the inside, suggests that at least some Jews were keen on differentiating themselves from the latter.

Acts evidences a distinct pattern of hostility against the gospel which emerges as the Lukan author consistently portrays certain Jews as stirring up local crowds against Paul and his companions and accusing them before local leaders or civic authorities, in an effort to undermine their efforts to affirm the gospel's continuity with and place within Judaism.[14] Moreover, the fact that the Lukan texts depict Jews, at times, in league with gentile leaders in the cities and, at other times, making allegations couched in Roman ideology (e.g., Acts 17:7), suggests an attempt on their part to turn an inter-religious dispute into a public matter involving issues of political and social import.[15] Public order and subversion of imperial authority were issues of grave concern to Rome.[16] The Lukan author notes that envy (ζήλου, ζηλώσαντες), presumably of Paul's missionary success (Acts 13:45; 17:5), and the conviction that the apostle's preaching, teaching and/or own personal actions entail beliefs and practices contrary to Jewish law (Acts 18:12; 21: 28; 24:6; 25:7–8) were the primary source of Jewish hostility. Whether or not the fear of being associated with a potentially dangerous or subversive sect presented yet another motivating factor in prompting some Jews to stir up public opposition to the Christ movement is not clear, although it is possible.[17]

---

13. The Lukan author refers to Christianity as a sect (αἱρέσεως αἵρεσιν̓) (Acts 24:5, 14).

14. Tellbe, *Paul between Synagogue and State*, 64, 67. Acts 13:44–52; 14:1–7, 19–20; 17:1–9, 10–15; 18:5–7, 12–17; 21:27–36; 22:6–22, 30; 23:1–22; 24:1–9. 25:1–12.

15. Tellbe, *Paul between Synagogue and State*, 64, 67.

16. Tellbe, *Paul between Synagogue and State*, 67.

17. Tellbe, *Paul between Synagogue and State*, 67. Tellbe suggests that this is the primary motivating factor.

What is clear from the evidence in Acts is that there were Jews in many cities of the empire who were adamant on drawing a distinct line between Judaism and Christianity, a line bold enough to be seen and accepted by outsiders. Moreover, whatever their specific motivation may have been, the particular strategy of opposition engaged, which included the involvement and encouragement of gentile opposition, including gentile civic authorities, suggests that these Jews were also concerned with preserving Judaism's protected status within the empire.[18]

Jewish opposition to the Christ movement in Rome is not explicitly addressed in Acts. However, the Jewish leaders in Rome, who came to see Paul at his bequest during his house arrest, express their awareness of the notoriety of the sect (Acts 28:22), with a number of them refusing to believe (28:23–24). Of particular note is that Lukan author ends the exchange with Paul making reference to the Holy Spirit and the prophet Isaiah, underscoring the continuing recalcitrance of the Jews and the consequent sending of salvation to the gentiles (28:25–29). This suggests that many, though, perhaps not all Jews (28:30), remained not only unmoved by the apostle's message, but also, by implication, hostile to the beliefs and practices of the Christ movement. The fact that such persons were leaders in the community also suggests their influence over members who, in all probability, had some point of contact with believers and the opportunity to respond to them in a negative way.

In addition, there is some evidence that Judaism and Christianity were differentiated early on in the capital city making it possible to distinguish members of the Christ movement at an early stage. First, by 64 CE, less than a decade after Paul presumably penned his letter, Roman believers appear to have been an identifiable group distinct from Roman Jews, since they alone were blamed by Nero for the fire. In addition, the fact that they were assessed to be credible scapegoats for the Emperor suggests that they were sufficiently unpopular with the masses by that time.[19] Even if they were still viewed by outsiders as a sect within Judaism, they were nevertheless seen as being somehow different, in a negative sense, from it. It is unlikely that this distinction and the accompanying hostility flowered suddenly and unexpectedly in 64 CE Rather, it was rooted in conceptions and prejudices planted in the preceding decade.

Second, the Antiochian origin of the name "Christian" in Acts 11:26 suggests that the distinction between Christians and Jews had become a matter of public discourse among outsiders by the early to mid-first century. It is likely that this

18. Tellbe, *Paul between Synagogue and State*, 114. Thus, I agree with Tellbe that Jewish opposition or persecution of Christians without the support of local authorities might have involved potential risk in a Greco-Roman city.

19. Tellbe, *Paul between Synagogue and State*, 64–65, 190. It is possible that the label "*Christiani*," as it appears in both Tacitus's report of the great fire (*Ann.* 15.44) and Suetonius's reference to Nero's persecution of believers (*Nero* 16.2), both written in the early second century, may be an anachronism when applied to the Christ movement in the early and mid-first century. However, the fact that Josephus and other Jewish writers do not refer to this incident, suggests both that Roman Jews were spared, and that Christians were not only seen as a distinct group, but that they were also known by this name.

discourse was known in other cities, including Rome, given the network of communication via messengers, who traversed the well-protected and maintained imperial roads. This would explain why Paul does not refer to his audience as Christians. It also suggests a reason why the Jewish community would seek to distance itself from the Christian movement either by attempting to pressure believing Jews to renounce the Christ movement and rejoin their former community or by securing the aide of gentiles in persecuting the believing community, while legitimizing their own efforts to disband the community and/or put it in the spotlight of Roman authority. Measures taken against Jewish communities in Rome and Alexandria in the 30s and 40s CE suggest that it was important for diaspora communities to safeguard their social and legal status by avoiding any activities that would draw negative Roman attention.[20] During the reign of Nero (54–48 CE) the Jews lived in general tranquility and may even have gained access to the imperial court. In this context it would have been imperative for Jewish leaders to safeguard their rights and privileged status. Moreover, Roman administration of non-Roman religions and the vicissitudes of the Jews under the Julio-Claudians suggests that there may have possible Jewish involvement in Nero's persecution of believers in 64 CE[21] If this was the case, then nonbelieving Jews in Rome would have begun distancing themselves from the Christ movement in the decades preceding their execution by Nero.[22] This in turn suggests that the believer community in Rome was experiencing some degree of hostility from the nonbelieving Jewish community.[23] It also indicates that Paul was writing to encourage the community in the face of potential persecution by Jews via the gentile community and/or civic authorities.

---

20. Tellbe, *Paul between Synagogue and State*, 63, 152, 188–89. During the first century CE, Roman authorities took a definite stand against the Jewish community in Rome in the form of expulsions by Tiberius (19 CE) and Claudius (c. 49 CE), threatened expulsion under Sejanus (30–31 CE), and a ban on Jewish meetings (41 CE) under Claudius. The main reason given for these civic actions against the Jewish community seems to have been the disturbance of civic order. In addition, Peter Richardson argues that the Jewish community at the end of the first century BCE and the beginning of the first century CE was sufficiently connected politically that it named two of its synagogues after the most powerful individuals in Rome: Augustus and his son-in-law, Marcus Agrippa (Richardson, "Augustan-Era Synagogues in Rome," 17–29). Furthermore, one of the synagogues was called "synagogue of the Herodians," while another may have been named after the governor of Syria, Volumnius (White, "Epilogue as Prologue," 361–87).

21. Walters, "Romans, Jews, and Christians," 175–95.

22. Walters, "Romans, Jews, and Christians," 180–81.

23. Tellbe, *Paul between Synagogue and State*, 189, 196–97, 286. Tellbe argues that Paul's positive assessment of Jews in Rom 9–11 makes it unlikely that the opposition against the Christian community in Rome is of Jewish origin. However, he assumes that when Paul wrote Romans some of the Christians in the community were still attending synagogues and that only in the long term would the consistent confession of Christ by Jewish Christians have elicited hostile reactions from the Jewish community.

3.1.2 Textual Evidence of General Persecution

The absence of empire sanctioned persecution of believers in Rome before 64 CE has by and large led interpreters to assume that Paul's references to suffering and hope in Romans do not relate to any specific sociohistorical reality. Although some interpreters make note of the references to suffering, more often than not this is described as the sort of general tribulation that believers experience as the result of their existence in a world that has not yet been fully redeemed.[24] Yet, there are two reasons that warrant caution in drawing the too hasty conclusion that persecution of the believing community in Rome is not in view. First, writers tend to return to the same theme or topic and/or to repeat terms when these are central to the issue(s) they are addressing. Paul's repeated return to the theme of suffering and his utilization of terminology related to endurance, perseverance, and hope points to the importance of this topic and, in turn, to the sociohistorical situation behind the text. Second, as the preceding section indicates, hostility toward the believing community by the larger nonbelieving community is to be expected given the socioeconomic and political dynamics of first-century life in the Roman capital. As I will demonstrate in what follows, Paul's choice of terms and their appearance in both his introductory and concluding remarks, and at points throughout the letter, indicate that the apostle's purpose in writing to the Roman believers is to encourage them to persevere in faithful obedience to the gospel in the face of adversity and hardship.

3.1.2.1 *Paul's Stated Purpose: Rom 1:8–17, 15:14–33, and 16:25–27*

Leaving aside the issue concerning the limits of Rom 1:8–17, there is general agreement that these verses, taken as a whole, indicate the purpose of the letter and reveal the concerns Paul perceives to be important for the letter's recipients.[25] Furthermore, Rom 15:14–33 returns to and expands upon issues and themes introduced in 1:1–17 and expanded upon in the epistle, as a whole, forming an *inclusio* with the latter. That is, Paul's statement regarding the goodness and knowledge of his audience (15:14) reflects his statement regarding their faith in 1:8. Likewise, he reiterates the basis of his authority in addressing them (15:15–16; 1:13–14). In addition, the apostle returns to the themes of obedience of faith and his call to proclaim the gospel to the gentiles (15:18; 1:13–15); the power inherent in the gospel (15:19; 1:16); boasting in Christ/God/the gospel (15:17–18; 1:16); and mutual care of one another (15:30–32; 1:11–12). He also expands on the statements he made in 1:10 and 13 regarding his delay in coming to them (15:18–24). This suggests that 1:8–17 and 15:14–33 should be read together, since each serves to illumine the other. Similarly, 16:25–27 contain the apostle's concluding remarks and, as we will see, not only summarize the main

---

24. For example, Jervis, *At the Heart*, 77–127.
25. Stowers, *Letter Writing*, 21–22.

ideas of the epistle but also reflect key terms and themes found in Paul's opening remarks.²⁶ In sum, all three of the above pericopes function together in revealing the apostle's intent and are best examined together.

In relation to the larger question of the letter's purpose, there are two sub-issues that must be addressed. First, there is the question whether 1:11–12 and 1:13 constitute one purpose or two distinct but related purposes and what is this purpose(s)? Second, is this purpose(s) identical with that of Paul's heretofore delayed visit to Rome? In other words, is there some sense in which the letter itself fulfills the objectives of the pending visit? I begin with the first question.

Paul commences the thanksgiving section by praising God for the saints in Rome because (ὅτι) their faith (πίστις) is proclaimed in the whole world (1:8). Since faith is a primary theme in this letter, it is noteworthy that the apostle introduces it here in relation to his audience. This suggests that Paul's audience is comprised largely of relatively mature believers and that his intent in addressing and/or visiting them does not involve the making of converts. Rather, his desire to proclaim the gospel to them (1:15) stems from his apostleship (1:5) and is for the purpose of strengthening (στηριχθῆναι), that is (τοῦτο δέ ἐστιν) for mutual encouragement through each other's faith, both Paul's and his audience's (1:11–12). That the sharing of a certain spiritual charisma (μεταδῶ χάρισμα ὑμῖν πνευματικὸν) refers in some way to the proclamation of the gospel is evidenced in several ways.

Paul states that he received his apostleship in order to bring about the obedience of faith among all the gentiles (1:5; 16:26). Although the meaning of the phrase "obedience of faith" is debated, it is best to take the genitive construction as including both the sense of a "response which is faith" and "obedience which stems from faith,"²⁷ with obedience referring to a lifestyle that exemplifies that belief; that is, a life conformed to God's will. This comports with the ancient understanding of πίστις, where the term could refer to an interior belief but, more often than not, was used to refer to specific character traits and resulting behavior stemming from that belief.²⁸ Since the apostle's ministry is linked to his duty to proclaim the gospel (16:25–26), note his reference to the prophetic writings in 16:26, which are directly linked to the gospel in 1:1–2,²⁹ this ministry includes both a summons to place one's trust in the

---

26. Similarly, Erwin Ochsenmeier concludes that although the authenticity of Rom 16:25–27 continues to be debated, these verses form an appropriate ending to the letter, "summarizing its main ideas, echoing some of its main terms (power, strengthening, gospel, message of Jesus Christ, revelation, prophetic writings, etc.) and sending the reader back to 1:1–7" (Ochsenmeier, "Romans 1:11–12, 395–406).

27. Dunn, *Romans*, 1:17.

28. Hodge, *If Sons, Then Heirs*, 83. In antiquity, the term could express a range of related concepts: trust, faithfulness, steadfastness, and loyalty. The verb form could denote the following: to trust, to be faithful to, to be steadfast, and in some cases, to believe. Thus, translations such as "faithfulness" or "trustworthiness" and "to trust" or "to be loyal," are best used to connote this particular disposition which in turn is bound up with a specific way of life or behavior.

29. According to Paul, the gospel was promised beforehand through the prophets in the holy

gospel and the demand to live a life of obedience that exemplified that trust. This is reflected in the multifaceted nature of Paul's mission strategy, whereby he often stayed in the cities he traveled to for a lengthy period of time, in order to share his life and to form relationships with those to whom he preached. That is, Paul's initial proclamation of the gospel was embedded within a comprehensive ministry, which included, in addition to the sharing of daily life, theological reflection and debate, ethical instruction, and the sharing of spiritual gifts.[30] In this sense, his mission strategy is multidimensional, in that it reflects the commitment to attract other people not only to the believing community's beliefs but also to its life-style. This is seen in 1 Thess 2:9-12 and in 2 Cor 4:5 where Paul refers to himself as a slave of the people to whom he ministers.[31] In other words, Paul's apostolic duty included proclamation aimed at both nonbelievers, for the purpose of conversion, and at believers, for the purpose of strengthening or increasing their trust in and obedience to God, with the latter in view in Romans.

According to Paul, this strengthening of trust and obedience is accomplished through his sharing with them of some χάρισμα πνευματικὸν (1:11). In Pauline usage, a χάρισμα is a concrete realization of God's grace.[32] The term also refers to the grace and power of God which believers communicate to others through the exercise of individual spiritual gift(s) bestowed upon each of them by the Spirit at the Spirit's discretion.[33] Although Paul does not specify the exact nature of this spiritual gift, the larger context suggests that Paul's proclamation of the gospel, or the exercise of his apostolic office, in some way functions as the means whereby God's grace is actualized for those who hear his message, resulting in their being strengthened by God, as the passive στηριχθῆναι indicates (cf. 16:25; also 15:19). Moreover, the immediately following phrase, τοῦτο δέ ἐστιν συμπαρακληθῆναι ἐν ὑμῖν διὰ τῆς ἐν ἀλλήλοις πίστεως ὑμῶν τε καὶ ἐμοῦ (1:12), indicates that Paul's act of sharing is a demonstration of his faith for the purpose of encouraging his audience. In addition, the reference to mutual encouragement (v. 12) exemplifies the apostle's understanding of spiritual charisma as divinely given gifts to be shared with other believers (Rom 12:4-5; 1 Cor 12:14-26).[34] In other words, although God strengthens the faith of believers through the gospel by means of Paul's apostolic ministry, believers also participate in this process by mutually encouraging each other, presumably by confessing God's trustworthiness and Jesus's lordship and by demonstrating their own belief and trust in God in the concrete actions of daily life. More specifically, Paul

Scriptures (1:1-2).

30. Rabens, "'Von Jerusalem und rings umher,'" 219-37.
31. Rabens, "'Von Jerusalem und rings umher,'" 219-37.
32. Dunn, *Romans*, 1:30.
33. Byrne, *Romans*, 51.
34. Dunn makes a similar point (Dunn, *Romans*, 1:31).

demonstrates his faith by living faithfully according to his apostolic calling to bring all the gentiles to the obedience of faith (1:5-6; 15:15-19).

This suggests that the apostle's reflections on his own past ministry in the East (15:19b-23) not only provide his audience with the reason for why he has often been hindered from coming to Rome (1:13a; 15:22-23), but also function as a demonstration of his unswerving faithfulness to his commission to proclaim the gospel to the gentiles. As such, they provide an example of faithful living for his audience. Paul's reference to his delivery of the collection to Jerusalem (15:25-29) serves a similar function. That the apostle devoted much energy to the collection (1 Cor 16:1-14; 2 Cor 8–9)[35] and that he viewed the gentile churches as debtors (ὀφειλέται) (15:27) to the saints in Jerusalem suggests that he saw the collection as part of his apostleship and his duty to call the gentiles to the obedience of faith. It was by means of the collection that gentile Christians could express in a concrete and practical way their love for and indebtedness to their fellow Jewish brothers and sisters in Christ,[36] with whom they share spiritual blessings, most likely those of the gospel.[37] Paul's perseverance in collecting the contributions from the gentile churches and his resolve to deliver the collection to Jerusalem, despite the hostility he is likely to experience from unbelieving Jews and the possibility that the collection may not be acceptable to the Jewish saints (15:31), evidences the apostle's own faithful obedience. Likewise, Paul's reference to his future plans to proclaim the gospel in Spain (15:23-24, 28) intimates his continuing faithfulness to his calling to proclaim the gospel to the nations. In other words, the travel itinerary, past, present, and future, exemplifies the apostle's own faith or trust in God, even in the face of potential adversity. By the same token, Paul's appeal for prayer on his behalf in the face of anticipated adversity from unbelieving Jews and even possibly from Jewish believers (15:30-32) signals his mutual reliance on the faithfulness of his audience.

Moreover, the apostle is careful to point out that although he has reason to boast of his work or service to God, his boast is solely in Christ (15:17) and in what Christ has brought about or accomplished (κατειργάσατο) through him (15:18-19a). The phrase Χριστὸς δι᾽ ἐμοῦ indicates Paul's belief that anything that has been done in his service to the gospel has been done by Christ. Nevertheless, the agency remains Paul's.[38] In recounting his past ministry, it is telling that he does not mention the trials and tribulations that often accompanied it (e.g., 1 Cor 4:9-13; 2 Cor 11:23-26). This is especially striking, since the Pauline mission strategy evidences flexibility in its plan-

---

35. Dunn, *Romans*, 2:872. The fact that Paul does not need to explain the nature of the collection suggests that his audience had already heard about it. This in turn suggests that they had heard of his efforts and resolve to secure it.

36. Moo, *Epistle to the Romans*, 903.

37. This agrees with Paul's insistence that salvation is through a Jewish Messiah and the fulfillment of promises made to Israel (Rom 1:16; 4:13-16; 11:17-24; 15:7-8).

38. Dunn, *Romans*, 2:862.

ning and implementation due to the conflict and adversity that often accompanied it, mandating a quick change in plans.³⁹ In other words, the apostle deliberately chooses not to mention the very things that have kept him from coming to Rome. Rather, Paul describes his past missionary endeavors in positive, exuberant terms, underscoring the point that his confidence rests in the fact that it was Christ who accomplished it all. In other words, Paul makes clear that the boast in his faithful service to the gospel is grounded in the God who sustains that ministry. Likewise, his hope that the collection will be acceptable to the saints in Jerusalem, that he will be saved from the unbelieving Jews there, and that he will move on to faithfully proclaim the gospel in Spain has its foundation in the faithful God in whom his boast rests.

This notion agrees with and exemplifies Paul's statement in 1:16 where he unequivocally states that he is not ashamed of the gospel, οὐ ἐπαισχύνομαι τὸ εὐαγγέλιον, since it is the power of God into/for salvation for all who have faith, Jew and Greek (1:16).⁴⁰ In the OT, the idea of shame is often used within the context of an individual's faith in or relationship with God. The notion of not being shamed by God is parallel to hoping or trusting in him. In other words, "that one's hope does not shame means that it is trustworthy and utterly reliable, since God himself upholds it" (e.g., LXX Pss 21:6; 24:2–3, 20; 30:2).⁴¹ Moreover, reading this clause as an example of *litotes,* in view of the boasting motifs which follow (2:17, 23; 3:27; 5:2, 3, 11),⁴² what Paul essentially states is that he boasts in the gospel. Hence, similar to his boast of his past work for God and hope for his future ministry in chapter 15, Paul's hope in the gospel has its foundation in the faithful God in whom his boast rests. This is underscored by the phrase which immediately follows, δύναμις γὰρ θεοῦ ἐστιν εἰς σωτηρίαν, and which gives the reason for the apostle's hope or boast. Paul's confidence in the gospel rests in the fact that it is the very power of God (also, 15:19).

For Paul, the term δύναμις refers to the divine force that transforms people at conversion (1 Cor 2:4–5; 1 Thess 1:5); sustains them as those who live a qualitatively different life in Christ (1 Cor 1:18; 2 Cor 4:7, 6:7, 12:9, 13:4; 2 Thess 1:11); and effects complete transformation at the resurrection (Rom 1:4; 1 Cor 6:14, 15:43; 2 Cor 13:4; Phil 3:10).⁴³ In other words, according to the apostle, the gospel is not merely the presentation of an idea. Rather, when it is preached something happens, in that the believer is saved from the power of destruction and transferred to the new age.⁴⁴ This comports with Paul's understanding of salvation as having past, present, and future

---

39. Rabens, "'Von Jerusalem und rings umher,'" 220, 234.

40. Verses 16 and 17 will be examined in more detail in chapter 4, particularly in regard to Paul's reference to both Jews and Greeks and the seeming priority of Jews.

41. Heil, *Romans,* 14.

42. Byrne, *Romans,* 51.

43. Dunn, *Romans,* 1:39. The power of God is a repeated concept in Paul (particularly Rom 1:20; 9:17; 1 Cor 1:18, 24; 2:5; 6:14; 2 Cor 4:7; 6:7; 13:4).

44. Ochsenmeier, *Mal, souffrance et justice,* 66.

aspects. For example, he speaks of salvation as something that has already taken place (e.g., Rom 8:24; 1 Cor 3:15, 5:5); as a present, unfolding reality (e.g., Rom 1:16–17; 1 Cor 1:18); and as pointing to a future culmination (e.g., Rom 13:11; 1 Cor 15:42–44; Phil 3:21). Hence, salvation is a journey from conversion up into its full realization at the eschaton as the preposition εἰς connotes. In common ancient usage, the term salvation denoted physical health, bodily preservation and safety from destructive forces. Although Paul retains some of the term's physical signification in the sense of deliverance from peril and restoration to wholeness, his usage is primarily eschatological in that it refers to deliverance from God's wrath and final destruction at judgment and full entry into the kingdom of God.[45]

Thus, for Paul, the gospel has the power not only to establish the people of God but also to sustain believers on their journey through their present life, in an, as of yet, not fully redeemed world, toward their future fully realized salvation at the eschaton. That this power is God's very own confirms the utter reliability of the gospel to do what it purports to accomplish both now and in the future.[46] Paul's exuberant expression of his own faith or trust in the gospel suggests that he desires that his audience share this same confidence. Much like his description of his faithful service to God in chapter 15, this demonstration of his trust in God's word serves to encourage his audience to persevere in their own faithful obedience. Moreover, given that God's power is mediated through its proclamation, in turn, suggests that Paul believes that his audience can and will be strengthened by hearing its message. However, since he is not speaking to potential converts, the proclamation of the gospel message would in all probability consist of an explication of its implications for believers who are in a situation that requires that they be strengthened. That this is what Paul intends to accomplish among the Roman believers is further evidenced in 1:13.

The reference to τινὰ καρπὸν, in this instance denoting "some appropriate or beneficial outcome or return," appears both to reiterate Paul's concern in verses 11–12, in more general terms, and to reinforce the point that his apostleship gives him the authority to address the Roman community, not as potential converts, but as faithful believers (1:13b–15, cf. 15:14–16). That is, an appropriate outcome of his proclamation of the gospel to those who are already believers would be the strengthening of their trust in and obedience to God. Interestingly, the type of fruit Paul expects to harvest among the Roman believers remains indefinite, as does the spiritual gift the apostle intends to share. In both cases the emphasis falls not on how and what Paul intends to accomplish but on the apostle's certainty that God's grace will work through him in some way and will result in some form of strengthening. Thus, this strengthening may occur through Paul's exercise of the charisma of teaching and/or exhortation.

---

45. Byrne, *Romans*, 51; Dunn, *Romans*, 1:39.

46. As Dunn points out, Paul's notion of the power of God as embodied in and mediated through the gospel accords with the OT understanding of the effectiveness of God's word (particularly, Ps 107:20; Acts 10:36–38) (Dunn, *Romans*, 1:39).

Similarly, the anticipated fruit may consist of individuals being strengthened, in some cases, in relation to their faith or trust in God and in the gospel, in others, in relation to their active obedience to God's will and, in still other cases, in relation to both their trust in and obedience to God. The fact that both sets of verses, 11–12 and 13–15, express the apostle's desire to visit Rome and come one after the other suggests that the strengthening of the Roman members of the Christ movement is his most pressing concern.[47] Consequently, this raises the question: Why did Paul think the Roman believers needed strengthening?

As we will see, Paul's choice of verbs and OT passages provide clues to the situation in Rome that Paul is addressing. However, before exploring this textual evidence, we need to address the issue pertaining to the relationship between Paul's intended visit to Rome and the letter itself. Does the letter itself fulfill the objectives of the pending visit?

Some interpreters have argued that Paul indirectly intends his letter to the Romans to function as a means of sharing with them some spiritual gift.[48] However, this view has been critiqued on the grounds that verses 11b–12, *stricto sensu*, relate the sharing of the charisma with his visit and not with his letter.[49] Nonetheless, there are several reasons why it is correct to think that the epistle fulfills, at least to some degree, Paul's objectives in visiting Rome.

First, in antiquity, letters were commonly though of as a substitute for the sender's actual physical presence. In other words, Paul's audience would have readily linked the letter to the apostle's desire to visit them. Thus, there would have been no reason for Paul to state explicitly that the purpose of his letter was identical to that of his visit. Second, there are indications in the letter that suggest that Paul has already received encouragement from the Romans and expects more in the future. At first glance, the reference to the mutual sharing of faith in 1:12 appears to challenge the view that the purpose of the letter and the intended visit are equivalent.[50] However, the fact that Paul makes note of the Roman community's faith suggests that the very news of their notable faith has already encouraged Paul, as he indicates in his prayer of thanksgiving

---

47. Although καρπός could refer to money given in recompense for a received ministry (Rom 15:28; 1 Cor 9:7; 2 Tim 2:6), as Robert Jewett suggests, (Jewett, *Romans*, 130n4), it does not fit this context. It is hard to see how Paul's pending request for financial help is related to his eagerness to proclaim the gospel (vv. 14–15) and the mutual encouragement of faith (vv. 11–12). Moreover, it is unlikely that verses 13–15 refer to the apostle's desire to gain gentile converts in the wider milieu of Rome as Brendan Byrne suggests (Byrne, *Romans*, 50). This is improbable given Paul's statement in 15:20.

48. For example, Fitzmyer, *Romans*, 248.

49. Ochsenmeier, "Romans 1:11–12," 399. Also, Witherington and Hyatt, *Paul's Letter to the Romans*, 43–44. Although Ochsenmeier acknowledges this grammatical issue, he nevertheless maintains that it "may be right to remain as indefinite (ti) as Paul" and take the spiritual gift as including "the message, content or results of the letter."

50. Witherington and Hyatt, *Paul's Letter to the Romans*, 44.

where he praises God for this state of affairs (1:8).⁵¹ In addition, Paul specifically asks the Romans to pray on his behalf (15:30–31), presumably with the assumption that their faithful obedience would lead them to do so, thereby encouraging him in his own obedience to his calling. Finally, the content of the letter accords with what Paul says concerning the objectives of his delayed visit. Unlike other Pauline Letters, Romans abounds with vocabulary related to affliction, hope, and perseverance.⁵² It is to this vocabulary to which we now turn.

3.1.2.2 *Evidence of Affliction and Oppression: Rom 16:17–20 and 13:1–7*

There is no explicit mention of persecutors in Paul's letter to the Romans. However, there are striking thematic and verbal parallels between Rom 1:8–17, 15:14–33, and 16:25–27, and 1 Thessalonians where both persecutors and persecution of the community are expressly mentioned (1:6; 2:14–16; 3:2–4).⁵³ Before exploring the similarities between the two letters and their significance for determining the historical situation of Romans, it is essential to ascertain whether Rom 16:17–19 refers to persecutors or, at the least, to persons intent on drawing believers away from the gospel.

3.1.2.2a COVERT HOSTILITY: ROM 16:17–20

Although it is not unusual to encounter severe warnings towards the end of Pauline Letters (1 Cor 16:22; Gal 6:12–13; Phil 3:2), some scholars maintain that these verses are a later interpolation.⁵⁴ However, it is not clear that the passage as a whole is untypical of Paul. For example, many interpreters recognize the affinity of Rom 16:17–18 with the content of Phil 3:19. Moreover, the position of the warning in the letter and its themes, vocabulary, and style are sufficiently Pauline to warrant the conclusion that they are original. In the case of Romans, unlike that of the letter to the Philippians, Paul is most likely warning his audience against deceptive outsiders (i.e., nonbelievers). The apostle clearly states that these persons are to be avoided (16: 17b), unlike members of the believing community who are to be welcomed (e.g., Rom 15:7). In addition, Paul gives no indication that any of the weak or the

---

51. Similarly, as Erwin Ochsenmeier points out, in 2 Cor 7:13–14, Paul speaks of having been consoled in the midst of afflictions by Titus's arrival, and the good news that the Corinthians responded positively to his letter (Ochsenmeier, "Romans 1:11–12," 404).

52. Ochsenmeier, "Romans 1:11–12," 404. Similarly, Craig S. Keener notes that although Paul speaks in general terms of "some" Spirit-inspired gift and of mutual encouragement by the others' faith, he nevertheless offers specific exhortations in his letter (12:1; 15:30; 16:17). Moreover, all of these verses use a cognate of the verb for "encourage" (Keener, *Romans*, 24).

53. Since Ochsenmeier has already investigated and noted the parallels between Romans and 1 Thessalonians, I will rely on his work, supplementing it as necessary.

54. For example, Byrne argues that despite some affinity in content with the warning in Phil 3:17–19, much of the language in 16:17–19 is not typical of Paul, which suggests that these verses are best viewed as a Deutero-Pauline interpolation (Byrne, *Romans*, 456).

strong are behaving in ways egregious enough to call for their exclusion. Moreover, dissensions within the community need not necessarily arise from within and may well be caused by outsiders. The reference to these deceivers as those who do not serve Christ (16:18), mark the contrast between those who serve Christ (insiders) and those who do not (outsiders).

Paul does not specify who these persons are or whether they are Jews or gentiles. However, the article τοὺς (16:17a) indicates that his audience would have understood to whom he was referring.[55] This suggests that the apostle is addressing a situation that the Roman believers are facing and will perhaps continue to face for some time. The reference to Satan and his impending defeat by God in verse 20 also points to an event that is currently unfolding and implicates the deceivers as acting under the influence of Satan (cf. 2 Cor 11:14–15).[56] Although the phrase, God will crush Satan under your feet soon (16:20), evinces apocalyptic language referring to the eschatological victory of God over Satan, this does not rule out the possibility that it refers to the resolution of some specific problem in Rome. With regard to this point, it is important to note that the admonition in verses 17–18 is quickly followed by praise (v. 19) which alludes to the community's current state of obedience (ὑπακοὴ) and is known to all (i.e., their obedience of faith [1:8]). In other words, Paul does not indicate that he is asking the Roman believers to remain in their obedience as insurance against future attacks. Rather, he urges them to remain obedient now, knowing that they stand firm in the hope that such evil will, in time, be utterly destroyed.[57] The reference to the eschatological defeat of Satan thus serves as a source of hope in a present, difficult situation. Consequently, the Roman believers can be certain that they will be fully liberated from this evil regardless of whether this vindication occurs at some point in this lifetime or the next.

Thus, it is unlikely that Paul is issuing a nonspecific warning against a potentially dangerous condition that may arise in Rome at some later unspecified time.[58] For all that, the question remains as to what the apostle's timely warning is directed against? Aside from the description of the deceivers' speech as being eloquent but false (χρηστολογίας καὶ εὐλογίας) (i.e., deceptively persuasive) (16:18b) and being contrary to the teaching they have learned (i.e., contrary to the gospel and Christian tradition), the apostle does not give any specifics regarding its content. However, if Paul's audience was aware of who these people are, then it is likely that they were

---

55. Fitzmyer, *Romans*, 745.

56. The word "Satan" appears elsewhere in Paul in 1 Cor 5:5; 7:5; 2 Cor 2:11; 11:14; 12:7; and 1 Thess 2:18.

57. It is not clear whether ἐν τάχει, "soon," refers to preeschatological or imminent eschatological defeat. The phrase may also indicate how something happens, that is, "quickly." The eschatological context suggests the former.

58. E.g., Dunn argues that Paul is drawing on his accumulated wisdom and experience as an apostle in order to pen this broad and nonspecific warning, rather than on events occurring in Rome (Dunn, *Romans*, 2:904).

cognizant of the content of their message, which explains why the apostle does not set forth its components. Moreover, there are clues in the text that indicate that the purpose of their false teaching was to persuade the believers with their beguiling speech to return, at least to some degree, to their prior affiliations and lifestyle, even perhaps to the point of severing their affiliation with the believing community.[59]

The reference to τὰ σκάνδαλα (v. 18a) suggests that the deceivers are attempting to persuade believers to sin by conforming to beliefs and engaging in behaviors and practices that are contrary to the gospel and tradition; that is, contrary to serving Christ. This comports with what Paul writes in chapter 6, 7:5–6, 8:1–13, 12:11, and 14:8 where he exhorts the believers to remain enslaved to God/Christ for the purpose sanctification as they walk in accordance with the Spirit. The exhortations to serve/follow the Lord/Spirit are contrasted with serving/following sin, passions, and/or the flesh. This contrast is echoed in 16:18 where the deceivers are described as those who do not serve Christ in contrast to the obedient believers. In addition, the reference to teaching (διδαχὴν), hearts (καρδίας), and obedience (ὑπακοὴ) in 16:17, 18, and 19, respectively, recalls 6:17 where Paul contrasts his audience's former condition of being slaves to sin with their new condition marked by obedience from the heart (ὑπηκούσατε ἐκ καρδίας) to the form of teaching (τύπον διδαχῆς) to which they were entrusted.[60] In addition, the exhortation to be wise in what is good and unmixed or untainted in what is evil (16:19b) sums up an important theme of the letter—that of the mind focused on and transformed by God, which is the only kind of mind capable of discerning God's will *and* living accordingly; that is, a mind capable not only of discerning evil but also of directing the individual in ways that are good (1:21–23, 28; 7:16–25; 8:5–8, 26–27; 12:2–3, 16; 15:14).

In addition to denoting temptations to sin, τὰ σκάνδαλα could also refer to enticements to apostasy.[61] That this meaning is in sight is signaled by 16:18b. The term κοιλία denoting gluttony or domination by self-directed animal appetites and passions is characteristically Pauline (cf. Phil 3:19), and reflects a type of censure prevalent in first-century Jewish polemic against apostasy (Philo, *Virt.* 182; 3 Macc 7:11; T. Mos. 7.4).[62] The notion of remaining unmixed or untainted (ἀκεραίους) by evil suggests that continued participation in the behaviors and life style patterns advocated by the deceivers

---

59. Douglas J. Moo's suggestion that Paul's description of the stumbling blocks as being "against the teaching that you learned" indicates that the apostle has mainly false doctrine in mind, evidences the modern split between belief and practice that did not exist in antiquity (Moo, *Epistle to the Romans*, 930).

60. Here, the reference to τύπον διδαχης most likely refers to the imitation of Christ. The use of τύπος in the Pauline corpus almost always refers to the emulation of a particular individual who provides a pattern of conduct (Witherington and Hyatt, *Paul's Letter to the Romans*, 171). For example: Rom 5:14; Phil 3:17; 1 Thess 1:7; 2 Thess 3:9; and Col 2:6 (Dunn, *Romans*, 1:343–44).

61. BDAG, "σκάνδαλον," 926.

62. Dunn, *Romans*, 2:903. Also, Hultgren, *Paul's Letter to the Romans*, 593, and Sandnes, *Belly and Body*, 165–80.

eventually results in renunciation of the gospel/Christ and the believing community. The fact that Paul makes reference to the deceivers' particular affect on the innocent or unsuspecting (ἀκάκων) suggests not only that his warning is meant to inform the believers of their true intent but also that their teaching is particularly insidious in that it appears to have their interests and well-being in sight. That is, unlike overt, hostile opposition, which relies on negative pressure in the form of oppression and affliction, this type of opposition assumes the strategy of beguiling persuasion, making it particularly insidious and, thus, dangerous. This explains why the admonition occurs at the end of the letter, appears so abruptly, and portrays the opponents in such negative terms. Paul is especially concerned with this type of covert hostility.

All of this indicates that the apostle is aware that the community in Rome is presently experiencing opposition in the form of persuasive argumentation aimed at pressuring individual believers to resume their previous affiliations and prior life in a way that would compromise their faithful obedience to the gospel. It would not be unusual to issue a general warning in such a situation given the various forms such deceptive argumentation might take due to the variety of previous relationships and particular life situations represented in the believing community. Moreover, it is likely that individual believers would be in different stages of compromise with the deceivers, ranging from those who completely disregard them to those who are close to fully embracing their false teaching. Moreover, it is quite likely that such a situation would create divisions among believers regarding the extent or degree to which compromise is allowable within the community. Given that this community is composed of both Jewish and gentile believers, it is also possible that these deceivers represent both Jews and gentiles.

As evidenced in his letter to the Romans, Paul was a Jew who remained loyal to his people (e.g., 9:1–5). However, he could be critical of both believing and nonbelieving Jews who opposed and interfered with his mission to the gentiles (e.g., Gal 6:12–13; Phil 3:2–3; 1 Thess 2:14–16, 3:5). As noted above, there a certain significant parallels between Romans and 1 Thessalonians (discussed below). One such parallel may be drawn between Paul's reference to Satan in Rom 16:19 and his mention of the tempter (ὁ πειράζων) in 1 Thess 3:5 (cf. 1 Cor 7:5).[63] In the latter, Paul relates to the Thessalonians his fear that somehow the tempter has succeeded in tempting them, so as to render futile his and Silvanus's and Timothy's ministry among them. As in Romans, there is the notion that Satan works through persons who are opposed to the gospel. In this case, these people are unbelieving gentiles (ἰδίων συμφυλετῶν) who are hostile to the believer community in Thessalonica (2:14). What is important for this discussion is the analogy Paul draws between the suffering the Thessalonians experienced at the hands of these people and that experienced by believing Jews in Judea. Although there are interpreters who regard 1 Thess 2:14–16 as a later insertion

---

63. In addition to "the tempter," Paul refers to Satan as "god of this world" (2 Cor 4:4) and "Beliar" (2 Cor 6:15).

due to the severe language about Jewish persecution of believers, it is more likely that these verses reflect the tension between unbelieving Jews and the apostles that is evidenced in Acts, particularly Acts 17:5–13. As discussed in the previous section, Jewish authorities and teachers would have reacted strongly against both the apostles' preaching of a crucified carpenter from Nazareth as the Jewish Messiah and the communities that worshipped him as Yahweh's son.

Thus, although Paul maintains the priority of the Jews in God's plan of salvation and insists that all Israel will be saved (Rom 11:26–29), he nevertheless recognizes that those of his kins-people who actively oppose God's purpose and plan through Jesus Christ, by persecuting his appointed servants and followers, are working on the side of Satan who himself works in opposition to God (cf. 1 Thess 2:15–16). The personification of death and sin as cosmic powers exercising dominion over creation, which are also implicitly linked with the rule of Satan over the world (cf. 2 Cor 4:4), is another important theme in Romans and lends credence to this conclusion.

Given that Paul would not regard the practice of the Torah as evil (Rom 7:7, 12, 14, 16, 21; 14:5–6), if Jewish deceivers are in view, then it is most likely that they are promoting teachings that either deny or seriously question the lordship of Jesus and/or the legitimacy of the gospel and/or the believing community in an attempt to persuade believing Jews and perhaps former gentile proselytes, to renounce the teachings and practices of that community. Paul's reference to slanderous persons who wrongly accuse him and his co-workers of antinomianism (Rom 3:8) may point to such nonbelieving Jews. It is telling that the apostle describes these persons as falsely quoting him by saying: Let us do evil (τὰ κακά) so that good (τὰ ἀγαθα) may come. In Rom 16:20, in the context of his warning against the deceivers, Paul exhorts his audience to be or remain wise in what is good (τὸ ἀγαθόν) and untainted by what is evil (τὸ κακόν), a reversal of what the slanderers claim against Paul's teaching. Moreover, promotion of such persuasive covert teachings aimed at effecting defection from the believing community could also serve as a mechanism for differentiating mainstream Judaism from emerging Christianity and it is possible that the slanderers/deceivers also had this goal in mind.

Similarly, if gentile deceivers are in view, then it is likely that they are attempting to persuade gentile believers to compromise their monotheistic beliefs and practices. According to Paul, gentile believers are to remain gentiles, as his negative stance toward gentile circumcision indicates (e.g., 1 Cor 7:18; Gal 5:2–4). Nevertheless, gentiles would necessarily have to give-up many of their former associations, social and religious practices, and related beliefs in order to become and remain members of the believing community. In this case, as in that of the former, succumbing to such teachings would result in serving the self and sin rather than Christ.

3.1.2.2B The Language of Hostility and Hope

Although Paul's reference to the deceivers in Rom 16:17–19 does not tell us all that we would like to know about the situation in Rome, there is further evidence in the text that suggests that Romans was penned within the context of opposition and affliction to serve as a source of hope and encouragement to those living in its midst. Erwin Ochsenmeier has documented the parallels between Rom 1:8–17 and 1 Thessalonians, noting both the thematic and verbal analogs. With regard to the thematic parallels, he observes that Paul writes to the Thessalonians in order to encourage them by strengthening their existing faith (3:1–3a; 10), which is renown (1:8).[64] Furthermore, similar to his disclosure in Romans, the apostle relates that he desires to come and see them but has, as of yet, been unable to do so (2:17–19). Nevertheless, he is encouraged by their strong faith which remains in good repute despite the afflictions they endure (3:6–7).[65] To these observations may be added 1 Thess 2:1–2 where Paul states that he and his co-workers, Silvanus and Timothy, were enabled by God to proclaim the gospel in Thessalonica despite great opposition, and prior shameful mistreatment in Philippi. As in Romans, the success of the apostle's ministry is attributed wholly to God and apparently functions as an example of perseverance in affliction that is grounded in a hope firmly undergirded by God.

While these parallels are interesting, it could be argued that they reflect little more than basic Pauline themes, much like Rom 16:17–18 echoes the content of Phil 3:19. However, Ochsenmeier notes that the relevance of these parallels to discerning the purpose of Romans is given weight when the verb στηρίζω is considered. This term appears in the Pauline corpus in only Rom 1:11, 16:25, 1 Thess 3:2, 13, and 2 Thess 2:17, 3:3. Although the term has a range of meaning, in many instances in the NT it is used in the context of believers under assault who are in danger of becoming uncertain or apathetic in their faith in terms of both doctrine and praxis.[66] Moreover, the four uses of the cognate ἐπιστηρίζω in the NT (Acts 14:22; 15:32, 41; 18:23) occur in contexts associated with the Pauline mission. Although trials are explicitly in view only Acts 14:22, it is possible that they are also in view in the three remaining passages.[67] In addition, passages that combine στηριζ- and παρακαλέω/παράκλησις, aside from Rom 1:11–12 and Acts 15:32, both of which offer little contextual information, all occur within the explicit context of oppression and affliction of believers (Acts 14:22; 1 Thess 3:2, 7; 2 Thess 2:17). Thus, just as the Thessalonians's persevering faith

---

64. The meaning of the verb ἐζήχηται, which is a hapax in the NT, is usually understood as either referring to the Thessalonians' work of evangelism or to the report of their faith which has spread (Ochsenmeier, "Romans 1:11–12," 397).

65. Ochsenmeier, *Mal, souffrance et justice*, 58–59, and "Romans 1:11–12," 396–97.

66. Ochsenmeier, *Mal, souffrance et justice*, 59. Hardship and affliction is explicit in six of the eleven uses outside of Romans (1 Thess 3:2, 13; Jas 5:8; 1 Pet 5:10). It is also likely that opposition is linked with the verb in Luke 9:15 and 2 Thess 2:17.

67. Ochsenmeier, "Romans 1:11–12," 398 and 398n4.

was an encouragement to Paul (1 Thess 3:6), it is possible that encouragement in the context of hostility is meant in Rom 1:12.[68] As noted above, Paul's own example of perseverance in the context of adversity (15:30–32) serves as encouragement to the Roman believers, satisfying the condition set forth by the apostle that such encouragement be mutual (Rom 1:12).

Furthermore, the vocabulary of love, faith, and perseverance used in a context of adversity in 1 Thess 3:6–8 is also present in Romans (5:1–8; 8:18–39; 15:4, 13). Moreover, Rom 1:11–12 uses the pair παρακαλέω-πίστις as found in 1 Thess 3:7.[69] In addition, there are repeated allusions to suffering and affliction in Romans (5:3–5; 8:17–23, 31–36; 12:12, 14, 17–21; 15:31; 16:4, 7). As mentioned above, these are often taken as referring to the general difficulties that believers face due to the present reality of life in a world that awaits full redemption. However, when these passages are read with Paul's intentions in coming to Rome in mind, they are just as likely to have some reference to an actual situation of affliction that the Roman believers are facing. Moreover, although it is possible that the exhortations to bless persecutors and to show kindness and mercy to enemies (12:14–21) are meant to remind Roman believers of Jesus's teaching on such matters (e.g., Matt 5:44), it is just as likely that such persons are actually present and active in Rome. Accordingly, believers are to act toward these persons in a way that reflects dominical teaching. It is noteworthy that this appeal ends in an exhortation to overcome evil (τοῦ κακοῦ) with good (τῷ ἀγαθῷ) (12:21). This echoes both 3:8 and 16:19, which, as discussed above, refer to a situation involving covert opponents and hostility. In the case of 12:14–21 the opposition is overt and unmistakably hostile, suggesting that Paul might be referring to both covert and overt opponents in Rome.

In addition, it is important to note that this exhortation and its concluding appeal falls within a section of the letter that deals with genuine love (12:9—13:10) of others both within and without the believing community (e.g., 12:13, 17–18). This section is bound by an inclusio, 12:9–13 and 13:8–10, that explicitly links genuine love to love of neighbor, which includes both fellow believers and strangers, and in the case of the latter, encompasses both friendly and hostile persons. In this pericope the emphasis is clearly (note the number of verses dedicated to this topic) on relations with members outside of the believing community, who are either belligerent or potentially so (13:1–7, discussed in more detail below). All of this suggests that Paul's primary concern is the believing community's response to actual and potential hostility. In this regard, we may make note of the apostle's exhortation to hate what is evil (In this case, the synonym πονηρόν is used) and to hold fast to what is good (τῷ ἀγαθῳ) (12:9b), which is sandwiched between the exhortations to genuine love (12:9a) and to love for one another (12:10a), including the showing of proper honor (12:10b, τῇ τιμῇ), which links to 13:1–7, specifically verses 3–4 (references to good and evil, ἀγαθον, ἀγαθός)

---

68. Ochsenmeier, *Mal, souffrance et justice*, 59–60. Also, Ochsenmeier, "Romans 1:11–12," 399.
69. Ochsenmeier, "Romans 1:11–12," 399.

and verse 7 (reference to honor, τὴν τιμήν). Thus, genuine love, more broadly speaking, is doing good (and shunning evil) which includes loving persecutors and enemies and showing due honor, in very concrete ways (13:7), to civic authorities. As noted above, the good-evil pair occurs in situations where conflict is quite likely in view, suggesting that such a context is in view in this extended pericope.

The repeated allusions to suffering and affliction in Romans noted above are matched by the frequency of references to perseverance and hope.[70] This is all the more significant since ἐλπι- vocabulary is relatively scarce in the NT.[71] Moreover, in Romans, hope is forged and finds its meaning within the context of suffering and affliction (5:3–5; 8:18–24), which suggests that Paul writes to the Roman believers in order to remind them of their hope in God's saving actions in a situation which seems to contradict his power, provision, and mercy.[72] Furthermore, Paul explicitly links hope to the Scriptures and implicitly to the gospel, which itself was promised in the scriptures (1:1–2; 3:21–22). In fact, the very purpose of the scriptures is to provide hope to believers (15:4).[73] In addition, this hope is linked with faith, whereby the sustained act of hoping in God and his promises results in the strengthening of faith (e.g., 4:18–24). In this case, the story of Abraham, who hoped against hope for the promised heir, provides hope for Paul's audience, whose perseverance under circumstances that appear to deny the faithfulness of God's will, as in the case of the patriarch, result in a reckoning of their faith as righteousness through Jesus Christ (vv. 23–25).

It is telling that this story from the scriptures is directly followed by 5:1–11, which features an exuberant declaration of believers' present peace with God through Christ, their access to his grace, and their boastful hope in the future sharing of his glory (5:1–2). However, this boast is immediately followed by a second, in which Paul posits suffering as the context within which this hope is formed and sustained (5:3–4). This hope is certain because it has as its foundation a faithful God who has demonstrated his love through his acts in Jesus Christ (5:6–10), whose love believers have already experienced for themselves through the Spirit (5:5). Consequently, both the boast in future glory and that in present suffering are ultimately a boast in God (5:11). After describing in detail precisely how God demonstrated his love in and through Christ, Paul once again makes scriptural allusions in the persons of Adam and Moses, whereby Adam's death dealing work, and implicitly the ministry of Moses, is explicitly compared to the life giving, unsurpassable work and ministry of Christ (5:12–21). Thus, for Paul, the scriptures are the foundation of hope, since they not only provide

---

70. Ochsenmeier, "Romans 1:11–12," 400. The term ὑπομονη, is found in 2:7; 5:3,4; 8:25; 15:4; ἐλπις in 4:18; 5:2, 4–5; 8:20, 24; 12:12; and ἐλπίζω in 8:24–25; 15:12, 14.

71. Ochsenmeier, "Romans 1:11–12," 400n22, 400. The verb ἐλπίζω occurs nineteen times in the Pauline corpus out of the thirty-one occurrences in the NT. While ἐλπις appears thirty-eight times in Paul out of the fifty-three uses in the NT.

72. Ochsenmeier, "Romans 1:11–12," 400.

73. Ochsenmeier, "Romans 1:11–12," 401n22.

exemplars of hope but also point to the ultimate source of this hope, a faithful God who has effectively dealt with death and sin in all its manifold concrete manifestations in and through Jesus Christ.

Thus, when both the lexical and thematic data are considered in tandem, the parallels between 1 Thessalonians and Romans are striking. This notwithstanding the fact that Romans, unlike 1 Thessalonians, makes no direct reference to oppressors, Jewish or otherwise. The marked difference in tone with respect to unbelieving Jews represented in these two letters may be attributed to the fact that in Romans Paul is seeking to establish in-Christ identity as having some continuity with Judaism[74] and to explain the continuing place of Israel in God's salvific plan. Any kind of polemic aimed specifically at Jews would defeat this purpose. Thus, he avoids any hint of anti-Jewish sentiment, tempering it in the form of diatribe with an imaginary interlocutor (i.e., the teacher who represents Israel under the Mosaic covenant).

Finally, it is important to note that the vocabulary of perseverance (τῆς ὑπομονῆς), encouragement (τῆς παρακλήσεως), and hope (ἐλπίδα) also occurs within the context of Paul's exhortation for unity between the weak and the strong (15:4–5). This suggests that the purpose of the letter is specifically focused on encouraging unity among the believers in Rome. However, although it is clear that this is an important concern, it is nevertheless one of several and, as such, cannot account for either all the allusions to suffering and hope, or the exhortations in 12:9—13:14. Moreover, the larger context indicates that this disunity between the weak and the strong is itself part of Paul's larger task of reminding his audience of the hope and power they have in Christ.

Romans 14:1—15:6 and 15:7–13 and their place and function within the letter is discussed in greater detail in chapter 6. What is important for the current discussion is that in this extended pericope, Paul presents Christ as an example to the Roman believers of an individual, who like the psalmist (Ps 68:10 LXX), suffers insult and persecution because of his selfless devotion to the service of God (15:3). This typological interpretation, which sees the psalmist (the suffering righteous person) as a type of the suffering Jesus,[75] agrees with Paul's understanding of the gospel as promised in the scriptures and explains how the scriptures function as instruction for present believers (15:4a). In other words, Christ illustrates that the choice to please God, rather than oneself, can even lead to death, in this case death on a cross.[76] It is precisely in this fashion that Christ bore the failings of humanity; that is, its sins against God. Consequently, through perseverance in pleasing God, specifically by building-up the neighbor, and through the encouragement provided

---

74. The points of continuity and discontinuity that Paul draws between Judaism and the Christ movement are discussed in greater detail in chapters 4 through 6 of this work.

75. Dunn, *Romans*, 2:839.

76. Dunn, *Romans*, 2:839. Dunn points out that the psalm is one of the most quoted in the NT, with the most explicit allusions making direct reference to Christ's passion and related events (Mark 15:23; John 2:17; 15:25; 19:28–29; Acts 1:20).

by Scripture, in this case Christ's own example of self-giving devotion to and trust in God, believers may have hope (15:4).

Although it is possible that the first διά clause indicates attendant circumstances, rather than cause, the latter is more likely given Paul's argument in Rom 5:3–4. In this rhetorical *sorites*, the apostle links suffering to hope, hope of the glory of God (5:2), via perseverance and the production of character. According to Paul, the sequence is a matter of common agreement, εἰδότες, (5:3). The basis of this common knowledge most likely rests on the presumed acceptance of the idea of disciplinary suffering found in the Jewish wisdom tradition and in Stoic thought which held that character is refined by steadfastness in trial and suffering.[77] Particularly in the martyr theology of Judaism, the term ὑπομονή has a double reference to fortitude in suffering and trust in God for ultimate deliverance. It is this fortitude and trust in God which produces δοκιμή, denoting what results from being put to the test—a proven or firm character.[78] In other words, in the context of 5:3–4, hope of the eschatological glory of God is the product of a lived choice to trust God in situations which appear to deny his existence, his faithfulness, and/or his power to save. The ultimate grounds for this hope are christological, since God has already proven himself in Christ (5:6–11).

It is likely that Paul has this causal sense in mind in the first διά clause in 15:4. As in the case of Rom 5, the ultimate ground of hope is Christ, specifically Christ's example of the righteous sufferer who is ultimately vindicated by God. The emphasis in this case is not on suffering per se but on self-denial (in a sense, a form of suffering) for the sake of pleasing God. Thus, perseverance in self-denial of one's freedom with regard to food and drink and the observance of days/the day, according to the pattern of Christ, for the sake of building up one's neighbor produces a proven character, that of a person devoted to God rather than to him or herself. When an entire community actively engages in this Christ-centered pattern of self-denial for the purpose of building-up the neighbor; that is, by putting aside opinions regarding these specific worship practices, unity of mind in accord with Christ and unity in glorifying God is the result (15:5–6).

At first glance, it is not entirely clear how self-denial in the area of food, drink, and observance of days/the day relates to the production of hope. However, in 15:13 Paul conveys a prayer wish wherein he beseeches God to grant that for which he prays—hope. The ground for this hope is the gospel which proclaims that God's actions in and through Christ have resulted, as promised in Scripture, in the unification of all the peoples of the world (15:8–12). In other words, the specific differences Paul sets out in 14:1—15:6 are implicitly generalized to include all differences of opinion regarding customs, habits, and practices, and the beliefs that underlie these, which would naturally result from the unification of people of diverse ethnicities.

---

77. Byrne, *Romans*, 166 (Deut 8:2–5; Prov 3:11–12; Sir 2:1–5; 4:17–18; 18:13–14; 23:1–3; Wis 3:1–6; 11:9–10; 2 Macc 6:12–16; 7:32–33; Pss. Sol. 10:1–3; 14:1).

78. Byrne, *Romans*, 170 (4 Macc. 1:11; 9:8, 30; 15:30; 17:4, 12, 17, 23; Job 14:19; T. Job 1:5; 4:6; 5:1).

These differences are to be accommodated as long as these do not in any way threaten, diminish, or tarnish commitment to Christ. This is possible in a world where such differences seem to inevitably result in either aggression, war, and/or the all out oppression and subjugation of one group by another because God has already established unity in Christ and believers are empowered by the Holy Spirit to do the same (15:5 (God); 15:13b). That Paul intends a generalization of difference in 15:7–13 is given credence by the explicit exhortation to welcome one another (15:7) which echoes that given in 14:1. In both cases the verb προσλαμβάνω is used. However, in the former, the welcome is generalized—extended to all and not just to the one who is weak, thus embracing all such differences (i.e., those that do not compromise one's commitment to Christ) under the general principle of unity in Christ by humble self-denial for the sake of building-up the neighbor.

In sum, perseverance in doing God's will within the context of adversity, whether caused by hostile outsiders or disagreements among insiders, as in the case discussed above, gives rise to a character devoted to God and conformed to the pattern of Christ. Believers' hope of the glory of God has its foundation in God's own actions in and through Christ as proclaimed in the gospel promised beforehand in the scriptures. As Christ was ultimately delivered from and vindicated for his suffering, so will believers, here, if they continue in obedience of faith. However, Paul is well aware that the present Christian life involves living out the demands of the new age amidst the realities of the present world.

3.1.2.2c Rom 13:1–7: An Example of Living Peacefully in a Hostile Context

Besides 1 Thessalonians, only in Romans does Paul exhort nonretaliation and active love for enemies and persecutors (5:15).[79] In 1 Thess 4:1–12 proper behavior toward outsiders is described as living quietly, minding one's own affairs, and working with one's hands. Within the context of affliction, any action on the part of the believing community that might be interpreted as hostile or aggressive would only serve to fan the flames of outsider hostility. More importantly, such behavior on the part of believers would distort or even destroy the message of the gospel. For Paul, the peace of the gospel is to be evidenced within the community itself and in the community's relationships with those outside of it (1 Thess 5:13b–15; Rom 12:16–18). Thus, it is quite conceivable that Paul's somewhat defensive exhortation to civic loyalty in Rom 13:1–7, unprecedented in any other letter in the Pauline corpus, expresses a concern for the believing community's public image,[80] particularly in the sense that this image should reflect that of Christ. If this is the case, then this passage provides further indirect evidence of outsider hostility toward the Roman believers.

---

79. Seyoon, *Christ and Caesar*, 57.
80. Osiek, "Romans 'Down the Pike,'" 153.

There are several notable thematic and verbal links between Rom 13:1–7 and both 12:9–21 and 13:8–10, suggesting that it is integral to Paul's larger argument.[81] Both the theme of doing good-forsaking evil and that of giving others due honor and respect, which is a form of showing love, runs across 12:1—13:10. Moreover, remaining subject to governing authorities provides a specific example both of living peaceably with those outside of the believing community and of not taking matters into one's hands with respect to vengeance (12:17–21). The injunction to live quietly, in peace with the Roman Empire and its authorities, is particularly salient if we accept that the most plausible historical setting for this passage is the social unrest in Rome in the late 50's generated by abusive taxation on the part of the state.[82] The thematic unity is further strengthened by several terminological links. The term "wrath" (ὀργή) appears in 13:4–5 and 12:19. In addition, ἀποδίδωμι and ἔκδικος/ἐκδικέω are found in 13:7 and 12:17 and in 13:4 and 12:19, respectively. Finally, ὀφειλή/ὀφείλω are present in 13:7 and 13:8, in reference specifically to governing authorities, in the case of the former and, more generally, to all persons, in the case of the latter.

Thus, the thematic and verbal linkages suggest that despite the lack of explicit grammatical connections between the three exhortations in 12:9, 13:1, and 13:8 there is a unity to the three sections of instruction each headed by their respective injunctions. We have already seen that 12:9 and 13:10 form an inclusio. The word "love" (ἀγάπη) appears as the first word in both instances. Similarly, the exhortation to hate what is evil (12:9) and the statement that love does no wrong to the neighbor (13:10) bracket this section and sum up both the theme of loving the neighbor (inclusively defined as fellow believer, outsider, and enemy) and serving the Lord (fulfilling the law), both of which amount to doing what is good. This suggests that the issue of why Paul includes the injunction to submit to the governing authorities is best resolved by considering how the payment of taxes to the Roman state may be regarded as love of neighbor.

It is important at the outset to recognize that the purpose of this passage is to shape the conduct of the audience rather than to provide general instruction on the

---

81. Several recent exegetes have argued that the passage is an interpolation by a later hand eagerly advocating Christian submission to state authority. This is evidenced by the fact that removal of the passage from the letter does not affect the intelligibility or logic of the argument (Byrne, *Romans*, 385, 386). However, as appealing as the interpolation theory may be in effectively removing a difficult and contentious passage from the Pauline corpus, there is neither textual warrant for regarding it as a later interpolation, nor for setting it aside as long as there is some plausible explanation for its inclusion in the letter. Also, Tellbe, *Paul between Synagogue and State*, 172–73.

82. Tacitus, *Annales* 13.50–51; Suetonius, Nero 10.1. The plausibility of this historical setting is acknowledged by many if not most interpreters (e.g., Keener, *Romans*, 154–55; Byrne, *Romans*, 386; Tellbe, *Paul between Synagogue and State*, 177–82; Witherington and Hyatt, *Paul's Letter to the Romans*, 310; Talbert, *Romans*, 296; Fitzmyer, *Romans*, 662; Dunn, *Romans*, 2:766, 772; and Jewett, *Romans*, 798–99. However, not all interpreters agree. For instance, both Douglas Moo and Ernst Käsemann maintain that certain charismatics in Rome had interpreted Paul's eschatological teachings as advocating the rejection of social norms and conventions, including the state and its governing authorities (Moo, *Epistle to the Romans*, 791; Käsemann, *Commentary on Romans*, 351, 359).

nature and function of the state and its relation to the people of God.[83] In other words, the apostle's theological propositions which speak of the state as the divinely appointed human agent of God serve primarily as a warrant for Paul's exhortation urging his audience to pay the taxes due to the Roman state. That this is the case is evidenced by the fact that Paul draws on familiar Greco-Roman and Jewish thought and language which describe traditional standard duties toward governing authorities acknowledged to be constituted by God/gods and under divine authority.[84] Moreover, 13:6–7 is prefaced by διὰ τοῦτο γάρ, which looks both retrospectively and prospectively, indicating the climax of the apostle's argument and working out the practical implications of 13:1–5. The concluding exhortation in 3:7 functions as a specific application of the general imperative in 13:1a, which together bracket 13:1–7.[85] Thus, part of Paul's argumentative strategy is to use conventional, largely uncontested propositions to buttress a specific argument that ties love of neighbor/serving the Lord (two sides of the same coin) to the contested issue of paying taxes.

Although the issue of which taxes Paul is referring to, direct, indirect, or both, remains a matter of debate, it is clear that the apostle is urging the Roman believers to pay the taxes that they owe. Three times he warns his audience not to disobey the authorities (13:2, 3, 4), which suggests that not all of the members of the community agree that these taxes should be paid.[86] This comports with the above-mentioned historical setting. In the context of abusive taxation, the temptation to evade this duty in an act of civil disobedience would have been appealing, even for believers. This would explain the pains Paul takes to couch the issue of paying taxes within the greater context of one's obligations to God, specifically the duty to honor and respect his agents on earth and to love one's neighbor as the fulfillment of the law.

In Rome, tax evasion was a punishable criminal offense. Hence, Paul's reference to the ruler's right to bear the sword (13:4), probably to the extent of inflicting capital punishment.[87] Thus, given the high-profile nature of this offense, civil disobedience would be sure to draw unwanted attention to the Christian community, even if only a handful of believers failed to pay their taxes. As mentioned above, the continued existence of the believer community in Rome was dependent on avoiding any suspicion of subversive activity on the part of its members.

Obedience to God in the form of paying taxes to secular authorities is but one prong of Paul's argument against tax evasion, which is itself couched within the larger exhortation to love one's neighbor. In one sense, love of neighbor includes

---

83. Tellbe, *Paul between Synagogue and State*, 176.

84. For example, Byrne argues that the closely parallel instructions in 1 Pet 2:13–17, 1 Tim 2:1–3, and Titus 3:1–3 suggests that there was even a set pattern of instruction across a range of early Christian communities (Byrne, *Romans*, 386).

85. Tellbe, *Paul between Synagogue and State*, 175.

86. Tellbe, *Paul between Synagogue and State*, 176.

87. Tellbe, *Paul between Synagogue and State*, 180.

giving due honor to others (12:10b), which would include giving due honor and respect to governing powers by submitting to their tax laws (13:7). However, there are indications in the text that Paul has something additional in mind—primarily, to urge those inclined to civil disobedience to lay aside their convictions regarding the proper response to abusive taxation for the good of those believers who have chosen to submit to state rule.

It is notable that the exhortation in 13:7 concerning secular rulers is immediately followed by the exhortation to love one another (13:8a). The two verses are closely linked by the use of ὀφειλάς and ὀφείλετε, respectively, indicating that 13:8–10 is a continuation of 13:1–7. The phrase ἀλλήλους ἀγαπᾶν signifies that Paul is referring to members of the believing community. Although the apostle describes love of neighbor as including those both inside and outside of the Christian community, in 13:8–10 his focus is specifically on fellow believers. Moreover, obedience to God, defined as fulfillment of the law, is accomplished by loving one's brother and sister in Christ (13:8b, 10). Thus, obedience to God is exemplified not only by submitting to secular law regarding taxes, a specific instance of obedience, but also and more fully by loving one's fellow believer, which includes among many other things, choosing a course of action that is likely not to bring harm to him or her—in this case, paying taxes, despite one's personal convictions to the contrary. A decision to engage in civil disobedience would likely have major repercussions for the believing community as a whole, including those members who remained obedient with regard to the issue of paying taxes.

In sum, this passage is a carefully crafted argument ultimately aimed at shielding the Christian community from further potential hostility from outsiders. The course of conduct that Paul urges the Roman believers to take is that which is pleasing to God in that it fulfills his will as it is expressed in the law and summed-up in the command to love one's neighbor, particularly one's fellow brother or sister in Christ. Moreover, the argument is context specific. Given the particular environment of civic discontent in Rome at that time and the Christ community's precarious position at the borders of both Judaism and Greco-Roman society, the choice to adhere to Roman tax laws in effect fulfills God's law, since obedience to secular authority in this case is ultimately a choice to love fellow members of the believing community.

3.2 Set Apart for the Gospel: Establishing the Credentials of an Ethnographer

As Paul's purpose in writing to the Roman believers, namely, to strengthen and encourage them as a people faithful to the gospel in a hostile environment, gives credence to the ethnographic character of Romans, evidence pointing to the substantiation of his role as an ethnographer likewise achieves the same goal. As discussed in the previous chapter, the credibility of native ethnographers was rooted in the authority they had as accurate and reliable interpreters of their own traditions (e.g., Josephus, *Ag. Ap.* 1.53–54; *Ant.* 1.5,

16.84, 20.261–65). That Paul crafts his letter in continuity with the Jewish scriptures is evident throughout the letter. From the opening words of his missive, Paul presents "his apostolic mission as one that proclaims and interprets the gospel and Israel's scriptural traditions."[88] Moreover, he sees himself as called to a divinely ordained task (Rom 1:1; 15:15b–16). In other words, like Strabo, who relates that the founders of Massilia acted under the direction of Artemis (*Geogr.* 4.1.4), Paul presents himself as a locus of divine activity through whom God works to establish and maintain believing communities throughout the Mediterranean basin (1:5; 15:18–19); his itinerant proclamation extending from Jerusalem as far as Illyricum (15:19).

Thus, in experiential terms, Paul presents himself as more than qualified as an ethnographer. Not only has he personally encountered divine power in his apostolic role, but he has also taken the gospel message in a grand sweep across the entire Eastern Mediterranean. Even if it is unlikely that Paul began his mission to the gentiles in Jerusalem (cf. Gal 1:22), with these two geographical references simply indicating the outer limits of his itinerant ministry,[89] the picture that he paints is that of a travel-seasoned man, operating under divine mandate, whose wisdom, by implication, is as broad as the extent of his sojourns. The wide compass of the apostle's personal witness of God's creative power operative in and through the gospel in inaugurating and sustaining believing communities is reinforced both by the statement that this extensive and productive activity is the very thing that has prevented him from coming to Rome (15:22). Moreover, with his work in these regions complete, the apostle intimates that he plans to extend his fruitful mission onward to Spain (15:23–24).

In intellectual terms, Paul's credibility as a reliable interpreter of his traditions is further buttressed by his reference to this mystery (τὸ μυστήριον τοῦτο) (Rom 11:25), that, by implication, he is uniquely privileged to receive and pass on to God's people, as he does in the following verses. Here, as in late-biblical and Jewish apocalyptic literature, τὸ μυστήριον refers to God's hidden plan for the final consummation, revealed to divinely ordained seers or prophets, for the comfort of the faithful community.[90] Similar to Josephus, who sees his surrender to the Romans as obedience to God's call to the prophetic office (*J.W.* 3.340–408), affording him the opportunity to reinterpret the sacred tradition of the Jews under the new age of Roman rule (*Ag. Ap.* 1.37, 40–41), Paul similarly claims a place in the prophetic tradition. In this way, he firmly establishes his credentials as interpreter of the life of his people, Jew and gentile alike, under the eschatological rule of Christ's rule; a life that itself must be interpreted in light of the revered, sacred tradition of the Jews. His role as a prophet dovetails with his role as ethnographer in that his ministry looks to the divinely conceived future, while simultaneously viewing the past, as both perspectives converge

---

88. Wagner, *Heralds of the Good News*, 1.

89. Byrne, *Romans*, 438.

90. Byrne, *Romans*, 354 (e.g., Dan 2:18–30, 47; 1 En. 16:3; 41:1; 2 En. 24:3; 2 Bar. 48:3; 81:4; 1QH 2:13; 4:27–28).

on the present, bringing it to light. Earlier in the letter, Paul alludes to his prophetic role with the reference to Moses (Rom 10:5). In this verse and that which follow, he sets-up a contrast, δέ (v. 6), between Israel's first and greatest prophet and himself, portraying himself as divinely called to reinterpret righteousness in light of Christ (vv. 6–13). Taken together, a picture emerges of an individual standing in the line of Israel's prophets who, at the same time, surpasses the tradition in which he is rooted, in the sense that the content of his divinely given revelation represents the culmination of God's hidden plan for all of humanity.

In addition to his prophetic role, Paul refers to his ministry of proclamation in priestly or cultic terms (Rom 15:15b–16). Similarly, Josephus offers his status as a priest as that which qualifies him as an authoritative translator and interpreter of the Jewish sacred texts (*Life* 1–8; *Ag. Ap.* 1.53–54; *Ant.* 1.5, 16.84, 20.263). Moreover, unlike the Greek historians, who neglected "to keep official records of current events," valuing literary flourish over accuracy, in order to outshine their rivals, (*Ag. Ap.* 1.15–25), the Jews "preserved with scrupulous accuracy their history" due to the fact that their record keepers are "chief priests and prophets" (1.29). The priests are "men of the highest character, devoted to the service of God," while the prophets obtained "their knowledge of the most remote and ancient history through the inspiration which they owed to God" (*Ag. Ap.* 1.30, 37). Whatever other significance this priestly metaphor has in the apostle's argument, the image conveyed, when combined with his prophetic role, is that of a divinely ordained representative of Israel who is responsible for ensuring that what was offered by God's people is acceptable to him. In this case, it is believing gentiles, suggesting Paul's specific role in fostering their sanctification.[91] Given that he is writing to relatively mature believers, and not to potential converts, the casting of his ministry in cultic terms substantiates his claim to provide a credible account of the believing community that establishes its legitimacy. In other words, as a priest of the new, eschatological community, Paul is uniquely qualified to provide his people with the teaching and praxis that leads to their sanctification.[92] Thus, the apostle's audience may rest assured that the ethnography he provides for them, in which he establishes both the identity of the people of God and the customs and way of life by which that identity is embodied, is accurate reflection of the people of God.

---

91. Byrne, *Romans*, 435–36. The verb ἱερουργέω is always used in the LXX and related literature (Philo, Josephus) in reference to the offering of sacrifice by Israel's priests, lending a cultic sense to the entire clause.

92. Although Paul casts his ministry as that specifically directed to the gentiles (Rom 1:5), his role in the sanctification of believers should not be seen as limited to gentile members. In the same way that Paul proclaimed the gospel in the synagogues, his exhortations to holy living are directed at all the members of his audience.

3.3 Conclusion

Indigenous ancient ethnographers wrote for the purpose of defining and legitimizing a particular people group with its unique laws, customs, and way of life, within the larger context of a new world order that claimed cultural, political, and economic superiority. It was imperative for these writers to buttress group affiliation, mainly by providing a positive identity for their people, against the pressures of cultural and social assimilation. This was especially important for groups, like the Christ movement, existing on the fringes of Greco-Roman society and culture. The objective of this chapter was to set the stage for further exploration of the ethnographic characteristics of Romans, primarily by reexamining the textual evidence pointing to the letter's primary purpose and by bringing to light the various ways that Paul establishes his credibility as a reliable interpreter of his people's history and traditions.

With respect to the letter's purpose, its ethnographic characteristics have been obscured by the tendency to view Romans as dealing primarily with salvation. This is true, whether one begins with justification by faith as Paul's main premise or with gentile inclusion, moving to the underlying theology of incorporation. In both instances, interpretation proceeds within a soteriological framework. However, a careful examination of the text shows that the Roman believers were facing social ostracism and general persecution perpetrated by nonbelieving friends, neighbors, business associates, and family, including nonbelieving Jews. It is this historical reality which Paul seeks to address by exercising his apostolic authority and duty in proclaiming the gospel of hope. Redefining the purpose of Romans in this way shifts the interpretational lens away from a too narrow focus on soteriology, broadening it in a way that can account for the epistle's form and content and its theological depth and complexity. The goal of ethnographers was not so much about engendering group unity, although that is a concern, or explaining how certain members became incorporated into the group. In these writings, the integrity of the group in question is a presupposition. Its legitimacy and, thus, its *continuing* coherence as a distinct group, is not, and it is with these issues that these authors are concerned. Accordingly, in his letter to the Romans, Paul sets about the task of constructing a positive group identity for the new movement, legitimating its place within the broader culture, so as to strengthen the Roman believers to continued faithful obedience.

Although determination of a literary work's purpose is instrumental in determining its genre(s) (and vice-versa), it is not the only factor involved. The interpretation of any work is colored, to one degree or another, by what the exegete assumes about its primary occasion and purpose. Yet, the validity of this determination and that of a writing's genre(s) is judged in relation to other evidence in the text, such as the presence of motifs and literary constructs and strategies commonly associated with the identified genre(s). This initial foray into the letter's ethnographic purpose and Paul's credentials as an ethnographer has served to bring to the surface the substructure undergirding the ethnographic framework composed of the more specific and discrete ethnographic motifs and strands of ethnic discourse that are woven throughout the text. Examination of Paul's specific use of these common conventions is the task of the following chapters. As I will demonstrate, when Romans is viewed as standing in some continuity with and in relationship to the broader genre of first-century ethnography not only are its purpose and content brought together but also its form and content. It is within this structural context that the dichotomies between law-faith (works-grace) and Jew-gentile are best understood.

CHAPTER FOUR

The Historical Legitimacy of the Christ Movement (Part I)

Law and Faith: Establishing Points of Continuity and Discontinuity between God's People in the Past and the Present (Rom 1–5)

FOR THE ANCIENTS, THE new was acceptable as long as it proved to have ties with the esteemed past. The same would have held true for the Christ movement. As we have seen, indigenous ethnographers, including Josephus, established historical legitimacy by arguing that their respective people groups were the most ancient and that all of the world's history could be traced to them. Accordingly, Josephus posits Noah's sons as the ancestors of all the people groups of the earth, tracing their descent from Adam, to Seth and his progeny (*Ant.* 1.120–47). Simultaneously, he accuses the Greeks of usurping the glories of the past "as though they [humanity] were descended from themselves" (*Ant.* 1.121). Similarly, Paul begins with the assumption that the Jewish scriptures provide the only valid frame of reference for the world's history. In them, he finds an account of both the universal human condition and God's work in rectifying that condition as promised and foretold through the prophets. Utilizing this frame of reference and drawing upon common ethnographic motifs and strategies of discourse, the apostle not only establishes the antiquity but also the universality of the Christ movement. He does this in two ways: first, by providing an interpretation of prior, Jewish history that finds its climax in the eschatological present; second, by providing an etiological account of the new movement with roots in two divinely instituted founding figures—one penultimate, Abraham, the other ultimate, Christ.

Accordingly, the focus of this chapter will be on key sections of Rom 1–5. An analysis of the ethnic discourse that Paul utilizes in accomplishing his task will bring to light the strategic role that the law-faith dichotomy plays in the apostle's effort to redefine traditional, intragroup construals of Jewish self-identity as the chosen people of God in light of the eschatological present. As we will see, this dichotomy is crucial for both his larger ethnographic aims and for the construction of the Spirit-wrought, allocentric self-identity by which he characterizes the people of God in the present.[1]

---

1. This identity will be examined in some detail in chapters 5 and 6 of this work.

4.1 Israel's Past Reinterpreted in Light of the Unfolding Eschatological Present: To the Jew First and also the Greek (Rom 1–3)

For Greco-Roman ethnographers the mythic past was important because it accounted for the present state of affairs. As we have seen, Greek myths of origin were interpreted and reformulated in the present light of unifying Roman power so as to bring diverse people groups under the umbrella of a universal world history centered on Rome. For example, Dionysius of Halicarnassus transforms each barbarian people group affiliated with the founding of Rome into a Greek one (*Ant. rom.* 1.9–70; 1.21.1–2), in order to remove "erroneous impressions" about the status of the Roman people as "barbarians" and "to substitute true ones" (1.5.1). That is, he seeks to show that Rome from its very founding, "produced infinite examples of virtue in men" which "no city either Greek or barbarian, has ever produced" (1.5.3). However, the Roman people, despite the Greekness of their ancestry, customs, and traditions, remain distinctly Roman. Rome "advanced to so great dominion," according to the "universal law of Nature," which "ordained that superiors shall ever govern their inferiors" (1.5.2). These inferiors included the very Greeks to whom Rome owed its illustrious past, since the Roman people excel in "piety," "justice," "life-long self-control," and "warlike valor" (1.5.3). For this reason, Rome "rules every country that is not inaccessible or uninhabited, "making the risings and the settings of the sun the boundaries of her dominion," drawing "to herself the neighboring nations" (1.3.3–4), who retain their ethnic identity as they are simultaneously identified as Roman subjects.

With respect to the Christ movement, the Jesus tradition could not provide an adequate foundational account on its own for the simple reason that it was new and lacked the weight of antiquity requisite for legitimacy. As Aristotle notes, "not even those descended from good ancestors are noble, only those who have among those ancestors originators who are good" (*On Nobility,* frag. 94).[2] Accordingly, what was needed was an interpretation of God's historical dealings with Israel that finds its climax in Jesus.[3] By using the Jewish scriptural texts as the authority and norm for constructing a universal world history, Paul provides the new movement, including its central founding figure, with ancient roots sunk deeply into the rich soil of a venerable Jewish tradition, while simultaneously presenting the Christ movement as the culmination of its engendering tradition.

---

2. Hodge, *If Sons, Then Heirs*, 31.

3. Lieu, *Christian Identity*, 89–94. The author argues that, although Paul considered the life, death, and resurrection of Jesus as the foundation of his gospel and knew and utilized some Jesus traditions, the apostle did not use the narrative traditions about his life as a source of history for the new movement. This continues into the second century, where neither the apostolic fathers, nor the apologists use the life of Jesus in making their case for Christianity. In other words, the early church did not trace its history only from the appearance of Jesus, but also from Israel's past. In this sense, Christianity appropriated Israel's history, as it retold it in light of Christ. The church's rejection of Marcion is a case in point.

4.1.1 Paul's Universal Perspective of the World

The universal scope of the apostle's perspective is evident in the opening words of his letter where the good news (εὐαγγέλιον) concerning Jesus Christ is described as God's own good news (Rom 1:1)—the God who is God over all peoples (3:29–30) and whose good news is for Jew and Greek alike (1:16). This inclusive perspective is also evident in the stock phrases, "Greeks and barbarians" and "wise and foolish" (1:14), and the category specifically used by Jews to denote all non-Jews, gentiles (1:5, 13). Ancient authors could, and often did, use the terms "βάρβαροι" and "ἀνοήτοις," like the term "τὰ ἔθνη," with a derogatory intent.[4] However, there is no indication in the text that Paul is accepting the viewpoint of the Greeks or designating particular ethnoracial groups as barbarians, foolish and/or invariably wicked. Rather, the use of these commonplace binary categories appears to reflect standard, first-century ways of denoting humanity in its entirety.[5] The apostle's repeated use of them, emphasizes the ethnoracial inclusiveness of God's good news. Moreover, it seems that the categories Greek and gentile are used interchangeably (e.g., Rom 2:9–10 and 2:14). Although Paul's employment of the term "Greek" may indicate a special deference to the ethnoracial identity of certain members of his non-Jewish audience, the overall effect is to highlight their present inclusion among God's people as gentiles.

Recall that Virgil's hero, Aeneas, embodies Roman attitudes and values, without any diminishment of his Trojan heritage (*Aen.* 3.167; 7.207; Book 8) and that Rome's noblest families, following suit, conceived of themselves as both Trojan and Roman. What this suggests is that Romanness, however defined, is achievable/available for all people as a universal ideal, irrespective of any particular ethnoracial identity, which need not be discarded but may be nested within the overarching Roman identity. This idea of synthesis, or world-wide unity of diverse people, under the aegis of Roman rule, without loss of ethnic distinction is also evident in Strabo, who depicts Rome, represented by the *pater orbis*, as the center to which various people groups are connected as distinct spokes to a wheel (*Georg*, 17.1.35–36; 3.24). Similarly, Dionysius of Halicarnassus writes that Rome "did not become entirely barbarized," after receiving a variety of barbarian people groups, who "differed from one another both in their language and habits," and their diverse ways of life (*Ant. rom.* 1.89.3–4). For Paul, the tension between the universal and the particular is held in tension by the one God, who is the God of both Jew and gentile (3:29–30). He, and not the Roman *pater orbis*, is the one who unifies all of humanity under his rule as its Creator and Lord. The apostle's introduction of the universal, expressed in terms of inclusivity of all of humanity, in the opening chapters of the letter, signals that the gospel that he is about

---

4. With respect to the first two, these could be used to indicate Greek cultural and intellectual superiority over and against non-Greek people groups. Similarly, the term "gentile," could be used to portray all non-Jewish "others" as sexually and ethically immoral, godless, and hence, uniformly wicked and unrighteous.

5. Dunn makes a similar point (Dunn, *Romans*, 1:32–33).

to present is unique in that it is the good news of a God, who is unlike any tribal and/or national deity, in that he is neither associated with only one, particular people group (the Jews), nor with a body of related ethnoracial entities. As the apostle will make clear in the arguments that follow, this God not only provides an overarching or supraordinate identity for his people, as his children, but also mandates the continuing validity of subgroup particularity, in term of ethnoracial identity, as necessary to his present work in and through Christ.

Of equal note is the apostle's opening statement in which he explicitly links this universal good news to what was promised beforehand through the prophets in the Jewish scriptures (1:1). Exactly in what sense the gospel stands as the fulfillment of prophetic promises, Paul will make clearer as his argument progresses. What is important here is that with this introductory statement the apostle establishes a climactic link, in the sense of promise-fulfillment, between God's good news concerning his son and Yahweh's historic dealings with the Jewish people, beginning with Abraham and extending into the present time. The heavy reliance on scripture evident throughout the letter, and particularly the frequent invocation of Isaiah, not only through direct quotations but also through allusion and intertextual echo, serves as a constant reminder for Paul's audience that the gospel stands in direct continuity with Jewish history and tradition. Moreover, this opening statement sets the tone for all that follows as the apostle interprets Israel's scriptural tradition in light of the unifying action of God's work through Christ, drawing all the world's people together under his lordship.

In this regard, brief mention may also be made of the verses immediately following this statement where Paul pointedly represents Jesus Christ as both a descendant of David according to the flesh and as the appointed Son of God in power, raised from the dead by the Spirit (1:3–4). Despite the exegetical difficulties associated with these verses, the kinship language of descent (γενομένου) and sonship (υἱοῦ Θεοῦ) clearly point to both Jesus's decidedly Jewish ancestral roots (ἐκ σπέρματος Δαυὶδ κατὰ σάρκα) and his more universal kinship ties with all believers, representing the firstfruits of the future resurrection of all the children of God (Rom 8:9–11, 14–17).[6] In other words, Paul portrays the movement's founding figure as having biological kinship ties with the Jewish people (ascribed/fixed), while simultaneously bringing non-Jews into this same ancestral line by positing common reception of the Spirit (achieved/fluid). Similar to Dionysus, who gives the Roman people a Greek ancestry, in order to bolster Rome's status as a non-barbarian people group, while simultaneously maintaining Roman ethnoracial distinctness (*Ant. rom.* 1.5.1, 9–70; 1.21.1–2), the apostle uses aggregative discourse to unite Jewish and gentile believers under a decidedly Jewish founder who nevertheless has universal kinship ties with all persons who believe in him; a complex theme that Paul will unpack as his argument progresses. This, combined with the close link he establishes between the Jewish scriptures and the gospel, in terms of

---

6. The role of the Spirit in Paul's larger argument is discussed in greater detail in chapters 5 and 6 of this work.

promise fulfillment, serves to bolster the believing community's status as a distinct people group possessing both a venerable ancestry and an equally venerable founder, who is no less than the appointed son of God.

Thus, from the start, Paul casts a universal vision wherein humanity as a whole stands united under the auspice of the gospel. The details of this vision, including the question of the status of nonbelieving, Jewish members of humanity are carefully worked out by the apostle in the arguments that follow. As I will demonstrate below, Paul's oeuvre, set within the framework of Jewish scriptural tradition, reaches back to mythological time to the Creation and the first human, Adam, touches on Abraham and pre-exilic Israel under the law, and references the Jewish people after the exile, reinterpreting the revered past within the present framework of God's universal redemptive work through Christ and the inauguration of the eschaton. However, before examining the ethnographic character of Rom 1–5 in greater detail, several general, introductory observations are in order regarding space and time as these relate to Romans.

First, as previously noted, geography and history, and past, present, and future time overlap considerably in ethnographic works from this period. Paul, like his contemporaries, casts his ethnography against the backdrop of a vast, encompassing scope of space and time. With regard to space, and unlike the founding of Greco-Roman people groups and their related cultic sites, the founding of the Christ movement is not tied to any specific place. Rather, although the movement originates in one place, Jerusalem, right from its inception, the intent is that it should spread from there to all the ends of the earth (Acts 1:6–8; 8:1, 4; 9:15, etc.). Accordingly, the geographic centrality of Jerusalem, Mt. Zion, and the Temple in the Jewish scriptural tradition is recast in light of the Christ event, and expressed in theological and/or metaphorical terms. Similarly, Paul extends the redemptive power of the gospel to embrace all of created space (and nonhuman creatures), linking creation's redemption to the future, full redemption of the children of God (Rom 8:19–23).[7] In essence, all space is/will be sacred by virtue of the centrality of the person of Christ and his relation to God's children, through whom it will be set free from sin and death. Consequently, the centrality of the Temple in the Jewish sacred tradition as the place where Yahweh dwells among his people (e.g., 1 Kgs 8:10–12; Ezek 43:7, 44:4) is replaced by the idea that believers themselves are the temple of God with the divine presence dwelling among them, wherever they are (e.g., 1 Cor 3:16–17; 2 Cor 6:16). In the temple and cultic site-replete first century, this idea of divine presence attached to geographically diverse people groups, rather than to a specific place and/or physical structure, would have had profound symbolic value in, signifying the vast scope and reach of the Christ movement as embracing all of the world and its peoples.

---

7. There has been considerable debate over the meaning of κτίσις. It is probably best understood as referring to nonhuman creatures and nature in general (e.g., Witherington and Hyatt, *Paul's Letter to the Romans*, 222–23).

This brings us to the next two, related observations which pertain to the conception of time in eschatological terms. The first of these relates to the fundamental understanding of the historical trajectory of Israel's covenantal relationship with Yahweh. As already mentioned, Paul works within a distinctly Jewish frame of reference in constructing his ethnography. Broadly speaking, one of the basic, scripturally based narratives common to a wide range of Jewish groups in existence during this period was the story of Israel's recurring disobedience and unfaithfulness to Yahweh, its failure to heed prophetic warnings and its subsequent experience of divine punishment in the form of exile, and the promise of a future restoration by God. The reality of subjection to Rome had the effect of pushing the full realization of this restoration to the future, introducing the element of eschatological hope.[8] It is this larger narrative that lies behind Paul's own particular version of the story, which sees the promised, hoped-for in-breaking of future, eschatological time into the present by means of the inaugural event of Christ's death and resurrection.[9] Central to this history, both in its original, prophetic version and, as we will see, in the apostle's reinterpreted version, are the related notions that it is God himself who will cleanse his people from their sinful disobedience (e.g., Jer 33:8; Ezek 36:24–25, 33), giving them a new heart and placing his Spirit within them, so that they might acknowledge him as God and live in obedience to him (e.g., Jer 31:33; Ezek 36:27).

In addition to this larger narrative is another, smaller sub-narrative, which Paul adopts and works within, of openness to the foreigner and foreign people groups. Its prevalence throughout the OT, particularly in Isaiah where there is a distinct element of contingency about gentile otherness that will be fully resolved in the eschatological future, has been noted.[10] Central to this narrative is the idea that nonelect peoples are full participants in the divine plan for humanity, with Israel specifically called to work out its destiny in relation to them, while simultaneously remaining separate (e.g., Exod 12:48–49; Ezra 6:21; Neh 10:29; Isa 56; Ezek 47:22–23).[11] A second, fundamental, and related aspect of this story is the idea that foreigners who attach themselves to Israel and its God, nevertheless maintain their own ethnoracial distinctiveness, with Israel retaining its unique status (e.g., Isa 66:22–23; Zech 14:16–21).[12] As we will see, Paul draws on this sub-narrative, while at the same time expanding it in an unprecedented way by dissolving traditional, ethnic oppositional strategies and creating new ones, in

---

8. Wagner, *Heralds of the Good News*, 29–30.

9. Wagner, *Heralds of the Good News*, 29–31. A full discussion of Paul's use of the Jewish Scriptures and his reliance on common, contemporary Jewish narratives is not possible, given the limits of this work. J. Ross Wagner's work addresses some of these lacunae.

10. Lieu, *Christian Identity*, 287.

11. Kaminsky, "Israel's Election and the Other," 17–30.

12. Kaminsky, "Israel's Election and the Other," 19–20, 22. It must be acknowledged that juxtaposed against these positive images of gentile inclusiveness are texts that portray the other more negatively and, in some cases, envision the total destruction of certain non-Israelite peoples.

order to construct a fresh understanding of the people of God that includes diverse ethnoracial groups, yet maintains Israel's special status.

The explanatory power of these two narratives derives from the fact that they allow for a reinterpretation of the past in light of a future that is itself interpreted as an already present, unfolding eschatological reality. For Paul, the future promise of a restored and renewed people of God is being presently fulfilled among the ethnoracially diverse members of the Christ movement who represent the culmination of God's historic plan for Israel. Past, present, and future time converge as the apostle's rendering of the Jewish scriptural tradition, which, while it acknowledges the unique place and role of Israel as the locus of divine action on behalf of humanity, nevertheless emphasizes the universal Lordship of Yahweh which embraces all of creation. Although the universal dimension of God's sovereignty runs like a red thread throughout the OT, global acknowledgment of that Lordship is portrayed as a future hope in the prophetic tradition. However, for Paul, who works within this frame of reference, the world, including both its people and places, lends itself to a universal history when God reunites it in and through Christ, bringing this future hope, as foretold by the prophets, into the present, while acknowledging that its fullest expression, nevertheless, continues to remain in the future.

In sum, like his Greco-Roman and Jewish contemporaries, Paul's universal perspective of the world emerges from within the context of the interplay between revered tradition and its associated narratives and the present reality of a unifying, new world order. Moreover, like his contemporaries, Paul is fully aware that his universal claims stand in tension with the reality of ethnoracial difference. In keeping with the ethnographic tradition of his time, the apostle carefully works through the intricacies of the relationship between the Jewish people, and their particular and distinct role in history, and believing gentiles, who stand both in continuity with and in discontinuity from Israel. It is to these points of continuity and discontinuity that we now turn.

4.1.2 Establishing Points of Continuity between Past and Present

In the Greco-Roman ethnographical tradition, universal unifying power is symbolized by Rome, the Roman Empire, and/or the person of the emperor. Accordingly, and in its starkest, simplest terms, the ethnically diverse people groups subject to Roman rule are seen as comprising the in-group, while the out-group is defined as consisting of unconquered, barbarian, people groups. A case in point is Strabo, who classifies unconquered people groups as unprofitable and undesirable (*Geogr.* 4.5.3–4; 15.1.1–26). The defining characteristic is membership in or affiliation with, whether forced or voluntary, the empire. For Paul, it is the unifying power of sin, alienation from God, and resultant enmity between the Creator and his creation that unites all of humanity, including the Jews (e.g., Hos 2:18–22). This idea of a universal alienation from God has its roots in the OT and especially, in the prophets, who decry Israel's persistent idolatry and lack of trust in God, practices which evoke divine wrath and judgment, placing Israel on par with idolatrous gentile nations, despite their elect status.

However, for Paul, humanity's past and present alienation from its God is decisively dealt within and through Christ, as God works to renew and restore his historical people, along with all gentiles who acknowledge his sovereignty. However, this redrawing of the boundaries of the people of God to include all who acknowledge him inevitably collides with the historical reality of Israel's election. Although this issue will be dealt with extensively in Rom 9–11, the apostle lays the groundwork for that task in the opening chapters of the letter. In these chapters, Paul sets out to establish a scriptural basis for universal inclusion that points to an active trust in God, manifested as obedience to him, as the primary identifying characteristic of his people, both in the past and in the present—thus, drawing a historical line of continuity between Judaism and the Christ movement. Consequently, the place of the law in this scheme and, by the same token, the unique role of the Jewish people raises the issue of discontinuity.

I will demonstrate that careful examination of the ethnic discourse in the first five chapters of Romans indicates that the apostle's primary strategy in establishing points of continuity and discontinuity resides in an effective dismantling of a particular Jewish intragroup stereotype of election that is no longer valid, based as it is on a failure to recognize the provisional role of the law in defining the people of God. In this way, Paul maintains the law's saliency as providing a source of valid ethnoracial identifiers, while simultaneously reinterpreting its past, historical role in defining the people of God in light of the present.

4.1.2.1 *All Who Have Faith (Rom 1:16–17): God's People, Past and Present*

In the previous chapter, I argued that Paul's main purpose in writing to the believers in Rome is to provide them with a positive social identity in order that they might be encouraged to persevere in faithful obedience to the gospel. Like his contemporaries, Paul constructs this positive identity by providing his audience with an ethnography aimed at legitimizing the Christ movement and as a consequence, its members. The purpose, so defined, dovetails nicely, with what most commentators see as the thematic statement of the epistle. Although several, well acknowledged exegetical difficulties have tended to muddy the interpretative waters, what is clear is the importance of faith to the apostle's thesis, with the word "πίστις" and its cognates occurring four times in the span of two relatively brief verses. Moreover, the last of these occurrences appears in a quotation from the Jewish scriptures (specifically, Hab 2:4) where the terms "faith," "righteousness," and "life" form an important cluster of meaning.

Faith, faithfulness, and the associated notions of trust and/or belief in is pervasive in the OT and, especially, in the prophets. In antiquity, the term "faith" was used to express a range of concepts, including, trust, faithfulness, steadfastness, and loyalty.

Likewise the verb was used to express the related ideas of: trust in; to be faithful to; to be steadfast; and to believe. Thus, in the ancient context, faith refers less often to mental ascent to, or belief in, some doctrine or truth, and more to a particular disposition of character, which is itself manifested in a certain way of behaving in the world. Thus, the understanding of faith as an abstract, private disposition of the mind is a modern notion.[13] The ubiquity of this theme may be attributed to the fact that it is one of the quintessential characteristics of both the divine and human side of the covenantal relationship where both parties were expected to demonstrate faithfulness toward one another by maintaining their respective responsibilities. In the prophetic tradition, Israel is portrayed as historically unfaithful in relation to Yahweh and his covenant. Its people forsake their God, choosing instead to worship the gods of other nations, and fail to honor and obey God both by disregarding his law and by engaging in prescribed religious rites and rituals, while failing to practice justice and righteousness, rendering its worship of God empty of true devotion (e.g., Amos 5:21–26). Although there is invariably a faithful remnant who choose to trust in and wait upon God, and/or who either forsake idolatry and/or repent of such things, on the whole, Israel's behavior toward Yahweh and, consequently, its members' behavior toward one another and, especially, toward the marginalized, is deemed unrighteous by the prophets.

As the prophetic tradition shows, human righteousness, although it can be more narrowly associated with and defined by obedience to the precepts of the law, also refers more broadly to an abiding trust or faith in and loyalty to its God that shuns the worship and supplication of other gods, seeks economic, political, and social justice according to Yahweh's standards, and refuses to make treaties with foreign nations in disobedience to the divine word, despite the apparent direness of the situation (e.g., Isa 1:4, 17, 23). In other words, the characteristics of human righteousness and faithfulness are tightly linked and often interchangeable (e.g., Isa 1:26),[14] in that behavior deemed righteous before Yahweh springs from a faithfulness or loyalty to him that actively seeks to enact his will in the world. As we will see, Paul argues that God's righteousness, which humans are to emulate in both their human relationships and in their dealings with God, and which was revealed in the past in the written law, is now being revealed in the gospel. What has changed is not the demand for an active faith in God which results in righteous affections and behavior, but the means through which God's own righteousness is revealed. In other words, the traditional dichotomy between law and faith as representative of two diametrically opposed religious systems, Jewish-Christian, that are further defined as legalistic versus grace-based, and ethnically particular versus universal, does not appear to be supported by the prophetic tradition to which Paul appeals. This becomes more apparent, as I will show, when the ethnic dimensions of his argument are brought to the forefront.

---

13. Hodge, *If Sons, Then Heirs*, 82–83.
14. In this verse, Israel is referred to as the City of Righteousness, the Faithful City.

In stark contrast, within the same prophetic tradition, Yahweh's faithfulness is portrayed as being tantamount to his righteousness. Although God's righteousness, his faithfulness, is often linked to his saving and liberating acts on behalf of beleaguered, exiled Israel, revealing him as unremittingly faithful in terms of his covenantal relationship with his people (e.g., Isa 40–55), in other instances, it is linked specifically to his acts of judgment.[15] This is apparent particularly in the apocalyptic sections of Isaiah, where in addition to God's salvific acts, there is the accompanying idea that *all* persons, Jews and gentiles, alike, who persist in doing evil will face imminent divine judgment that will result in their destruction; an idea that links unrighteousness in God's eyes to death (e.g., Deut 30:6, 15–20; Prov 21:21; Wis 1:15, 5:1–5, 15; 15:3).[16] Conversely, righteous persons, who exhibit active faith and trust by acknowledging God as God and by doing what is lawful and just in his eyes, no matter what the circumstances, reap the benefits of life (e.g., Ezek 18:5–9; 33:10–20).

Saved humanity, within the framework of the Jewish tradition within which these scriptural texts were interpreted, consisted primarily of faithful Jews and, in some cases, included gentiles affiliated with the Jewish community and its God. However, the sub-narrative of gentile inclusion remained just that, a sub-narrative. And as we have seen, although biblical texts that speak of gentile inclusion point to their inclusion as gentiles, their exact place within and status among the people of God remained a contested issue within the Jewish communities of the first century. In this rendering of the prophetic tradition, the in-group clearly consists of a central core comprised of faithful Jews, claiming biological, Jewish descent, with gentile sympathizers and proselytes standing at a variety points somewhere nearer to the periphery of the boundary, depending on how these boundaries were defined. Conversely, the out-group consisted of all non-Jewish persons; that is those who could not claim Jewish ancestry and/or who did not exhibit any degree of adherence to Jewish law, religion, or custom.

Against this background, Paul's thematic statement, while evoking an important cluster of related OT terms, "faith," "righteousness," "life," that outline the basic trajectory of Yahweh's historic dealings with Israel, simultaneously disrupts and reconfigures the cast of human characters. Moreover, his reinterpretation of the tradition results in the sub-narrative of gentile inclusion coming to the fore, where it becomes a central theme, driving the plot. Paul boasts in the gospel (Οὐ ἐπαισχύνομαι may be read as an example of *litotes*) because it has the power to save all people, who have faith in it and in the God of whom it speaks. God's righteousness, which in the past was quintessentially revealed in his saving acts toward Israel, is presently being revealed (ἀποκαλύπτεται) in the gospel, which expands beyond the horizon

---

15. In this tradition, salvation broadly refers to God's rescue of his people not only from worldly political and military oppression, but also from divine wrath and judgment in the face of national covenant failure and apostasy.

16. Bernhard W. Anderson considers the final apocalyptic relecture or rendering of the book of Isaiah in great detail (Anderson, "Apocalyptic Rendering," 17–38). Also, Byrne, *Romans*, 52–53.

of Israel to include all of humanity. Most likely, Paul is referring to God's righteous character here, given the OT citation which follows. As already noted, God's saving acts, his righteousness, and faith formed an important cluster of concepts in the Jewish scriptures. Standing centuries after these words were first penned, modern readers need to be reminded of how unsettling this would have been to an ancient person, who despite the relative openness of Greco-Roman religion, nevertheless tended to associate particular gods with specific people groups—the God of the Jews being no exception. Dionysius of Halicarnassus illustrates this principle when he identifies the Pelasgians as Greek due to the manner in which they conduct their sacrificial ceremonies (*Ant. rom.* 1.21.1–2). As this example illustrates, membership in a particular ethnoracial group was often signaled by discrete worship practices which expressed loyalty to a people group's identifying god(s).

Paul's use of the common binary oppositional categories, Jew and Greek, underscores the fact (Of note is that these categories follow quickly on the heels of the categories of Greek-barbarian, wise-foolish, mentioned in v. 14) that what he has to say in the argument that follows has great import for the issue of social identity, more broadly, and for ethnoracial identity, in particular. What is important to note is that these binary opposites not only denote a reference to all of humanity but, more importantly, that under the unifying characteristic of faith they no longer denote traditional, Jewish oppositional, us (Jews) and them (gentiles), categories of persons. Paul's subtle use of ethnic discourse in this instance foreshadows his dismantling of these oppositional strategies in the argument that follows. As we will see, the defining characteristic of faith is what allows him to link members of God's people in the past, who were predominantly Jewish, to those in the present, who are both Jew and gentile. At the same time, by means of this trait, the apostle will create new oppositional categories that both definitively define the members of the Christ movement and account for the status and place of nonbelieving Jews within the framework of the present in-breaking of eschatological time.

Thus, although the apostle will flesh-out his re-interpretation of this basic OT narrative as his argument progresses, verses 16–17 set the stage for what follows by introducing two points that are crucial for his argument: faith, defined as active trust in God, as the defining characteristic of the elect, both in the past *and* in the present; and the universal and unifying scope of God's work in and through Christ, as announced in the gospel.[17] The centrality of faith as a characteristic of the people of God is underscored by the phrase "ἐκ πίστις εἰς πίστις" in verse 17.[18] Although the precise meaning of the phrase continues to be debated, it is best taken in the intensive

---

17. As I pointed out in chapter 1, we may assume that after several readings and expositions, Paul's hearers would have gained sufficient familiarity with the letter in its totality, which would have allowed them to see the outline of his argument in 1:16–17 and how what he says there is tied to his opening statement describing the gospel as God's good news promised beforehand through the prophets.

18. Byrne, *Romans*, 54.

sense, underscoring the centrality of faith.[19] In other words, the ability to perceive the gospel as the power of God for/into salvation is dependent on trusting or believing that God indeed has revealed his righteousness or his power to save humanity in it. Moreover, it is important to note that nothing in the immediate context suggests that Paul is speaking of Christ's own faith. Rather, both the context of the letter itself and that of the OT point to human faith. The reference to Hab 2:4, which immediately follows, underscores this.[20] The prophet's dialogue with God, as it appears in the Jewish scriptures, portrays Habakkuk's perplexity in the face of Yahweh's decision to punish Judah's wickedness by means of the Babylonians, who are even less righteous (Hab 1:6, 12–13), his learning to wait in faith (2:3–4) for Babylon's eventual punishment (2:4a, 5–13, 15–19), and the ultimate revelation of God's universal lordship and rule (2:14, 20). This text underscores the link between human righteousness and human faith/trust in God in a situation that appears to call God's own righteousness and justice into question. This would resonate with a present-day audience facing general, social persecution by both Jewish and gentile neighbors who find the message of the gospel and its crucified Messiah preposterous; especially, given the fact, that this Jewish Messiah has been rejected by a majority of his own people.

Both the flow of Paul's Greek version of the verse and the Hebrew of the MT suggest that "by faith" should be taken with ζήσεται. The argument that the phrase describes how one is righteous, that is, by faith, stems from a reading of Romans that presupposes that Paul is concerned with establishing how one obtains a righteousness that leads to eternal salvation, through faith, as opposed to, through works of the law. However, as I have argued, the prophetic tradition links faith, life, and righteousness in a way that belies such a dichotomy between faith as a form of mental ascent to the sovereignty of God and obedience to the will of that same God. Rather, the righteous person is righteous both in the sense that he or she trusts fully in God and lives in a way that evinces such trust or belief in his sovereignty. For Paul, it is not an issue of whether the Romans should continue to live by faith in order to be righteous or whether they are already righteous because they believed/believe in the Gospel. Rather, as in the OT, and particularly in Habakkuk, the righteous person trusts in/ has faith in God *and* lives accordingly—this may properly be described as an active faith. Although we cannot be entirely certain why the apostle chooses to omit the pronouns found in the original text, it is plausible that he does do so in order to underscore the centrality of faith in God, and specifically in his present salvific work in and through Christ, and its inextricable link to righteousness and life in the eyes of that same God.

In sum, what emerges from this brief, yet powerful, thematic statement is the notion of faith, defined as an active trust/and or belief in God, linked with righteousness

---

19. Byrne, *Romans*, 54.

20. Paul's rendition of the verse omits all pronouns attaching to the original, both as it appears in the Masoretic Text ("his faith") and the LXX ("my faith"), an omission that has spurned considerable debate over whether ἐκ πίστις attaches to the verb or to the subject of the sentence.

and life, as the defining characteristic of his people, both in the past and present. Paul will develop this notion further, playing it against the law, in an effort to define members of the Christ movement more clearly, drawing a line of temporal continuity between the faithfulness of God's people in the past and that of his people in the present, in the extended argument which follows. The phrase, Ἰουδαίῳ πρῶτον (v. 16), hints at this temporal continuity.

Paul will pick-up on the theme of Jewish priority, both temporal and hierarchical, at several points in his argument. Here, the phrase, Ἰουδαίῳ πρῶτον, seems to indicate not only that the Jewish people are presently the first addressees of this good news, but also, and more importantly, that they represent the very people who first heard this news, in the form of a promise, in the past, through the prophets (Rom 1:2). As the apostle emphatically notes, it is the Jews, who were entrusted with the oracles of God (3:2).[21] In other words, those Jews (the OT remnant) who responded in faith to the prophetic word, τὰ λόγια, of hope of salvation in the past, stand in continuity with those in the present, both Jew and Greek, who respond in faith and hope to this same God, who has accomplished a new work in and through Christ, as announced in the gospel.[22] Paul will return to this theme of a Jewish remnant in chapters 9–11, developing it in greater detail. What is important to note here, is that although the remnant of the past did not specifically hope and trust in the work of God through Christ, they nevertheless hoped and trusted in a gracious God who could and would ultimately restore them to their previous status as his people. For Paul, this gracious God has already acted through the death and resurrection of Christ, preserving a remnant of believing Jews. Thus, faith in this God, both in the past and in the present, is what identifies those who were, are, and will be his.[23]

---

21. In the LXX and in extrascriptural Jewish literature, the oracles of God could denote the entirety of the divine word embodied in the Law and the prophets. In most instances, the term is accompanied by a reference to the promise of salvation based upon Israel's unique covenantal relationship with God (Byrne, *Romans*, 112).

22. The concept of a remnant who survive God's wrath and judgment against a largely apostate Israel runs throughout the prophetic tradition and serves to vouchsafe God's promise to restore his people. For example, Isaiah holds out the promise that once God has removed the wicked from Israel's midst, those who repent will be forgiven, wiped clean of all their sins, and restored (Isa 1:16–20).

23. The centrality of faith, or what Paul means by the phrase, "from faith into faith," becomes more clear in Rom 4 where the apostle discusses Abraham's and David's faiths, linking them to Christ's faith. In this way, he draws a continuous line from the OT to the present. It has and always will be faith in God, the God who presently has brought about the promised new age of the Spirit.

4.1.2.2 *God of Both Jews and Gentiles: Dismantling Ethnoracial Oppositional Strategies*

4.1.2.2A The Leveling Effect of Foundation Myths: The Decline of Humanity into Wickedness and Impiety

Romans 1:18–32 is often interpreted as an indictment against gentile idolatry and the vice and wickedness caused by the pagan failure to acknowledge God as Creator and Lord. The numerous parallels between this text and that of the Wisdom of Solomon are cited as evidence for the conclusion that Paul's purpose in this portion of the argument is to demonstrate that God's wrath against the gentiles is just.[24] Accordingly, the unidentified interlocutor in 2:1–16 is typically viewed as being a Jew,[25] although some scholars identify this imaginary person as a gentile.[26] The purpose of the two diatribes (1:18—2:16 and 2:17—3:20) taken together is to establish God's righteous judgment of humanity, as a whole, which is guilty of a failure to worship God as the Lord, as evidenced in gentile idolatry and in misguided Jewish moral superiority.

This interpretation has some merit, despite the fact that the ethnic identity of the first interlocutor remains debatable and although there are scholars who have argued that 1:18–32 references Israel's idolatry, particularly the golden calf incident.[27] My intent is not to provide a detailed critique of these positions, since this would involve the type of detailed exegesis that is beyond the scope of the present work. Rather, by focusing on the ethnographic elements present in both of the passages mentioned above, and in their wider context, mainly 3:21—5:21, I hope to bring clarity to several of the contested issues by providing an alternative reading that better accounts for the passage itself and its wider context. I will demonstrate that in the first five chapters of Romans, Paul presents his audience with a sweeping history of humanity, beginning in mythological time at the Creation up until the present age of Christ and encompassing the foundation of Israel and the giving of the law. Like his contemporaries, the apostle's account maintains a loose chronology (cf. Strabo, *Geogr.* 4.1.11; 4.6.10; 6.1.6; 6.2.1) that focuses on moments of foundation, change, and transformation and the key biblical figures associated with these events (cf. Josephus, *Ant.* 10.147–48). Strabo utilizes the Trojan war, the heroic age, the mythical return of the Heracleidae, along with the battle of Actium to indicate time (*Geogr.* 8.5.5; 8.6.15; 8.7.5; 10.5.8; 13.4.5; 15.3.2), rather than specific dates. Similarly, Josephus's account of the Babylonian exile, consists of key events in the life of Israel (*Ant.* 10.147–48), which he strategically arranges according

---

24. E.g., Sanday and Headlam, *Romans*, 51–52.

25. Francis Watson notes Jewish identification as the consensus (Watson, *Paul, Judaism, and the Gentiles*, 197).

26. E.g., Esler, *Conflict and Identity in Romans*, 151; Witherington and Hyatt, *Paul's Letter to the Romans*, 76.

27. Lucas, "Reorienting the Structural Paradigm," 121–41, is an excellent example.

to his ethnographic purposes. As discussed below, Paul proceeds in a similar fashion. Within the context of this historical-mythological-ethnographical account, Paul dismantles traditional, Jewish oppositional strategies, while simultaneously redefining the salient criteria identifying the people of God.

Paul begins his sweeping account with a thematic statement (1:18–19) focused on the eschatological present-time revelation (ἀποκαλύπτεται) of God's righteous wrath against humanity as a whole. This wrath is justified because it is in response to humanity's suppression of its knowledge of God, which God himself has made plain. Moreover, as will be made clear in verses 20–31, sexual immorality and vice is the result of human failure to properly honor and worship God, despite clear knowledge of who he is. Of note is Paul's use of the term ἄνθρωπος and related ethnically neutral pronouns, which continue throughout a major portion of the passage that follows. In fact, there is no mention of ethnic categories until 2:9–11 where the apostle discusses God's impartial judgment of the both the Jew and the Greek. Thus, 2:9–12 forms an inclusio with 1:16–17—the gospel is for all people, because all persons will be subject to final divine judgment at the eschaton. The present revelation of God's wrath against human wickedness and impiety is meant to lead to repentance before the arrival of that auspicious day (2:4).

Although it is not explicit that this wrath is revealed in or through the gospel, with the reference to heaven most likely underscoring the fact that this wrath has a divine source, the context suggests that the good news consists of both God's righteous anger against sinful humanity and his kindness and forbearance. This notion is prevalent in the prophetic texts where Yahweh's acts of salvation are often simultaneously associated with his judgment of Israel and/or the nations and his forgiveness and mercy (e.g., Isa 12:1–6; Jer 12:14–17, 30:12–24; Ezek 36:16–38; Amos 9:8–15; Mic 7:8–13, 18–20; Zech 14:1–11). The gospel, then, like the prophets of the past, issues both a word of warning and of comfort, at least to those who heed its admonition. However, for Paul, the day of the Lord has already come to pass in and through Christ, although its complete fulfillment lies in the future. Thus, there is both a present judgment and a future judgment. It is the present judgment, via the gospel, that, according to Paul, fulfills the prophetic promise of judgment-renewal/restoration of Israel, and in some cases, of Israel's enemies, as in the case of Egypt and Assyria (Isa 19:16–25).

Paul continues his reinterpretation of the Jewish scriptures in light of the present by linking God's present righteous wrath against human impiety and wickedness to its mythological past, with the reference to the creation, ἀπὸ κτίσεως κόσμου, in 1:20. The transition to the past tense (ἐδόξασαν) in verse 21 signals that the apostle has shifted to speaking of humanity at the beginning of time (at least, from the human perspective) when its failure to acknowledge God as God led to idolatry and moral decline (vv. 22–31). Of note is that the past tense continues from verse 21 through verse 31, with a shift to the present (εἰσίν; συνευδοκοῦσιν) in verse 32, which signals that Paul is once again speaking of persons in the present. As noted above, the numerous parallels between this text and Wisdom of Solomon may suggest that Paul is speaking implicitly of gentile idolatry. However, although it is clear that he borrows from the latter, it is not entirely clear that he has only gentiles in mind. There are no explicit ethnic references to indicate that he is referring solely to non-Jews. Rather, as noted above, he employs deliberately inclusive pronouns and terms, beginning and ending with the binary categories of Jew and Greek, which themselves signal a reference to humanity as a whole. Although it is possible that this critique of wicked humanity is meant to either quash gentile ethnic superiority or trap an unsuspecting Jewish audience as part of a larger campaign to enkindle gentile and Jewish rapprochement, it is equally probable that it is a foundational account. First, Paul is addressing mature believers who neither need to be convinced that they need the gospel nor to be reminded that they, in the case of gentiles, worshipped idols before becoming believers. Second, the apostle's vague (in modern terms) indicators of time would have alerted an ancient audience that he was speaking of humanity's mythological origins.

Myths related to humanity's religious, moral, political, and social decline after its initial inception abound in both Classical and Greco-Roman literature (e.g., Hesiod, *Op.* 90–93, 120, 176–78; Seneca, *Ep.* 90.5–6, *Phaed.* 486, 527–28; Ovid, *Metam.* 1.127–50, 15.99–103). There is also evidence that the ideal of Rome's Golden Age, coupled with an aniconic exemplar of religion, existed in the first century CE (Plutarch, *Is. Os.* 378.67, 379.70–71; *Num.* 13.6, 16.1–4, 19.5—20.7).[28] For example, Plutarch writes:

> And in a like manner Numa forbade the Romans to revere an image of god which had the form of man or beast. Nor was there among them in this earlier time any painted or graven likeness of deity, but while for the first hundred and seventy years they were continually building temples and establishing sacred shrines, they made no statues in bodily form, convinced that it was impious to liken higher things to lower, and that it was impossible to apprehend deity except by the intellect (Plutarch, *Def. orac.* 436.48).

Moreover, from an early date, ancient philosophers viewed traditional iconic, polytheistic religion with a critical eye, since it was dependent on things other than the intellect, which they maintained was the only human faculty capable of apprehending the supreme, ineffable principle[29] Similarly, Josephus depicts humanity's decline after creation (*Ant.* 1.60–62; 72–73). For example, he writes that, Cain "put an end to the simplicity in which men lived before the invention of weights and measures: the guileless and generous existence which they had enjoyed in ignorance

---

28. Jewett, "Corruption and Redemption of Creation," 25–46.

29. Athanassiadi and Frede, *Pagan Monotheism in Late Antiquity*, 7–8. The editors note that, at the same time, these philosophers condoned traditional religion either on the ground that it constituted the nearest form in which the uneducated could understand the truth, or because it was socially useful, or for both reasons. They justified their actions by either arguing that what was really being worshipped under various names and through historically sanctioned forms of cult was the one ineffable principle of things, or that these beings formed a hierarchy subordinated to the supreme god.

of those things he converted into a life of craftiness" (1.60). Furthermore, in the course of time, during Noah's life, the people "abandoned the customs of their fathers for a life of depravity" (1.72).

Thus, it is conceivable, that in Rom 1:20–31 Paul is arguing that polytheistic worship is a distortion of the original vision of an aniconic, monotheistic, and rational religion for humanity.[30] The reason he does this is to underscore the basic gospel teaching that monotheism represents the original, divine intent for humanity. This building of a common ground among all people groups lying not in an exclusively Jewish monotheism, but in monotheism as such,[31] would have served as a powerful weapon in the apologetic arsenal of early evangelists, such as Paul, who proclaimed the difficult message of a crucified, Jewish savior of the world. Indeed, Paul explicitly states that he desires to proclaim the gospel to the believers in Rome (1:15). And it is quite conceivable that he is doing just that in these opening chapters, although in a way that suits his ethnographic aims. Granted, it is difficult to assess whether Paul has Rome's Golden Age specifically in mind here. However, it is plausible that Paul's audience would have made this association. This would only serve to strengthen the link that the apostle later makes between reason, the proper worship of God, and a lifestyle reflective of the Deity, which is itself a form of rational worship (Rom 1:21–32; 12:1–2).

Consequently, Paul's censure of idolatry and polytheism represents a convergence between Jewish and Greco-Roman thought, deliberately made by him in an effort to reach his mixed audience.[32] The fact that Paul presents this commonplace, Greco-Roman idea utilizing the symbolic and linguistic framework of a largely Jewish narrative (cf. Josephus, *Ant.*) accords with the frame of reference that he is working with and, consequently, indicates that Paul did not intend his audience to read/hear this section of the letter as an example of Jewish, anti-gentile polemic. Rather, Paul's reference to the time of creation suggests that he is referring to the time in Israel's past before the giving of the law. That is, he is alluding to the very earliest stages leading to Israel's emergence and founding as an independent nation. It was precisely during this key pre-foundational period, that the people comprising the incipient nation of Israel participated in the worship of other gods during their sojourn in Egypt (Ezek 20:4–9) and continued to indulge in such behavior while their divinely appointed lawgiver, Moses, was in the process of receiving its divinely instituted laws (Deut 9:7—10:11; Ps 106 [105]:20–23). It is quite conceivable that the members of Paul's audience, who were well-versed in the Scriptures, would have linked the apostle's excoriation against

30. Van Kooten, *Paul's Anthropology in Context*, 343.

31. Van Kooten, *Paul's Anthropology in Context*, 344.

32. Yet, unlike Greco-Roman moral philosophy, which argues that the supreme deity can only be apprehended by means of the intellect, Paul maintains not only that this deity has been revealed in the man Jesus, but that believers participate in the risen Christ in a transformative way, such that they presently experience newness of life and will experience even more complete renewal in the future. This idea of transformative participation pushes Paul's conception of conformity to Christ beyond the boundaries of the Greco-Roman philosophical ideal of imitation of the supreme deity.

πᾶσαν ἀσέβειαν and Moses's intercessory prayer in which he asks Yahweh to overlook Israel's ἀσέβημα (Deut 9:27).[33] Moreover, beginning with Deut 9:1–6, the idea that the impending destruction of the nations is due to their ἀσέβεια is repeatedly stressed in this text, drawing both incipient Israel and the gentile nations into the category of the impious.[34] The recitation of Israel's idolatry and rebellion against Yahweh throughout its history in both Ezek 20:1–29 and Ps 106 resonates with the picture of the decline of humanity as a whole due to idolatry as portrayed by Paul in Romans and by the prophets who depict apostate Israel in equally harsh terms (e.g., Jer 4:22; 5; 7:28; 9:3–21), even accusing Yahweh's chosen people of wickedness exceeding that of the gentiles (Ezek 5:5–7).

It is important to keep in mind, in this regard, that Paul has already directed his audience's attention to the prophets and their writings in the opening verses of the letter, which suggests that this is the framework, and not the much more flattering portrayal of Israel in Wisdom of Solomon, within which the first chapter is to be understood. The apostle's concluding statement (1:32) underscores the historical reality of humanity's general inability (Note the indefinite pronoun οἵτινες) to see itself as it truly is, in the eyes of God—a blindness that continues into the present, to which Paul now turns his attention.

4.1.2.2B Dismantling Ethnic Stereotypes and Redefining Jewish Self-Identity as the Elect: Judging the Other and the Impartial Judge

As discussed in the previous chapter, binary divisions, such as Jew-gentile and Greek-barbarian, are part and parcel of the oppositional strategies common to ancient ethnic discourse and are used to assert a people group's self-identity. The strategy is effective for the reason that it employs powerful stereotypes that function to negate the collective other, while simultaneously asserting the collective self. For example, Hellenistic Judaism generally maintained that gentiles had no natural knowledge of God. Jews alone had access to the truth about Yahweh, through his self-revelation to Israel, which marked them as the chosen people.[35] According to Josephus, the ancestors of the Jews received God's law "from the very mouth of God" (*Ant.* 3.93), which came down to their progeny through the scriptures (*Ant.* 3.280, 286, 322; 4.302), where it is "engraved" on the "souls" of the Jewish people (*Ag. Ap.* 178), in its original form (*Ag. Ap.* 183). Thus, as an ethnoracial entity that lives under a theocratic constitution, the Jews are a people who have both a singular grasp of who God is and unique knowledge of the divine intent for humanity. Similarly, Greco-Roman writers disputed Jewish access to genuine knowledge of the divine, claiming that such knowledge was the

---

33. Lucas, "Reorienting the Structural Paradigm," 136.
34. Lucas, "Reorienting the Structural Paradigm," 136.
35. Jewett, *Romans*, 154.

purview of philosophically educated and, thus, not available to fools and barbarians.³⁶ Accordingly, Greeks could become barbarians by failing to "acknowledge the same gods" and "the same equitable laws," which came down from these gods, "by which most of the spirit of the Greeks differs from that of barbarians" (Dionysius, *Ant. rom.* 1.89.4). Likewise, the Jewish peoples' purported access to the divine could be called into question either by disputing the legitimacy of their lawgiver (Josephus, *Ag. Ap.* 2.145) and, hence, the divine origin of their law, or by claiming that present day Jews no longer followed the divinely prescribed mandates given to their ancestors by their lawgiver, Moses (Strabo, *Geogr.* 16.2.39).

Paul calls into question these common stereotypes underlying traditional ethnoracial categories by claiming that all people have knowledge of God and all have suppressed the truth about him. It is important to note here, that Paul is not speaking of individuals. Clearly, he is not speaking of those Israelites who did not participate in the idolatry at Sinai, nor is he making reference to the faithful remnant in the prophetic tradition. Nor, for that matter, is he speaking of the morally upright and virtuous gentile or gentile proselyte. His point is that both Israel and the nations have failed to honor and worship God according to the knowledge they have of him. All of humanity is guilty of this, to one extent or the other, and, as Paul will make clear, the Torah did not, does not, and cannot save Israel from this general human condition.

In light of this, 1:32 not only underscores humanity's blindness on this point, but also suggests that such blindness underlies the ethnoracial stereotyping that sees the self as immune from such ignorance. Hence, the apostle's reference to applauding others who practice such things appears as an ironic statement pointing to the misplaced attitude of religious superiority over the other prevalent among Jews and gentiles alike. In the eyes of both groups, it is the other, and not the self, who deserves to die for its superstition/paganism, vice, and immoral/atheistic practices. Thus, both Jew and gentile, in their blindness, applaud their own respective group, unaware that each is subject to God's wrath for suppressing the truth about him and doing those things they think the other is guilty of. Accordingly, Paul moves on to address the issue of judging in 2:1, concluding that God is the only impartial judge of humanity (2:11).

The censure of the blind, hypocritical interlocutor (2:1–11) is best read in light of the preceding indictment, with διό suggesting a causal relationship between this passage and the indictment against idolatry and human vice. That is, the judging of any group by another is excluded because the above indictment applies to all of humanity. The alteration between ποιέω and πράσσω in relation to τὰ αὐτά and τὰ τοιαῦτα also suggests such a linkage, while the term ἀναπολόγητος (2:1) recalls 1:20.³⁷ As noted above, the ethnic identity of the interlocutor remains an issue of debate. However, given what precedes and Paul's continued use of ethnically neutral terms, ὦ ἄνθρωπε (2:1, 3), which recalls (1:18), and pronouns and his return to the

36. Jewett, *Romans*, 154.
37. Lucas, "Reorienting the Structural Paradigm," 134.

binary categories of Jew-Greek in 2:9–10, which recalls 1:16, it is best to see the interlocutor as a representing the basic human propensity to view the ethnic other as inferior. As such this imaginary person represents the vice of pretentiousness familiar from Hellenistic philosophical literature.[38]

This apostrophe was commonly used to typify particular vices or behavior which the writer or teacher desired his or her audience to refrain from.[39] It is possible that Paul is addressing pretentious behavior among believers. However, given that he is addressing an audience that has already accepted the gospel, and whom he commends for their faith, makes it unlikely that he is concerned with attitudes and behaviors among believers that evidence a refusal to acknowledge human failure to confess and worship God as God. Rather, and as I have already maintained, Paul's statement that he is eager to proclaim the gospel to the communities in Rome (1:15) suggests that he is doing just that, but as part of his larger goal of encouraging them to remain faithful to it. In other words, the diatribes in 2:1–16 and 17–29 represent how the gospel might be preached to an audience of unbelievers in an effort to convince these persons of their need for it. However, in this specific case, Paul's reiteration of a fundamental teaching of the gospel, that is, that all of humanity is guilty and subject to God's righteous wrath, is part and parcel of his reinterpretation of the Jewish scriptures in light of the new eschatological age. Thus, Paul preaches the gospel to his audience, but, as we will see, in a way that emphasizes its continuity with a Jewish past that itself evidences elements of contingency with respect to the gentile other. In other words, he preaches it in light of his ethnographic aims.

As noted above, traditional oppositional categories, both of the Jewish and Greco-Roman variety, associated ignorance of the divine and the resulting impiety and wickedness with the ethnic other. Paul in effect dismantles these categories by maintaining that God will judge each person without respect to his or her ethnic affiliation(s). The apostle's accusation that the ethnically unidentifiable interlocutor is practicing those things for which he or she condemns the ethnic other, relates to the preceding argument which established the guilt of humanity as a whole in suppressing the truth about God, and specifically to 1:32. The main thrust of 1:32 and 2:2 within the context of the larger argument is to underscore the fact that any supposed knowledge of God and his righteousness is not enough. What is crucial is whether or not that knowledge translates into attitudes and behaviors that are righteous according to divine standards. This cuts right to the heart of the Greco-Roman notion that knowledge of God was for the intellectually superior Greek or Greek-educated person. No matter, both the Greek and the barbarian will be judged according to his or her deeds and not according to his or level of theological acumen (2:6). The same holds true for the Jew, a point Paul will return to, as discussed below. What is important in this regard is that Paul expands the Jewish notion of judgment according to deeds to include

---

38. Stowers, *Rereading of Romans*, 34, 101, 144–48.
39. Stowers, *Rereading of Romans*, 101.

the idea of gentiles who essentially do what the law requires, despite the fact that they are gentiles and do not possess the written law as a source of knowledge of God's will (2:12–16); a move which pointedly dismantles the ethnic stereotype of the Torah-free, wicked gentile. Moreover, as the apostle audaciously asserts, it is the doers of the law who will be counted as righteous at the Last Judgment, regardless of ethnic identity and regardless of whether the law that is kept is in its written form or that present in the heart and conscience. There is nothing in the context that suggests that Paul is speaking of gentile believers in 2:14–16. Rather, the use of these binary categories indicates that the apostle is referring to humanity as a whole.

Thus, Paul establishes three key points which he will develop in the arguments that ensue. First, knowledge of God and the divine will (i.e, what God requires of humanity as its Creator and Lord) is available to all peoples and is not limited to the Jews, although they are the only group who have it in its written form. Second, humanity as a whole, Jews included, has suppressed this knowledge, embracing attitudes and engaging in behaviors contrary to divine intention and, as a consequence, has been allowed by divine fiat to spiral down into moral and sexual degeneracy. Third, nevertheless, all of humanity, in all of its ethnic diversity, will stand before the judgment seat of an impartial God who is the only one capable of assessing an individual's moral and ethical culpability. The tension between the second and last points is more apparent than real, since the fact that all persons are under the power of sin (Rom 3:9) means that no one is capable of meeting the expectations necessary for fulfillment of the divine will, whether in its written (law) or spiritual (heart and conscience) form.

As in ancient ethnographic works in general, the past (the decline of humanity), the present (the revelation of the righteous wrath of God against the consequent wickedness and impiety of humanity), and the future (the Last Judgment) are reinterpreted in light of the present eschatological reality of the gospel. Paul's main point in this rehearsal of the basic premises of the gospel, which we may assume are familiar to his audience, is to underscore the Jewish roots of the new movement (Rom 1:2), while simultaneously deconstructing traditional oppositional categories premised on a common, Jewish construal of Israel's chosenness as definitive of Jewish self-identity. Both of these aims come to a head in 2:17—3:19 where the apostle redefines this self-identity according to the prophetic tradition as reinterpreted in light of the Christ event. In doing so, he reconfigures and expands Jewish self-understanding as the elect people of God in a way that allows for the inclusion of non-Jewish ethnic groups.

Paul's dialogue with the imaginary Jewish interlocutor is best understood within the context of the larger argument beginning with 2:1 and Paul's indictment of the ethnic pretentiousness characteristic of humanity in general. Accordingly, in 2:17, he turns specifically to address Jewish ethnic pretension.[40] In view of the diatribe in

---

40. Historically, scholarship has shifted from viewing this passage as Paul's general critique of Jews and legalistic Judaism as such, to reading it in a more narrow sense as referring to a specific type of Jew—the arrogant or hypocritical teacher who considers him or herself superior to the gentile "other."

2:1–11 in which Paul denounces the basic human propensity to stereotype the other as inferior, it is possible that the apostle has Jews as a people group or Israel as a nation in view here. This is not to say that the apostle is critiquing Judaism as such. The introduction of the law in 2:12 has interjected an important element into the conversation that needs further consideration. The term νόμος has several meanings in Romans that are best determined by context. It may refer to: the written law or Torah; some part of the Jewish scriptures; or to a principle or rule. It is difficult to determine if Paul has the Mosaic law specifically in mind here. However, since the Mosaic law includes a constellation of Jewish, inter-subjective, ethnic criteria and, given that circumcision appears throughout the opening chapters of the letter and that these chapters are concerned with a decidedly Jewish foundation account, it is likely that the apostle, at the least, has the Mosaic law in mind, even if he is also considering the Torah in its entirety. This is especially true given that the Abraham account in Genesis serves as a Jewish foundation myth, which includes circumcision, in much the same way as the giving of the law at Sinai signifies the foundation of the nation of Israel.

Moreover, as discussed below, this element is central to the interlocutor's conception of Jewish self-identity. That this is the case is not surprising, given that indigenous ethnographers maintained the superiority of their respective people group on the grounds that their divinely given laws established both their legitimacy as a people/nation and their status as the source of knowledge and truth about the divine, rendering them the font of human civilization and learning. According to Josephus, the Jewish law-giver, Moses, is remembered not only by the "Hebrews alone but even by alien nations" (*Ant.* 2.216) for his beauty (2.230–31), his valor and sagacity as a general in the Egyptian army (2.243–53), and his confidence in God's promises (2.275), who could "hear the speech of God himself" (4.329–30). This illustrious law-giver received God's law and delivered it, in its fullness, to the Jewish people (*Ant.* 3.89–90, 93–94), who hold it presently, in its entirety (3.280, 286, 322; 4.302). Moreover, *all* who conform to God's will by observing his law and learning from this account of the Jewish people, who serve as *exempla*, will prosper (*Ant.* 1.14, 346; 4.185; 11.169; 18.309), suggesting that the God of the Jews and his laws are for all of humanity. Israel, or the Jewish people, thus, stand as the source of knowledge of the divine and the Deity's intent and will for human civilization.

Given that Paul is in some sense preaching the gospel to his Roman audience, the issue of the law in relation to the gospel becomes paramount, not only for Jewish unbelievers, who are not members of the apostle's audience, but also for believing members of a movement claiming Jewish roots and embracing Jewish sacred texts. Although a first-century Jew might readily admit Israel's historic complicity in the worship of graven images and in the disobedience of God indicative of the larger gentile world, the postexilic denouncement of idolatry and renewed return to the law would in all probability limit that admission as applicable only to Jews in the past. In addition, for both the believing and the unbelieving Jew, the law prescribed the customs, ways of communal life, and worship practices that identified the Jews as an ethnoracial group, raising the issue of the continuation of Jewish ethnic identity in the absence of the law.

According to outsider reckoning, Jews are "those who have and observe Jewish sacred things" (Josephus, *Ant.* 14.228, 234). Similarly, both Philo and Josephus describe Judaism as a *politeia*, with its citizens participating in its institutions and conventions, as these are explicated in the law (Josephus, *Ant.* 12.142, 15.253; Philo, *Spec. Laws* 1.9.51). That Paul considers the law a key element in relation to both the issue of identity and to his larger ethnographic aims is evidenced by the fact that it functions as the central nexus linking the preceding arguments to the idea of faith in Jesus Christ in the arguments that follow.

As we will see, by means of this dialogue with his imaginary Jewish interlocutor, the apostle preaches the gospel in a way that links the Christ event to an event described in the prophetic tradition in a way that relegates the written law to a subsidiary position, in temporal terms, in God's dealings with humanity (a point which he will return to again and again) while allowing it to retain its significance in terms of defining Jewish ethnic identity. This is imperative for Paul's ethnic discourse and the dismantling of traditional oppositional categories, given that the law contained a constellation of identity markers that functioned to define the Jews not only intersubjectively as an ethnoracial group but also played a key role in constructing the central intragroup stereotype defining them as the elect people of God. When the apostle's ethnographic aims are considered and careful attention is paid to the discourse, whereby he skillfully refashions the concept of Israel's unique status as the people of God in light of the fulfillment of prophetic tradition, any notion that this passage evidences anti-Semitic tendencies evaporates.

That the written law and the Jewish people's unique relationship to it is primarily in view here is indicated in several ways. This passage, particularly when viewed in relation to the ethnically neutral passage which precedes it, is richly embossed with ethnically charged motifs. First, in verse 17 the list of identifying characteristics of those who adopt the ethnic designation, "Jew," for themselves (ἐπονομάζῃ) both begins and ends with a reference to the law. According to the imaginary interlocutor, possession of and instruction in the law determines the Jewish people's unique relationship to God, their knowledge of him and what he desires and expects from them, and their ability to discern what is essential. Ancient ethnographers identified particular ethnic groups not only by common ancestry but also by regional laws and customs, including, and especially, religion and its associated cults, rituals, and forms of worship. For example, Herodotus identifies common purpose and language, shared sacred spaces and sacrifices, and similar ways of life or customs, in addition to shared ancestry, as an important criteria defining Greek ethnicity (*Hist.* 8.144.2). According to Dionysius of Halicarnassus, the Greekness of Roman customs, temples, images of gods, and worship practices serves as conclusive evidence of the Roman people's true ancestry as descendants of the Greeks and not of base barbarians (*Ant. rom.* 1.5.1, 9–70; 1.21.1–2). In addition, outsider texts more often than not defined Jewishness in terms of the observance of Jewish laws, customs, and sacred things. By the same token, Jewish writers focused attention on the divinely given law as that which established the legitimacy of the Jewish race as a distinct people and/or a *politeia*. In terms of social identity construction, the Jewish law, with its observable religious and social customs and practices, functioned as the intersubjective nexus in the dynamic interplay between in-group and outsider assessment of the salient criteria defining Jewish ethnicity. Put simply, both Jews and non-Jews would agree that Jews were Jews because they followed their own particular law with its own peculiar requirements.

However, and second, according to social-identity theory, the prominent role of the law in this process of social categorization, suggests that the intragroup understanding of this stereotype be strongly biased towards a favorable self-evaluation, so that a positive social identity might be created that enhances the distinctiveness and status of the Jewish people in comparison to other, contemporary people groups. Thus, it would be natural for Jewish writers to depict the law as conferring a unique character and status to the Jewish people in relation to their gentile neighbors and, as has been already amply demonstrated, Josephus's works stand as a prime example of this. The verb ἐπονομάζῃ suggests that Paul is referring specifically to those characteristics which Jewish insiders would use in reference to themselves. Although most Greco-Roman outsiders would readily admit that the ethnic-group Jews was largely characterized by the peculiar customs and ways of life mandated by their laws, they would, in all probability, be much more reluctant to admit that, because of this, the Jews possessed a superior level of discernment and a unique relationship with and knowledge of the divine. Rather, and more often than not, although Jewish piety and morality were appreciated by some non-Jews, particularly God-fearers and proselytes, on the whole, they were seen as a superstitious group, governed by laws which resulted in the practice of strange customs and an anomalous way of life.

Third, that Paul is referring specifically to an insider assessment of Jewish self-identity is also apparent in the following two verses. Once again, the positive distinctiveness of the Jewish law is emphasized. The imaginary interlocutor, in effect, downplays outsider evaluation of the law as promoting superstition and strange customs and practices, by reinterpreting its characteristics as representing the embodiment (μόρφωσιν) of knowledge and truth. Thus, the law, rather than relegating the Jews to the level of a strange and superstitious group, who can be easily dismissed as such, gives them preeminent authority as teachers over foolish, unschooled, and immature gentiles, who lack the wisdom embodied in the Torah (2:19–20). As Josephus points out, because the law is "engraved" on the "souls" of the Jewish people (*Ag. Ap.* 2.178) in its original form (2.183), they live under a theocratic constitution that cannot be improved in any way (2.184–85). Given that the elect status of Israel was largely understood within the framework of its covenant with Yahweh and the ensuing obligations and responsibilities as defined by the law, what the interlocutor essentially offers is an understanding of Jewish election premised on the belief that the law provides a unique source of knowledge and truth about the divine unavailable to any other people group. What is important to note is that Paul's interlocutor does not mention any of the intersubjective criteria that were commonly assumed to define the Jews as an ethnic group. Rather, the focus remains on the intragroup stereotype of the Jews as the chosen people of God by virtue of their possession of the written law. In other words, the issue is not about supposed ethnic superiority as such, grounded in certain observable ethnic markers found in the law, such as circumcision, Sabbath and food laws, but about insider understanding of the precise relationship between Israel's election and the law. According to the apostle, this particular construal of self-identity is problematic because it fails to take into account both Israel's and the law's place on the timeline of God's dealings with humanity. Paul addresses the former in 2:25—3:31 and takes up the latter in chapter 7.[41]

The argument in 2:25-29 recalls what the apostle has already said in regard to God's impartial judgment of humanity at the eschaton within the specific context of the promise of a renewed heart given to Israel at its inception as a nation (Deut 10:16, 30:6) and reiterated in the prophetic tradition as the divine solution to its recurring disobedience (Jer 4:4, 9:25–26; Ezek 44:7, 9). Paul has already established two points which serve to deconstruct the above mentioned, insider construal of Israel's chosen status. First, knowledge of and truth about God is available to all of humanity. Second, what ultimately matters, in terms of eschatological judgment before an impartial God, is whether or not this knowledge translates into corresponding attitudes and behavior.

The rapid succession of accusatory questions in verses 21–23 once again brings to the fore the indictment against Israel's disobedience as it is found in the prophetic tradition, linking it to the interlocutor's misconstrued self-conception. The references to Jews stealing and engaging in sexual immorality appear to be specific examples of the more general indictment against backsliding and apostasy found in the prophetic tradition. The charge of temple robbing is more obscure. However, the pilfering of sacred objects from cultic sites was one of the most serious crimes in the ancient world.[42] Within the context of Israelite conquest of the Canaanite nations, Deut 7:25-26, God instructs the Israelites neither to take for themselves the gold and silver on their enemies' idols nor to bring the objects themselves into their homes. In the later prophetic tradition, Israel is accused of numerous acts of idolatry, which recalls this mandate and Yahweh's warning that taking possession of such sacred objects would result in Israel becoming ensnared to foreign gods. Furthermore, the charge of robbing temples suggests the selling of these stolen goods

---

41. For the purposes of this chapter, I will focus on Israel's present location on this timeline and will take up Paul's argument in Rom 7 in greater detail in chapter 6 of this work.

42. Byrne, *Romans*, 100.

for a profit, which recalls the more general prophetic indictments against Israel's participation in illicit gain. The fact that the pilfering of temples was a serious crime in the ancient world only serves to underscore the point that Paul is making. Israel's self-assessment as a superior guide to the nations has no basis in historical reality, since God's chosen people have engaged in acts contrary to the law they purport to understand and to teach to others. The first and last questions are particularly pointed, revealing the insider assessment of the group-self for what it really is, an empty construct with no basis in historical reality.

Thus, the teacher (i.e., Israel or the Jewish people) is not really a teacher, since he or she has failed to master what he or she purports to teach. Boasting in the law, as that which sets the Jewish people apart from all other people groups, is in reality an empty act of self-glorification, since God himself, whom Israel claims to have unique knowledge of and to be in a special relationship with, is dishonored as a result, recalling the blindness that Paul excoriates in 1:32—2:3. Even more egregious is the fact that this blindness also results in an assessment of the group-self that completely contradicts the perception of those outside of the group. Like the rest of humanity, Israel's knowledge of God, in this instance, as it is specifically revealed in the law, did not result in the honoring of his name, recalling 1:21. Just the opposite, Israel's just punishment by exile resulted in nothing less than the dishonoring of God's name among the nations, who mistakenly attributed Israel's conquest to a weak and ineffectual God, who was powerless to protect his people from military defeat and foreign oppression (Isa 52:5; Ezek 36.20). That Paul interprets the LXX phrase of Isa 52:5 "on account of you" as "because of your fault" transforms what was originally an oracle of compassion into one of judgment.[43] This recalls 2:6–11 and the fact that Israel, despite its elect status, will stand in judgment before God on the last day.

The theme of judgment according to the law continues in the next section of the argument and is introduced with a reference to circumcision and uncircumcision that recalls 2:9–11 and 2:13–15. Here, Paul draws a careful distinction between physical and spiritual circumcision based on the distinction drawn in the prophetic tradition, which is itself reinterpreted in light of the present unfolding eschatological reality. Two things are of note. First, Paul is not arguing about the saliency of physical circumcision as an ethnic identity marker. The description of the hidden or inward Jew as one who receives praise not from others but from God (2:29c), introduces a theme that Paul will continue to develop as his argument progresses (especially, chapters 9–11). Namely, it is God, who not only initiates election, but, more importantly, defines and sustains it; and it is he who determines who will be included among the elect. In this instance, the apostle makes the point that Jewish self-identity as the chosen people derives from the righteous God, who has already promised that he will forgive, cleanse, and renew his people by circumcising their hearts. Not only does Israel's state of election spring from God (Deut 10:14–15), but more importantly, it is sustained by

43. Byrne, *Romans*, 101.

him and, consequently, its meaning is defined by him. In other words, it is not the law that ultimately confers and sustains Jewish self-identity as the elect, but rather God himself, who is the only one able to confer inward circumcision by the Spirit. This is in contrast to the law, which only mandates physical circumcision, which, accordingly, is a penultimate marker of Jewish chosenness; a point Paul will return to several times as the argument progresses. The preposition, ἐν (v. 29), may be taken instrumentally. Even if it is taken in the local sense, the implication remains that the Spirit is operative in circumcising the heart in distinction to the written law which calls only for physical circumcision. Paul will make the contrast between the age of the law and that of the Spirit as his argument continues to unfold. Consequently, the circumcised heart is the ultimate marker of the Jewish people of God in the eschatological present, as foretold and promised in the scriptures.

Second, in this passage, Paul is not replacing the Jewish people of God with righteous and/or believing gentiles. In other words, he is neither redefining the term "Jew" in a way that includes gentiles (righteous/law-keeping gentile = true Jew), nor is he annihilating Jewish ethnic identity (true Jew = nonethnic/universal believer). In the first place, I have already argued that Paul is specifically addressing the Jewish intragroup stereotype of Jews as the elect people of God by virtue of covenant and law. Accordingly, the reference to the uncircumcised, who as the result of keeping the requirements of the law, are accounted as circumcised specifically recalls 2:13–15 and anticipates 3:9 and 3:22–23. Paul's point is that the intragroup stereotype of Jewish election premised on the law might have had some validity, but only if Israel had kept the law. Given that the apostle maintains that both Jews and gentiles are under the power of sin suggests that the so-called righteous gentile does not represent an actual category of humanity, but rather functions in the apostle's ethnic discourse to underscore the point that election is solely within God's purview and power. In this instance, the question, "Who are the elect?," will be determined at the eschaton by the impartial judge. In other words, Paul is dealing with hypothetical situations, since neither Israel, as its history amply demonstrates, nor gentiles are capable of obeying the requirements of the law, written or otherwise.

Moreover, Paul's audience, familiar with the gospel and its message of an unfolding eschatological present, would not have taken this passage as a re-definition of the Jew, so as to annihilate Jewish ethnic identity, as such. Rather, what Paul will state explicitly in 3:21–26 is anticipated in the reference to the circumcised heart, which believers, mature in the faith, would most likely recognize as the divine promise given specifically to the Jews and fulfilled in and through Christ.[44] Accordingly, the apostle's

44. The book of Acts provides us with a sampling of evangelistic speeches, including some made exclusively to a Jewish audience (e.g., 2:14–39; 7:2–53) and one judicial defense speech, containing evangelistic elements (26:27). In these, reference is made to God's impartiality (10:34); Israel's primacy (2:39; 10:36; 13:17, 23, 26, 46–47; cf. 18:5–6); its idolatry and disobedience (7:40–43, 53); the testimony of the prophets concerning Jesus Christ (2:25–28, 30, 34; 7:52; 10:43; 13:32–33, 35, 38–41; 26:6–7, 22, 27); and the gift of the Holy Spirit poured out upon all of humanity as a sign of the present

critique of the intragroup stereotype of Jewish election would not have been heard as a critique of Israel's election as such. In other words, Paul is not implying that Israel's election has been revoked and/or that the Jewish people have been replaced by another group on the grounds that their election is based either on a condition impossible to fulfill and/or on a faulty understanding of what it actually consists of. Rather, what is implied in the apostle's dialogue with the interlocutor, thus far, is that Jewish self-identity is misconstrued because it fails to recognize that the divine promise of future forgiveness of Israel's sins of idolatry and disobedience and the cleansing and renewal of its people has become a present reality in God's work through Christ; a point Paul will drive home in 3:21–26. In other words, Israel cannot atone for its disobedience by more strident, postexilic attempts to keep the law, since God has provided a different means, as foretold in its own scriptures. It is here that faith comes in, or trust in what God is presently doing (3:28), allowing Paul to link God's past dealings with Israel to his present actions toward humanity as a whole.

However, before bringing his particular proclamation of the gospel to its climax, the apostle sets forth a definition of Jewish self-identity as the elect that agrees with his larger ethnographic aim of establishing continuity between the past and the present in an effort to provide historical legitimacy for the Christ movement, while preserving Jewish primacy. Deconstruction of the Jewish perception of the group-self naturally raises the issue of the validity of Israel's unique status, past, present, and future, as Yahweh's chosen people (3:1). Thus, Paul's Jewish dialogue partner, either unfamiliar or in disagreement with the gospel and its eschatological message, is perfectly justified in protesting against the apostle's assessment of his group's self-identity. This evaluation not only suggests that the biblical notion of Israel's election is empty, at best an ephemeral dream shattered on the rocks of the historical reality of its sinfulness, but also that the prophetic promises of divine forgiveness and renewal are similarly empty, since God appears to have reneged on the foundational, covenant promise of Israel's supposedly enduring status as the chosen people of God. The interlocutor's reference to physical circumcision in 3:1, which in this context most likely refers to its saliency as a marker of belonging to the chosen people, underscores his/her concern with maintaining a traditional understanding of Jewish intragroup identity.

Leaving full resolution of God's covenantal faithfulness or righteousness in the face of Israel's sinfulness aside until 3:21–26, Paul responds to the interlocutor's objection by maintaining that Jewish self-identity, including its primacy as a people group, is established by the fact that Israel was entrusted with the oracles of God (3:2).[45] The

---

eschatological age (2:17–21; 10:45). In sum, a common theme in these speeches is the gospel's fulfillment of promises foretold in the Jewish prophetic tradition, and the expansion of these promises to include non-Jewish peoples without the negation of Israel's primacy as God's chosen people. Thus, we may assume that these teachings were part and parcel of the gospel message, and that Paul's Roman audience would have been well versed in them.

45. A full discussion of 3:3–8, which is concerned specifically with the important theme of the righteousness of God, is not possible here, given the purpose of this study. The objections raised in

entirety of the divine word embodied in the law and the prophets, along with the promise of salvation, was given to the Jews by God to hold in trust, presumably not just for Jewish posterity, but also for all of humanity. In other words, Israel's special status is defined by God's choice to reveal to them his pledge of salvation. The verb ἐπιστεύτησαν connotes the Jews' unique position among the nations as the people group through whom God's salvation would be accomplished, something Paul has already hinted at in 1:1–4. As Paul will make clear, the Jewish people are first both temporally and hierarchically. They were the first to receive the gospel in its promissory form in the prophetic tradition and, thus, are the first to whom it is proclaimed in its fullness. In terms of rank, the key founding figures involved in God's salvific plan for both Israel and humanity as a whole claim Jewish descent. In other words, the Jewish people are unique because they provide the human, mundane entry point and context for the revelation of divine salvific action in human history. It is through this people group that God chooses to act to redeem the world from both its willful ignorance of him and its disobedience to him.[46]

Of note is that Paul does not explicitly address the interlocutor's question regarding the value of circumcision. What is implied, and what will be further addressed in 4:10–12, is that although circumcision retains its saliency as a sign of the covenant, it is not instrumental in establishing Israel's self-identity as the chosen people of God. Rather, it is God alone who establishes, defines, and sustains their elect status. Thus, the purpose of the law is not to confer a special status upon Israel as an authority over the nations concerning the truth about God, as the interlocutor believes. Rather, its purpose, according to Paul, is much more narrow, both in terms of what it actually accomplishes, bringing knowledge of sin (3:9–19 and 20b), and with respect to its limited temporal span in the history of God's dealings with humanity.

In Rom 3:9, Paul once again raises the issue of Jewish privilege. In this instance, unlike in 3:2b, he appears to deconstruct any notion of such a thing. Aside from the fact that this verse appears to contradict what the apostle has already established regarding the Jews' unique status, there is some debate over not only how to translate the Greek but also its place in the argument.[47] Although the question parallels that in 3:1, it is best taken as introducing a section of dialogue separate from that coming before. However, since it continues the topic of Jewish privilege, it also serves as a

---

these verses most likely reflect those that might be raised by Jews in response to the gospel premise of universal human sinfulness. That Paul raises them here need not imply that he expects his audience in Rome to do so. Rather, if indeed he is preaching the gospel, his reference to them simply serves to remind his audience that these objections are unwarranted, given the fact that God has more than adequately "defended" his righteousness in and through Christ.

46. Paul returns to this and expounds on it in 9:4–5 where he details the prerogatives of the Israelites. I will discuss these in more detail below. In sum, each of these stems from the Scriptures and each points to the priority in rank of the Jewish people in terms of God's dealings with sinful humanity.

47. I take the verb προεχόμεθα as a middle form with an active sense. Neither Dunn's ("What then do we plead in our defense?") nor Fitzmyer's ("Are we [Jews] at a disadvantage?") translations, although grammatically possible, fit the context (Dunn, *Romans*, 1:144; Fitzmyer, *Romans*, 330–31).

bridge, linking these two sections of dialogue.⁴⁸ In the first, the intragroup stereotype of Jewish privilege is redefined to reside in the fact that the Jews represent the people group entrusted with the oracles of God. The repetition of a similar question and answer in the second part of the dialogue need not be taken as a contradiction of what Paul has already established. Rather, its presence in the text, allows Paul to draw his audience back to the issue of election, so that he may elaborate on his redefinition of it, linking it to 2:25—3:8, while anticipating the climactic summary of the gospel in 3:21–31. The catena of scriptural texts in 3:10–18, serves to underscore a point Paul has previously and repeatedly made: Israel's own sacred tradition attests to its covenantal disobedience, making it equally culpable before the God who judges Jew and gentile impartially. This was true not only in the past, but also in the present: whatever the law (in this context, scripture) says (λέγει), it is speaking (λαλεῖ) to those who are under the law (3:19).

Thus, any notion that Israel's postexilic repentance from idolatry and return to the law somehow re-confers its unique status as elect among the nations is misguided. Why? The law brings knowledge of sin as a transgression against God's will (5:13), making Israel unique among the nations in the sense that it alone was entrusted with this knowledge. It is through the Jewish people that humanity's sinfulness was and is made plain. Thus, the law in this very narrow sense confers Jewish privilege, although in the way specifically defined by Paul. The shift to the future in verse 20a (δικαιωθήσεται) recalls 2:5–6 and 2:27 and anticipates 7:14–25 where the apostle will return to the issue of the law's inability to confer a spiritual circumcision of the heart. Once again, Paul draws on the revered past, in this case, Ps 143 (LXX 142), introducing the quotation with the phrase, ἐξ ἔργων νόμος, directly linking the doing or keeping of the law with the absence of righteousness on the day of judgment. The phrase works/deeds of the law should not be restricted to particular observances of the law, such as circumcision and food laws, that served as markers of ethnoracial identity.⁴⁹ As I have argued, Paul is not dealing with intersubjective ethnoracial criteria in these chapters. Moreover, the immediate context suggests that he is speaking of the law in its entirety and not just specific aspects of it. This is true, because God has already revealed through his prophets that the ultimate resolution of the crisis of universal disobedience of his precepts lies in an inward renewal of the heart, wrought by the Spirit (cf. Rom 8). This transformative renewal, as Paul will make clear, makes possible the fulfillment of the requirements of the law. Thus, the apostle is not condemning the keeping of the law as the means of both establishing Jewish ethnic identity and of maintaining covenantal responsibilities. Rather, his point is that a new age has dawned, with a new covenant of the Spirit, which not only makes a radically new type of obedience to the intent of the law possible (Rom 10:4; 13:10),⁵⁰ but also guarantees

---

48. Byrne makes a similar point (Byrne, *Romans*, 119).

49. E.g., Dunn, *Romans*, 1:53–54.

50. I will explore the precise meaning of this in the chapters that follow.

the Jewish people's continued existence as an ethnic group and continued primacy as the people of God.

Paul's emphatic switch to the present (νυνὶ), in 3:21a, signals his return to the eschatological present, which brings his proclamation of the gospel to its climax. Of note is both the reference to the law and the prophets (3:21b), which recalls 1:2 and the Jewish scriptural tradition, and the cluster of OT terms mentioned at the beginning of the letter; that is, righteousness, both God's (3:21a, 22a, 25b, 26a) and humanity's (3:24, 26b), faith (3:22a, 25a, 26b) and implicitly life, by means of the reference to Christ's atoning sacrifice for sin (3:24–26). The debate over what Paul means by the term δικαιόω and what exactly Pauline justification entails begins with Martin Luther, extends down through proponents of the New Perspective, and on to their critics. A discussion of this topic is beyond the thesis of this work. That being said, it is important to note several things. Paul's construal of God's grace through Christ could be taken to mean that works play no role in justification, both initial and final. However, the apostle also makes clear that God will not ignore immoral or unrighteous attitudes and the behavior stemming from such, at the final judgment (Rom 2:6). These two aspects need to be held in tension. As I have already mentioned, Paul maintains that election (getting in or initial justification) is solely the purview of God; a theme, as we will see, he returns to again and again. Thus, it may be viewed as a gift, apart from any form of human merit. Yet, the apostle is clearly concerned with the quality of life that both Israel, in the past, and believers, in the present, manifest as a result of this gracious act. Speaking of believers, John M. G. Barclay puts it this way: "the basis for that fit, the foundation and frame of the patient good work that leads to eternal life, is a act of divine power, an incongruous gift to sinful humanity whose transformative effects will be evident at the judgment."[51] I will touch upon this at various points in the chapters that follow, as Paul himself develops the notion of election by grace, through faith in Christ and what is expected of believers, as a result, in terms of obedience to God.

For the apostle, sin is inextricably linked with death (5:12). Similarly, Paul brings his recitation of human history to a climax, achieving his ethnographic aim of linking the Christ event to an event described in the prophetic tradition. Moreover, this climactic summary of the gospel serves as a segue to the apostle's decisive dismantling of Jewish oppositional strategies. Boasting, recalling 2:17 and 23, in the elect or privileged status of the Jews before God and over the rest of humanity by virtue of the law is, according to Paul, excluded by the law (in this context, principle) of faith (3:27). In other words, if faith in Christ is characteristic of the people of God in the eschatological present, then it follows that the law does not and cannot confer superiority to the Jewish people not only because Israel failed to keep it, being under the power of sin, with the law bringing knowledge and the reckoning of sin (5:13), but also because God has fulfilled the prophetic promise of a renewed and transformed

---

51. Barclay, *Paul & Gift*, 473.

heart through Christ. Thus, verse 28 sums up what Paul has already said regarding the law. While it continues to have saliency as an ethnoracial identifier, it no longer marks the eschatological elect of God, a topic Paul will discuss in more detail and in a more nuanced fashion in chapters 9–11.

More importantly for the apostle's ethnographic aims, the fulfillment of these scriptural promises calls for a response of faith to what God is doing in the present, linking Israel's past faithfulness to Yahweh and the covenant with its law to faithfulness to Christ in the present. Moreover, by relegating the law to a penultimate position, and positing faith in God's present eschatological dealings with humanity, including the reception of the Spirit, Paul opens the door wide to the inclusion of non-Jewish people groups. In this regard, and in characteristic fashion, the apostle substantiates his position with a reference to a core, Jewish scriptural teaching. In this instance, he draws upon the tradition that maintained that God is the Creator and sovereign Lord of all people and of all of creation (e.g., Gen 1:1—2:4; Deut 6:4; Pss 9:20; 33:6–8, 13–15; 47:2, 7–9; 67:2–5; 94:8–10; 96:1–5, 7–10) (3:29, 30a), reinterpreting it in light of the eschatological present, so as to bring to fore the acknowledgment of this state of affairs among the nations. Moreover, in accordance with the scriptural framework within which the apostle is working, the eschatological incoming of the gentiles and their worship of Israel's God occurs with the retention of full ethnoracial distinctiveness (e.g., Isa 66:22–23; Zech 14:16–21). In this sense, the gospel necessitates the continuing saliency of subgroup particularity, since, for Paul, it signals the already present, unfolding eschatological reality foretold by the prophets in the scriptures. Accordingly, both the uncircumcised and the circumcised will be set right by faith (3:30), underscoring the fact that everything he has said thus far about the law is in relation to its function in defining Jewish self-identity as the chosen people and not to its saliency as a source of ethnoracial identifiers.[52] Just the opposite, Jew and gentile, the circumcised and the uncircumcised, remain distinct people groups under the lordship of the one God.

In sum, Paul simultaneously unifies all people groups both under the rubric of wrath, judgment, and death and also under the rubric of the good news of the gospel—judgment and salvation, two sides of the same coin, a concept also seen in the OT, particularly in relation to the faithful remnant, a notion he will return to and expand on in chapters 9–11. By opening the door wide to gentile inclusion, the apostle essentially dismantles the Jewish intragroup stereotype of election as conferring Jewish religious and moral superiority over the nations by virtue of the law. However, his introduction of the principle of faith in opposition to the law has laid the foundation for a different oppositional strategy that will allow him to categorize humanity into

---

52. The future in this instance need not be read as referring to final judgment. Paul has already established that the present setting right of individuals is by faith apart from works (3:28). Rather, verse 30 spells out one of the consequences of the core belief that God is one; that is, he justifies the circumcised and the uncircumcised on the ground of faith.

three essential groups, while maintaining ethnic distinctions. These are: the people of God, consisting of both believing ethnic Jews and gentiles; the unbelieving people of God, those under the law (i.e., unbelieving ethnic Jews and, presumably, God-fearers and proselytes); and unbelieving non-Jewish persons. As I will argue in chapters 5 and 6, faith as the characteristic of the elect people of God is further elaborated by Paul where he explicitly associates it with adoption into the family of God and reception of the Spirit. Thus, faith is concretely manifested in believers, identifying such ethnically diverse persons, as those transformed by the Spirit, who evidence knowledge of God, obedience to his requirements, and proper worship of him, as a result of their new Spirit-wrought, allocentric identity. As we will see, faith and the Spirit are inextricably linked and both function in tandem as markers of the believing community. Faith cannot be severed from reception of the Spirit and one cannot have the Spirit without faith in Christ.To speak of faith as the marker of God's present people necessarily implies that they have the Spirit and vice versa. Consequently, the use of either term serves as an abbreviated notation of the fuller descriptor of the believing community, as that marked by faith-Spirit.

Thus, in light of the above, the law-faith dichotomy does not function primarily as a shorthand form describing two diametrically opposed paths to salvation, one right (i.e., Christian, dependent on grace, nonethnic) and the other wrong (i.e., Jewish, legalistic, nationalistic). Paul's reference to justification through Christ as a gift of God's grace in Rom 3:24 need not be read as completely opposed to Jewish scriptural tradition. That God's act of atonement in and through Christ originates solely by divine fiat and, as such, constitutes a gift, recalls the prophetic texts which emphasized that Israel's future forgiveness, restoration, and renewal was likewise according to divine fiat, a work wrought solely by God, who would act, simply because he is supremely righteous, apart from any merit on Israel's part. In this sense, Paul stands in some continuity with the OT tradition, as I have noted at the start of this chapter. However, there is discontinuity between this tradition and the apostle, who reinterprets the OT notion of the remnant in light of the unfolding eschatological present inaugurated by Christ's death and resurrection.

The OT texts were largely concerned with the preservation of the people of God, via the remnant, and not with their final salvation. Thus, Paul's rendition of this tradition appears to stand in more continuity with certain Second-temple texts, which pushed the OT promise of the restoration and renewal of Israel into the eschatological future (e.g., 2 Bar. 32:1–7). Paul states in no uncertain terms that Christ's sacrifice of atonement is for past sins that God had purposefully chosen to pass over. These would include the sins of Israel. The apostle simply states that this was done to show God's righteousness. Although theologically dense and stated without elaboration, this would make sense within the framework of Jewish tradition that he is working in and that he is reinterpreting and appears to be a summary of teachings his audience is already familiar with. This will become clearer as Paul's arguments progress. These arguments will be examined in the following chapter of this work. According to Paul, judgment will be according to deeds; a point which is underscored by his insistence that the law is not overthrown by faith, but, on the contrary, is upheld (3:31). Rather, when examined in light of Paul's ethnic discourse, these terms signify both the Christ movement's continuity with its Jewish roots, faith in Yahweh and in his dealings with humanity, and its discontinuity with it, in terms of the law's provisional nature with respect to God's salvific actions.

4.2 Israel's Etiological Accounts Reinterpreted in Light of the Unfolding Present: Abraham and Christ, Divinely Instituted Founding Figures (Rom 4–5)

Divinely appointed founding figures figure prominently in foundation accounts. In these accounts the founder functions as the locus of divine activity through whom the intentions and purposes of the gods in establishing a new community are accomplished; thus, lending credence to the community's social, cultural, and political arrangements, especially, and including, its religious practices and observances. Dionysius of Halicarnassus attributes the founding of cities in Italy by the Pelasgians to an oracle (*Ant. rom.* 1.19.3) by which "heaven itself was guiding them into this one particular country" (1.20.1–2). By the same token, the Pelasgians later lost control of the region due to "calamities inflicted by the hand of Heaven" (1.23.1). They were replaced by the Tyrrhenians, who took control over Italy, led by the founding figure, Tyrrhenus, "the fifth in descent from Zeus" (1.27.1). In both Homer and Virgil, the role of the pantheon in orchestrating the principle events surrounding the major characters is direct and dramatic (e.g., *Aen.* 1.8–33, 125–41, 225–96; *Od.* 1.15–20, 45–70; *Il.* 1.44–47, 206–9), while Herodotus focuses on the divine ordering of human history (*Hist.* e.g., 9.100–1). Like these and other contemporary, indigenous ethnographers, Paul draws on key biblical figures, Abraham, David, and Adam, because these scriptural persons not only represent important characters in the divine-human drama, but also because they point to moments of foundation and transformation in this unfolding drama that have import for the present life of the believing community. Although Paul appears to have little to say about David apart from Christ's Davidic descent (Rom 1:3), his appearance in Abraham foundation narrative accedes to his pivotal role in Israel's history. Thus, Paul's relatively brief mention of David serves to strengthen the line of continuity between the new movement and its ancient historical roots and the Deity responsible for constituting the people of God, both in the present and past.

As we will see, Paul essentially repeats the story he has already told in Rom 1–3 in chapters 4–5 but draws in the founding figure and patriarch, Abraham, in order to show that it is God alone who establishes that the line of descent will be reckoned via faith or trust in him, both in the past and in the present. However, rather than portraying Christ as the promised seed of Abraham, as he does in Gal 3:15–16, the apostle highlights his role as God's established means of setting right the unrighteous in the present time and, thus, as the divinely ordained founder of a new community of people, who stand in both continuity (descendants of Abraham) and discontinuity (joint heirs with Christ, Rom 8:17) with the historical people of God. By deemphasizing the ancestral line of descent between Abraham and Christ, Paul, in effect, places the emphasis on God, who himself is the link between the new movement and its Jewish past. It is this God, who foretold this present work through his prophets, bringing it to completion in Christ. There is no stronger link than this, given that the same God, in effect, founds both movements by choosing and establishing founding figures and working through them as he sees fit in a manner that demonstrates his own unfailing righteousness. In this way, Paul simultaneously constructs a venerable ancestry for the members of the new movement that links them to their Jewish past and provides divine legitimation for its founding figure, Jesus. Moreover, by introducing the figure of Adam as the counterpoint to Jesus Christ, the apostle maintains a universal perspective both in terms of humanity's universal condition and God's universal solution to the problem of sin and death.

4.2.1 Abraham, the Ancestor of All Who Have Faith: Paul's Aggregative Discursive Strategy

As discussed in the previous chapter, although ethnoracial self-definition occurs vis-à-vis the other, an alternative, equally prevalent strand of thought affirmed inclusivity, primarily by positing common genealogies. Such aggregative, etiological genealogies not only allowed Greco-Roman ethnographers to connect the glorious past of the Greeks to the new age of Roman rule, but also allowed them to link the other to the self, without the loss of ethnic distinction. Accordingly, Virgil refashions the Greek accounts of Aeneas into an epic that ties the Roman people, who remain distinctly Roman, to the Trojan legends (*Aen.* 1.1–7), in order to provide them with a glorious past suitable to Rome's present greatness. Similarly, Josephus posits Noah's sons as the ancestors of all the people groups of the earth, rather than the Greeks, who imposed on the nations "forms of government, as though they were descended from themselves" (*Ant.* 1.20–147). Accordingly, all people groups could trace their genealogy to one of these Jewish scriptural ancestors. Yet, each group retained its ethnoracial particularity in relation to the Jews, who are superior in terms of ancestral primacy.

For Paul, the retention of ethnoracial distinctiveness among the people of God is equally important. However, for the apostle, the retention of ethnic particularity is not enmeshed within an argument for ethnoracial superiority. Ethnic particularity is to be retained because it is mandated by the scriptures and, hence, accords with divine intent and purpose. Since the gospel represents the fulfillment of the scriptural promise regarding the eschatological incoming of the nations into the people of God, Israel simply serves as the particular, mundane entry point for God's universal, salvific action for all of humanity, in all of its diversity. Consequently, if Israel's God is the one true Lord and Creator of the world, then this God cannot be viewed as a tribal or national Deity associated explicitly with Israel and the Jewish people. Rather, his universal lordship, which in the past was made manifest through his dealings with Israel (e.g., Exod 7:5), is now manifest in and through the gospel, which is good news for both Jew and gentile. Accordingly, Israel's great founding figure, Abraham, to whom God promised that he would become the ancestor of many nations (Gen 17:4), can no longer be reckoned as the ancestor of Israel, exclusively. Rather, he is to be reckoned as the father of many nations.

This type of aggregative discourse, which posits a common genealogy in order to unite diverse people groups, may be contrasted to that which utilizes a common purpose to achieve ethnoracial unity. An example of the latter is Thucydides's account of Hermocrates's address to the Sicilian Greek cities, wherein he asks the Dorians, Ionians, and Chalcidians, and so forth, to set aside their ethnoracial differences and place their identity as Sicilian above their particular ethnicity in order to resist a common enemy, the Athenians, even as he recognizes that they may go to war against each other in the future (Thucydides, *Hist.* 4.59.1—4.64.5).[53] In this instance, a common identity is foregrounded for the purpose of attaining a mutually beneficial goal without the erasure of other, in this case, sub-identities.[54] By the same token, the category, Sicilian, functions as a temporary, unifying identity that can be set aside as soon as the common goal is met. This may be contrasted to the more permanent common identity constructed by means of a shared genealogy, with its emphasis on the ascribed end of the identity spectrum.

As we will see, particularly in Rom 12–15, in-Christ identity is both permanent (however, the potential for apostasy on the part of believers remains) and primary, whereby ethnoracial identity is retained, yet, *in all instances*, remains secondary to in-Christ identity. For Paul, there is one God, who is the Lord of all people groups, whose founding figures, Abraham (penultimate) and Jesus Christ (ultimate) serve to unite all of humanity, in all of its diversity, under one ancestor, in the case of the former, and into a single, Spirit-constituted family, in the case of the latter. As illustrated in the example of Hermocrates's speech to the Sicilians, the establishment of a common genealogy is essential for the construction of a permanent supraordinate identity. Hence, Paul's insistence on Abraham's universal status as the father of many nations. Moreover, for in-Christ identity to be not only permanent but also primary, all ethnoracial identities must be relativized. This requires more than a change of thinking regarding the ethnic other, as seen in Hermocrates's appeal for unification made to the various Sicilian people groups, where the subordination of ethnic particularity continues only as long as Sicilian unity is politically expedient. It requires nothing short of a divinely wrought transformation, as Paul will make clear in the arguments that follow. At this point in

53. Hodge, *If Sons, Then Heirs*, 118–19.
54. Hodge, *If Sons, Then Heirs*, 119.

the letter, his goal is to establish the ancestral lines that underlie the in-Christ identity that he will explicate in the following chapters.

Thus far, Paul has established the binary categories of faith and law, allowing him, to implicitly categorize members of the Christ movement, both Jew and gentile, under the rubric of faith, in opposition to nonbelieving Jews, and, presumably God-fearers and proselytes (cf. Rom 9:32; 10:3). The introduction of Abraham serves a dual purpose in the apostle's ethnography. The first capitalizes on the usefulness of aggregative discourse in constructing kinship ties between Jews and gentiles in a way that will allow Paul to think and argue in terms of family resemblances between believing Jews and gentiles, in effect, tightening the link between the Christ movement and its Jewish roots. The second, although related to the first, pertains more specifically to the apostle's task of constructing a respectable, principle or primary identity for the believers in Rome.

As noted in the previous chapter, ethnicity-race constitutes an individual's most basic social identity, orienting all other social identities, by answering the question, "Who are my people?" Moreover, since ethnic identities were not necessarily exclusive, individuals could and did claim multiple ethnoracial identities. For example, Dorians, Ionians, and Chalcidians also claimed to be Sicilians, foregrounding the former or latter identity in accordance with the shifting political landscape (Thucydides, *Hist.* 4.59.1—4.64.5). Although Paul does not explicitly refer to believers as an ethnoracial group, his recourse to kinship terminology suggests that he regards in-Christ identity as the community's chief identity, orienting other social identities, including the ethnic categories of Jew and gentile, in a way that both preserves these social identities, yet transforms them. Thus, believing and unbelieving Jews continue to constitute an ethnoracial group in distinction from other people groups, while simultaneously constituting two distinct groups, with the former having kinship ties with believing gentiles. This amalgamation of diverse ethnic groups without the loss of distinction, as I have argued, was possible due to the double-natured, seemingly paradoxical character of kinship or ancestry as it was perceived in antiquity. Paul harnesses the power of this aggregative discourse bringing it to bear on the Jewish peoples' preeminent founding figure.

4.2.1.1 *Fluidity in Kinship Construction: The Faith of Our Forefathers, Abraham and David*

Abraham is a figure of great importance in the OT where he is portrayed not simply as the ancestor of Israel, but as the divinely appointed mediator through whom God acts to establish his own chosen community of people. He is the one who received the covenant and the promises on Israel's behalf and it is through him that Israelites are reckoned as heirs to a divinely bequeathed inheritance. Consequently, the significance of Abraham's ancestral role takes on an active saliency in the present in the sense that his dealings with God remain determinative for the Jewish people and, especially, for the glorious Israel of the messianic age.[55] Given the pivotal, transhistorical role that Abraham plays in the life of God's people, Paul cannot do otherwise than appropriate him as a key founding figure of a new movement that bridges Israel's past and its future messianic fulfillment. Accordingly, Paul sets out to do two things. First, in light of the larger argument he is making, he establishes the temporal primacy of Abraham's act of faith, relegating his obedience to the law, as evidenced in his acceptance of circumcision, to a secondary position; thereby, introducing faith as the prime criterion defining the people of God. This is central to the argument Paul is making, since a frequent motif in the Jewish literature of this period is the portrayal of Abraham as the paradigm of faithfulness and obedience to God.[56] For example, Abraham's faith spoken of in Gen 5:6 is coupled in intertestamental writings with his acceptance of circumcision, which is interpreted as anticipatory fulfillment of the Torah. In addition, his continued faithfulness under testing and trials (Gen 22:1–18) was viewed as meritorious for both for him and his posterity (e.g, Sir 44:20–21).[57] Second, the apostle links Abraham to Christ in a way that guarantees the preeminence of the latter as a divinely appointed founding figure of a movement firmly rooted in the promises given to Israel in the past.

Paul signals his intent to turn to issues regarding ancestry and descent with the phrases τὸν προπάτορα ἡμῶν and κατὰ σάρκα (4:1). The false inference in 3:29 that God is the God of the Jews only, implies the corollary statement that Abraham is the father of the Jews only,[58] presumably in the sense that he received the covenant and the promises on this peoples' behalf—theirs and their blood descendants. The phrase κατὰ σάρκα signals that Paul is preparing to challenge this level of understanding Abrahamic descent solely in ascribed terms. Although the translation, "Then what shall we say? Have we found Abraham to be our forefather according to the flesh?" makes good sense of the larger context, it is best translated, for grammatical reasons, as: "What then shall we say that Abraham, our forefather according to the flesh, has discovered?"[59] If the infinitive was meant to be read as a predicate, then forefather

---

55. Byrne, *Romans*, 142.
56. Das, "Paul and Works of Obedience," 795–812.
57. Byrne, *Romans*, 142.
58. Cranford, "Abraham in Romans 4," 71–88.
59. Barclay, *Paul & Gift*, 483. Verse 1 has generated some debate over punctuation and translation of the infinitive and the corresponding position and meaning of the phrase κατὰ σάρκα. For a discussion of the textual problem associated with the infinitive ευρηκέναι, see Cranfield, *Epistle to the Romans*, 1:226–27; Metzger, *Textual Commentary*, 450; Barrett, *Epistle to the Romans*, 81; Käsemann, *Commentary on Romans*, 106; Barth, *Epistle to the Romans*, 117. There is some consensus among scholars that the manuscript evidence favors retention of the infinitive (Hays, "Have We Found Abraham?," 80, 83). Richard B. Hays has made the argument for both the punctuation and syntactical structure of the infinitive clause as they appear above in the first translation, and for taking κατὰ σάρκα as modifying Abraham. Similarly, see Jipp, "Rereading the Story of Abraham," 217–42.

would not have a definite article.⁶⁰ As discussed below, what Abraham discovers, or more precisely, what Paul wishes his audience to recognize, is that God's intent all along was for Abraham to be the father of not just the Jews but of a multiethnic people via faith (and, thus, neither via the law nor via blood) in the God who would bring all of this about. In other words, in the arguments that follow, Paul draws a line of continuity between the founding figures Abraham and Christ, and their ethnoracially diverse descendants, which establishes the preeminence of the latter founding figure. In light of this, the phrase κατὰ σάρκα is best taken as referring to both physical descent and physical circumcision. God's promises to Abraham as recounted in Gen 17 are inextricably bound to this rite. In antiquity, such patrilineal rites functioned as mechanisms regulating descent.⁶¹ Accordingly, verses 2–3 may be taken as stating a reason, as the γὰρ indicates, why Abraham cannot be regarded as a forefather solely in ascribed terms; a reason Paul will elaborate in the ensuing verses. It should be noted that, there is insufficient reason to presume a grace-works antithesis in verses 2–10. Abraham had reason to boast in his good works as all Jews did, but as Paul makes clear in verses 3–5, he could not boast of his righteousness towards God, since it was given to him by God as a gift.

As discussed below, Paul's point is that Abraham is the founding figure of both the Jewish people and members of the Christ movement, in the sense that God's promise to him that he would inherit the world (4:13) springs or descends from faith, so that all who share in this family trait of faith or trust in God are heirs of the promise which, according to Paul, finds fulfillment in God's work in and through Christ. As the apostle will make clear in 8:14–17, believers, because they are united with Christ, represent the progeny of God, not Abraham. Moreover, as Paul will later argue, unbelieving Jews, although they are able to claim physical descent from Abraham, are not his true descendants, since they lack this family resemblance in that they fail to trust God in his present work in and through Christ. In ancient thought, a person's character, and not simply physical attributes, was deemed as an inherited give. For example, people "were virtuous because they were sprung from virtuous men" (Plato, *Menex.*237A).⁶² In other words, virtuous people came from virtuous families and thus, true descendants were expected to act in a way that reflected this familial trait. In this way, the apostle establishes Christ as the preeminent, divinely appointed founding figure of God's people in the new age. What Paul is doing here is capitalizing on the double character of ancestry/kinship; that is, he is taking the basic belief that kinship depends on blood or seed (fixity) in order to give real substance to the ancestral identity he is constructing for the Roman believers, while simultaneously introducing a criterion (faith or trust in God) that functions to give fluidity to his construction, allowing him to incorporate both believing non-Jewish peoples and believing Jews

---

60. Barclay, *Paul & the Gift*, 483n88.
61. Hodge, *If Sons, Then Heirs*, 26–28.
62. Cited in Hodge, *If Sons, Then Heirs*, 80–81.

into the Jewish family tree. Later in chapters 9–11, he takes the same criterion and uses it to justify the conclusion that nonbelieving Jews have been temporarily broken off from that same family tree.

The issue of boasting in 4:2, recalls 2:17, 3:9, and 3:27 and the matter of traditional Jewish self-understanding as the chosen people of God vis-à-vis the covenant and the law. Having previously deconstructed this particular intragroup stereotype on the grounds of Israel's failure to keep the law, Paul drives the final nail into the coffin by establishing that Abraham's status as founder of Israel, in the sense of both ancestor and mediator of God's promises, was purely a gift, conferred upon him according to God's will, on the basis of his trust that God would keep his promises. In other words, the apostle argues that Abraham became a chosen person of God, prior to any act of obedience with respect to the law, as evidenced by his circumcision. Accordingly, the above mentioned intragroup stereotype is invalid at an even more profoundly fundamental level than Paul has already argued, in the sense that God never intended the law to function as the ultimate criterion defining his people, as evidenced by his dealings with Abraham. Thus, the reference to boasting in 3:27 and 4:2, need not be construed as a pejorative reference to works of the law.[63] Rather, the apostle's point is that election, both in the past and the present, falls solely within the purview of God. This indicates that Paul is neither interested in proving the superiority of justification by faith over works, nor in establishing that Jewish reliance on ethnic boundary markers does not work in securing salvation. Rather, he is interested in making clear that all boasting must be grounded in God (4:2; 5:11), including boasting about the status as the chosen people of God. In both 2:6–11 and 3:20 the type of works or deeds under consideration are not restricted to those designed to maintain ethnic boundary markers. Moreover, readings which maintain that the term "ἔργων" in 4:2 refers to ethnic boundary markers neither adequately explain the bookkeeping metaphor of 4:4–5, nor offer an acceptable exegesis of the reference to David and Ps 32 in 4:6–8 and the connection made (via the reference to the blessing in 4:9) between 4:9–12 and the previous section.[64] The apostle's point that election lies solely within the purview of God is made clear in verses 4–5 and the reference to David in verses 6–8.

Given that the language of verses 4–5 is commercial crediting language, the key issue here is reckoning according to obligation versus reckoning according to favor.[65] In other words, the bookkeeping metaphor is used to clarify the meaning of the verb λογίζομαι, particularly as it is used in verse 5 where Abraham's righteousness is seen

---

63. Glen N. Davies notes that this noun occurs in only one other place in the letter—15:17—where the context suggests the appropriateness of boasting (Davies, *Faith and Obedience in Romans*, 119). The act of boasting is not inherently bad, given that the Jewish boast in God is approved in the OT and in the literature of the Second Temple period and by Paul himself (Deut 10:21; 26:29; Sir 39:8; 50:20; Pss. Sol. 17.1; Rom 2:17, 23; 15:17). This is contra Joseph A. Fitzmyer, who maintains that chapter 4 demonstrates how all human boasting is excluded (Fitzmyer, *Romans*, 369).

64. Visscher, *Romans 4*, 218.

65. Cranford, "Abraham in Romans 4," 80; Jewett, *Romans*, 312–13.

as freely credited or given as a gift. Verse 3 is a quotation of Gen 15:6 LXX which is best read together with verses 4–5. Accordingly, since this gift was given to Abraham when he was one of the ungodly, he must be the forefather of the Jews on a basis other than, or in addition to, physical descent. Paul will take this up further beginning with 4:9. Here, in verses 6–8, he applies the Rabbinic exegetical principle of *gezerah sawah*, interpreting Gen 15:6 in light of Ps 32:1–2; in effect, stating that the reckoning of righteousness is equivalent to the nonreckoning of sins.[66] Of note is Paul's explicit reference to David, another key founding figure from Jewish history, who also has eschatological significance, since it is from his line that the Messiah was expected to come. In the psalm that Paul makes reference to, emphasis is placed on the psalmist's acknowledgment and confession of transgression and God's freely given forgiveness. There is no mention of the sacrificial system of atonement, as prescribed by the law. Rather, Paul refers to David as one who experienced blessedness as God's reckoning of righteousness apart from works (4:6). This anticipates and recalls the eschatological promise that God would freely forgive Israel's sin, if its people should repent, suggesting that, although the law provided a system for atoning for sin, the forgiveness of this sin ultimately resides in God who is free to establish any system of atonement he sees fit, including the present sacrificial atonement of Christ (3:24–26). Recall that Paul has already referred to God's forbearance in passing over previously committed sins until the present (3:25–26), pointing to the penultimate status of the levitical sacrificial system of atonement. As Abraham was reckoned righteous based on his trust in God's promises, similarly, David was reckoned righteous due to his trust that God forgives the repentant sinner. Moreover, in the case of the latter, whose double sin of premeditated adultery and murder could not be atoned for under the Mosaic law (Acts 13:39),[67] simultaneously underscores the degree of reliance on or faith in God that this founding figure exemplifies, particularly in light of his dire situation, and the mercy and faithfulness of the God upon whom he relies and in whom he trusts.[68] In this way, Paul draws a line from Abraham to David and, ultimately, to Christ via faith or trust in God as the one who both establishes and restores his people. Faith or trust in this God, then, is the trans-historical criterion identifying the people of God.

4.2.1.2 Fixidity in Kinship Construction: Abraham, the Ancestor of Both the Circumcised and the Uncircumcised

In 4:9–12, as in the previous arguments in 2:17—3:21, Paul is referring to circumcision more specifically as a marker identifying Jewish election. Central to the

---

66. Davies, *Faith and Obedience in Romans*, 160; Byrne, *Romans*, 146.
67. I am indebted to Ben Witherington III for this observation.
68. Both the theme of trust in God in dire circumstances and that of the infinite mercy and faithfulness of this righteous God are brought up by Paul time and time again as his arguments proceed. Moreover, both of these themes relate to his larger ethnographic aims.

apostle's argument is Gen 15, specifically, the fact that Abraham's response of faith to God's promise that he and Sarah would have an heir comes before any mention of circumcision (cf. Gen 15:1–6 and Gen 17:9–14) and before the narration of covenant making.[69] Circumcision was believed not only as necessary for establishment of the covenant, both Abrahamic and Mosaic, but as some of the intertestamental literature suggests was also seen as providing access to heaven or the messianic kingdom.[70] The continuing viability and validity of this intragroup stereotype as a marker identifying the people of God in the eschatological age is something Paul would not agree with. As the apostle points out, it is Christ who confirms (βεαιῶσαι) the promises given to the patriarchs (Rom 15:8). It is important to keep in mind that he is not critiquing the rite of circumcision in and of itself, only the accompanying Jewish idea that the present people of God are identified by this physical sign as an indication of their special status.

Thus, Paul's aim in 4:9–12 is to reinterpret the traditional understanding of Abraham in Gen 17:11, whereby it was believed that his covenant with Yahweh was established through circumcision. By invoking the notion of kinship/blood/seed, Paul gives substance to a line of descent that is actually by means of a common faith/trust in God and his promises. This is accomplished by invoking Gen 15:6 and focusing on the exact point in time when Abraham was circumcised (v. 10), while simultaneously making recourse to the terms σημεῖον in relation to circumcision and σφραγῖδα with respect to the righteousness of faith (v. 11). After noting that Abraham was reckoned as righteous before he was circumcised, Paul carefully distinguishes the sign of circumcision, which invokes the terminology of Gen 17:11 from the seal of the righteousness of faith.[71] The term σημεῖον refers to a distinguishing mark which identifies someone or something,[72] while the term σφραγῖδα designates the confirmation or authentication of a state of affairs.[73] Accordingly, circumcision functions as confirmation of a spiritual state of affairs that existed prior to and independent of it, supporting the conclusion that Abraham was reckoned righteous before being circumcised. Thus, although circumcision functions as the mark physically distinguishing the Jew as a member of the covenant people, more importantly, it confirms the fact that Abraham was reckoned righteous apart from it, emphasizing that is God

---

69. The former read within the broader context of the latter emphasizes Abraham's role as the central ancestor through whom Israel's special status as elect is mediated. Moreover, numerous Jewish documents suggest that the rite of circumcision was that which confirmed God's promises to Abraham (Jdt 14:10; Esth 8:11–17; Josephus, *Life*, 113, 149; Gen 17:11; Sir 44:19–20; Jub. 15:26) (Jipp, "Rereading the Story of Abraham," 224–25).

70. Witherington and Hyatt, *Paul's Letter to the Romans*, 126 (CD 16:4–6; Jub. 15:31–33).

71. Although Dunn cautions against seeing a distinction between the terms "sign" and "seal," Cranford is correct in his assessment that the lexical evidence permits finding a difference in Paul's use of the terminology (Dunn, *Romans*, 1:209; Cranford, "Abraham in Romans 4," 84).

72. Rengstorf, "σημεῖον," 7:200–69.

73. Barrett, *Epistle to the Romans*, 86–87; Moo, *Epistle to the Romans*, 268–69; Cranfield, *Epistle to the Romans*, 236; Fitzer, "σφραγίς κτλ," 7:939–53.

alone who confers the status of righteousness. The purpose of this pre-circumcision reckoning of righteousness was to make Abraham the ancestor of the gentile who has been set right by God and does not bear the physical sign; and of the Jew who has also been made righteous by God but bears the physical mark. The common denominator in both cases is God, who reckons his people as righteous based on their trust or faith in him. By highlighting the temporal sequence of God's dealings with Abraham, Paul implicitly contrasts God's consistent response to human trust in him with the temporally limited signification of circumcision.

Of note is verse 12, where Paul refers to Jews, as indicated by the phrase ἐκ περιτομῆς or "from (the) circumcision." The preposition ἐκ is ubiquitous in the context of descent and kinship as it is found in the ancient texts where the object of the preposition functions to indicate the source or origin of the person or group in question, which can be either a parent or an ethnic group.[74] For example, Josephus observes that, Jews and Lakedaimonians come from one descent group (ἐκ ἑνὸς εἶεν γένους), coming from a common descent relationship via Abraham (ἐκ τῆς πρὸς Ἄβραμον οἰκειότητος) (*Ant.* 12.226). For Paul, Abraham is the father of the circumcised, who are described as those who not only spring from the circumcision but who also follow in his footsteps (ἐκ περιτομῆς), μόνον ἀλλὰ καὶ τοῖς στοιχοῦσιν τοῖς ἴχνεσιν τῆς ἐν ἀκροβυστίᾳ πίστεως τοῦ πατρὸς ἡμῶν Ἀβραάμ). In this case, "[the] circumcision" functions as an ethnic group, indicating its continuing validity as a criterion of ethnic identity. However, the qualifying phase, "but who also follow in the footsteps of the faith that our ancestor Abraham had before he was circumcised," explicitly posits active faith or trust in God as that which determines true Abrahamic descent (cf. Rom 9:7–8). In other words, faith, not circumcision/works of the law, is the central identifying marker of the people of God. Moreover, this is an active faith, as the term ἴχνος demonstrates. Here, it is used metaphorically and denotes "the trace left by someone's conduct or journey through life."[75] This suggests that not only is faith active, but also that it includes an element of obedience.[76] Moreover, the idea of faithful obedience recalls the notion of spiritual circumcision which Paul connects with obedience in 2:26–27 and which becomes more prominent in chapter 6, where baptism into Christ's death (6:3) results in enslavement to God and obedience into sanctification (6:22). The apostle's reference to following in the footsteps of the faith, evidenced by Abraham in verse 12 alludes to such a continuing perseverance in righteousness as evidenced in obedience.

In this way, Paul uses the criterion of faith/faithful obedience to draw a line of descent between Abraham and the Jewish people and Abraham and the gentiles. What ties the Jewish people of God, both in the past and the present, to the gentiles is both

---

74. Hodge, *If Sons, Then Heirs*, 80–81, 86–91. Hodge also sees a wordplay in Paul's use of "from faith" and "from law," but interprets them differently.

75. Stumpff, "ἴκανος," 3:402–6.

76. Dunn, *Romans*, 1:212.

a common founding ancestor (fixed end of the spectrum) and active, obedient faith or trust in God (fluid end of the spectrum), with Paul moving between the two ends depending on where he is in his argument. This is comparable to the shifting saliency of ancestry in the *Roman Antiquities*, where either a common genealogy, in the case of the Romans, or common customs and worship practices, in the case of the Greeks, is foregrounded, depending on the point the author wishes to make: to disprove barbarian ancestry, in the case of the former, and to prove a loss of Greek identity, in the case of the latter (Dionysius, 1.9–70; 1.121.1–2; 1.89.4). Moreover, in this way, Paul provides a legitimate ancestor for the new movement that also finds its roots in an ancient religion, which, in ethnographic terms, gives the Christ movement historical legitimacy. By redefining Abrahamic descent as based on faith, thereby, disengaging the traditional link between such descent and physical circumcision, Paul simultaneously redefines Abraham's trans-historical ancestral role, broadening it, so that his dealings with God remain determinative not only for the Jewish people as a whole and, especially, for the Israel of the messianic age, but also for the gentiles. Romans 4:13–18 functions to solidify lineage via faith, where Paul engages in word play based upon the idea of kinship and descent, with respect to the law.

This is the first time that the word νόμος appears in this chapter (v. 13) and most likely refers not only to the covenant command of circumcision given to Abraham (Gen 17:11) but also to the Mosaic law. Paul's point here is that God's promise to Abraham was given before either of the two covenants. As he has already argued, the Scriptures, particularly Gen 15:6, teach that Abraham was set right by faith. Thus, if Abraham's heirs spring from the law (ἐκ νόμου), then this means that God has reneged on his promise to Abraham of an heir and descendants. In this instance, the phrase from the law indicates the ancestral source, parent or ethnic group, from which Abraham's heirs would spring, if their status as heirs was reckoned according to descent from the law. For Paul, the law works wrath (v. 15), because it brings knowledge of sin (3:20). Thus, those who spring/descend from the law are heirs of God's wrath rather than heirs of the world, as promised to Abraham.[77]

Verse 16 is elliptical, lacking an express subject. Although it is possible that the phrase from faith refers to the promise mentioned in verse 13, given that ἐκ πίστεως parallels ἐκ νόμου in verse 14 and completes Paul's ancestral-based wordplay, it is more likely that the subject is comprised of those heirs who spring from faith. Similarly, by way of contrast, Rom 16b–c provide the reasons why descent is to be reckoned according to faith, just as verse 15 states why ancestry cannot be traced through the law. Accordingly, those who spring/descend from faith, since faith relies on and trusts in God, inherit grace, God's free gift (v. 16); in Abraham's case it was the gift of

---

77. Κόσμος most likely refers to the future restoration of physical creation. Some strands of early Judaism had already expanded the promise of Gen 22:17–18, and the promise of land to include the whole world (Witherington and Hyatt, *Paul's Letter to the Romans*, 126). Thus, Paul is referring to the eschatological promise given to Israel that it would inherit the world, which he sees as having already been inaugurated in and through the death and resurrection of Christ.

an heir; in the believer's case, it is the gift that comes in and through Jesus Christ himself (5:15). The references to the one from the law and also to the one from the faith of Abraham in verse 16b most likely refer to nonbelieving Jews and believing Jews and gentiles, respectively, given that Paul sees God's promise to Abraham confirmed/fulfilled in Christ's death and resurrection and that he believes that nonbelieving Jews continue as heirs of the promise, despite their temporary exclusion from the people of God (Rom 9:4-5; 11:1-2, 17, 25-29). The apostle's appeal to both ends of the fluidity/fixity spectrum gives substance to his construction of Abrahamic kinship based on the criteria of faith. Simultaneously, his appeal to temporal sequence, in relation to Abraham's acts of faith and circumcision, allows him to craft two lines of descent from a single ancestor, with the latter functioning in a penultimate role within the larger context of God's ultimate plans and purposes for humanity.[78]

In addition, the above word-play serves to emphasize a point Paul has already made; namely, that Abraham's and, consequently, Israel's election is based solely on God's initiative, and that he and his descendants are to trust in this God and in his ability to bring his promises to fruition by whatever means he chooses (vv. 13–14). Consequently, although interpreters are correct that Paul is concerned with making clear that Abraham is the forefather of both Jews and gentiles, it is important to note that this claim falls within the context of an even larger claim that he is making. Abraham's faith is described for the purpose of showing that God reckons righteousness to those who trust in him both in the past and the present (v. 23). In other words, the faithfulness of God guarantees that what was true for Abraham is also true for his descendants. Paul has already made clear that the object of faith in 4:1–12 is God; whereby David's and Abraham's sins are forgiven on the basis of trust of their trust in him. Moreover, according to Paul, this past forgiveness is itself based on the future death of Christ (3:25–26). Central to Paul's logic is the affirmation that there is one God who acts in a manner consistent with past promises and, because of this, he is able to maintain that the gospel is not only consonant with the Jewish scriptures, but also upholds them, including the law.

This suggests, that Paul's primary purpose in invoking Abraham is neither to offer him as an example of faith (as opposed to works) that is to be imitated by believers or to prove the eschatological equality of Jews and gentiles.[79] Rather, his point is to

---

78. Paul will again draw on this notion of faith in chapter 9 where he will further clarify, using kinship language, those who presently belong to the people of God (the elect). Here, as we will see, adherence to the law becomes the criterion identifying those who have been temporarily broken off from the people of God because they have failed to trust in God's present work of right-setting in and through Christ. Hodge makes a similar point regarding the two lines of descent, although her argument, as a whole, differs (Hodge, *If Sons, Then Heirs*, 90–91).

79. Although the patriarch's significance to Paul's overarching argument is uniformly acknowledged among scholars, the reason why he is invoked remains a subject of debate. A prevalent view is that Paul appeals to the story of Abraham in order to present the paradigmatic example of justification by faith (e.g., Käsemann, *Commentary on Romans*, 118; Moo, *Epistle to the Romans*, 273). Some scholars maintain that Abraham is the *typos* of either the new people of God (e.g., Schliesser,

demonstrate that the believers in Rome can trust that God reckons them righteous in the present, through Christ, because the same God reckoned Abraham as righteous in the past. The parallels that Paul draws between Abraham and the Roman believers and the precise way in which he traces them evidence his concern with depicting the faith of the people of God, both in the past and the present, as premised on God's own faithfulness. This then becomes the basis of believers' hope, a theme Paul expounds on in 5:2b–5. This makes sense in light of Paul's broader ethnographic aims in that, the new movement finds its legitimacy in the fact that it is established by God himself, who not only revealed his design for humanity to his people in the past, but who himself established its founding figures according to his plan and purposes alone. Moreover, the new movement's self-identity as the people of God is secure, since it is established and maintained by a righteous God, faithful to his promises.

Thus, Paul's description of Abraham's faith in God as beyond hope in hope (v. 18) serves more specifically as an example of perseverance that is itself grounded in a faithful God, for the eschatological people of God, who like Abraham must walk in obedient trust (vv. 23–25), regardless of how things may appear. Of note is that the faith that results in righteousness, both in the case of Abraham and of believers, comes out of a situation strongly contradictory to what has been promised.[80] In Abraham's case, the promise entails a descendant. However, Abraham and Sarah are physically incapable of reproduction. Analogously, for believers, the promise is abundant life. Yet, the members of the Roman community faces various social pressures, making life difficult at best, and, at worst, impossible. In this respect the language of νέκρωσις (4:17, 19) is suggestive. Such terminology is not typically used to describe the natural decay of sexual organs. Rather, it is language normally reserved for describing a corpse.[81] This use of death terminology appears to underscore the continuity between Isaac's miraculous birth from the corpses of Sarah and Abraham and Jesus's resurrection from the dead, both of which are dependent on the God who promises and is able to bring life from death. The phrase τοῦ ζωοποιοῦντος τοὺς νεκροὺς καὶ καλοῦντος τὰ μὴ ὄντα ὡς ὄντα (v. 17) points to the power of God demonstrated both in producing an heir from two corpses and in raising Jesus from the dead, a power akin to the power of creation *ex nihilo*,[82] evoking the redolent cluster of terms, life-death, righteousness-faith introduced in the opening paragraphs of the letter.

Abraham's Faith in Romans 4, 393, 395; Adams, "Abraham's Faith and Gentile Disobedience," 47–66) or the *typos* of Christ (e.g., Hays, "Have We Found Abraham?," 92, 98). Hays also refers to Abraham as a representative figure of believers. Those who reject the notion of typology often speak of Abraham as a representative figure, an exemplum or paradigm of or for the Christian. Alternatively, others propose interpretations that emphasize the corporate character of Rom 4 (e.g., Forman, "Politics of Promise," 301–24).

80. Lowe, "Oh διά!," 149–57.
81. Moo, *Epistle to the Romans*, 284.
82. Witherington and Hyatt, *Paul's Letter to the Romans*, 128.

However, although Paul draws a line of continuity between the founders, Abraham and Christ and, thus, between Judaism and the new movement, the apostle is careful to establish the preeminence of the latter in keeping with the eschatological framework within which he is working. Although verses 17–22 remain tied to the Genesis narrative, they nevertheless demonstrate a shift in Paul's thought toward christological concerns. Not only are these verses framed by two christological passages, 3:21–26 and 4:23–25, but, as noted above, the death language found in 4:17–23 and 4:24–25 and the allusions to God's life-giving, creative power, suggest that Paul's christological conclusion in verses 24–25 needs to be integrated into the broader argument.[83] Of note, in this regard, is Paul's idealization of Abraham's faith. The Abraham of Romans stands in contrast to the Abraham of Scripture who tries to procure God's promise through Hagar (Gen 16:1-6) and who laughs at God's promise of a son (Gen 17:17).[84] Equally of note is the apostle's description of the basis of Abraham's conviction; that is, that the patriarch was fully convinced that God was able to do what he had promised (v. 21). The διό immediately following links this clause to its result (v. 22), with emphasis falling not on faithful Abraham but on a faithful God who acts righteously towards his people. Verse 23 points to a similar conclusion. Here, once again, the emphasis is not on Abraham's faith, as portrayed by either the scriptures or Paul, but on the reckoning of righteousness, an act performed by God. The apostle deftly ties this past act of divine right-setting to the present, again positing God as the object of faith. However, at this juncture in the argument, the reckoning of faith in the present time is specifically defined as trust in the God, who raised Jesus from the dead (4:24).

Moreover, although it is God who is the object of faith throughout chapter 4, the use of διὰ πίστεως in 3:25 within the context of sacrificial language suggests that it is Jesus's faithfulness which is in view in that verse and in 4:16.[85] This is supported by the phrase εἰς τὸ εἶναι βεβαίαν τὴν ἐπαγγελίαν; that is, the promise is certain because it is premised on Jesus's own faithful death and resurrection. Thus, although Abraham's faithfulness is the means by which God's promise is mediated to both Jews and gentiles, Jesus's faithfulness is that which confirms this promise and makes it certain for those who trust in God. Thus, both temporally and hierarchically, Christ stands as the preeminent founding figure.

---

83. Jipp, "Rereading the Story of Abraham," 217–22, 228. A majority of interpreters fail to integrate verses 23–25 into Paul's larger argument, presumably because its meaning is taken as obvious: as Abraham believed and was set right, so too believers are set right by faith.

84. Jipp, "Rereading the Story of Abraham," 236.

85. Paul makes the claim that God's promise to Abraham and for all his seed is ἐκ πίστεως. A number of scholars have argued that this phrase, taken from Hab 2:4, refers to Christ's own faithfulness (Jipp, "Rereading the Story of Abraham," 232). In constructions where πίστις is followed by a genitive noun of person, Paul implies the subjective genitive (Rom 3:3; 4:12).

4.2.2 Christ, God's Ultimate Founding Figure: Faith, Righteousness, Life, and Reconciliation to God

4.2.2.1 *Christ's Temporal Preeminence*

In 5:1–2, Paul simply states, without elaboration or apology, that believers are justified by faith, suggesting that he is not interested in presenting a defense of justification by faith as opposed to works. Rather, his interest lies in drawing lines of continuity between Judaism and the Christ movement, similar to that seen in chapters 1–3, by demonstrating that the eschatological promise of restoration and renewal given to Israel by God, as foretold by the prophets, has been fulfilled in and through Christ. The numerous thematic and linguistic parallels seen in 5:1–11 and chapter 4 underscore the points of continuity between Abraham and Jesus, while simultaneously presenting Christ as God's present means of reconciliation, in this sense superseding that provided by the covenant and the law in the past.

Broadly speaking, scholars tend to overlook the significance of the οὖν which introduces Rom 5:1 and the implications thereof.[86] Similar to the οὖν in 3:27 and 4:1 the οὖν of 5:1 functions to take Paul's argument one step further, suggesting that the analogy with Abraham is not limited to chapter 4.[87] More specifically, the phrase, δικαιωθέντες ἐκ πίστεως (5:1), echoes a theme which pervades Rom 4 and Abraham's relationship with God described as enmity in terms of ἀσέβεια (4:5) is echoed in 5:6.[88] The previously mentioned parallel between Abraham and believers in relation to hope in the face of contradictory situations, appears in 5:1–5. The reason why believers have such hope is given in 5:6–11 which parallels ungodly Abraham's freely given reconciliation to God as the basis of his hope. The οὖν in 5:12 moves the argument forward by spelling out how this reconciliation through Jesus occurs and harkens back to 4:24–25. 5:13–14 echoes 4:14–15 and gives the reason why Abraham, the obedient patriarch, needs forgiveness. 5:17b emphasizes that righteousness is a free gift, a theme which harkens back to 4:3–5. Moreover, this free gift of righteousness comes from God (4:3–5, 6–9, 16), although for believers it is now through the one man Jesus Christ (5:15–17). Thus, the themes of 5:20 harken back to 4:14–15. Romans 5:1–11 serves to flesh-out the initial righteous-ing discussed in 4:1–17 and is linked to chapter 4 via 4:24–25. This throws the faith of Abraham into relief. It is not a faith that is antithetical to works. That is not Paul's point here. Rather, the point is that the

---

86. Sandnes, "Abraham, the Friend of God," 124–28.

87. Sandnes, "Abraham, the Friend of God," 124. See also, Dunn, *Romans*, 246.

88. Sandnes, "Abraham, the Friend of God," 125–26. Although Sandnes focuses his work on the role of Abraham in divine reconciliation, there are parallels between chapter 4 and chapters 5 and 6, which suggest that Paul invokes the story of Abraham not only to describe initial righteousing, but also to highlight the necessity for perseverance in faith. Thus, 4:18–25 previews the argument for obedient faithfulness that Paul develops in chapters 5 and 6.

promise made to Abraham is both confirmed and fulfilled in Christ. Jesus's hierarchical superiority as a founding figure is elaborated in 5:12–21.

4.2.2.2 Christ's Hierarchical Preeminence

As noted above, the οὖν in 5:12 moves Paul's argument forward by further elaborating on God's reconciliation with humanity through Jesus by comparing the effects of his obedience and righteousness to the disobedience of Adam, the first human. The introduction of Adam at this point is incongruous in the sense that his role as the progenitor of the human race clearly precedes that of Abraham. However, as noted in the previous chapter, the primary intent of ancient ethnographers was not to recount the past systematically but rather to safeguard the memory of events worthy of being remembered for the very reason that they performed an important role in shaping the self-understanding of the community in the present. In the case of both Strabo and Josephus, key events and the persons associated with them are used to indicate time (e.g., Strabo, *Geogr.* 12.8.16; Josephus, *Ant.* 10.147–48). Moreover, precise chronological sequence is of lesser importance than the preservation of the history and traditions associated with key figures (e.g., Strabo, *Geogr.* 12.8.16).

In this instance, the apostle makes recourse to Adam to draw his audience back to humanity's mythological origins and the intrusion of death and sin into the world in order to highlight Christ's unique standing as the only one through whom the basic human condition of sinfulness and unrighteousness is rectified. According to both Paul and the prophets, the problem of human sin finds its ultimate solution in God and, for the apostle, God has provided a remedy in and through Christ who reestablishes humanity's rightful dominion over creation.

Like his Jewish contemporaries and near-contemporaries, Paul creatively constructs a portrait of Adam suitable to his rhetorical[89] and, in this case, ethnographic aims. First, he attributes the presence of sin and death in the world to Adam, specifically, to Adam's transgression, which presumably refers to his failure to keep God's command regarding the tree of knowledge (Gen 2:16–17; 3:6).[90] Central to the apostle's

---

89. John R. Levison offers a compelling critique of the use of early Jewish texts by NT scholars to provide background material for Paul's letters. This practice, he argues, has led to both a failure to recognize the diversity of interpretations of Adam in early Judaism, and to a distortion of the meaning of Adam in these texts. When individual interpretations of the biblical Adam, which are themselves a product of the aims and purposes of any given author working with the Genesis narratives, are considered within the shared perspectives and traditions which control particular schools of thought within early Judaism, what emerges is great diversity within a limited unity (Levison, *Portraits of Adam*, 159–60).

90. Wisdom writers did not attribute the origin of death to Adam's transgression, regarding mortality as a natural feature of human existence, while Josephus exhibits little interest in the effects of Adam's sin. Paul seems to take a position similar to that found among apocalyptic authors who attributed death in the present, evil age to Adam's sin in the garden (Levison, *Portraits of Adam*, 158–59). Less evident in the Jewish tradition is the idea of Adam's responsibility for the prevalence of sin among

argument, thus far, has been the notion that all of humanity has failed to properly acknowledge and worship God, a state of existence that the law could not remedy; its limited purpose, as the apostle reiterates, being to reckon sin as sin (Rom 5:13–14, 20). Accordingly, he attributes humanity's fundamental state of unrighteousness to its originator, Adam, without any explanation of how Adam's transgression translates into individual culpability among his progeny.[91] This attribution of humanity's proclivity toward sin to Adam suits the apostle's ethnographic purposes. He has already argued for humanity's unrighteousness in the old age, both before and after the giving of the law. Accordingly, he attributes this state to the original founder of the human race. The lack of elaboration on this point, coupled with the personification of death and sin as ruling authorities or kings, ἐβασίλευσεν, (5:14, 17, 21), suggests that Paul's main objective parallels his larger ethnographic aims. The apostle's point is that the community that Adam established, which encompasses all peoples, including Adam himself, throughout history, up until the present time, is characterized by its submission to these two rulers who, as ruling powers, prescribe the laws and customs, or way of life, that define this universal community. Moreover, according to Paul, through his transgression, Adam relinquished his and, consequently, humanity's divinely given dominion over creation (Gen 1:26; cf. Rom 8:20–21) to these destructive powers.

Thus, sin and death, not Adam, stand as the ruling heads of the old order. Like many of his Jewish contemporaries Paul assumes that all people groups ultimately trace their ancestry to Adam (e.g., Josephus, *Ant* 1.120–47). However, the apostle's purpose in referencing the entry of sin into the world through the first human is to underscore the distorted nature of the old age, ruined by Adam's transgression. All humans are abdicators of their rightful dominion over creation in the sense that they are the subjects of sin and death. The law, rather than overturning this destructive, subversive reign, serves only to reveal its true nature. This portrait of Adam that Paul draws is in keeping with the depiction of humanity presented in chapters 1–3. Adam's and his posterity's subjection to sin and death is ultimately attributable to God's righteous judgment (Rom 5:16; cf. 1:24, 26, 28), which only God himself is able to reverse or rectify. However, the reference to Adam's abdication of the rule originally given to humanity at this juncture in the argument allows Paul to speak of Christ as the founder of a new community through whom God reestablishes humanity's rightful dominion.

Accordingly, Christ is greater than Abraham not only in the sense that it is through his faithfulness that God conquers the ubiquitous power of sin and death but, more importantly, in the sense that he stands as the head of a newly created community composed of diverse people groups who are characterized by their faith

---

humanity. However, 4 Ezra 3:21–22 and 4:30–32 refer to the transmission of a sinful tendency (Byrne, *Romans*, 174–75).

91. Although Paul does state that all have sinned (Rom 3:23), this does not explain how Adam's specific sin was "inherited" by his progeny.

in a God who delivers on his promises. As the apostle makes clear, it is through the one, Jesus Christ, that those who receive grace and the gift of righteousness exercise dominion in life (5:17). Christ not only confirms the promises made to Abraham but also brings them to fruition by establishing a community, appointed by God, to exercise its rightful rule over his creation. Thus, the Roman believers are reminded not only of their ties to an ancient, venerable religion and its preeminent founder, Abraham, but also, and more importantly, of their royal status in Christ, God's ultimate and preeminent founder. In ethnographic terms, their preeminent status as a people group is grounded in God himself.

4.3 Conclusion

For both Paul and Greco-Roman and Jewish ethnographers, etiological accounts, establishing the antiquity and, thus, the historical legitimacy of a given people group played a central role in constructing a positive identity for the ethnoracial groups for which they were advocating. As social identity theorists point out, individuals will seek to identify with groups that are defined by what are perceived to be positive rather than negative characteristics. In cases where the in-group is seen to lack positive distinctiveness, a decrease in affiliation with or even alienation from the group is inevitable. Historically, the Jewish people perceived themselves as the elect of God. They identified themselves as Yahweh's chosen people, with the covenant and the law standing as the major attestation to this unique divine-human relationship. Accordingly, in his effort to strengthen group affiliation among the believers in Rome, Paul seeks to present the Christ movement as representative of the people of God in a way that stands in some continuity with this revered Jewish self-perception, yet, acknowledges the reality of the new age where the past is reinterpreted in light of the present.

Skillfully employing the tools of an ethnographer, the apostle portrays the members of the Christ movement as the locus where all history converges and receives its meaning via its divinely instituted founding figure, Christ. For Paul, humanity's alienation from its God is decisively dealt with in and through this founder, who stands as both the confirmation and fulfillment of God's promises to Abraham and, thus, to Israel. In accordance with the historical framework within which the apostle works, God's identity as the one Lord and Creator of the cosmos, necessitates the continuation of ethnoracial distinctiveness within the people of God, since his work in and through Christ represents the incoming of the nations foretold in the Jewish scriptures. The fact that humanity's salvation is accomplished through a founder of Jewish descent underscores God's sovereignty in accomplishing his salvific purposes, a theme Paul continues to develop in the arguments which follow. Throughout this grand portrait of Israel's and, ergo, humanity's history, Paul weaves a complex pattern of ethnic discourse by which he effectively dismantles the Jewish intragroup stereotype of election vis-à-vis the law, on the grounds that the status of Israel as the elect is, in its entirety, a work of God, who alone determines who will be included and on what grounds. Accordingly, God's people, both in the past and the present, consist of those who exhibit trust or have faith in him, with faith understood in the active sense, as that exemplified by obedience. Although the law continues to have saliency with regard to the inter-subjective criteria defining Jewish ethnoracial identity, its divinely purposed, provisional nature renders it unsuitable as a trans-historical criterion of the people of God.

In sum, thus far, in his bid to secure historical legitimacy for the nascent movement to which his audience belongs, Paul has effectively tied the Christ movement and its founder to their Jewish roots. Simultaneously, he presents the former as surpassing the latter in the sense that the new represents confirmation/fulfillment of past, divinely given promises, raising the issue of the status of unbelieving Jews in a continuing narrative within which they were initially cast in the leading role. This issue becomes particularly acute in Rom 8:14–17 where Paul brings his kinship discourse to a climax, defining divine filiation in terms of Christ and the Spirit. Examination of Paul's answer to the question of Israel's place in the new age of the Spirit is the task of the following chapter. In Rom 9–11, Paul not only recapitulates the basic themes set forth in the first five chapters but also provides an explanation for why the majority of Jews have failed to accept their Messiah. The latter serves the important aim of further legitimating in-Christ identity and strengthening the faith of his audience, since Paul portrays this failure as according to divine purpose and plan. Moreover, the law-faith dichotomy not only continues to play a role in the apostle's identity discourse but also serves to establish the priority, both temporally and hierarchically, of the Jewish people. In this sense, Rom 9–11 stands as the second part of Paul's ethnographic effort in establishing the historical legitimacy of a new movement, which is itself grounded in the God of Israel, the God of both Jews and gentiles.

CHAPTER FIVE

The Historical Legitimacy of the Christ Movement (Part II)

Establishing a Positive Identity (Rom 6–8 and 9–11): Children of God Apart from the Law

THUS FAR, PAUL HAS argued that the traditional Jewish intragroup stereotype of election via the law is flawed due to the law's provisional nature in the larger scheme of God's dealings with humanity. It is the sovereign God who defines, establishes, and maintains the elect status of his people. The historical legitimacy of the believing community inheres in the fact that its members, like God's people in the past, exhibit faith in this God and his ways, with this faith understood in the active sense, involving both a trusting disposition and behavior that reflective of such a mind-set. Election is thus a complex interplay between divine sovereignty and the human response of faith or trust in its expression at any given point in salvation history; a notion Paul will continue to unfold and develop as his argument proceeds.

However, the provisional nature of the law raises an acute issue. In ethnographic terms, a legitimate people have legitimate, that is, divinely mandated, laws. It is these, divinely appointed, laws which circumscribe and define a given people group by spelling out the worship practices, norms, customs, and way of life that make them a distinct community. Thus, Josephus, in his attempt to legitimate the Jewish people, takes great pains to refute Apion's charges against the legitimacy of Moses as a divinely appointed lawgiver (*Ag. Ap.* 1.1; 2.154, 157–58, 162–67), pointing out, in no uncertain terms, that, "the original institution of the Law was in accordance with the will of God." Accordingly, there cannot be "a finer or more equitable polity" (*Ag. Ap.* 2.184–85) than that of the Jewish people, who are identified as "those who have and observe Jewish sacred things (Josephus, *Ant.* 14.228, 234). Since the laws and traditions of any given people group function to give the community its identity, in the case of the believing community, what then is to guide this emerging entity in its religious, communal, moral, and ethical self-definition, given, as Paul has argued, that the Jewish law is provisional?

More specifically, how is walking righteously before God defined and manifested in a community free from the provisions and stipulations of the old, written law?

These questions are critical, given Israel's identity as the righteous people of God in distinction to the nations, who are often portrayed as unholy and unrighteous, in large part, due to the fact that they do not possess the written law. In this regard, it is helpful to consider 1 Cor 9:21 and Gal 6:2. In these texts, Paul makes reference to the law of Christ, which suggests that he is not replacing the OT law with faith, with the latter understood as cognitive assent to the truth of the gospel. In both cases, the law of Christ refers to the ethical and moral imperatives given by Jesus or by his example that believers are required to follow as a result of their acceptance of God's good news.[1] The law of Christ is qualitatively different from the old, written law not only because of the operation of the Spirit, who makes fulfillment of it possible, a fulfillment which includes satisfaction of the intent of the OT law (Rom 13:10), but also because this new law is itself operative under a new covenant instituted by God in and through Christ (2 Cor 3:6, 9–14).[2] However, despite its difference from the old, written law, it is continuous with the latter in the sense that it, like the Mosaic law before it, reflects God's will for his people.

Although the phrase law of Christ does not appear in Romans, the related ideas of new covenant and new law are implicit in Paul's argumentation, as discussed below. At this point in the letter, the question of what is to replace the OT law, given its provisional nature, has been raised by implication, in light of the larger ethnographic context; that is, by the fact that a legitimate people need legitimate laws. Paul's answer, as we will see, is subtle, given the need to keep continuity between Judaism and the new movement and discontinuity between the two, in tension. That the apostle has already noted the provisional nature of the Jewish law makes a delicately nuanced answer even more imperative.

Consequently, it is these issues which guide Paul's construction of believers' identity in Rom 6–8 and, to some degree, his refinement of that identity vis-à-vis that of unbelieving Israel in chapters 9–11. These two sets of chapters work in tandem, each addressing one side of the group self-identity coin. The first three are aimed at constructing a favorable in-group bias, while the second set is aimed at dispelling the out-group antagonism that accompanies the evaluative process associated with the former. For the apostle, the Christ movement represents God's ultimate purpose for humanity. Yet, in this portrait of God's people in the present, Israel paradoxically retains its priority.

5.1 Constructing a Favorable In-group Bias: Living Righteously Apart from the Law (Rom 6–8)

Following a long argument aimed at deconstructing the false conclusion that freedom from the Jewish law equates to moral and ethical lawlessness, the apostle's ethnic

---

1. Witherington, *Conflict and Community in Corinth*, 213.
2. Witherington, *Conflict and Community in Corinth*, 379–80.

discourse reaches its climax in his identification of believers as the sons (and daughters) of God by the Spirit in 8:14–39. No less than descendants of the great patriarch Abraham, they are the children of God, joint heirs with their founder, Christ. Moreover, for Paul, this Spirit-wrought identity confers upon believers the ability to walk before God in righteousness apart from the old, Jewish law, which is provisional. In terms of social identity theory, what the apostle accomplishes in chapters 6–11 is to establish positive distinctiveness for the believing community over and against the Jewish unbelieving community, by portraying the former as embodying the relevant comparative dimensions, righteousness and divine filiation, to a superior degree and, most importantly, apart from the law of the old, Mosaic covenant, which historically functioned as the decisive factor in Jewish self-definition as the elect of God.

At this juncture, it is important to keep in mind that Paul is not discarding the idea of law per se, although his arguments, thus far, seem to imply that he is, at least as far as the Jewish law is concerned. Rather, he will demonstrate that believers are to obey God, living in accordance with his will, under the new covenant instituted by the death and resurrection of Christ. As noted above, the idea of a new covenant is implicit, since Paul does not use that term. However, the eschatological framework within which he operates strongly suggests that the old covenant has been replaced by a new covenant characterized by the outpouring of the Spirit, who makes obedience to God's law, as revealed in the law of Christ, possible. As discussed below, the old, written law, given to the Jewish people, is brought to its end in/by Christ (Rom 10:4) and believers are empowered to fulfill its divinely established intent (Rom 13:10). In other words, there is both a new covenant and a new law that is both continuous, in one sense, and radically discontinuous, in another sense, from the old, written law.

Recall that the degree of group affiliation is dependent on the perception that the group is capable of supplying satisfactory aspects of an individual's social identity. Since social change is inevitable, group-identity insecurity is also inevitable, creating the need for a search for positive distinctiveness among competing groups; in this case, between the believing community and the unbelieving Jewish community, from which it springs. Accordingly, Paul portrays the emerging community as manifesting the characteristics of eschatological Israel. This background of traditional Jewish images, perspectives and interpretations provides a matrix common to both subgroups within which Paul delineates points of convergence and divergence between the two groups within a presently unfolding eschatological perspective. This, in turn, allows him to securely establish the identity of the believing community within the larger framework of Jewish, traditional, self-identity in a way that intensifies believer affiliation with the new, emerging community.

Thus, Paul argues that, believers, both Jew and gentile, are empowered to walk righteously before God not only apart from the old, written law but also to an extent not possible for God's people in the past. For the apostle, freedom from the rule of sin, which dominated God's people in the past, is secured in Christ through whom believers enter into a new life of obedience made possible by the eschatological giving of the Spirit. It is this same Spirit who establishes the kinship ties necessary for opening the door to living a life that bears a family resemblance to that of Christ's own faithful obedience to God. Accordingly, the OT motif of Israel as God's child or son, which in the post-biblical tradition, in dependence upon the promise contained in Hos 1:10 (MT 2:1), came to be associated with eschatological Israel, is portrayed, by Paul, as presently fulfilled in the believing community.[3]

The idea of kin resemblance is important in ancient thought. The notion of progeny existing in ancestors explains the related belief that nonphysical attributes, such as character, are inscribed in the genetic makeup of the family and can be passed down from ancestor to descendant. For example, Aristotle writes that offspring are both in and come out of their parents, with the mother and father contributing different attributes. The mother contributes the parts of the body, while the father provides the shape and character of the child (Aristotle, *Gen. an.* (737a23; 767b15).[4] Similarly, Philo notes that "kinglike potentialities" are inherited:

> From the cradle I [Gaius] have had a host of teachers: fathers, brothers, uncles, cousins, grandparents, ancestors, right up to the founders of the family, all my kinsmen by blood on both the maternal and paternal sides, who attained to offices of independent authority, apart from the fact that in the first begetting of their seeds kinglike potentialities for government were contained.[5]

As these examples illustrate, in ancient understanding characteristics such as the ability to rule are present in the seed itself and are transmitted through conception.[6] Accordingly, offspring reflect the character of the family from which they came. Moreover, as discussed below, this is no less true for the children of God, the siblings of Christ.

5.1.1 Faith and Identity: Walking before God in the New Age

As discussed above, in antiquity, identity is strongly linked with kinship in that nonphysical traits were thought to be passed on along family lines. Family resemblance was conceived not only in terms of shared physical characteristics but also in terms of such shared attributes as status, personality, character, intellect, and emotional make-up.[7]

---

3. E.g., Exod 4:22-23; Deut 14:1; 32:5-6, 19-22; Isa 1:2-4; 30:9; 63:8; Hos 1:10 [MT and LXX 2:11]; Wis 12:7, 21; 16:10, 21, 26; 18:13; 19:6; Sir 36:17, where the son of God motif denotes a privilege reserved to Israel precisely as God's people. Examples from the post-biblical tradition include: 1 En. 62:11; Jub. 1:24-25; 2:20; Pss. Sol. 17:30; As. Mos. 10:3; 4 Ezra 6:58; 2 Bar. 13:9; Bib. Ant. 18:6; 32:10; Sib. Or. 3:702; 5:202; 4QDibHam 3:4-6; 3 Macc 6:28 (Byrne, *Romans*, 249).

4. Hodge, *If Sons, Then Heirs*, 94-95.

5. Philo, *Embassy* 54, cited in Hodge, *If Sons, Then Heirs*, 95.

6. Hodge, *If Sons, Then Heirs*, 95.

7. Hodge, *If Sons, Then Heirs*, 17, 25, 31.

Accordingly, birth into a noble or royal family carried the expectation that its members would think and act in a manner consummate with such an illustrious pedigree (Aristotle, *On Nobility* frag. 94).[8] This explains why Greco-Roman ethnographers were intent on providing an illustrious genealogy for the Roman people (e.g., Homer, *Il.* 6.145–211); for instance, providing proof that the founders of Rome "were Greeks," who had "come together from nations not the smallest nor the least considerable," bringing "customs and institutions by virtue of which their descendants advanced to so great dominion" (Dionysius, *Ant. rom.* 1.5.1–2). This served to validate Rome's status as the legitimate world power, since its eminence was seen to rest on the fact that its rulers and authorities were descents of Greek gods, demigods, and heroes.

Accordingly, for Paul to refer to believers as children of God (τέκνα Θεοῦ) (8:16) indicates that their identity is not only bound-up with their privileged designation as the people of God, but also that, as God's people, they mirror divine righteousness both in their relationships within and without the community and in their laws, customs, and way of life. However, the apostle has already argued that the Jewish law, which was meant to guide God's people in righteousness in the past, serves only to bring knowledge of sin, suggesting its impotency in the face of sin's power (7:1–25). As such, it is powerless to shape the behavior of those under it, raising the question of what is to guide believers in walking righteously before their God in the present. As Paul will argue, in the new age, the Spirit not only replaces the old, written law as a moral and ethical guide, but more importantly frees believers to live the life of righteousness envisioned in the OT law but never attained by Israel.

As discussed in more detail below, the Spirit, who characterizes the new covenant, empowers believers to live according to the moral and ethical teachings and example of Christ. As already noted, the law of Christ is not mentioned in Romans; rather, the emphasis is placed on the transformative power of the Spirit. It is the Spirit, who reconfigures believers' identity, so that they are able to fulfill the intent of OT law in a radically new way, a way not possible for God's people in the past. For Paul, the intent of the OT law is fulfilled (Rom 13:8–10) as believers live according to Christ's teachings and example (6:17). Moreover, the Spirit, in a manner akin to the law of Christ or to his teachings and example, directs believers to walk in a way pleasing to God; that is, in a way that does not gratify the self and its desires (8:5–8). As Paul will argue, the written law did not have the power to break the dominion of sin. God dealt with sin in and through Christ, so that believers are now enabled to walk according to the Spirit (8:3–4). Thus, the Spirit works in tandem with Christ and with his teachings and example, in the sense that he guides and enables believers to live according to the τύπον διδαχῆς (6:17); that is, to live in conformity to Christ. It is in this sense that the Spirit (in tandem with Christ, both of whom characterize the new age with its new covenant) replaces the old Jewish law and the old covenant. As we will see, Paul refutes the notion that the written law of the old covenant was

---

8. Hodge, *If Sons, Then Heirs*, 31.

sufficient to overcome the self's fleshy desires. That is, he refutes the idea of the OT law as a means of mastering the passions. According to the apostle, the ability to live to God is given to believers under the new covenant of Christ and the Spirit, both of whom work in tandem to constitute a new law for the people of God in the new age, who are divinely empowered to live accordingly.

In these chapters, as in Rom 1–5, the apostle reinterprets the past in light of Christ, reframing the identity of God's people in terms of his death and resurrection. His argument occurs in three distinct movements all aimed at dispelling the notion that believers' freedom from the Jewish law equates to lawlessness, in the sense of wickedness; that is, in ethnographic terms, to an illegitimate people group. These movements are examined in the sections which follow below and function to lay the groundwork for Paul's climactic reference to believers as the children of God; that is, as a people bearing the stamp of God's own holiness apart from the Jewish law.

The question of what is to guide the behavior and shape the character of the believing community in lieu of the OT law touches upon civic identity which includes the norms, laws, and customs that define a particular people group's communal mode of life. In antiquity, civic identity is intimately bound-up with what we think of as religious and ethnic identity. Thus, Josephus writes that, the Idumeans became citizens of the Jewish *politia* by adopting "the customs and laws of the Jews," including the worship of the God of Israel (*Ant.* 15.253). Belief in this God is central to membership in the community, so that "when Achior saw all that the God of Israel and done, he believed firmly in God," "was circumcised and joined the house of Israel" (Jdt 14:10). Recall that in ancient thought these so-called types of identity intersected each other in such a way that all three, in some fashion and to some degree, depending on the ethnographer and his or her aims, worked together to form the ethnoracial identity of a given people. Accordingly, Paul draws on the previously introduced notion of dominion/rule, and on conceptions of slavery and marriage, relationships instituted, understood, and circumscribed within a civic or political context, to define the freedom of believers in a way that ensures that it is conceived in terms of conferring upon them the ability to live for or under the rule of God. Living under the rule of God implies that the believing community also has a set of norms, customs, and laws, however conceived and defined (an issue Paul will deal with in length beginning in Rom 12), which govern its communal life. In other words, it implies that God's people in the present are a legitimate people group.

As mentioned above, the apostle's argument may be divided into three sections. The first movement consists of defining believer's identity in terms enslavement to God (Rom 6:1–23); with the second, further redefining this slavery as occurring under the rule of the Spirit (7:1–6); while, in the third division (7:14—8:13), Paul revisits the foundation narratives, both past and present, introduced in the first portion of the letter, retelling them expressly in terms of the law, Christ, and the Spirit. As people with a law, although of a law qualitatively different from that of the old written code, believers are the people of God in the present precisely because they are able to fulfill the requirement of the law given to Israel in the past. As in the first chapters of the letter, Christ stands at the nexus of past and present, continuity and discontinuity. The coming of the Messiah brings the outpouring of the Spirit, promised and foretold in the Scriptures, two events which result in a complete reconfiguration of the law from a written code associated with death to a life-giving mode of existence in the Spirit, who himself enables a life of righteousness. In the new age of the Spirit, believers' union with Christ in his death and resurrection opens the door to the possibility of a radical obedience to God that not only fulfills the intent of the old law but also represents an inner transformation of believers such that they bear a family resemblance to Christ in their orientation to and actions within the world. They are the children of God in a sense that was never possible for God's people in the past, who lived under the old written code.

5.1.1.1 *Under the Rule of God (Rom 6:1–23)*

As in Rom 5, sin, in chapter 6, is personified as a ruling power. However, in this chapter, the relationship between sin and believers and believers and God is more narrowly defined in terms of the slave-master relationship, particularly in 6:15–23, where slave imagery predominates. In addition, Paul links the rule of sin with existence under the (rule) of the law (6:14).[9] This rule is contrasted to that of grace which is associated with the rule of God (v. 14). Moreover, the emphasis in Rom 6 is on believers' obligation to resist the rule of sin in their bodies, refusing to stand alongside of it, no longer placing themselves at the disposal of a slave master bent on making them ready participants in its system of domination.[10] The mixed metaphors of ruling power-subject and master-slave are used by the apostle in a creative way to establish the fact that the believing community, living under grace, lives under the rule of God. In this sense, it is not lawless; that is, its members are not living in disobedience to God, despite their freedom from the written law. What this new type of law consists of and exactly how believers fulfill its requirements is explained in greater detail later in the argument. In this chapter, Paul's focus is on the fluid end of the identity spectrum, such that identification with the believing community is portrayed as attainable through a common life of walking righteously before God defined apart from the written code, yet, nevertheless, not lawless, given members' identity as slaves of righteousness.

---

9. Although the word κυριεύσει is not used in reference to the law, the preposition ὑπὸ, in this context, connotes rule. As Jewett notes, the phrase "under law" appears to follow an early rabbinic interpretation of Exod 19:17 and Deut 4:11 that viewed the law as a threatening thing suspended over Israel's head (Jewett, *Romans*, 415).

10. Dodson, *"Powers" of Personification*, 129. In Rom 5, the agency of sin and death over and against that of God and Christ is emphasized.

Although the word "faith" does not appear anywhere in Rom 6, it is presupposed, and all who have this faith enter into a new reality through Christ such that their identity as citizens or subjects of sin's realm is exchanged for a new identity characterized by the rule of God. This identity, which has a distinctly civic cast, is couched within an overarching theological framework. The christological basis for a life of obedience to God apart from the written law, presented in 6:1–14, is what makes the community's identity as slaves of righteousness (6:15–23) a possibility. Thus, Paul's answer to the false inferences presented in the opening verse and in verse 15 comes in two parts. Its overall purpose is directed at addressing the absurdity of thinking that being under grace, rather than under the law, equates to being under sin. As the apostle makes clear, existence under the rule of grace is in reality a transfer from the rule of sin to the rule of God—a rule that lies at the core of the identity of the people both in the past and the present. Moreover, it is a transfer that entails a transformative death and resurrection within believers—a notion that Paul will further develop in the following chapter.

5.1.1.1A Theological Basis: Unity with Christ in His Death and Resurrection

The opening objection (v. 1) appears to arise out of the strong emphasis Paul has just placed on God's seemingly unlimited supply of grace in the face of increasing transgression and sin under the law (5:20–21). From this, an erroneous deduction could be drawn that life lived under the rule of grace (ἡ χάρις βασιλεύσῃ) essentially equates to a life free of the moral and ethical restraint provided by the law (cf. Rom 3:8), since continuing in sin would only result in an increased supply of grace—a good thing. Although it is possible that Paul is responding to a real antagonist, it is also possible that the rhetorical question is aimed at providing a segue to a fuller discussion of believers' behavior in lieu of the law—an issue that has been lurking in the background, thus far, and, in terms of the apostle's ethnographic purposes, in need of explanation. The apostle's response in verse 2 is not only emphatically negative, but also serves as an adumbration of the argument that follows in 6:3–14 and forms the theological basis for the identity Paul begins to construct in 6:15–23.

The christological basis for the community's new identity is directly linked to its founding experience. Paul has already established the defining events of the believing community's history: Jesus's death, burial, and resurrection. According to the apostle, each of these events is appropriated by the believer by his or her participation in them, such that each member becomes a part of the community.[11] The reference to baptism into Christ Jesus and into his death (6:3) is most likely a passing allusion to the rite of Christian initiation with which Paul's audience would have been familiar. Paul links death with Christ with future victory over death (vv. 5 and 8). The phrase τῷ

---

11. Talbert, *Romans*, 161–62.

ὁμοιώματι τοῦ θανάτου αὐτοῦ (v. 5) refers not to baptism or what happens in baptism but to the continuing existence (note the perfect γεγόναμεν) of baptized persons living in the form of Christ's death. Here dying and rising, ultimate victory over death, are not one event. Rather, there is union with Christ's death now, which results in present newness of life (v. 4), followed by a future bodily resurrection.

Some of Paul's writings imply that the ritual itself represents dying and rising with Christ: being baptized entails dying with respect to the structures and powers of the world (Col 2:20); taking off the old human with its vices, divisions, and entanglements; and putting on a new life in Christ (Col 3:9–10).[12] However, baptism is not the theme of this passage. The ultimate basis for Paul's appeal in this chapter is not what happened when his audience was baptized, but what happened when Christ died and rose.[13] Moreover, Paul likens baptism to burial with Christ, but refrains from saying that baptism is the means by which or through which believers are raised in him.[14] The tension between the present newness of life and the not yet complete conformation to Christ, which will occur only at the resurrection, agrees with Paul's understanding of salvation. What is significant is that the apostle equates this rite with being baptized into (εἰς) Christ's death. This suggests that initiation into the community involves more than being joined to Christ in a static spatial sense. It also involves the dynamic sense of actual participation in Christ's overall career of death, burial, and risen life.[15] The old self and the body of sin (6:6)[16] refer to the legacy of Adam that all of humanity shares in common, and it is precisely by participating in Christ's death and resurrection that this essential nature is changed.[17]

Some scholars argue that the old self and new self are not ontological but rather relational or positional in orientation. Thus, these terms do not speak of a change in nature but a change in relationship.[18] Although transfer of domains is useful for understanding the meaning and ramifications of union with Christ, it does not exhaust Paul's understanding of what it means to be united with Christ's death. The verb συνθάπτω (v. 4) denotes the act of being buried in a shared grave, and although Paul's use is metaphorical, it nevertheless conveys the idea of a real death.[19] Furthermore, when Paul refers to an ethical tension in the Christian life, he speaks of it in two ways: as a tension between the flesh and the Spirit (Gal 5:16–25); or as a contrast between the mortal body, which is subject to suffering, death and decay, and the resurrection

---

12. Meeks, *First Urban Christians*, 102.
13. Moo, *Epistle to the Romans*, 355.
14. Dunn, *Theology of Paul the Apostle*, 470.
15. Byrne, *Romans*, 190.
16. The "body of sin" may be seen as the whole person orientated toward the world and toward self-satisfaction.
17. Witherington and Hyatt, *Paul's Letter to the Romans*, 157.
18. E.g., Moo, *Epistle to the Romans*, 370–73.
19. Jewett, *Romans*, 398.

body (2 Cor 4:7–12). He does not speak of it as a tension between the old self and the new.[20] The ontological aspects of Paul's thought become even more apparent when the role of the Spirit, who energizes this transformation, is considered. Although there is no explicit mention of the Spirit in chapter 6, Gordon Fee points out that the linguistic correspondences between this chapter and the Spirit language in 7:5–6 and 8:1–30 suggests that the Spirit has been a presupposition behind Paul's argument in 6:1–23. For example, the empowering presence of the Spirit is implicit in 6:4 where he refers to Christ being raised from the dead through the glory of God, so that believers might walk in newness of life. In this way, the Spirit as the agent of Christ's resurrection is linked to that of believers. Moreover, when the apostle comes to the section where the work of the Spirit is predominant in the argument (8:1–30), he references some of the critical language of chapter 6 to the Spirit.[21]

How this transformation is effected and by what agency is described in detail beginning with 8:1, culminating in Paul's reference to believers as children of God and joint heirs with Christ, where he appeals to ascribed kinship (the fixed end of the identity spectrum) in order to lend authority and credibility to the achieved (or fluid) end of his identity construct. However, at this juncture of the argument, his focus remains on the fluid end of the spectrum, where freedom from the rule of sin is the identity criterion that distinguishes the believing community from all other people groups. Thus, Paul constructs the binary categories of those under the rule of law-sin-death and those under the rule of grace-God-life, dividing humanity accordingly. Implicitly, the two categories also reflect on ontological contrast which Paul will further develop in 8:1–17. Here the emphasis is on Christ's work as the basis and mechanism for a change in identity, which goes back to what the apostle argued in chapters 1–5. Christ is God's solution to the historical disobedience of his people. Whereas sin reigned in God's people in the past due to the law's limited role of providing knowledge of sin, sin rules over believers only if they accept its reign (6:12–14).

In essence, the death of the old self through union with Christ's death results in the transformative birth of the new self which makes the doing of the exhortations in verses 12–13 possible. Thus, Paul sees death of the old self with Christ as a gateway to life, a new life that begins in the present and culminates in the future, at the eschaton when the mortal body is raised from the dead (6:4–5, 8, 22). Since believers continue to live in a mortal body which is not immune to sin and temptation, the same body that has been freed from its servitude to sin (6:6) is nevertheless a body that still participates in the weakness, suffering, and dissolution of this age.[22] The battle against the present age is cast in civic terms and is fought by believers placing their members, i.e. their whole person, as weapons (ὅπλον) in the service of God (6:13).[23] On the

---

20. Witherington and Hyatt, *Paul's Letter to the Romans*, 160.
21. Fee, *God's Empowering Presence*, 499–500.
22. Witherington and Hyatt, *Paul's Letter to the Romans*, 162; Moo, *Epistle to the Romans*, 383.
23. Jewett, *Romans*, 410. Jewett notes that Paul's use of the metaphor of weapons in 2 Cor 6:7 and

other hand, to place oneself at the disposal of sin would be to participate willingly in the war against God and to deny the reality of Christ's redemptive act. The idea of bearing arms in allegiance to one's king is reflected by the verb παρίστημι which has the connotation of being at the disposal of or yielding oneself to a regent. It is important to note that the righteousness in 6:13 is personified as the force wielding the weapons, implying that believers are to reckon themselves as weapons in the hands of God to be used for his purposes and according to the norms and laws that govern his realm. Thus, to stand alongside the power of sin or the will of God means to serve the purposes of either kingdom.[24]

5.1.1.1B Believer's Identity: Slaves of God, Slaves of Righteousness

The controlling metaphor throughout 6:15–23 is that of slave-master, rather than that of subject-ruler, which predominates in 6:1–14. Although slavery was an accepted social institution in antiquity and did not necessarily equate to maltreatment and involuntary servitude, it was a form of bondage, resulting in an inferior status that stood in stark contrast to the ideals of freedom and full citizenship. Paul has just argued that believers are subjects of God, implying their status as citizens of a desirable realm in contrast to that of the oppressive dominion of sin. In light of this, he most likely takes up the image of slavery to underscore the point that life under grace is a live of obedience, since slavery necessarily entails obedience to a master.[25] Consequently, the false inference in verse 15 is given the strongest possible rebuttal in verse 16. One is either a slave to righteousness or a slave to sin. There is no other alternative. The ontological and relational change wrought by believers' participation in Christ's death and resurrection means that they have become slaves of righteousness (6:18). Although, as Paul has already argued, the possibility of re-enslavement to sin remains.

More importantly, the slave-master metaphor allows Paul to craft an identity for his audience that evokes a powerful image from the Jewish scriptures of the servant or slave of God. The apostle has already established that enslavement to sin is a highly undesirable state, leading as it does only to death. Recall that, in antiquity, the state of enslavement resulted in the effacement of the enslaved individual's past history and social connections and affiliations. It was possible for this state to be reversed through the legal process of manumission, whereby a slave would become a member of his or

---

10:4 and the use of ὅπλον to refer to military armor in Rom 13:12 suggests the translation of "weapon" in Rom 6:13. Although Cranfield admits that Pauline usage favors translation of ὅπλον in its particular sense of "weapon," he argues that the general sense of "instruments" is more appropriate here in view of the references to the service of slaves in this chapter (Cranfield, *Epistle to the Romans*, 1:318). However, the predominating metaphor in 6:1–14 is that of subject-ruler, rather than slave-master as in 6:15–23.

24. Jewett, *Romans*, 409–11.

25. Byrne, *Romans*, 200.

her master's community, taking on the identity of that particular group. This transformation of identity was often more gradual than it might first appear, since enslaved persons, and, especially, household slaves, tended to adopt the religious practices and cultural norms of their master, while in bondage.²⁶

Analogously, slaves of sin would be expected to exhibit a way of life commensurate with that of their master; while slaves of God would be expected to reflect his righteousness. Thus, when believers experience manumission from enslavement to sin through Christ's death, they become free persons (Rom 8:1–2, 15, 21; cf. Gal 4:1–11; 4:21—5:1; 5:13). However, their identity, rather than being defined by their previous master's community, in this case, disobedience, death and the law, is transformed into that which reflects the righteousness of the one who effects their manumission and, to whom, they become enslaved.²⁷ The designation δοῦλος of God in the LXX did not carry the negative connotations associated with slavery in the Greco-Roman world. In the OT, the title is used in connection with the prophets (Amos 3:7; Jer 7:25; Dan 9:6), Jewish worshippers (Neh 1:6, 11; Pss 19:11, 13; 35:23, etc.), and for Israel as a whole (Ps 135:22)²⁸ Akin to the slaves of Caesar, whose social and economic status was higher than most of the free population in the Empire, due to the fact that their master was a son of god,²⁹ the designation, "slave of Yahweh," bestowed special privilege upon Israel and the individuals who bore the title. Thus, the contrast between these two identities not only serves as a powerful tool in evoking the proper response in Paul's audience, the choice not to serve sin (i.e., remain faithful to the gospel), but also and, more importantly, further substantiates his argument that freedom from the law does not equate to a state of lawlessness. God's people in the present, as in the past, are identified as the people or slaves of God by their obedience to him.

Moreover, in the present age, the people of God are to be obedient from the heart to the τύπον διδαχῆς to which they have been handed over (v. 17). Here, the reference to τύπον διδαχῆς most likely refers to conformity to Christ, both to his teachings, as the term διδαχή suggests, and to his example. Since the use of τύπος in the Pauline corpus in most instances refers to the emulation of a particular individual who provides a pattern of conduct, this suggests that the Pauline notion of the law of Christ (1 Cor 9:21; Gal 6:2) is in view.³⁰ Thus, believers are to live according to the pattern of Christ;

---

26. Dohrmann, "Manumission and Transformation," 59, 61. For example, Roman slaves, in addition to adopting Roman religion, were given a new Latin name and imitated local dress and customs, becoming part of the household. Some learned Latin and Greek. Upon manumission, the now-freed slave did not revert to his or her previous ethnic status, but became a Roman citizen subject to Roman law. Similarly, non-Jewish slaves in Jewish households learned the law and observed both the Sabbath and holy days, stepping easily into the Jewish community when manumitted and upon circumcision and immersion.

27. For Paul, one is either enslaved to sin or to God. As noted above, there is no other alternative.

28. Jewett, *Romans*, 100.

29. Jewett, *Romans*, 100.

30. Witherington and Hyatt, *Paul's Letter to the Romans*, 171. E.g., Rom 5:14; Phil 3:17; 1 Thess 1:7; 2 Thess 3:9; and Col 2:6.

that is, they are to live in conformity to his moral and ethical teachings and example. It is in this sense that Christ constitutes the new law, which governs the new people of God. Furthermore, the language of being "in Christ" and of "dying with Christ," and the like, represent different expressions of the conformity to Christ theme, signifying the need for believers to live a life reflective of the life of Christ. That is, a life that is righteous (vv. 13, 18–19, 20–22), patterned after the God who is righteous (3:25–26). Thus, the idea of being united with Christ's death points to the whole of Jesus's life on earth, who lived his life righteously, as one dead to sin and alive to God.

What is implicit here is the idea that Christ replaces the Jewish law as a pattern to be emulated; a concept Paul states more explicitly in Rom 10:4.[31] In this regard, Philo portrays the Torah as the ideal law not only because of its divine origin, but also because it, in contrast to the laws of other nations, the Jewish law best produces self-mastery.[32] It is an antidote to desire in that the stipulations of the law not only serve as exhortations addressed to reason but also embody the constitution of the ideal commonwealth dedicated to the promotion of self-mastery.[33] Similarly, in 4 Maccabees, discipline and education in the Torah produces virtue, since the law operates to raise reason to the point where it masters the emotions (1:1; 5:16; 9:17–18; 13:22, 24).[34] Accordingly, the Jewish people are fittingly described as "a race of most righteous men," "always concerned with good counsel and noble works," caring "for righteousness and virtue," by "fulfilling the word of the great God," the law (Sib. Or. 3:218–25, 234–47).[35]

For Paul, Christ is the end of the law, not in the sense that there is now no need for believers to progress in virtue, particularly the virtue of love (13:8–10), but rather in the sense that he both embodies it and supersedes it, bringing it to its ultimate fulfillment (3:21–22; 10:4). Moreover, Jesus Christ is simultaneously the virtuous person who reflects the character of the Deity in human attitudes and patterns of behavior and also the divine pattern of excellence itself. Thus, it is conceivable, given the points of contact with Greco-Roman moral philosophy present in Romans, that Paul's audience, Jew and Greek, would readily associate Christ with the pattern of excellence to be emulated. In Greco-Roman moral philosophy, progress in virtue is often associated with the process of assimilation by human beings to divine habits and character. Both Paul and the moral philosophers see this assimilation/imitation as a dynamic activity involving a progressive element marked by constant vigilance, struggle (e.g., Rom 6:15–19), and the need for wisdom/reason (e.g., Rom 1:18–32 and 12:1–2) in choosing the course of conduct which leads to an ethical life reflective of

---

31. The idea that conformity to the Torah leads to wisdom and, consequently, a life lived in accordance with God's will, is prevalent in the Jewish writings of this period. Gathercole, *Where Is Boasting?*, 161–82, provides a helpful summary of this literature. Romans 10:4 is discussed in more detail below.

32. Stowers, *Rereading of Romans*, 58.

33. Stowers, *Rereading of Romans*, 61, 64. Stower notes that Josephus also presents Judaism as a philosophy of self-mastery. See also, Gathercole, *Where Is Boasting?*, 171–72.

34. Gathercole, *Where Is Boasting?*, 170–71.

35. Gathercole, *Where Is Boasting?*, 173.

divine characteristics or virtues. According to the moral philosophers, to condemn actions which "the world admires is quite impossible without real and solid wisdom" (Plutarch, *Virt. prof.* 78.6). Moreover, although the paradigmatic pattern of virtue to be emulated is exemplified by the supreme deity, persons of exemplary virtue also serve as a kind of intermediary pattern of emulation, in that such individuals embody in human form the habits and character of the god that is revered.

Furthermore, for Paul, this life of obedience is from the heart, in contrast to the servile, often external, obedience of the slave, engaging the entirety of the person.[36] The passive, παρεδόθητε, suggests the action of God who places believers in a situation where Christ can place the τύπος of his own obedience upon their lives.[37] Instead of the written law, they are "given up to a new ethical force, the obedience of the risen Lord welling up in within them."[38] Accordingly, the role of the Spirit in Paul's thought pushes beyond the boundaries of the Greco-Roman ideal of assimilation to the divine, in the sense of imitation, to include the believer's actual participation in the life of Christ both in the present and, more completely, at the eschaton. For those ὑπὸ χάριν (v. 14) committing sinful acts matters greatly, since a person is the slave of whichever power he or she chooses to obey. This notion that to be under God's grace is to be under obligation to obey him is highlighted by the phrase ὑπακοῆς εἰς δικαιοσύνην which is contrasted to obedience to ἁμαρτίας εἰς θάνατον (v. 16). Here Paul contrasts sin as a master with obedience (rather than God) as a master, thus placing the emphasis on the believer's continued obedience.[39]

The phrase ὑπακοῆς εἰς δικαιοσύνην should not be translated as "obedience which leads into righteousness." That Paul exhorts believers to commit themselves to God as weapons and slaves of righteousness (vv. 16, 18), suggests that righteousness is not the goal of obedience but its presupposition. This is made clear in verse 17. Thus, the sense of this phrase appears to be that obedience to God is necessary for maintaining the status of righteousness.[40] In verse 16, Paul places a stark choice before his audience: to return to their former condition of being slaves to sin or to live out their new situation as slaves of Christ. The verb παριστάνω "place oneself at the disposal of" in the context of δοῦλος εἰς ὑπακονή connotes a voluntary placement of oneself at the disposal of another. One means of replenishing the supply of slaves, who were often manumitted at the age of thirty or forty, was the enslavement of debtors and the voluntary selling of oneself as a slave. This usually happened out of economic necessity, but there were cases of persons selling themselves or family members into particular forms of slavery, such as service to a distinguished patron, in the hope of economic and social advancement. This is the social reality underlying

---

36. Byrne, *Romans*, 202.
37. Byrne, *Romans*, 202.
38. Byrne, *Romans*, 202.
39. Cranfield, *Epistle to the Romans*, 1:322–23.
40. Furnish, *Theology and Ethics in Paul*, 175, 195–96.

the comparison Paul draws with service to sin.⁴¹ In other words, although believers have been buried with Christ and have crucified the old self, they are still free to choose to whom they will remain enslaved.

Hence, Paul's exhortation to the Roman believers to present their members as slaves to righteousness into sanctification (v. 19) points to the human response demanded by the divine action in verse 18.⁴² Instead of libertinism or lawlessness, union with Christ leads to the service of righteousness, sanctification, and its end, everlasting life (vv. 22–23).⁴³ Thus, although the nature of the law, understood as that which provides a pattern of conduct to be followed, to which believer's are subject is radically different from that of God's people in the past, their basic identity, like Israel in the past, stems from their relationship to God which is manifested in a righteous and holy manner of life. However, according to Paul, this relationship to God is qualitatively different from Israel's relationship in the past, in that the slaves of God in the new age enjoy this privileged status in the new life of the Spirit and not under the old written code (7:6).

5.1.1.2 *Widowed from the Law, Wedded to Christ (Rom 7:1–6): An Analogy from Marriage*

In seemingly abrupt fashion, Paul returns to the law and its provisional nature, using the metaphor of marriage to describe believers' freedom from the law and relationship with Christ in conjugal terms.⁴⁴ This is important for the identity he is constructing for several reasons. Most obviously, reintroduction of the law at this point in the argument provides the apostle with the opportunity to further explain and clarify the law's connection with sin (3:20, 4:15, 5:20; 6:14).⁴⁵ More importantly, it allows Paul to present the exact nature and substance of the new code governing life in the present age in a way that evidences a continuity with the past, even as its represents something new. To this end, Paul presents the law as a negative foil to the Spirit,⁴⁶ who essentially replaces the written law as the moral guiding force, an event foretold by the prophets, harkening back to Paul's statement in Rom 2:28–29. Thus, in one sense, the discontinuity between the age of the written code and that of the Spirit is not as complete

---

41. Jewett, *Romans*, 416.
42. Cranfield, *Epistle to the Romans*, 1:327.
43. Cousar, *Theology of the Cross*, 102–3.
44. Paul addresses his audience as those who know the law (7:1). Both Jewish auditors and gentile God-fearers would know that the law was binding only while one was alive. This view is expressed in later rabbinic writings (Sabb. 30a; Nid. 61b; B. Pesah 51b; Kelim 9:3) (Talbert, *Romans*, 172). The idea that death cancels the rule of the law is one that could be easily explained to gentiles not familiar with this teaching. Thus, it is not necessary to take this passage as specifically addressing Jewish believers and, perhaps, former gentile proselytes.
45. Byrne, *Romans*, 209.
46. Also, Byrne, *Romans*, 209.

as it may appear at first glance. However, it is profoundly radical in the sense that it is rooted in a tradition that it surpasses even as it fulfills it.[47] In addition, the analogy from marriage underscores Christ's role as the nexus between past and present, the old age and the new aeon, the age of the written code and that of the Spirit, the rule of sin and death and the rule of grace and life.

Evident throughout Rom 7 is the rhetorical technique of antithesis, whereby Paul sets life under the law (negative) in contrast to life in the Spirit (positive).[48] By setting the positive over the negative, the present situation over the past, he highlights the superiority of the new to reinforce the hope it contains.[49] In this sense, what the apostle offers in Rom 7 is not really an apology for the law, although he does disentangle it from a simple identification with sin (7:7–12), finding a place for it within a wider divine purpose (7:13)[50]—the law, a good thing, served to reveal sin as sin. This hope, embodied in the person and work of Christ, is part and parcel of Paul's ethnographic purpose of constructing a positive identity for his audience; an identity that points simultaneously both to its traditional past and to the future fulfillment of the promises in its scriptural heritage.

As noted above, Paul's focus, thus far, has been on the fluid end of the identity spectrum, such that identification with the believing community is portrayed as living righteously before God apart from the written code. The community is not lawless, given members' identity as slaves of God/righteousness. At this juncture in his argument, the apostle takes up the kinship relationship of marriage in order to give substance to the achieved identity he has thus far constructed. The kinship discourse retains a subtle, civic cast given Paul's appeal to the law and its description of a married woman's legal status in relation to her husband (Num 5:20–29 LXX).[51] In this case, union with Christ's body results in death to or freedom from the law (Rom 7:4). In some Jewish traditions, the Torah is portrayed as God's daughter, Israel's bride (e.g., Sipre Deut. 345.2.2; Pesiq. Rab Kah. 12:11, 26:9).[52] Accordingly, Israel's identity as the people of God stems from its union with the law; a union that is portrayed in the most intimate terms. That is, the houses of Israel and God are joined via the kinship bond of marriage through the Torah. In Paul's rendition of the analogy, because believers

---

47. This, once again, raises the issue of Israel's place in the new aeon, an issue that has been lurking in the background through much of Paul's argument and one he will soon address. For now, his focus remains on driving home the point that not only is believers' freedom from the written law acceptable in both ethnographic and theological terms, but also, and more importantly, that the present people of God have something even better, something that was given to them according to God's plan and purposes.

48. Byrne, *Romans*, 209.

49. Byrne, *Romans*, 209.

50. Byrne, *Romans*, 209.

51. Witherington and Hyatt, *Paul's Letter to the Romans*, 175. Under Roman law, a woman could initiate divorce, while under Jewish law, it was the husband's prerogative (cf. Deut 24:1) (Byrne, *Romans*, 213).

52. Keener, *Romans*, 85.

are the widowed wives, who have died through Christ (6:2–11; 7:4) to their husband, the law, they are free to give themselves to Christ, without fear that the law will judge them as being adulterous persons (7:1–4).[53]

It is likely that the explanation of marriage given in Gen 2:24 underlies both versions of the metaphor. It is equally likely that behind the image of believers' marriage with Christ lies the OT motif of of Yahweh's marriage to Israel (Isa 54:5–6; 62:1–5; Jer 2.2 [cf. 3:1]; Ezek 16:8–14; Hos 2:16–20).[54] This image of the one flesh union of husband and wife provides an even more powerful impression than that of shared blood in giving substance to a people's identity as the slaves of God, in the past, via their conjugal union with the law, and, in the present, via their marriage to Christ. The passive verbal form, ἐθανατώθητε (v. 4), strongly suggests that believers' death to the law is the result of divine initiative,[55] underscoring Paul's point that the law was always meant to be provisional within the divinely ordained scheme of things. The marriage of believers to the one raised from the dead (v. 4) goes to the core of their transformed identity as slaves of God. The image of one flesh conveys the idea of marriage as involving the totality of the persons joined.[56] Accordingly, believers' conjugal relationship with Christ results in the bearing of offspring (καρποφορήσωμεν) to God, where these offspring are understood as acts of obedience (vv. 5–6).[57] It is this totality of union, involving the heart, mind, and body, with Christ which enables believers to be the slaves of God in a way that was never possible for his people in the past; a point, Paul will drive home in 7:7—8:13.

The reason why such radical obedience is possible (γὰρ) is because believers no longer live in the flesh, but in the new life of the Spirit (vv. 5–6). Thus, the conjugal relationship between Christ and believers results in the promised, eschatological circumcision of the hearts of God's people by the Spirit (Jer 31:31–34; Ezek 36:26–27; cf. Rom 2:29). Paul associates the past with life in the flesh and life under the law (v. 5), anticipating 7:7–25, which is contrasted with the present and associated with life in the Spirit (v. 6), anticipating 8:1–13. The phrase ἐν τῇ σαρκί is used in a negative sense, here, as designating human existence hostile to God as characteristic of the old

---

53. Paul's analogy is not perfect. However, it drives home the point that it is through their union with Christ that believers are free from the law. The same metaphor appears in 1 Cor 6:15–18, where, citing Gen 2:24, Paul uses it to illustrate the unacceptability of union with a prostitute (cf., 2 Cor 11:2). This relationship between bride (believers) and body (Christ) is spelled out explicitly in Eph 5:28–31 (Byrne, *Romans*, 214; Keener, *Romans*, 85–86). The reference to Christ's body, διὰ τοῦ σώματος τοῦ Χριστοῦ, need not be taken as referring to Jesus's physical body on the cross. The wider context suggests (especially, 6:12–13) that Paul has in mind the idea of Christ as a personal and communal sphere or domain of salvation into which believers have been brought. This sphere encompasses his life, death, and resurrection (Byrne, *Romans*, 211).

54. Byrne, *Romans*, 214.
55. Jewett, *Romans*, 433.
56. Jewett, *Romans*, 434–35.
57. Byrne, *Romans*, 211.

age initiated by Adam.⁵⁸ In this era, the law functioned as a tool of sin. The union between humanity and the law, whether in the form of the Jewish law or that present in the gentile conscience (2:12–16), bore death as its offspring (καρποφοπήσωμεν). This was the only result possible, because the only life possible was that in the flesh, as Paul has already argued in 1:18—3:19 and 5:12–14. The phrase τὰ παθήματα τῶν ἁμαρτιῶν is unclear. The genitive could be one of quality (sinful passions). However, the plural is awkward. It could also be understood as an objective genitive and translated as "sin-producing passions."⁵⁹ In either case, these passions are understood in a negative sense. Moreover, Paul does not seem to imply that the passions have their origin in the bodily parts, but rather that they are given expression by means of these parts or members.⁶⁰ Verse 6 states explicitly that believers' identity as the slaves of God is a present reality, since their union with Christ results in the new life of the Spirit. The phrase παλαιότητι γράμματος echoes 2 Cor 3:6, calling to mind Paul's reference to the old covenant in 2 Cor 3:14 and the old leaven in 1 Cor 5:7, which are defined by their opposition to the new revelation in Christ. In Romans, this reference harkens back to the theme of the old man that was crucified with Christ in 6:6.⁶¹ Thus, letter refers to the old covenant that came to an end with Christ and the giving of the Spirit.⁶² The law is old because it has been eclipsed by Christ and the Spirit, as foretold by the prophets.

In sum, God's people in the present, free from the law, which has come to an end, are, nevertheless, a legitimate people in a way both continuous with and discontinuous from God's people in the past. They, like God's historic people are his slaves, who walk in righteousness before him. Yet, unlike Israel in the past, they are no longer Yahweh's slaves under the old written law, but under the Spirit. In other words, the present people of God are a renewed and restored people, who have experienced the promised, eschatological circumcision of the heart through the life, death, and resurrection of Christ.

---

58. Byrne, *Romans*, 212. In Paul, σάρξ can refer to the realm of the physical and finite, carrying no negative connotation. It is also used by Paul to describe a lifestyle where humans turn to the realm of flesh and absolutize it, worshipping creatures, including serving themselves, and creation instead of the Creator. In other words, to live according to the flesh was to engage in idolatry, regardless of whether one served idols, one's own ego and desires, or both (Talbert, *Romans*, 172–73). However, this should not be taken to mean that "flesh," for Paul, simply denotes "sinful nature," as something with no connection to the physical body. Rather, according to Paul, a believer's way of thinking should not be dominated by the flesh (i.e., one's desires, which have a legitimate place, but not as ruling factors) but by the Spirit (8:5–9), which involves a renewed mind (12:2). This renewed mind guides believers in presenting their physical bodies and its members to God, in his service. In other words, for the apostle, "flesh" includes a bodily dimension in addition to its attitudinal and affective dimensions (Keener, *Romans*, 95–97).

59. Byrne, *Romans*, 215.
60. Jewett, *Romans*, 437.
61. Jewett, *Romans*, 439.
62. Witherington and Hyatt, *Paul's Letter to the Romans*, 177.

Thus, the law-faith dichotomy, similar to its role in Rom 1–5, serves to illustrate these lines of continuity and discontinuity between the past and the present. Although faith is not explicitly mentioned in the passages discussed above, it is implicit in that the renewal and restoration of God's people occurs via Christ and their trust in the God who has provided this present means of salvation. Moreover, this new people of God includes members of historic Israel, to whom the promise of restoration and renewal was first given—an important line of continuity that Paul will address in some detail in chapters 9–11. Thus, active faith or trust in God remains as the principal line of continuity between the past and present. However, since Paul's task in chapters 6–8 is to establish a positive identity for his audience as the children of God, he must necessarily address the issue of living righteously before God apart from the law. Thus, unlike in chapters 1–5, where election via the law functions primarily as a foil to election via trust or faith in the God who alone decides the mechanism of election, the law, in these chapters, functions as a foil to the Spirit. This is to be expected given the task at hand. In neither case does the apostle present the law as a reality diametrically opposed to faith in God/Christ. Rather, the importance of obedience to God, whether under the old written code or under the Spirit remains of prime importance. Thus, believers are exhorted to remain enslaved to God, since, as the apostle has already clearly stated, they will be repaid according to their deeds (2:6–11). For them, a life lived righteously before God, upon which the hope of salvation rests, is a real possibility because of the presence of the Spirit.

5.1.2 Origins and Identity: Foundation Narratives Revisited and Contrasted

As previously noted, foundation narratives or myths address the issues that are fundamental to a community's self-understanding in categories that are relevant to the group in question as it defines itself in relation to the tradition in which it is rooted and from which it diverges as an emerging entity. An excellent example of this is Virgil, who, in his effort to legitimate the Julio-Claudian line, provides Rome with a foundation account that ties the Roman people and the Empire to the Trojan legends (*Aen.* 1.1–7; 3.167; 7.207; Book 8), linking Rome to a glorious, Greek mythic past, including its pantheon and thereby, legitimating its place as the world power. Moreover, ancient Mediterranean people assessed themselves in terms of stereotypes derived primarily from family history.[63] Accordingly, virtuous persons were thought to descend from virtuous families (Plato, *Menex.* 237A), while those possessing the necessary attributes for ruling came from families whose seed contained "kinglike potentialities for government" (Philo, *Embassy* 54).

---

63. Talbert, *Romans*, 187.

Thus, an emerging community's account of origins is an integral part of its identity and it is for this reason that Paul recounts the foundation narratives at this juncture of his argument. As in chapters 4 and 5, Paul draws on Israel's/humanity's and the new movement's origins not only for the purpose of defining the lines of continuity and discontinuity between past and present, but, more importantly, for the purpose of underscoring the superiority of the present situation. In this instance, the point of comparison is between the law (past) and the Spirit (present). The retelling of the foundation narratives in these terms, thus, functions to underscore the major points made in Rom 6:1—7:6. By utilizing these myths, Paul goes to the heart of the believing community's self-understanding as the Spirit-wrought, children of God.

Recall that, Paul's primary ethnographic purpose is to present his audience with a positive identity in order that they may persevere in obedience to the gospel in the face of social hostility. Believers' identity as slaves of God/righteousness and, as such, a legitimate people under lawful rule, is given substance by their union with Christ's death and resurrection. The apostle describes this union in conjugal, kinship terms via the metaphor of believers' marriage to Christ. Moreover, the apostle has tied this identity, whose roots go back to OT tradition, to the coming of the promised Spirit. What remains to be shown is that all of this is according to divine purpose and plan, since the believing community's hope rests ultimately on the God who establishes, maintains, and renews his people according to his promises. Paul's appeal for hope reaches its oratorical climax in 8:18–30, wherein he ties the themes of creation and election to the hope of believers. The cumulative effect is to emphasize to his audience that the divine plan to bring humanity to glory through Christ is currently being accomplished among them and is proceeding inexorably to its divinely purposed goal.[64] This is the true state of affairs, despite circumstances and appearances to the contrary. By returning to the foundation narratives in Rom 7:7—8:13, Paul's sets the stage for this hope, highlighting the role of the Spirit in renewing and restoring God's people to righteousness and obedience as foretold in the Scriptures. These two narratives, the negative 7:7–25 and, especially, 7:14–25, and the positive, 8:1–13, which function like panels of a diptych, each illuminating the other by way of contrast,[65] prepare the way for both Paul's climactic statement regarding believers' identity in 8:15–17.

---

64. Byrne, *Romans*, 254–55.
65. Byrne, *Romans*, 213.

ESTABLISHING A POSITIVE IDENTITY

5.1.2.1 *The Law: Community Identity in the Past*

5.1.2.1A ADAM, ISRAEL, AND THE LAW (ROM 7:7–13)

Here, as in verses 14–25, Paul uses the I as a speech-in-character (*prosopopoeia*).[66] To whom the I refers remains a subject of debate.[67] When the ethnographic character of Romans is considered and, particularly, when this passage is understood as Paul's retelling of a foundation narrative applicable to both humanity, in general, and to Israel, more specifically, it becomes clear that the I most likely refers to both Adam and Israel. There are several reasons why this is probable. First, the verbs in this passage are all in the past tense, signaling a shift in chronological time. There are clues that this movement is back to humanity's and to Israel's primeval origins. This brings us to the second point.

Many interpreters have found echoes of Adam and Eve's experience in the garden as related in Genesis. For instance, verses 8 and 9 speak of the I as alive apart from the law, then of the commandment's coming, and, thirdly, of sin's using it as an opportunity to deceive and kill the I (Gen 2:7, 2:16, 3:1–5, 3:22–24; cf. Rom 7:11 and Gen 3:13).[68] In addition, the primeval couple's coveting of the fruit of the prohibited tree is seen by both Paul and his Jewish contemporaries as a form of violation of the tenth commandment of the Decalogue (Exod 20; Deut 6; cf. Gen 3:5–6, 3:22; Apoc. Mos. 19:3).[69] Although these parallels have some foundation, some have also found echoes of the experience of ancient Israel in this passage.[70] That is, before the foundation of the nation at Sinai and the giving of the Mosaic law, nascent Israel may have been sinful, but it was not conscious of transgression, as Paul has already argued (cf. 5:14). With the giving of the Mosaic law, trespasses multiplied (cf. 5:20).[71] The final commandment of the Decalogue is cited in abbreviated form (7:7e). All the objects of coveting cited in Exod 20:17 and Deut 5:21 (cf. Rom 13:9) are omitted. In this way, the commandment prohibits all illicit desires. In ancient thought, especially in Stoicism,

---

66. Stowers, *Rereading of Romans*, 16–17, 264–79. See also, Talbert, *Romans*, 186–87, and Witherington and Hyatt, *Paul's Letter to the Romans*, 179–87. Most modern scholars understand Rom 7:7–25 as speech-in-character, rather than strictly autobiographical. However, some see the "I" as denoting Paul's and, presumably, every Jew's, solidarity with Israel (Moo, *Epistle to the Romans*, 426–31). Although it is true that Paul did not shed his identity as a Jew upon entry into the believing community, his own, presumably autobiographical, claims regarding his experience of the law (Gal 1:13–14; Phil 3:6) appear to be at odds with the pessimistic description in Rom 7. Also, it is not clear how a person like Paul, born a Jew, could be once alive apart from the law (7:9).

67. Byrne, *Romans*, 217–18, and Witherington and Hyatt, *Paul's Letter to the Romans*, 187–88, present concise summaries of options regarding the identity of the "I." Jewett, *Romans*, 441–43 provides a summary of the history of scholarship on this point.

68. Talbert, *Romans*, 187. Paul uses the Genesis account elsewhere in his letters (2 Cor 11:3; cf. 1 Tim 2:14).

69. Talbert, *Romans*, 187–88.

70. Talbert, *Romans*, 187–88.

71. Talbert, *Romans*, 188.

desire was seen as the root of all evil (e.g., Apoc. Mos. 19:3; Apoc. Abr. 24:9; Philo, *Spec.* 4.84–94; *Decal.* 142, 150, 173; 4 Macc 2:4–6; cf. Jas 1:15).[72] Accordingly, what Paul seems to have in mind is the idea that God's prohibition awoke a latent human propensity to rebel against dependence upon God such that, the I came to know and feel the desire lying at the root of all acts of disobedience. That is, the I experienced the desire to possess whatever it wanted and to do whatever it wished, without regard for God. For Paul, this is to know sin (cf. Rom 3:20).[73] Both Adam and Israel are portrayed in the OT as guilty of this.

Finally, both the Adam narrative and the Sinai involve community origins and both have been the focus of Paul's argument, as discussed in the previous chapter of this work. Moreover, both are inextricably linked, in so far as, Israel provides the human, mundane entry point and context for the revelation of divine salvific action in human history; while humankind is in need of salvation due to Adam's transgression. In other words, for Paul, human history finds its locus and meaning in Israel's history, given its special role in God's plans and purposes for humanity as a whole.

Given that Paul mentions Adam in Rom 5 and no other biblical figure is introduced between that chapter and the section under consideration, it is also possible that only Adam is in view. Even if this is the case, Adam as the progenitor of humanity is the exemplar of human experience with God's law before the coming of Christ. This would include both Israel and its law and gentiles, who have the law written on their hearts (2:15). However, brief mention is also made of Moses (a key founder in Jewish tradition) in 5:14, which suggests that both the Adamic and the Mosaic covenant are in view. They are linked in the sense that by breaking the first, Adam brought sin and death into the world, while Israel provides the mundane entry point for God's rectifying of this situation. The first two covenants, both broken by human unfaithfulness, with both renditions of God's law powerless to change the sin condition, cannot and do not compare to the new covenant of Christ and the Spirit. As such, it represents God's final solution to the problem of human unfaithfulness, sin, and death.

As I have already pointed out, ancient ethnographers placed all of humanity within the historic framework of choice, either Greco-Roman or indigenous, in order to construct a world map that endorsed the superiority of the people group in question while encompassing all of the known world's ethnoracial groups. Accordingly, Rome is depicted as ruling every country that is not inaccessible or uninhabited, drawing to herself the neighboring nations (Dionysius, *Ant. rom.* 1.3–4). Similarly, by linking Adam's experience of the law with Israel's, Paul draws all of humanity, Jews included, under the rubric of sin's hijacking of God's holy, just, and good law for its own evil purposes (vv. 12–13). It is this experience that is common to both Jewish and gentile human families. Thus, Paul is not singling out Jews in a negative sense or for reasons that may be construed as being anti-Jewish. Rather, he recapitulates what

---

72. Byrne, *Romans*, 219, 222.

73. Byrne, *Romans*, 219, 222.

he has already said regarding Israel and its historic disobedience under the covenant. Moreover, the promise of restoration and renewal by the Spirit was first given to Israel, a point he will return to in chapters 9–11. Like the OT prophets before him, Paul's critique of Israel need not imply anti-Semitic tendencies on his part.

It is this history of origins that defines and identifies all persons who lived prior to Christ—a point that Paul has more than sufficiently already made. Moreover, by wrapping Israel's foundation account within the larger folds of the Adamic account, Paul is able to draw lines of continuity (the promise of circumcision of the heart by the Spirit) and discontinuity (the written code) between Judaism and the ethnically diverse new movement. The cumulative effect of this negative account of humanity's experience of the law is not only to underscore the holiness of the law and the unholiness of sin but, more importantly, to highlight the superiority of the human condition under the Spirit, addressed in the previous chapters.

5.1.2.1B Life Under the Law (Rom 7:14–25)

The switch to the present tense in this passage need not be understood as signaling that Paul now intends the I to refer to either himself, believers, or both. First, verses 14–25 continue the argument begun in verses 7–13, with no indication that the apostle has ceased using the technique of impersonation. Paul's aim is not to relate an account of his own experience but to convey the powerful sense of ethical and moral impossibility under the law. That the passage reflects some aspect of Christian life or struggle is untenable, since Paul has already said that believers have died to the law (7:4–5) and are no longer under the law (6:14).[74] Moreover, it is probable that Paul uses the present to further accentuate the rhetorical vividness of the speech-in-character.[75] Thus, both Adam and, plausibly, Israel remain in view. Second, the use of the present tense allows Paul to describe from the inside the enduring consequences of sin's hijacking of the law.[76] That is, it signals that what is being said is true of some group of persons who are in relationship with Adam and Israel.[77] That is, persons, both Jew and gentile, who are outside of Christ (in Adam) and, thus, under the rule of sin, death, and the law, as Paul has already argued.

In sum, the ancient technique of speech-in-character allows for an especially vivid retelling of the two related foundation narratives, with the gripping account of personal struggle in this passage driving home the inferiority of life under the law both in terms of ethical and moral impossibility (7:15–23a) and in terms of the present eschatological reality of the giving of the Spirit through God's work in and through

---

74. Witherington and Hyatt, *Paul's Letter to the Romans*, 193–94; Byrne, *Romans*, 225.
75. Keener, *Romans*, 93.
76. Byrne, *Romans*, 225.
77. Witherington and Hyatt, *Paul's Letter to the Romans*, 193. Witherington maintains that only Adam is in view.

Christ (7:24b–25). In addition to the Jewish law, Paul has already established that gentiles have a form of the law of God inscribed on their hearts to which their conscience attests (2:14–16). In essence, Paul takes a standard *topos* of the ancient world, the conflict between knowing what is the right thing to do and not having the capacity to do it, and applies it to a description of life under the law, both the Jewish law, more specifically, and the law of God, more generally.[78] In verses 18–21, the struggle between what the I wills to do and what it actually does is expressed without specific reference to the law, suggesting a broader perspective than that expressed in verses 15–17. This broadening of perspective continues into verses 21–23 where the term νόμος (vv. 21 and 23, 3x) is best translated as "ruling principle" in distinction from the law of God (v. 22). The reference to the law of God agrees with the observation that the apostle is speaking of all persons, Jew and gentile, outside of Christ, since the law of God can refer to either the Mosaic law, or the Torah, or to the law in a more general sense, as that written on gentile hearts.

Thus, while the first passage relates the history of origins that defines and identifies all persons who lived prior to Christ, the second depicts the continuing effects of this family history on those who live outside of Christ, both Jew and gentile alike. This is not to say that Paul is describing his own experience as a Pharisaic Jew with the law or that he is implying that nonbelieving Jews would agree with his assessment. Rather, he is describing a theological reality that has been revealed by God through Christ and the Spirit, that is, through the gospel. This would be the case even if Adam, and not Israel, is in view, since Adam is the progenitor of the entire human race and the exemplar of human experience with God's law, whatever its specific form, apart from the transformative power of the Spirit. As noted above, ancients identified themselves in terms of stereotypes derived primarily from family history. Paul simply draws on this practice. Accordingly, the two passages work in tandem whose cumulative effect is to portray all humanity outside of Christ as bearing a family resemblance to Adam and, as such, as a people whose identity is wrapped-up with sin, death, and the law.

At its core, their identity is constituted by the fact that they are enslaved to sin (7:14) and, as such, unable to be obedient to the law, even though they know that what the law demands is good (7:16b). This bondage is so thorough that Paul also refers to it as an indwelling power (7:17, 20, 23), in the sense that a slave must be obedient to his or her master, regardless of what he or she may think or know regarding that person and his or her demands. This is expressed in the three dilemmas that Paul presents in verses 15–17, 18–21, and 21–23, in which the I behaves in a way contrary to what it

---

78. Paul's expression in verse 19 and similar formulations in verses 15–16, 18, 20a, and 21, have close verbal parallels in Epictetus (*Discourses* 2.26.1-2, 4-5). However, for Epictetus the issue is misperception, which confuses the will about what is in its best interest. For Paul, the issue is captivity to sin, an issue found in other Jewish works (e.g., 1QH 1:21-23, 26-27; cf. 1QS 3:13—4:26; 4 Ezra 3:20-22; 4:30) (Byrne, *Romans*, 228, 231; Stowers, *Rereading of Romans*, 260-64). The *topos* is given classic expression by Ovid: "I see the better way and I approve it; but I follow the worse" (*Metam.* 7.19-21).

intends or knows is morally right.⁷⁹ This need not be understood as saying that the I is not responsible for its acts, in that it is a helpless pawn in sin's hand. Rather, Paul's point is that the I, apart from Christ and the Spirit, is incapable of maintaining a consistent pattern of obedience to God, a point the apostle has already made. Knowing God and knowing what he demands is not enough. Knowledge must translate into concrete actions and patterns of conduct that directly express the content of that knowledge. Thus, Paul excoriates humankind for its idolatry, behavior it engaged in, despite the fact that it knew God (1:19–23). In literary terms, the apostle's presentation of the I's dilemma is hyberbolic.⁸⁰ The flesh (σαρκί), verse 18, and the members (μέλλεσίν), verse 23, each term denoting the part of the self that relates to and engages in concrete action in the world, obeys the slave master, sin, rather than rational and willing part of the I, which knows what God desires.⁸¹ Consequently, another, related aspect of this identity is its fleshliness (σάρκινός) (7:14b), which is closely tied to the state of bondage (7:14b). In light of 7:5–6, σάρκινός denotes the basic human condition of creaturely hostility to its Creator, broadly expressed as idolatry, that results in the self asserting what it wants over what God wills.

Of note is that Paul uses the metaphor of slavery, rather than a kinship trope, to convey the fundamental identity of Adamic humanity. This is important, since, in antiquity, the state of enslavement and the corresponding effacement of one's past identity was seen as a reversible condition. Upon manumission, the former slave received an identity commensurate with that of his or her former master. As noted above, for believers, manumission results in an identity commensurate with divinely defined righteousness. This comports with Paul's basic premise that the gospel represents God's good news for all humanity, in the sense that, reception of it, stemming from faith in the God who has acted through and in Christ, results in a fundamental transformation of identity. Although the apostle speaks of believers' identity in terms of enslavement to God, which picks-up on this idea of transformation and is, in turn, given substance by the notion of believers' unity with Christ, his construction of believers' identity, as discussed below, ultimately rests on the foundation of their filial relationship with God. This is no small matter, since the Jewish people not only viewed themselves as the slaves of God, but more importantly, as his children.

Paul begins to shift his focus from the family history of Adamic humanity to that of humanity in Christ in verses 24–25.⁸² In light of these verses, it is possible

79. Byrne, *Romans*, 227–29.

80. Keener, *Romans*, 93.

81. The military language in verse 23 is significant, since the usual fate of prisoners of war in antiquity was to be sold into slavery (Byrne, *Romans*, 228).

82. At first glance, these two verses are difficult to reconcile, since the grounds for thanking God (vv. 24–25a) do not immediately follow. Rather, Paul reverts back to describing the futile situation experienced by Adamic humanity (v. 25b). This has led some to conclude that verse 25b represents a gloss. However, there is no textual warrant for this conclusion. More problematic is verse 25a, which appears with some variation in the textual tradition. However, whether Pauline or scribal, it is an

to view the I of 7:14–25 as representing a person with a guilty conscience, on the point of conversion.[83] However, if Paul is contrasting humanity's (Adam)/Israel's foundation account with that of the believing community, then it is more likely that these verses and the corresponding I of this passage work in tandem to illustrate what the apostle has been saying all along. Adamic humanity, Jew and gentile alike, finds release from enslavement to sin and moral and ethical impossibility through the means that God has provided—that is, through faith and trust in his work in and through Christ. Verse 25b rounds off Paul's account of humanity's (Adam)/Israel's foundational history and its continuing effects, with verses 24–25a functioning to drive home the point that this condition will persist until and unless the I hears and accepts the gospel. Put differently, verses 24–25 provide a segue to the apostle's retelling of what he presents as the superior foundation account (8:1–13) and its effects on the people it both constitutes and defines.

5.1.2.2 *The Spirit: Community Identity in the Present (Rom 8:1–13)*

Paul signals his shift to the eschatological present with the chronological marker, νῦν, and his movement to a new, alternative foundation account by linking its divinely instituted founder (8:3), Christ, to those who are in him (8:1). With this powerful opening statement, which emphasizes the believers' freedom from divine condemnation (κατάκριμα), he sets the stage for the presentation of their identity in terms that starkly contrast with that of Adamic humanity, such that, its superiority in regard to its ability to constitute and define a people righteous before God is emphasized. In one sense, this passage brings to a close the apostle's defense of the necessity and possibility of living as a righteous (i.e., lawful) community before God that he began in 6:1.[84] In another sense, presenting it as the superior alternative to the previously narrated foundation account, allows Paul to also speak in terms of family history, which reaches its fullest expression in 8:14–17, bringing his historical account of the believing community, including its identity, to a climax.

Once again, Paul reiterates that believers' identity is rooted in God and his work in and through Christ, so as to condemn (κατέκρινεν) sin in the flesh, making it possible for them to live in conformity to God's will. The phrase, ἵνα τὸ δικαίωμα τοῦ νόμου, neither refers to the law in its entirety nor to any particular commandment but to what the law, in its totality required of God's people; that is, living righteously before him. The passive πληρωθῇ highlights the fact that this fulfillment is impossible

---

interjection that does not negate the overall Adamic thrust of the passage (Byrne, *Romans*, 223). See, Jewett, *Romans*, 455–58, for discussion of the textual history and the associated question of interpolation.

83. E.g., Witherington and Hyatt, *Paul's Letter to the Romans*, 198.

84. Similarly, Byrne, *Romans*, 235.

apart from the Spirit.⁸⁵ Thus, there is no condemnation for those who are in Christ (cf. 1:18–19; 5:16, 18) because God condemned the slave master, freeing those in bondage to it. God's condemnation of sin through his Son provides the entry point to the transformation of identity which occurs at manumission. It is by virtue of believers' existence in the founder of this new, transformed community that they take on the characteristics of their family of origin. Paul sets the primary characteristic of this new identity in contrast to the σάρκινός identity of those enslaved to sin. The fact that believers walk according to the Spirit (8:4) means not only that they are divinely enabled to live righteously before God, but also that their minds are renewed in a transformative way that allows for ethical and moral possibility (cf. Rom 12:1–2). The basic human condition of being σάρκινός means that the mind, although cognizant of God's law and its requirements, nevertheless habitually capitulates to the desires of the flesh due to enslavement to sin. In this sense, the σάρκινός person has a mind set on the things of the flesh (8:5a) and acts accordingly.

Here, Paul is using the language of ideal types; that is, he is using binary terms standard in his culture. For example, both Jewish wisdom and Stoic philosophers divided humanity into the wise and the foolish and, in the case of Jewish writers, into the righteous and the wicked. Yet, Jewish writers recognized that most or all people sinned and philosophers understood the truly wise person as an ideal.⁸⁶ Similarly, Paul uses the binary categories: those governed by the flesh and those governed by the Spirit. He is concerned with delineating two general patterns of conduct that conform to two states of existence. The question of whether persons without the Spirit can ever do good is not in view here. Moreover, Paul has already made clear that the possibility of once again becoming enthralled to sin remains for believers. Hostility to God is the defining characteristic of those who are σάρκινός, since these persons are incapable of submitting to his law (8:7).

By way of contrast, those who walk according to the Spirit have minds set on the things of the Spirit (8:5b). Release from slavery from sin results in a new mind that is not only free from bondage to sin, but able to discern the ways of the Spirit, who knows God's will (8:27), making it possible for believers to act according to the Spirit's guidance. Thus, believers are enabled to fulfill the righteous requirements of God's law in a way that was never possible for his people before. In the past, this possibility remained part and parcel of Israel's future hope of restoration and renewal. Paul's reference to God doing what the law was unable to do in that it was weakened because of sin dwelling in the flesh evokes the OT promise of when the law would be inscribed on the hearts of God's people by God himself (Jer 31:33; Ezek 36:27). As the apostle points out, the root problem had been sin dwelling in the I (7:14–25). The new situation, despite the fact that living in the flesh remains a possibility, is characterized by the replacement of sin by the Spirit, which Paul refers to both as the Spirit of God (v.

85. Byrne, *Romans*, 237.
86. Keener, *Romans*, 98.

9b, 11a) and the Spirit of Christ (v. 9c); thus, linking the OT motif of the Spirit of God directly to the person and work of Jesus.[87] The repeated references to the indwelling of sin (7:17, 19; cf. vv. 18 and 23) are matched by three allusions to the indwelling of the Spirit (vv. 9b, 9c, and 11a). Verse 10a simply states, if Christ is in you, and suggests an inextricable link between Christ and the Spirit.[88]

The link between the present situation and the promises given to Israel in the past is further sharpened by setting the two ways of living in terms of their eschatological outcome, death or life, with the latter denoted in the traditional language of life and peace, ζωὴ and εἰρήνη (v. 6).[89] As in the OT, what makes one of these two outcomes inevitable is the type of relationship to God at work in each of the contrasting mind-sets (vv. 7–8). It is the righteous, defined as those who have the Spirit of Christ and belong to him, who will experience eschatological salvation, including resurrection of the mortal body (vv. 10–11). Thus, according to Paul, tracing one's origins to the founder of the believing community opens the door to the possibility of eternal life, as long as one continues to live according to the Spirit (vv. 12–13), which itself is a condition of living that is made possible only in and through Christ. In these concluding verses, the apostle offers his audience a stark choice between death and life reminiscent of the exhortation in Deut 30:15, 19, with the concluding promise, you will live, echoing Hab 2:4, quoted in the thematic statement (1:17).[90] It is by faith that God's people, both past and present, receive the gift of eternal life.

In sum, in terms of the apostle's larger ethnographic purpose of establishing the historical legitimacy of the Christ movement, Rom 6:1—8:13 serves a dual purpose. First, by establishing precisely how the requirement of the law can be fulfilled in believers, Paul strengthens the link between past and present while simultaneously redefining the former in light of the latter. The righteousness that Israel could not manifest by obedience to the law in response to God's gift of election is now made possible in Christ, by the Spirit. In this way, the apostle rounds out his discussion of faith. Faith, in the present, as in the past, refers to both belief in God and, in this case, specifically, to belief in the gospel. This faith is manifested in a particular disposition of character, in this case made possible by the Spirit, who works within believers, so that the righteous requirement of the law might be fulfilled in them (8:4). In the present context, δικαίωμα is best translated as "commandment" or "requirement." By using the singular, Paul focuses attention on the essence of what the law required; a righteous life.[91] The use of the passive, πληρωθῇ, underscores the idea that righteous behavior is dependent both on divine initiative and empowerment and on a deliberate choice on the believer's part to conduct him or herself in the world in a way that

---

87. Byrne, *Romans*, 239–40.
88. Byrne, *Romans*, 239–40.
89. Byrne, *Romans*, 239.
90. Byrne, *Romans*, 241.
91. Byrne, *Romans*, 243–44.

pleases God.⁹² Although Paul never uses the term "covenant," it is implied in the sense that, the old covenant with its law is part of the old age. The new age has its own, distinct covenant characterized by the giving of the Spirit in and through Christ, such that the requirements of the law are fulfilled in believers apart from the written code. Although proper relationship to God continues to be understood in terms of walking righteously before him, the degree of obedience possible and, thus, expected, and the form that moral guidance takes in the new age is both quantitatively and qualitatively different. The stark contrast that Paul draws between the law and the Spirit attests to a radically new situation that, although it springs from the old, surpasses it, in the sense that, it fulfills the promises given to Israel in the past.

As we will see, with this discussion of the empowerment of believers to walk righteously before God, Paul lays the groundwork for the more specific ethic and the Spirit-wrought allocentric identity, that makes such an ethic possible, that he will develop beginning in Rom 12:1. This redefinition of the law in terms of both Christ and the Spirit not only provides the necessary theological framework for Paul's reconceptualized ethic, but also serves a second purpose, providing a segue to the apostle's discussion of the role of the Spirit in divine filiation, bringing the theme of election to a climax.

5.1.3 Spirit and Identity: The Children of God in the Eschatological Present (Rom 8:14–17)

Verse 14 is closely tied to verses 12–13, suggesting that the title, υἱοὶ Θεοῦ, and the privilege and status that accompanies it, is inseparable from both behavior and conduct in the present world and, in turn, with eternal life in the future. The γὰρ in both verse 14 and verse 15 substantiates Paul's statement in verse 12 that believers are no longer debtors to the flesh, both because they are led by the Spirit (v. 13) and because they are sons (and daughters) of God (v. 14).⁹³ This is in keeping with ancient notions of identity, whereby Israel's identity is viewed as not only bound-up with its designation as the people of God, but also that, as such, it mirrors divine righteousness in the laws, customs, and manner of its life in the world. Thus, according to Josephus, since the law is "engraved" on the "souls" of the Jewish people, in its original form, they are uniquely identified as the people who live under a theocratic constitution that cannot be improved in any way (*Ag. Ap.* 178; 183–85). Moreover,

---

92. Byrne makes a similar point (Byrne, *Romans*, 244).

93. In the Greco-Roman context, sons were usually adopted for the purpose of supplying an heir. Daughters were rarely adopted in ancient Greece. In the Roman period, daughters could inherit in the absence of a son, but they were rarely adopted for the purpose of inheritance. Paul chooses the gender-specific practice of adopting sons in order to communicate the full potential inherent in being joined with Christ (Hodge, *If Sons, Then Heirs*, 69). Thus, his choice of words does not signify that he intended to exclude women from this special status. Moreover, Paul uses the more gender-neutral "children of God" in two instances, 8:16 and 8:17.

their law and customs are not only ancient (*Ag. Ap.* 2.151–54) but also have a divine source (*Ant.* 3.89–90; 93–94).

For Paul, it is the Spirit that both enables righteous living and establishes the kinship tie that gives believers a singularly exclusive and intimate relationship with God, extending divine filiation to include both Jews and gentiles. In other words, by applying the OT image of Israel as God's child to the new community, Paul redefines election in terms of the Spirit and faith in God's work in and through Christ.[94] Thus, the law-faith dichotomy is implicitly at work here as the apostle crafts a favorable in-group bias of righteousness and divine filiation by the Spirit, in contrast to that by the law, as the fulfillment of traditional promises given to Israel. The OT promise of a righteous people/child of God is seen as fulfilled in the believing community both in terms of its conduct, the ability to walk righteously before God, and in terms of ancestral descent, by which they bear a family resemblance to the righteous and holy God.

The metaphor of the household, within which this Spirit-wrought kinship tie is enfolded, captures the dramatic change in status which accompanies believers' reception of the Spirit. The head of the household usually held the most authority, whereas slaves held the least, with sons, including adopted sons, standing to inherit.[95] In 8:15, Paul uses the term, υἱοθεσίας, which is a technical term for adopting a son in the Greco-Roman world.[96] In addition, it is likely that behind the literal, contemporary understanding of this term there stands the broad Jewish tradition of Israel, especially eschatological Israel, as son/child of God. This is suggested by Paul's listing of υἱοθεσίας as one of the privileges of Israel in 9:4.[97] In essence, members of the believing community are heirs of the filial privileges pertaining to eschatological Israel by virtue of the fact that they are co-heirs (συγκληρονόμοι) with Christ. That is, as the adopted children (τέκνα) of God, believers stand with Christ, the son of God and primary heir, to inherit the eschatological blessing of life, including eternal life, and the future world.[98] This dramatic change in status is underscored by Paul's reference to the spirit of slavery in verse 15. In one sense, the phrase functions as a reminder of humanity's pre-Christ condition as enslaved to sin. It is precisely the unlikelihood of

---

94. Paul will emphasize God's prerogative in defining the elect in Rom 9–11, especially chapter 9.

95. Hodge, *If Sons, Then Heirs*, 31, 69. Adopted sons shared the same rights and responsibilities as sons born into the family. In Judaism, although there is no law that explicitly addresses adoption, or any text that describes a ceremony of adoption, there is evidence that it was known among Jews. For example, Philo and Josephus recognize adoptions in the sacred text and in political events (Philo, *Moses*, 1.19; Josephus, *Ant.*, 2.232).

96. Hodge, *If Sons, Then Heirs*, 69.

97. Byrne, *Romans*, 250, 252.

98. Within the Jewish tradition, the motif of inheritance occurs frequently in conjunction with the promise God made to Abraham concerning possession of the land. In the later tradition, the land promise was broadened to include the present and future world, embracing the whole complex of eschatological blessings given to Israel (Byrne, *Romans*, 251). This agrees with what Paul says in Rom 4, especially vv. 13, 17, and 24.

slaves becoming heirs that is the point.⁹⁹ In another sense, the phrase functions as a foil to the Spirit of adoption, underscoring the fact that believers' present condition is incomparably better than their former existence. That is, their new status as sons of God by the Spirit is accompanied by the direct and vivid experience of a unique and intimate relationship with God, expressed in the cry "Abba, Father" (v. 15)—a cry of confidence (v. 16) that stands in direct contrast to the fear that more often than not accompanies the condition of being enslaved to another. Put differently, in legal terms, the adoption transaction is made official by the Spirit, who witnesses (συμμαρτυρεῖ) (8:16) believers' new status as children of God.[100] This witness confirms within believers that they are indeed under the protection and care of a divine father, presumably, and especially, when the sense of belonging is threatened by external circumstances that seem to indicate otherwise, as the reference to suffering with Christ (8:17) and the ensuing epideictic oration (8:18–30) suggest.

Thus, Paul rounds out the positive image of believers as slaves of God, enslaved to righteousness, grounding that identity in their foundational identity as children/sons of God. The two, seemingly dichotomous, images function in tandem to describe the rich relationship between God and his people, each bringing out a particular facet of it. Recall that in the OT, the notion of Israel as the servant/slave of God bestowed special privilege upon it and the individuals who bore the title. Moreover, in the scriptural tradition, the Jewish people not only viewed themselves as the slaves of God, but more importantly, as his children. Although it is true that God is not often referred to as father in the OT, nor invoked in prayer as father, there are filial references in both Deuteronomy and the late prophetic texts. Moreover, Paul explicitly states that adoption, that is, divine sonship, υἱοθεσία, belongs to the Israelites (Rom 9:4). This suggests that the scarcity of references does not necessarily mean that the filial relationship between Israel and God was unimportant in terms of shaping its identity as the people of God. For example, in Deut 32, God is described as a father who elects, founds, establishes, and sustains his children, Israel (32:5, 6–7, 19–20, 43), who are also referred to as his slaves (32:36). This is coupled with the particularizing effect of formulating the fatherhood of God in terms of God's choosing of Israel from among the nations (32:8–9).[101] The fact that this filial portrait is put in a context of a testimony, witness, and instruction that is to be recited, memorialized, and lived out within and by the community (32:45–47) underscores its function in shaping Israel's self-understanding in relation to God.[102] Even more importantly, this feature of Israel's identity is foundational.

---

99. Hodge, *If Sons, Then Heirs*, 69. I do not agree with the author that this adoption applies only to gentile believers.

100. Hodge, *If Sons, Then Heirs*, 72.

101. Mengestu, *God as Father in Paul*, 105. The same emphasis is found in the prophetic depictions of God as father (Isa 63:16 [twice]; 64:9; Jer 3:4–5, 19; 31:9; Mal 1:6; 2:10).

102. Mengestu, *God as Father in Paul*, 105.

That is, in the prophetic tradition, God's fatherhood, not his covenantal faithfulness, is presented as the basis for the request for forgiveness, rescue, and restoration (e.g., Isa 63:7—64:12). In Isa 63:7—64:12, God is identified as Israel's savior (63:8) and redeemer (68:9), while Israel is identified as his people and children (63:8, 14, 18; 64:9). More importantly, in 63:16, God's relationship to Israel as father is presented as the basis for the peoples' request that he return to them (63:15-19). Similarly, in Isa 64:8-9 the fatherhood of God is presented as the basis for the appeal that he forgive his people and rescue them. In essence, Isaiah appeals to the relationship God has with Israel as Father in creating them, loving what he has made as both head of the family and as the potter.[103] A similar theme is found in Jer 2:1—4:4 and Mal 1:2-6; 2:10-15, where both appeals for mercy, restoration, and deliverance and exhortations to honor God and fellow Israelites are grounded in God's relationship to Israel as father.[104] At the center of all of the pleas discussed above lies formative discourse that portrays the creation of Israel through the fatherhood of God; that is, the appeals focus on a familial relationship that existed prior to Israel entering into a covenant relationship with Yahweh (cf. Exod 4:22).[105] Thus, the plea for restoration is essentially a request for the restoration of the father-son relationship. The privilege is depicted among other things in terms of inheritance, protection, and hope of rescue, while the responsibility, generally speaking, is depicted in terms of Israel remaining faithful to Yahweh.[106] That the familial relationship is prior to the covenantal is indicated by the fact that that these pleas occur in the context of Israel's failure to keep the covenant.[107]

Similarly, for Paul, this filial relationship is not only the basis for the formation of a new people (election) but also functions as the underlying narrative that creates and legitimates their customs and manner of life as a distinct people group or community. In other words, the ascribed pole of the apostle's kinship discourse is given substance by the fact that it is grounded in formative discourse that appeals to shared blood via filial kinship ties. However, for the apostle, the key element which distinguishes the present family of God from that of the past is the bestowal of the promised Spirit upon believers via their affiliation with Christ. By harnessing the traditional formative discourse of Israel's divine filiation and applying it to the believing community within the context of the eschatological present, Paul accomplishes two things. First, by appropriating a self-identity and an understanding of election that reaches back, before the covenant and the law, Paul tightens the link between the past and the present, drawing a line of continuity between the believing community and its Jewish roots. This is in keeping with his argument concerning the provisional nature of the written law. Second, by applying this self-understanding within the context of an unfolding

---

103. Mengestu, *God as Father in Paul*, 106–7.
104. Mengestu, *God as Father in Paul*, 108–11.
105. Mengestu, *God as Father in Paul*, 112, 114.
106. Mengestu, *God as Father in Paul*, 112, 114.
107. Mengestu, *God as Father in Paul*, 112.

eschatological present defined by the Spirit's construction of divine-human kinship, Paul pushes past the particularizing effect of the traditional understanding of the family of Israel, expanding its boundaries so as to include all members of humanity who respond in trust to God's good news. This is in keeping with the traditional narrative framework, and respective sub-narratives, within which he constructs a legitimate history for the believing community.

Thus, the casting of believers' identity in terms of divine filiation is climactic in two other important respects. First, it creates a new unity among ethnoracially diverse people groups. Viewed in terms of the traditional, Jewish binary categories, Jews and gentiles are now ἀδελφοί (8:12), members of the same household, whose head is God. They are children of God, who are also either Jewish or gentile. As noted above, reception or possession of the Spirit marks the change into sons (daughters) and siblings, which is in keeping with prophetic texts which associate the giving of the Spirit with the restoration and renewal of God's wayward people; texts which also employ kinship language (e.g., Ezek 36:26–28). Moreover, in both Ezek 36:27 and Rom 8:4, those who receive the Spirit are enabled to keep God's law;[108] consequently, they bear a family resemblance to the righteous and holy God.

This reflects a conception of spirit as generative, a notion also found in descriptions of *pneuma* in Greco-Roman philosophical and medical texts. For instance, according to the Stoic theory of *krasis*, or blending, the permeation of beings by spirit effects a change in them, such that every part of the original body, while maintaining its own character, nevertheless participates fully in the mixture.[109] Philo exhibits a similar understanding of *pneuma* in his description of Abraham: "the divine spirit which was breathed upon him from on high made its lodging in his soul, and invested his body with singular beauty, his voice with persuasiveness, and his hearers with understanding" (*Virtues* 217).[110] Paul appears to draw on this contemporary understanding of *pneuma* in his representation of the Spirit as a binding agent who unites ethnoracially diverse believers as brothers and sisters by establishing kinship ties between them and the divine, both Christ and God the Father. Thus, the Spirit creates new kinship and does so materially, serving as a version of shared blood.[111] That is, for Paul, the divine-human kinship ties wrought by the Spirit are transformative in the sense that they both create a new, unified family of transformed persons without collapsing individual identity and ethnoracial diversity and that this divinely constituted family is no less real, tangible, and organic than its biological counterparts. Rather, although humanly constructed categories of persons,

---

108. Hodge, *If Sons, Then Heirs*, 72–73.

109. Hodge, *If Sons, Then Heirs*, 72–73.

110. Cited in Hodge, *If Sons, Then Heirs*, 75.

111. Hodge, *If Sons, Then Heirs*, 75–76. This suggests that an oppositional understanding of "physical" versus "spiritual" kinship, as it appears in Pauline scholarship, is a modern assumption based on a limited understanding of ancient conceptions of both *pneuma* and kinship.

regardless of how narrowly (family unit) or broadly (ethnoracial group) these are conceived, continue to exist within the unfolding eschatological present, the relationships and modes of existence which characterize them are circumscribed and reconfigured by the Spirit-wrought kinship ties that define the divine-human family.[112] Thus, this transformation occurs at both the individual and the group level, identifying all believers as members of a new community that is distinct from all other humanly constructed categories of persons.

Second, what emerges from this divinely constituted and reconfigured family is a new set of boundaries that essentially operates to divide humanity into three categories, in distinction from the traditional binary classification of Jew and gentile. These are: Jewish and gentile believers; gentile unbelievers; and Jewish unbelievers. Although Paul has not yet directly addressed the topic of majority Jewish unbelief, the historical and eschatological frame of reference within which he operates, based as it is on the traditional sacred texts, points to a view of the world that sees unbelieving Jews as standing apart both from believing Jews (and believing gentiles) and unbelieving gentiles. Moreover, the apostle's construction of a favorable in-group bias that defines self-identity in terms of divine filiation via the Spirit rather than the law, has raised the issue of Israel's past, present, and future identity as the children of God. That is, in the present, it is the Spirit who changes persons, both Jew and gentile, into sons and daughters of God, who, in addition and according to scriptural promise, bear a family resemblance in terms of conduct and behavior to their righteous and holy Father, apart from the written precepts of the law.

Thus, I do not agree with Hodge that the adoption of gentiles incorporates a new people into an already existing kin group. Although she is right to point out that Paul does not believe that gentile sons of God replace their Jewish counterparts, but share the inheritance with them, he is equally adamant that unbelieving Jews are presently branches that have been broken off (9:17–23).[113] In other words, the structure of the original family of God has been disrupted and reconfigured in the eschatological present. According to Paul, the outpouring of the Spirit through Christ creates a new family of God, which, although it contains members from the original, divinely constituted kinship group, is different in that these Jewish members possess the promised Spirit and have been transformed. This is what distinguishes them both from unbelieving Jews and unites them with believing gentiles. This is discussed in greater detail in the sections that follows. Furthermore, those who were never conceived as being members of God's people are now included, while those bearing historic membership in God's family are presently excluded. This latter group, from which the Messiah

---

112. How diversity in divine-human-family unity is achieved, maintained, and concretely manifested in and by the believing community is explored in the following chapter of this work, which deals with Paul's conception of a Spirit-wrought allocentric identity and its accompanying ethic, as it is presented in Rom 12–15.

113. Hodge, *If Sons, Then Heirs*, 76–77.

springs (1:2; 9:5) and to whom belong the adoption and the promises (9:4) stands in a unique position at the border between past and present—a distinct, divinely constituted people group whose liminal status Paul now addresses.

5.2 Identity and Out-group Comparison: The Place of Israel in the Eschatological Present (Rom 9–11)

As noted above, in-group identity is primarily about the ascription of positive characteristics to the group and not about disdain for or unfavorable representations of the other. However, since the establishment of a favorable in-group bias involves an inherently evaluative process, it is seldom sympathetic and often carries the potential for social tension and antagonism between the groups involved in the comparison. The often unintended result of this ordinary, adaptive, and functional psychological process is a conceptualization of the other as in some way inferior.[114] More specifically, this means that Paul's construction of Christ movement identity entails the inherit risk that the believing community would view itself as in some sense completely replacing or superseding historic, ethnic Israel as the people of God.[115] It is also possible that gentiles, especially, might come to think too highly of themselves, particularly if they were to view their believing Jewish counterparts as too closely connected to their unbelieving ethnoracial counterparts. This would be a pressing issue in cases where Jewish believers sought to maintain ethnoracial cohesiveness by practicing those aspects of the law which they deemed salient for defining and maintaining Jewish ethnic identity within the greater believing community.[116] Thus, by clarifying Israel's place in the new world order, Paul, in turn, clarifies the believing community's self-identity in this same new age.

According to Paul, the promises given to Israel by its God find their confirmation and fulfillment in God's work in and through Christ, suggesting that God's purposes for the nation find their expression in Christ, the promised Messiah, and those who belong to him by virtue of their faith or trust in God's work in and through him. Indeed, Paul's argument thus far appears to lead to the unavoidable conclusion that unbelieving Israel is a slave to sin, rather than to God and, as such, subject to God's wrath and, thus, no longer his children. Thus, even though the apostle has been careful to maintain the continuing saliency of the law in providing viable inter-subjective criteria for defining Jewish ethnicity, his effort to establish a line of continuity between God's people in the past and present via faith and a line of discontinuity via the law,

---

114. Kuecker, *Spirit and the 'Other,'* 30.

115. That Rom 9–11 forms a distinct unit within Paul's letter and that these chapters are related to his purpose in writing are not disputed. However, the question of whether and to what extent Paul maintains a place for Israel as a distinct ethnic entity and as the chosen people of God, apart from the Christ movement and the new people of God, remains a point of contention.

116. Paul addresses this very issue in Rom 14:1—15:13, which is examined in chapter 6 of this work.

could easily be misinterpreted. For instance, it could be wrongly interpreted as creating both a historical Israel, defined in terms of Jewish ethnoracial kinship and descent, and a new or spiritual Israel, one composed of Christ-believers of diverse ethnicities, with the latter having preeminence over the former.

However, as discussed below, this dichotomy is the result of a failure both to recognize the mechanisms involved in constructing kinship and lines of descent in antiquity and to carefully consider Paul's utilization of ethnic discourse in constructing a third category of humanity, unbelieving Israel, that has both temporal and hierarchical priority over the other two categories. As I will demonstrate, Paul's use of aggregative and oppositional strategies allows him to maintain the existence of one, historic Israel over time, grounding its continuity from the past, up and into the future in the electing work of a righteous God whose promises to and plans for his people stand firm.

5.2.1 Election and Identity: The God Who Levels All Human Evaluative Processes

5.2.1.1 Children of the Flesh and Children of the Promise: Divine Reckoning of Lines of Descent (Rom 9:1–29)

Here, as in chapters 2–4, Paul challenges the traditional Jewish understanding of election, in this case, by virtue of biological descent from Israel's patriarchs. As in the former case, the apostle places the emphasis on God who initiates, defines and maintains election according to his will. More specifically, even in the case of ascribed kinship, which gives substance and continuity to not only Jewish ethnoracial identity in general but also, more particularly, to Jewish identity as the elect, it is God who determined which of the biological descendants of Israel's primary patriarchs would provide the seed from which this elect people would descend. Paul's point is that all human evaluative processes, whether done in terms of ascribed or achieved kinship, are rendered moot in defining who the people of God are, since it is God alone who determines this. In other words, any human claims based on superiority via elect status whether based on Jewish biological descent or on gentile inclusion in the new age of the Spirit are leveled. Moreover, as Paul will demonstrate, any claim to superiority that Israel can rightfully make in terms of priority exists only by divine fiat. All is from God and depends on him and, as such, speaks to his unsearchable and inscrutable ways and his profound wisdom and knowledge (11:33–36).

The apostle accomplishes this task in a seemingly roundabout way. However, in actuality, and as discussed in the following sections, the seemingly circuitous route he chooses, allows him to construct the categories necessary for understanding Israel's temporary liminal status. In sum, he begins by reiterating the theme of God's sovereignty in relation to election and his freedom in establishing an eschatological people that is ethnoracially inclusive. According to Paul, this has always been the case, both in the past in relation to Israel (9:1–18) and in the present (9:19–29) in relation to the nations of the world. As in the previous chapters, in Rom 9–11, the apostle makes recourse to Scripture in order to draw a line of continuity between past and present. As before, continuity is grounded in a God who has already revealed his intentions and purposes for humankind in Israel's sacred texts. This God acts according to both the promises he made to Israel *and* to his eschatological plans for humanity as revealed by the prophets.

Paul then (9:30—10:21) turns to majority Israel's rejection of the gospel. By noting Israel's continuing, present zeal for God and its sustained pursuit of righteousness, unenlightened and misplaced as these attempts may be, he subtly, yet effectively, deflects in-group evaluation of the other as religiously and morally inferior. In addition, by couching Israel's disobedience to the gospel in a long scriptural argument, the apostle hints at and prepares the way for the culminating argument he will make regarding Israel's rejection of the gospel as according to divine plan and purpose, for the benefit of the world.

Having laid the groundwork for a more favorable, or, at least, a more neutral conception of the other, Paul finally makes explicit (11:1–32) Israel's favored status in terms of its continuing role in God's plans and purpose, its place in the eschatological age, and its divinely given hierarchical and temporal priority in relation to the nations. In this final tour de force he establishes that Israel's rejection of the gospel is temporary both in the sense that God has provided a remnant of faithful, believing Jews in the present and that all of Israel will be saved in the future. Thus, the Jewish other is not only the predecessor of the present believing community (11:17–18), this people also plays an integral, divinely mandated role in the process of the inclusion of gentiles within it.

5.2.1.1A In the Past (Rom 9:1–18)

In this section, Paul utilizes oppositional and aggregative discourse in a complex, creative way in order to drive home the point that human reckoning of lines of descent is trumped by divine choice. He begins with an acknowledgment of Israel's privileges as the chosen people of God (9:4–5). Thus, their hierarchical priority stems from God who has bestowed upon this specific ethnoracial group divine sonship (υἱοθεσία), the glory, the covenants, the giving of the law, and the worship and service of God. That these privileges continue, in some form and fashion, into the present is suggested by the fact that Israel was the first to receive the promises, which, Paul has argued, find their confirmation in Christ; that the patriarchs, from whom the believing community also descends, are Israelites; and that Jesus, the Messiah, the founder of the new community, also claims biological descent (κατὰ σάρκα) from this people group. Thus, right from the beginning, Paul establishes the hierarchical and temporal priority of Israel. Throughout the argument spanning chapters 9–11, this priority is held in tension with the apostle's vision of the believing community, as the eschatological people of God, as representative of a renewed and restored Israel within which gentiles, as gentiles, are also included; a vision, he will argue is grounded in and joined to scriptural tradition.

With respect to Israel's priority, it is also noteworthy that Paul, throughout this section and also throughout chapters 10–11, casts the traditional binary categories of Jews and gentiles in terms of Israel and the gentiles.[117] The self-designation Israel was especially employed in the period before the exile, with the designation Jews becoming more prominent thereafter. Accordingly, when the apostle evokes this specific title in relation to his kin according to the flesh (vv. 3–4), he evokes the traditional name given to Jacob by Yahweh (Gen 32:29), suggesting Israel's continuing validity as the people of God[118]—a point he will argue, extensively. Moreover, during Paul's time, Israel was the preferred self-designation among the Jewish people, with Jew/Jews being used mainly by outsiders.[119] By evoking this insider term, with all of its connotations of privilege, special status, and divine blessing, the apostle subtly reinforces Israel's priority in relation to the nations. In addition, by drawing upon this designation, he draws together believing Jews and their unbelieving ethnoracial counterparts into one, historic people group; thus, providing an important line of continuity between God's people in the past and those in the present, a line he delineates more clearly as his argument progresses. As we will see, for Paul, Israel is composed of both unbelieving and believing Jews, all of whom can trace their ancestry to Abraham and Jacob.[120]

Paul's reference to Israelites as my kin according to the flesh (v. 3), focuses on ascribed kinship and implicitly calls to mind the traditional binary categories of Jew-gentile. Taken in combination with the privileges listed in the verses immediately following, and the apostle's argument thus far, verses 3–5 suggest that these evaluative categories have validity in so far as they define a specific people group through whom God has chosen to implement his salvific plans for humankind. However, in verse 6, Paul quickly qualifies the importance of natural or biological descent in defining the people of God. On the surface, this verse appears to contradict what he has said regarding Israelite identity as ascribed. However, Paul's point is that the divine reckoning of elect status trumps all human reckoning of lines of descent. That this is so is evident right from the beginning of Israel's history as a people. What matters and has always mattered in the divine economy of things is the category of kinship according

---

117. This designation occurs twelve times in chapters 9–11.

118. Jewett, *Romans*, 561–62. E.g., Josephus uses the term "Israelite" 188 times in the early portion of the *Antiquities* down to the period of the Maccabees, and thereafter he uses "Jews" in reference to more contemporary history.

119. Jewett, *Romans*, 562; Byrne, *Romans*, 287.

120. As discussed below, for Paul, the people of God in the present consist of believing Israel and believing gentiles, while the children of the promise consist of all of Israel, both believers and nonbelievers, and believing gentiles.

to the promise, a point Paul has already established in chapter 4. Kinship according to the flesh, although valid as far as human reckoning of physical descent goes, is secondary to the former. Thus, although both Ishmael (Gen 16) and Isaac (Gen 21) are biological descendants of Abraham and, as such, Israelites in terms of ascribed kinship, it is God who established Isaac, the divinely promised child, as the seed from whom Israel would descend.

Similarly, with regard to the next patriarchal generation, Paul points out that God reversed the natural order by determining and revealing to Rebecca (i.e., promising to her) that the elder would serve the younger (Gen 25:23) before either child had the chance to do either good or evil, so as to merit either divine approval or censure (vv. 10–12). The reference to works (ἔργων) in verse 12 recalls works of the law in the earlier chapters of the letter. In this context, it is best understood as referring generally to human attitudes and behavior that are either pleasing or displeasing to God. Paul's point is that God's plans and purposes are sovereign in the sense that he is free to determine his course of action, without any regard for human thought and action, as verse 13 (Mal 1:2–3) makes clear. God's elective purpose (πρόθεσις), presumably referring to establishment of Israel as the people of God, proceeds from his own call (ἐκ τοῦ καλοῦντος), his own sovereign, creative, and sustaining initiative.

What is important to note is that, at this juncture of the argument, Paul does not explicitly identify true Israel (v. 6b) with any community or people group and, especially, not with the believing community. The immediate context suggests that true Israel consists of the descendants of Isaac and Jacob, rather than of those who come from the line of either Ishmael or Esau. Paul's point is that God, with respect to election, has always operated upon the principle of promise; that is, according to his own sovereign will. It is God who determined both that Isaac and Jacob would be the progenitors of Israel and that Ishmael and Esau would be the ancestors of the Ishmaelites (Gen 25:13–16; 1 Chr 1:28–31) and the Edomites (Gen 36:1), respectively, although all four can be correctly reckoned as descendants of Israel's first and primary patriarch, Abraham. In other words, according to Paul, God not only freely calls nations and people groups into being but also freely utilizes them for his own creative purposes. That this is the case is suggested by the apostle's reference to the Exodus narrative and the hardening of Pharaoh's heart (Exod 9:16) in verse 17.

This brief, rather abrupt, reference to the Exodus narrative is best read within the larger context of Paul's argument to this point, which hinges on the key figures of Abraham, Adam, and Christ, and on God's salvific acts towards humanity, including creation, as a whole. As in Genesis, the role of Abraham and his descendants is a central concern in the Book of Exodus where God's intentions to bless all of humanity through the seed of Abraham are thwarted by the unnamed Pharaoh, who does not know God and who, consequently, attempts to put himself in the place of God by oppressing the descendants of Jacob (Exod 1:1–5).[121] Accordingly, the battle God wages with Egypt, as

---

121. Creach, *Violence in Scripture*, 79–81.

represented by Pharaoh, is linked with God's purposes in the election of Israel.[122] God's hardening of Pharaoh's heart for the objective of making his power and name known (9:17), speaks to his salvific acts of setting creation right with its Creator, first through Israel, and ultimately through Christ.[123] It is precisely through Egypt's/ Pharaoh's desire for power and self-glorification that the true Lord is revealed.

Yahweh's prerogative in making himself known in whatever manner he chooses to whomever he pleases is underscored by Paul's reference to Moses, the representative of Israel, in verses 14–16 (Exod 33:18–19). In this case, Yahweh states in no uncertain terms that his granting of Moses's request to witness the revelation of divine glory, God himself, is based solely on the latter's own graciousness and not on any merit on Moses's/Israel's part. In the larger context, Moses intercedes on behalf of Israel when God threatens to remove his presence due to its sin. Thus, Yahweh's self-revelation to Moses correspondingly suggests that God's compassion toward his wayward people is similarly unmerited. God acts as he does, because he is God. In other words, God's elective purposes with respect to both Egypt and Israel have their sole origin in divine sovereign will. Yahweh freely chooses to show compassion to Moses/Israel and display his wrath against Pharaoh/Egypt for his own purposes. That Pharaoh/Egypt is portrayed as a force that opposes God's intention for humanity to be blessed through Abraham, suggests that God's opposition to this nation and its ruler should not be understood to indicate his hatred of or disregard for a particular people. Rather, it indicates divine opposition to a way of life based on injustice and unrighteousness that unduly promotes the self and results in the oppression of the other.[124] It is telling that the prophets accuse Israel of similar exploits, vividly describing the divine punishment that is to come if Israel fails to repent. In both scriptural instances, God's objective is the same—to make himself known, in the former case, by positive means and, in the latter, by negative means.

In addition, it may be noted that, the reference to God hardening Pharoah's heart, together with other like statements in the surrounding context, notably the Jacob-Esau contrast (vv. 10–13), the pot illustration in verses 20b–21, and the references to vessels of wrath and (v. 22) need not be read as supporting the Augustinian doctrine of Double Predestination. Such a doctrine goes beyond the point that Paul is making, that it is God's prerogative as God to act freely, without any need to give account for his actions to his human subjects. Thus, for the sake of the present argument, the apostle intentionally downplays human freedom and responsibility. However, he can readily make recourse to the human side of the equation when necessary (Rom 6:1—8:13; 2 Cor 5:5).[125] Moreover, Paul is speaking in terms of people groups and not of the eternal fate, salvation or damnation, of individuals. In other words, final salvation is

---

122. Creach, *Violence in Scripture*, 79.
123. Of note, in Exod 9:16, God shows mercy in not destroying Egypt (Keener, *Romans*, 119).
124. Creach, *Violence in Scripture*, 130–31.
125. Byrne, *Romans*, 298–99.

not even in view here—God's sovereign freedom in determining how, when, and by what means he implements his plans and purposes in human history is.

In sum, as scriptural tradition shows, God levels the human evaluative process of defining the self over and against the other in terms of ascribed kinship or ethnic superiority in two important ways. First, as Paul makes clear, there is another factor at play besides that of biological descendant in defining the true descendants of Israel; namely, divine prerogative, which operates independently from any form of human contribution, physical or otherwise. It is God who decides who will be included among the people of God, a decision that is by no means circumscribed by human reckoning of lines of descent, ascribed, achieved, or some combination of both (9:16). By redefining the traditional oppositional categories of Jew/Israel and gentile/the nations in terms of children of the flesh and children of the promise, Paul lays the groundwork for defining the people of God in aggregate terms. The people of God are those whom God freely chooses to be such, at any point in human history, and cannot be assumed to include all or only the biological descendants of Abraham. Unlike Abraham's faith in God's promise of a son, which Paul highlights in 4:16–22, the human response to God's promise, in the case of Abraham (9:9) and the response to God's word (9:10), in the case of Rebecca, is not emphasized in this portion of the argument, since the apostle is concerned with defending the unfailing nature of God's promises to Israel (9:6). However, the response of human faith or belief is implicit here, and becomes more prominent in chapters 10–11 where Israel's lack of faith in God's work in the present age becomes the defining issue regarding their present inclusion among the people of God. Moreover, the category, children of the promise, which opens the door to all people groups, regardless of their physical or biological descent, assumes that they trust in the God who instituted this ethnoracially diverse community in and through Christ. Paul has already made this clear.

Second, God's implementation of his salvific plans and purposes for humankind proceeds solely according to divine prerogative in that God freely chooses to utilize various people groups at certain times and for particular tasks in his effort to make himself and his name known to his recalcitrant creatures. As Paul will argue, unbelieving Israel continues to play a central, divinely mandated role in making God known to the gentile nations.

5.2.1.1B As in the Present (Rom 9:19–29)

Having taken up the objection that God's sovereign freedom appears to make it unreasonable for him to find fault with humans for their obstinacy, by reminding his audience of humanity's creatureliness (9:19–21), Paul links God's actions in the past to the present, laying the final necessary groundwork for taking up the issue of Israel's status in the new age. The reference to God's call (καλέω) in verses 24, 25, and 26 recalls what Paul has already said concerning God's sovereign freedom in summoning individuals and nations to particular tasks related to his salvific actions on behalf of humanity. God is consistent in exercising his freedom in that he presently calls both Jews and gentiles, as objects of mercy (ἐλέους). The reference to believing Jews and gentiles as objects of mercy recalls God's dealings with Moses in verses 15–16 and Paul's point that God acts with sovereign freedom apart from any human contribution. In this sense, both Israel and the believing community are of equal standing in that each is called, established, and sustained by a God who acts according to his own purposes without regard for human merit. Moreover, this ultimate sovereignty means that God is free to exclude and include people groups and reconfigure the people of God as he sees fit, as Paul argues, the scriptures themselves foretell (vv. 25–26; Hos 2:23 [LXX 2:25]; Hos 1:10 [LXX 2:1]).[126]

God's calling of the gentiles and their constitution as God's people and as his sons (and daughters), described in the apostle's reinterpretation of Hosea's warning to wayward Israel, suggests that these persons are also children of the promise, in the sense that they represent the fulfillment of God's promise to Abraham that he would be the father of many nations. That is, Paul has already established that Scripture indicates that God's promise and calling, rather than physical descent, mark the pattern of divine action.[127] Underlying this idea of children of the promise is the notion of the human response of faith in the God who makes such promises, which Paul will take-up in 9:30—10:21. Thus, the children of the promise, refers to both Israel, the physical descendants of Isaac and Jacob, believers and nonbelievers, and believing gentiles, a point the apostle will continue to return to as his argument progresses.

Although Paul identifies the vessels of mercy with the believing community, Jew and gentile, he does not explicitly identify those made for destruction with any particular people group and, especially, not with unbelieving Israel. Paul has already defended God's freedom to deal positively and negatively with individuals/nations according to his own will and purposes as something evident from the scriptures. Moreover, the apostle's previous references to God's wrath (1:18) and to his his patience in this regard (2:4–5), and the immediate context, which indicates that he is referring to God's actions in the present, new age, suggest that he is speaking, in a general sense, of those who have not yet accepted God's good news in Christ. That is, he is speaking of vessels presently positively related to God and those that are currently negatively situated in relation to him.[128] God's patience (μακροθυμία) (2:4; 9:22) with regard to the latter, also suggests that Paul does not have eternal salvation/damnation in mind, but rather the notion that God's wrath as revealed through the gospel has at its goal human repentance. Although

---

126. In this case, Paul applies a text explicitly referring to Israel's restoration to the gentiles. This reveals one of Paul's fundamental interpretive strategies, where Israel's Scriptures are read as a witness to God's acts of reversal by which individuals and/or people groups seemingly outside of God's favor or mercy, according to human standards of reckoning, are shown mercy and/or are included among those deemed to be his people (Wagner, *Heralds of the Good News*, 83).

127. Byrne, *Romans*, 292.

128. Witherington and Hyatt, *Paul's Letter to the Romans*, 253.

this category of currently unrepentant humanity would *implicitly* include unbelieving Jews, Paul, at this point in his argument, does not mention Israel specifically, since his goal is to draw a line of continuity between God's actions in the past and those in the present. The focus remains on God.

Thus far, Paul has more than adequately defended God's sovereignty with regard to election; a freedom that strictly circumscribes human ways of determining who the people of God are. Consequently, with regard to the issue of antagonism that accompanies out-group comparison, since past scriptural tradition demonstrates that elect status is something conferred by God, the present elect status of the believing community is neither merited, nor self-constructed and, as such, cannot be the grounds for self-promotion or boasting. In addition, all that the apostle has said regarding Israel, thus far, is that they are the descendants of Isaac and Jacob. Hence, they are children of the promise, who have both temporal and hierarchical priority as those to whom God first revealed his salvific plans and purposes and through whom he both initiated these plans and purposes and brought them to culmination in Christ, Israel's messiah. In no sense has Paul redefined Israel in terms of the believing community, so as to draw a distinction either between a historical Israel and a true Israel (i.e., the believing community) or between an ethnic Israel and a spiritual Israel (i.e., the believing community). What he has done by introducing the category of children of the promise and by emphasizing God's consistency in freely selecting individuals and people groups for particular purposes and tasks throughout history is to lay the groundwork for both gentile inclusion within a renewed Israel, composed of a Jewish remnant (discussed below), and Israel's continuing priority in the new age.

However, the reference to the vessels made for destruction has introduced an element of tension with regard to Israel's current status and its priority. If the majority of Jews are currently negatively related to God, in what sense is God faithful to his promises to Israel and, consequently, in what sense do they remain his people? Although Paul will take on this issue more directly beginning with 9:30, at this juncture in his argument, he introduces one more element fundamental to his defense both of God's faithfulness and of Israel's priority—the notion of the remnant.

As in his treatment of God's elective actions, Paul places emphasis on the historical facts of Yahweh's dealings with Israel, which indicate that God, in his judgment of a disobedient and apostate Israel, has consistently preserved a remnant of his people as a sign of his unerring faithfulness to Israel, as a whole (vv. 27–28 and 29) (Isa 10:22–23; 1:9). Verse 27b is taken from a similar expression occurring in Hos 1:10 (LXX 2:1), linking the Isaiah text to Hosea and suggesting the unity of the divine purpose in calling a diverse, composite people of God.[129] The preservation of a remnant is no less true in the present where the Jewish members of the believing community represent God's remainder. In essence, God's promise of a Spirit-wrought, renewed and restored Israel finds confirmation in these members. However, this is not God's

---

129. Byrne, *Romans*, 306.

last word in regard to Israel as a whole. As Paul will argue, the children of the promise, who are also currently vessels made for destruction, due to their unbelief, essentially form a third category of humanity that exists in a liminal state of being temporarily cut-off from the present people of God, yet remaining the people of God in the sense that their restoration lies in the future. In other words, God's promise of a renewed and restored Israel awaits it complete future fulfillment. Thus, within the Scriptures, Paul finds not only a precedent that accounts for the small number of Jews among believers, but also hope for Israel, as a whole.

In this regard, it is of note that, in applying the divine filiation privilege of Israel to the gentiles (vv. 25–26), nowhere does Paul revoke the original designation as applying to Israel, as a whole. Rather, verse 28 suggests that God carries out his purposes regarding Israel, the gospel, and humanity, in general, by the present diminishment of Israel in a quantitative sense.[130] Paul conflates Isa 10:23 with a form of Isa 28:22b in a way that it agrees neither with the MT of the latter nor the LXX. The meaning of the present participles, συντελῶν and συντέμνων are disputed. They may indicate that God's promise will see limited fulfillment via the remnant or that this promise will be fulfilled only for a limited number of Israel. Additionally, the participles may convey the notion that God has shortened the time of Israel's suffering and punishment.[131] Given that the idea of the remnant is central to Paul's argument regarding Israel's continuing place and role in God's present salvific acts and the fact that he appears to have adapted the OT texts in a creative way for his own purposes, suggests that he utilizes these participles to convey the idea that the present whittling down of Israel is part of God's larger purposes. That is, in the present new age, Israel is represented by the believing remnant, with the majority of Israel existing in a liminal state as temporarily cut-off from God's people. The latter are Israelites, being children of the promise, but they differ both from believing Israel and from non-Israelite persons, both believers and nonbelievers. This conception creates space for the argument that this liminal state is temporary (11:25–26); that unbelieving Israel, as an enemy of the gospel, nevertheless remains the beloved of God (11:28–29); and that, although unbelieving Jews are presently vessels made for destruction, they, unlike unbelieving gentiles, are the recipients of a past irrevocable divine calling and its accompanying gifts that makes them unique among the rest of currently unrepentant humanity (11:29). Appeal to the fluid end of the identity spectrum allows for the construction of this third, liminal group of humanity.

---

130. Byrne, *Romans*, 306.
131. Fitzmyer, *Romans*, 574.

5.2.1.2 Israel's Unenlightened Zeal and Misplaced Righteousness (Rom 9:30—10:4)

In the previous section, the emphasis on divine initiative in calling the people of God into being challenged the human evaluative processes involved in constructing group self-identity. According to Paul, the people of God, both past and present, exist as such solely by God's decision to freely choose particular individuals and people groups for specific tasks and by his creative power in establishing them for these purposes, apart from any human contribution. Consequently, even at the ascribed end of the identity spectrum, physical descent is circumscribed by divine prerogative. God not only determines the lines of descent with respect to those who constitute Israel but also has determined that the lines of descent with respect to the children of the promise will also include gentiles.

In this section,[132] the apostle shifts his focus to the fluid end of the identity spectrum by bringing to the fore the human response of faith to divine initiative as that which is characteristic of the eschatological people of God, returning to the themes of law and faith introduced in beginning chapters of the letter. Although the category children of the promise does not appear here, it underlies the discussion regarding faith and righteousness that runs through the entirety of this section of the argument. Paul has already established that God sovereignly establishes who the children of the promise will be both in the past and in the present. That is, he has demonstrated that the inclusion of gentiles into the eschatological people of God and the reduction of Israel to the remnant comports with God's salvific plan for humanity as foretold by the scriptures. The present section furthers the argument by reintroducing faith in the present work of God in and through Christ as that which distinguishes the people of God in the present. The introduction of this identity criterion gives Paul the flexibility needed to portray unbelieving Israel as distinct from both believing Jews and believing gentiles; in effect, further refining the category of children of the promise in a way that underscores majority Israel's liminal status. As discussed below, he does this in a way that simultaneously differentiates unbelieving Israel from unrepentant humanity; thereby, further leveling in-group antagonism toward the out-group.

In this regard, it is telling that the apostle couches his discussion in a contrast between believing gentiles and unbelieving Israel.[133] Paul has already demonstrated that faith in the present work of God, both as an attitude and as a pattern of conduct, is a characteristic of his people both in the past and the present. It is this element that simultaneously unites believing gentiles with believing Israel and differentiates this

---

132. The integrity of 9:30—10:21 is indicated by the question "What then shall we say?," which often marks a new argument. Moreover, the words "righteousness" and "faith" are central in this section, and are almost entirely absent in 9:1–29 and 11:1–36. Finally, in both 9:30-32 and 10:20-21, Paul contrasts the inclusion of gentiles with the exclusion of Israel (Moo, *Epistle to the Romans*, 617).

133. However, the emphasis remains on the problem of Israel's exclusion (also, Moo, *Epistle to the Romans*, 617).

group from unbelieving Jews. Drawing upon it once again in this section of his argument, he skillfully employs it to portray unbelieving Israel as misguided children of the promise, laying the groundwork for his climactic portrayal of it as both enemy of the gospel and beloved of God.

Paul begins by defining the issue in terms of the attainment of a goal; namely, righteousness. There is nothing in the context to suggest that Paul is speaking of righteousness only in a forensic sense.[134] Rather, the reference to a zeal for God suggests a pattern of life exemplified in loyalty and devotion to God. Moreover, righteousness is not strictly synonymous with salvation. Thus, Israel may not have obtained righteousness, but that does not mean that it is necessarily missing out on final salvation. Similarly, gentile believers may have obtained righteousness, but that is not a guarantee of salvation (cf. 11:17–24).[135] Gentiles have attained it without seeking it, while Israel pursuing a law of righteousness did not achieve that law (vv. 30–31). The genitive phrase "νόμον δικαιοσύνης" is controversial and can be taken in a variety of ways.[136] Given the context, it is best read as law resulting in righteousness. That is, the problem, according to Paul, is not that Israel strove to be righteous before God by keeping the law, but that the law was never intended to deal with human sin, despite its holy character. Thus, Israel could not reach the goal of the law εἰς νόμον οὐκ ἔφθασεν, no matter how earnest its efforts. As Paul will maintain, the goal/end of the law is Christ (10:4). It is through Christ that righteousness is attained. The righteousness in view in both cases is the same and refers to the state of living in right relationship with God, the difference lying in the fact that gentiles did not strive to fulfill the written law in order to live in such a manner, never having received it, in contrast to Israel, which did receive it. Rather, gentiles attained righteousness through faith in the gospel and the enabling outpouring of the Spirit. In 9:32, Paul draws a contrast between pursuing (the Greek lacks a main verb) righteousness either through faith or through works (of the law). Paul has already made clear that the problem is not works, in and of themselves, but the fact that Israel has failed to comply with the law due to the inescapable power of sin. That is, Paul is not indicting works, per se, but the failure to acknowledge, in faith, that God has done something new in Christ

By defining the contrast between believing gentiles and unbelieving Israel in this way, Paul couches the contrast between the two groups in eschatological terms, a maneuver that allows him to maintain the lines of continuity and discontinuity between the two groups, drawn in the previous chapters of the letter. More importantly, the contrast allows for the distancing of unbelieving Jews from unrepentant humanity, in general. Unlike unbelieving humanity, Israel has a zeal (ζῆλον) for God (10:2),[137]

---

134. Contra Moo, *Epistle to the Romans*, 618–19.

135. Byrne, *Romans*, 309.

136. Moo, *Epistle to the Romans*, 622–24, provides a summary.

137. "Zeal" is a commendable characteristic in the intertestamental period (e.g., 1 Macc 2:27; Jdt 9:4; Sir 45:23–24; Josephus, *Ant.*, 12.271), reflecting the unswerving loyalty to God exemplified in the

which presupposes that its people acknowledge him as God and are devoted to him, and that they continue to strive to exemplify this loyalty in walking righteously before him. The problem, according to Paul, is that Israel continues to use the law as its moral guide (9:31); thereby, stumbling on the stumbling stone of Christ (9:32c–33) and, consequently, missing out on the present, Spirit-wrought renewal and restoration promised to it in its Scriptures. In other words, its zeal is not according to knowledge (οὐ κατ᾽ ἐπίγνωσιν) in the sense that, unbelieving Jews have failed to discern God's present pattern of salvific activity in the world as it is revealed in the gospel. Unbelieving Israel has knowledge of the gospel in the sense that it has heard it (10:18). The problem is that it has failed to understand/accept its meaning and purpose for God's people. Paul spells this out in 10:14–21, where he argues that scripture foretells both the inclusion of gentiles and Israel's difficulty in accepting the gospel. Thus, Israel knew of the gospel, both in the sense that it heard it proclaimed and in the sense that it was foretold in the scriptures, but did not respond appropriately. Instead, unbelieving Jews continue to cling to the past. Thus, their attempt to attain righteousness, no matter how noteworthy in its single-mindedness and passion, is doomed to failure, given all that Paul has already said concerning the power of sin and the law's inability to rectify the basic human proclivity to sin. Paul will return to this point in 10:5–13 where he uses Lev 18:5, Deut 30:11–14, and Isa 28:16 as scriptural validation for God's present work in Christ as superseding the old age of the law.

Nothing Paul has said, thus far, is new. However, the positing of righteousness as the goal of both believing gentiles and unbelieving Jews, helps to neutralize the evaluative processes that lead to bias against the out-group. Admittedly, both groups have equal zeal for God, in that each seeks to walk righteously before him, the difference being that unbelieving Jews have failed to submit (ὑπετάγησαν) to God's present means/pattern of righteousness in Christ (10:3–4). It is in this sense, that they seek a righteousness of their own (10:2).[138] Moreover, nothing in the context suggests that Paul is rebuking the Israelites for being self-righteous. Such a view presupposes an understanding of the law based on the traditional reading of the law-faith dichotomy. Verse 4 is controversial.[139] However, given the eschatological context and Paul's entire argument to this point regarding the provisional nature of the law, it is best to read the verse as stating that in the present new age, Christ, not the law, is God's means/pattern of righteousness. Thus, τέλος is best translated as "end," in the sense that the old age of the law is over. However, there is continuity between the ages in the sense that Scripture foretells God's circumcision of the heart in the new age, by which the intent of the law would be fulfilled among God's people through the enabling work of the Spirit. It is in this sense, that Christ is the

---

OT figures of Elijah (1 Kgs 19:10) and Phinehas (Num 25:6–13). It is also praised in the NT (John 2:17; Acts 22:3; 2 Cor 11:2; Phil 3:6) (Moo, *Epistle to the Romans*, 632; Byrne, *Romans*, 311).

138. Contra Moo, *Epistle to the Romans*, 635.

139. Moo, *Epistle to the Romans*, 636–43, provides a summary of the various positions.

culmination of the law; that is, through his life, death, and resurrection God's intent or purpose regarding the law comes to full fruition.

Thus, to live in the new age as if it were still the old is to posit a human understanding of righteousness over that presently provided by God. It is important to note that, nowhere does Paul claim that unbelieving Israel is unrighteous, that is, wicked, in the sense that its people do not seek God and his will for them. Rather, their liminal status as the people of God is due to the fact that they continue to live as if the new age of the Spirit had not dawned. Due to God's past calling and promises, they remain Israel, children of the promise, neither superseded nor replaced by the gentile people of God. Yet, unlike their believing Jewish counterparts, they cannot participate in the present renewal and restoration of Israel, which now includes gentiles, due to their unbelief. Thus, as in the previous chapters, Paul utilizes the law-faith dichotomy to connect the past to the present, drawing lines of continuity and discontinuity between God's people now and then in a way that creates a distinct place for unbelieving Israel in the new age, allowing Paul to delineate its unique role in the unfolding eschatological present.

5.2.2 God's Beloved: The Remnant, the Root, and the Present and Future Restoration of Israel

Thus far, Paul has established that the existence of both Israel and the believing community is solely the result of God's creative and sustaining power, by which he freely brings into being and reconfigures the people of God according to his own salvific plans and purposes for humanity. In the old age, the people of God consisted of Israel which, in times of apostasy, was represented by the remnant. The children of promise consisted of both the physical descendants of Isaac and Jacob and the future members of the gentile nations promised to Abraham as his descendants. In the new age, the people of God consists of believing Jews, that is, the remnant, and the promised believing gentiles, with the children of the promise consisting of both of these groups, in addition to unbelieving Israel. By shifting the focus between God's elective actions and the human response to these actions, that is, by foregrounding either divine promise or human faith in that promise as two sides of the same intergroup criterion coin, Paul begins to sketch the contours of a portrait of Israel as occupying a unique place in the new age.

A lengthy interpretation of scripture (10:5–13) that establishes both the eschatological validity of righteousness through faith, and its superiority with respect to the old age of the law, particularly in the sense that it allows for the inclusion of diverse people groups among the people of God, adds further depth to the depiction of Israel's liminal state. The final section (10:14–21) of this phase of Paul's argument, a scriptural demonstration that points to Israel's own culpability in failing to enter into the new age, while simultaneously intimating that this failure is, in some sense, according to divine plan or intention (10:19; cf. 11:11, 13–14), completes this picture of Israel as standing at the nexus between the old and the new, as part of God's wider purposes, yet, as standing at a distance, due to its own response. With this image in place, Paul begins to unfold his climactic vision of Israel's place and role in the new age.

This portrait of Israel takes its final form as the apostle skillfully illustrates three aspects of its current identity that guarantee that God has not permanently rejected it; thus, dissipating any form of bias by the believing community, Jew and gentile alike, against the out-group. Paul's argument may be divided into three sections: God has not rejected Israel (11:1–10); Israel's stumbling has a wider purpose in God's plans for humanity (11:11–24); and all Israel will be saved, since God's gifts and calling are irrevocable (11: 25–32). The first two sections address potential Jewish and gentile bias against unbelieving Israel, respectively. The final section highlights the leveling effect that God's sovereign mercy has on human evaluative processes.

5.2.2.1 Leveling Jewish Believer Bias against Israel (Rom 11:1–10)

In this section, Paul's focus is specifically on the Jewish-believing remnant (vv. 2–6), who are referred to, specifically, as the elect (ἡ ἐκλογὴ) in contrast to unbelieving Israel, who are referred to as the ones who were hardened (οἱ ἐπωρώθησαν).[140] According to the apostle, the idea that God has rejected Israel is implausible for two reasons. First, God has preserved a remnant; hence, it cannot be said that he has abandoned all of Israel. Second, as for the rest of Israel, its hardening is part of a larger divine purpose, which suggests that God is not yet finished with it. In short, the apostle makes clear that the respective identities of Jewish believers as the elect and their nonbelieving counterparts as the hardened, are the result of God's sovereign decision regarding each of the groups and the particular purpose God intends for them.

The elect are the elect solely due to the selection of grace (κατ ἐκλογὴν χάριτος);[141] that is, apart from any human contribution, including compliance with the law (v. 6).[142] The scriptural example of Elijah's lament and God's response (1 Kgs 19:10, 14, 18) (vv. 3–4) underscores both God's enduring fidelity in preserving for himself (κατέλιπον ἐμαυτῷ) a people, even in situations that suggest the wholesale rejection by Israel of its God, and the fact that the people of God exist solely due to God's own initiating and

140. The term λοιποὶ indicates that the elect, in this instance, refers to the Jewish-believing remnant, specifically.

141. Fitzmyer, *Romans*, 605.

142. Although the term ἔργων may refer to works of the law, specifically, the context, which speaks of God's sovereign elective actions, a motif that Paul has consistently utilized and developed throughout chapters 9 and 10, suggests a broader understanding of works. Moreover, Paul utilizes the phrase ἐξ ἔργων in Rom 4:2 and 9:12 in reference to human behavior in general, regardless of whether these actions are carried out in accordance with the law or not (Byrne, *Romans*, 334–35). In other words, the phrase includes works of the law since this is the pattern of righteousness given by God to Israel, but given the emphasis on elective grace as solely the prerogative of God, it broadly encompasses all human actions.

sustaining power. Although Paul can also speak of the importance of human response to divine initiative, in this portion of the argument, he places emphasis on the divine aspect of the interplay between God's actions and human response.

Recall, that in Greco-Roman foundation stories, it is external forces and not the participants themselves who determine the necessity and course of founding a new community. However, this divine ordering of human affairs occurs without the negation of parallel human causation. For example, in neither Strabo's nor Herodotus's accounts does supernatural causation render human agency inoperative or replace empirical cause and effect. Rather, as in Greek thinking in general, these are seen as parallel sets of causation. A case in point is Strabo's narration of the founding of Massilia by the Phocaeans, who upon setting sail to their destination, receive an oracle from Atremis, commanding them to use a woman named Aristarcha as their guide (*Geogr.* 4.1.4). In order to accomplish this task, the Phocaeans must take decisive action. Accordingly, they elect to sail to Ephesus in order to inquire of the goddess where this women, who is to be their guide, can be found. Similarly, the woman, once found, is portrayed as an active participant in the divine-human drama. She consents to the voyage and procures the sacred images of Artemis that she is to take with her. Finally, Strabo relates that the Phocaeans and their guide settle the colony and build a temple to Atremis, whereupon they establish Aristarcha as the priestess; all according to their own volition (*Geogr.* 4.1.4). In sum, the oracle to the Phocaeans and Aristarcha's dream function to lend legitimacy to Massilia as a divinely founded city. Yet, the settlement of the colony and the building of the temple are attributed to human agency. Moreover, Strabo highlights either divine or human causation, depending on where is is in the narration and what point he is seeking to make.

Similarly, the biblical texts hold both of these poles, divine causation and human action in tension, as does Paul. In this way, the apostle levels any evaluative process, on the part of the Jewish believing remnant, that might lead to the conclusion that God has rejected unbelieving Israel on the basis of its negative reaction to the gospel. Thus, Israel's responsibility (9:30—10:21) is not excluded. It is simply not foregrounded in this part of the argument. Rather, unbelieving Israel's response to the gospel is but one factor in a complex divine drama of restoration and salvation. Similarly, the Jewish believing remnant is another such factor.

However, at the same time, Paul's identification of Jewish believers as the elect strongly implies that members of hardened Israel are no longer the people of God. This conclusion is also suggested by the apostle's statement that the elect have attained the status of righteousness before God, apart from any effort on their part, while the rest of Israel, in all its efforts to do so, has failed (v. 7). That is, the members of hardened Israel can no longer be considered God's people, since they have not achieved the level of righteous requisite in the new age. The context suggests that what was sought was righteousness, in the sense of right relationship or standing with God, in the present. Although righteousness before God is also a prerequisite for final salvation, Paul appears to be speaking of hardened Israel's present status. The elect remnant exist ἐν τῷ νῦν καιρῷ, a loose temporal marker, as does, implicitly, the rest of hardened Israel. Moreover, Paul attributes Israel's hardening to God, painting a rather grim picture of majority Israel's present condition. Not only is this condition the result of a deliberate, divine act, but it is also a state foretold by the scriptures and testified to by two of Israel's key founding figures, Moses and David (vv. 8–10).

Paul's introduction of Isa 6:9–10 into Deut 29:4 (LXX 29:3) in verse 8 transforms Moses's lament that God has not intervened to correct Israel's obtuseness into the stronger claim that this insensibility has been directly caused by God. That is, God has not merely withheld spiritual sight, but has deliberately dulled present day Israel's perception.[143] In verses 9–10, there is the suggestion that the curses that David, the righteous sufferer, called down upon his afflicters are presently manifest in Israel's hardening.[144] Given that some of David's tormentors were his own relatives, indicates that in these hostile kinfolk, Paul sees a prefiguration of those Jews who have rejected their own messiah.[145] Accordingly, unbelieving Israel's obtuseness is a present manifestation of a spiritual blindness that has been part of its legacy since its foundation. As a result, unbelieving Israel presently (διὰ παντός) stands in a hostile relationship to God's suffering righteous one, Christ, thereby suffering the curse of darkness and insensibility invoked by David.[146]

Yet, although this rather harsh censure seems to suggest that hardened Israel is more akin to unrepentant humanity than it is to the believing children of the promise, Paul preserves the basic contours of the picture of Israel's liminal status that he has been sketching in several ways. As already noted, he strongly intimates that this status, irrespective of Israel's own contribution, nonetheless serves a larger divine purpose. The apostle's reference to his own physical descent (v. 1c) harkens back to the children of the promise motif (9:3–5) and hints that God is not yet finished with unbelieving Israel. The latter, similar to himself and to his believing kinfolk, are children of the promise to whom belong all of the ancient privileges and promises. In this regard, it is telling that in all of the seemingly harsh discourse in 11:1–10, Paul neither conflates Israel with the Jewish-believing remnant nor suggests that unbelieving Israel is, in one sense or another, no longer Israel. Rather, he views Israel as divided between those who trust in God's present work in and through Christ and those who do not; a view for which he finds ample scriptural precedent. Similarly, the reference to God's

---

143. Wagner, *Heralds of the Good News*, 243–44.

144. The quotation agrees with LXX Ps 68:23–24 (69:22–23) and Ps 34:8. Paul, like other NT writers, appeals to the psalms of the righteous sufferer in order to elaborate the Christ story. The catchword "eyes" joins this psalm to the previous texts, Deut 29:4 and Isa 6:9–10 (Fitzmyer, *Romans*, 606). This suggests that Israel's hardening is the chief point being made. It is unclear whether all the details of the curse are meant to apply literally to unbelieving Israel (Byrne, *Romans*, 332–33).

145. Fitzmyer, *Romans*, 607.

146. Wagner, *Heralds of the Good News*, 261.

foreknowledge in verse 2[147] suggests that hardened Israel's refusal to embrace the new age is temporary and that it can be reversed. The scriptures foretell of Israel's eschatological renewal and restoration; a time when divided Israel, the apostate and the remnant, will once again be one. A time, which Paul will argue, is yet to come. Moreover, the larger stories of both Isaiah and Deuteronomy, which provide the scriptural framework for this portion of the argument, attest to God's fidelity to his people, a fidelity that eventually overcomes their unfaithfulness, so that those whom God has rendered insensible are redeemed and restored.[148] In the meantime, the Jewish believing remnant are to view themselves and their nonbelieving counterparts as part of a larger divine purpose and plan, within which each plays a unique role.

5.2.2.2 *Leveling Gentile Believer Bias against Israel (Rom 11:11–24)*

The specifics of the role hardened Israel plays and what purpose this hardening has in God's salvific plan have yet to be revealed. However, Paul has established that God has not entirely abandoned Israel in that he has made provision both for a remnant and for the continuing inclusion of the rest of Israel within the divine plan. As seen above, the apostle's leveling of potential Jewish-believing remnant bias against Israel has been suggestive, rather than explicit, particularly, when compared to the direct warning he gives to gentile believers (11:18). A higher probability of relatively strong gentile in-group bias against the out-group makes sense, given that ethnoracial identities were frequently nested in antiquity. That is, believing Jews would likely consider themselves both Jews and believers, making it less likely that in-group favoritism toward the believing community would result in strong out-group antagonism. Rather, Jewish believers would most likely be capable of negotiating the tension between membership in the new movement and their continuing identity as Jews. The apostle himself provides a good example of this. Conversely, gentile believers, who would not consider themselves Jews, despite their membership in and favoritism toward a group with distinctly Jewish roots, would be more likely to develop a stronger antagonism toward the out-group, given the lack of ethnoracial affiliation.[149] Consequently, in his

---

147. Divine foreknowledge reflects a biblical idiom where it connotes both choice and election (cf. Gen 18:19; Jer 1:5; Hos 13:5 (MT); Amos 3:2; 1QH 9:29–30) (Byrne, *Romans,* 272).

148. Wagner, *Heralds of the Good News,* 252–57.

149. In 16:3–16, Paul does not directly greet the personal friends he mentions, but rather he asks the believers in Rome to greet them. In addition, the list of twenty-six persons includes at least three Jewish believers whom Paul refers to as his kinsmen/women (Lampe, "Roman Christians," 218, 224–25). It is possible that in addition to the three people explicitly identified as Paul's kinsmen/women, there were others on the list who were Jewish Christians (Witherington and Hyatt, *Paul's Letter to the Romans,* 379–81). Regardless, the net effect of this indirect greeting is to effect unity among the believers in Rome. The verb the apostle employs does not mean merely to "greet" in a perfunctory way, but to "wrap one's arms around and embrace someone, and when coupled with the command to offer a holy kiss as well (v. 16), it amounts to a command to treat those named as a family" (Witherington and Hyatt, *Paul's Letter to the Romans,* 81). This directive suggests that Paul is intent on breaking down

bid to establish the place and role of Israel in the new age, Paul seeks to establish not only Israel's continuing significance, but also its temporal and hierarchical priority. Thus, he defines the place and role of gentiles in the new age in relation to Israel, which maintains its primacy.

Of note is that in this portion of his argument Paul neither refers to scripture, nor does he draw on the identity criteria he has used thus far in establishing the lines of continuity and discontinuity between God's people past and present. Rather, at the heart of his argument lie two metaphors by means of which he fills in the contours of the portrait he has thus far sketched of unbelieving Israel. This suggests that what he is attempting here is to explain the exact relationship between believing Jews, their unbelieving ethnic counterparts, and believing gentiles; closely related, but not identical, groups. Consequently, the question, "Whom does the olive tree represent?" may be misleading, since the point of the metaphor is not to establish a specific identity, but rather to explain the relationship between three distinct, but closely related, groups. The metaphor is dynamic, rather than static, spanning past, present, and future.[150] The apostle has already established that: all three groups are children of the promise; all three are descendants of Abraham; that the first and third group constitute the people of God in the new age; and that the second group, although descendants of God's people in the past, are no longer his people in the new age. The fact that they remain children of the promise indicates their liminal place in the divine scheme of things.

Paul's tripartite division of humanity underscores the flexibility of identity construction in antiquity. Although shared ancestry was a common standard of classification, it was not the sole or even definitive one. This criterion is more often than not interwoven, in ethnographic texts, with other salient standards to form either a backdrop or a foreground for the other criteria, depending on the author's purpose(s). For instance, Dionysius of Halicarnassus similarly creates a tripartite division of humanity, interweaving common ancestry with common customs, traditions, and worship practices, foregrounding either the former (*Ant. rom.* 1.5.1; 1.9–70) or the latter (1.21.1–2; 1.89.4) with respect to both Greeks and Romans, depending on where he is in his argument. What emerges is a tripartite division of humanity that has the traditional Greek-barbarian dichotomy at its base: barbarians, which include Greeks, who have abandoned their customs and worship practices, and all non-Roman people groups; true Greeks, who may be distinguished from Romans (e.g., 1.90.1); and non-barbarians, composed of all Roman peoples and true Greeks. He writes: "Hence from now on let the reader forever renounce the views of those who make Rome a retreat of barbarians, fugitives and vagabonds, and let him confidently affirm it to be a Greek city . . . for one will find no nation that is more ancient or more Greek" (1.89.1–2). Arguably, true

---

gentile antagonism toward the Jewish ethnic "other," both insider and outsider, which one would expect due to the lack of ethnoracial affiliation.

150. Fitzmyer provides a summary of the various positions on the above question (Fitzmyer, *Romans*, 609–10).

Greeks, living under present Roman rule, exist in a liminal state, since they are not barbarians, yet, by virtue of the fact that they are subjects of Rome, their previously unsurpassed glory is diminished in relation to the superior people, who now rule over them. "As for the Greek powers," "they gained neither magnitude of empire nor duration of eminence equal" to Rome, which "rules every country that is not inaccessible or uninhabited" (1.3.1–3). Continuity between past Greek glory and present Roman greatness is established via a common genealogy, customs, traditions, and worship practices. However, the latter is discontinuous from the former, in that its dominion is greater and more enduring than that ever established by the former. Implicitly, Roman identity as non-barbarian embraces Greek non-barbarianism, while simultaneously surpassing it by virtue of its present unsurpassed greatness.

Moreover, and similarly, Paul has established a line of continuity between God's people past and present via faith (defined as a disposition evidenced in behavior), with the written law serving as a provisional identity criteria and, as such, a point of discontinuity. Furthermore, the primacy of Israel is maintained. All of this lies beneath the surface of the picture Paul is painting. Thus, the metaphors are not so much about establishing group identity as they are about properly positioning related groups. Moreover, the metaphors are successful for the very reason that they preserve the distinction between Israel and believing gentiles. None of the three identities are conflated, even as each of the three is seen to spring from a single root.

5.2.2.2A The First Fruits Metaphor

The first metaphor (v. 16a) serves as a bridge between Paul's disclosure of the purpose of God's temporary rejection of Israel (11:11–15) and the olive tree metaphor. Referring specifically to unbelieving Israel and harkening back to the stumbling motif from Isa 28:16 in 9:33, Paul makes clear that the hardening of the majority of Israel is not permanent, since it occurs within a wider divine purpose (v. 11). The two verbs ἔπταισαν and πέσωσιν connote falling, but the context suggests that they operate in tandem to signal that although Israel has stumbled, this stumbling is not of such severity that it cannot be reversed.[151] Put differently, the issue is whether it is God's intention to bring Israel to final ruin. To this the apostle responds with a resounding "no." That Israel has been rejected by God is evidenced in verse 15. Although it is possible to read "their rejection" as referring to a rejection (of God, of the gospel) on the part of unbelieving Jews, in the second half of the verse, Paul contrasts this rejection by their acceptance. Moreover, Paul's emphasis throughout this section is on God's responsibility for Israel's spiritual stupor and obduracy.[152] Israel's trespass (παραπτώματι), most likely referring to its rejection of the gospel, has as its aim the salvation of the gentiles, with the latter's salvation having as its objective the provoking of the former

---

151. Byrne, *Romans*, 344.
152. Moo, *Epistle to the Romans*, 693.

to jealousy. The idea of provoking Israel to jealousy refers back to Deut 32:21, cited in 10:19, while the dative suggests that trespass is instrumental. Given the lack of an explicit time reference, salvation, in this case, probably refers to the whole span of gentile salvation, past, present, and future. Paul does not state the mechanism of this provocation. Perhaps, the idea is that Israel will be provoked by the fact that gentiles are receiving/ experiencing (via the Holy Spirit) the eschatological blessings originally promised to it. The idea being, that upon witnessing this, Israel will turn to the gospel. The apostle's phrasing may be compared to that in 9:30–33, where the failure of Israel to attain righteousness and gentile attainment of it were set in contrastive parallel. In this instance, Paul places the contrast within the context of the overall divine plan, finding a causal/instrumental connection between the two.[153]

Accordingly, the purpose of gentile salvation is explained explicitly in relation to Israel. Moreover, the former's salvation is not simply for its own benefit but has occurred, specifically, for the sake of members of the out-group. Put differently, according to divine intent, it is because of the out-group that gentiles are members of the in-group and their identity with the in-group serves in the interest of the out-group. By phrasing it in this way, Paul defines the place and role of gentiles in relation to Israel, which stands as the reference point. This is underscored by the πόσῳ μᾶλλον language (v. 12), which harkens back to 5:9–10, 15, and 17 and contrasts the benefits to the world, in general, and to the gentiles, more specifically, by majority Israel's rejection of the gospel with the benefits that will come with the latter's πλήρωμα (fullness). This term can be taken in both a qualitative and quantitative sense, completeness and full number, respectively. While πλήρωμα has a qualitative denotation, the context and the parallel with verse 25 suggests that this completeness is attained through numerical addition. In this case, Paul would be suggesting that the present defeat (ἥττημα) of Israel, signified by its reduction to a remnant, will be reversed.[154] Once again, the phrasing emphasizes Israel's priority. Not only does its rejection of the gospel, although a trespass, bring salvation to the rest of creation, but its own future eschatological restoration promises even greater blessings; namely, life from the dead—eschatological resurrection for the gentiles (v. 15).[155] In other words, Paul depicts Israel's liminal position as a nexus between the new age, in which it does not yet directly participate, and the fullness of the new age to come, where its participation is divinely guaranteed.

---

153. Byrne, *Romans*, 338.

154. Moo, *Epistle to the Romans*, 659–60.

155. The actual phrase, ζωὴ ἐκ νεκρῶν, never occurs elsewhere in the NT. The phrase "from the dead" is found forty-seven times, and every occurrence except one—Rom 6:13—comes in a phrase referring to the resurrection. Paul's other description of the process he depicts here suggests that "life from the dead" must be an event separate from Israel's restoration, involving the whole world, and occurring at the end of history. In Jewish apocalyptic thinking, the restoration of Israel is seen as an event bringing in eschatological consummation (Moo, *Epistle to the Romans*, 695–96).

Thus, by placing Israel's liminal status within the divine salvific-purpose framework that spans past, present, and future, Paul demonstrates Israel's continuing and pivotal place in the unfolding eschatological present. Its stubborn persistence in remaining in the old age serves as the point where God's present blessings flow out to wider humanity, with the language suggesting that it will stand there for as long as God wants it to and that its eventual restoration will not only usher in the end but will bring even greater benefits. In the present, Israel, by its rejection of the new age, ultimately serves it, and will serve it until the end. In sum, Israel, the people of God, part of it temporarily rejected, serves a role past, present and future. It remains the mundane entry point for God's salvific purposes, despite the rejection by some of its members of their messiah.

Paul underscores this point by offering his ministry to the gentiles as an example (vv. 13–14). Placing his mission to the gentiles within the wider context of divine purpose, he notes his reason for actively promoting the success of this ministry to the gentiles, namely, to provoke his fellow Jews to jealousy.[156] In essence, although, on the surface, it may appear that his ministry priority remains the gentile community, in reality, it is subordinate to the unbelieving Jewish community in the sense that his ministry's success among the gentiles is ultimately for the purpose of leading at least some Jews to salvation. Paul's appeal to his own ministry may also serve the related purpose of correcting gentile appeals to the apostle himself as a reason to disdain unbelieving Jews and, perhaps, even Jewish believers.[157] By defining his own ministry in terms of a wider divine purpose, he levels in-group antagonism for the out-group.

Thus, the first metaphor (v. 16a) rounds out what Paul has said thus far regarding the future acceptance of Israel and how this is related to the present acceptance of gentiles and also serves as a transition to the olive tree metaphor, which more clearly describes the dynamic relationship between these groups both in the present and the future. What is relatively clear is that the first fruits metaphor is meant to convey the idea that a holy portion, in this case, a portion of a community or group of people, conveys holiness to the whole. Whom this portion represents is less clear.

It is possible that the believing Jewish remnant ensures the continuing holiness of Israel, with holiness understood as being set apart for God. Thus, Israel is representative of the people of God in the present new age through the remnant and, given God's wider purpose, will reach its fullness, in terms of numbers, in the future consummation. Accordingly, unbelieving Israel, although occupying a liminal place in the new age, nevertheless remains set apart for God. This accords with everything Paul has just argued. However, verse 16b suggests that the holy portion refers to the patriarchs. That is, it is by faith that the patriarchs in the past were considered holy and, similarly, it is by faith that the remnant is holy. This harkens back to Paul's notion of the children of

---

156. The verb δοξάζω, in this instance, appears to reflect the sense of doxa, the opinion or repute one has in the eyes of another (Byrne, *Romans*, 345).

157. Moo, *Epistle to the Romans*, 691.

the promise, again emphasizing the idea that the children of the promise include hardened Israel. For Paul's audience, there is no question that the children of the promise include believing Jews and gentiles. The point of contention is the identity of unbelieving Israel and Paul has defined it within the larger context of salvation history, past, present, and future. Thus, it is possible that Paul has both in view here. That is, both the patriarchs of the past and the remnant in the present ensure the continuing holiness of unbelieving Israel, despite its current rejection by God. Having established this, Paul turns to further refine his explanation of the dynamic relationship between Israel and believing gentiles in the new age.

5.2.2.2B The Olive Tree Metaphor

As noted above, the point of the olive tree metaphor is not so much to describe a static entity, e.g., true Israel, as it is to describe the dynamic relationship between three related groups of humanity: believing Israel (the remnant); believing gentiles; and unbelieving Israel. This is part of Paul's overall bid to level antagonism toward the outgroup resulting from in-group bias. Paul had already established that all three groups are related as children of the promise via the patriarchs, and, especially, via Abraham. Two of the groups, unbelieving and believing Israel, are related in terms of physical descent, while the third, believing gentiles, remain gentiles in terms of physical descent, yet share ascribed kinship with members of believing Israel via faith. What remains to be made absolutely clear is Israel's continuing priority and its continuing identity as God's elect, despite God's current (yet, temporary, as Paul will drive home) rejection of the Jewish majority. In other words, the passage is not about ethnic identity per se and what happens to that identity in the new age when gentiles are included in Israel's promised restoration. For Paul's first-century audience, Jews are Jews, Israel is Israel, despite the fact that gentiles have been included in the family tree. Moreover, gentiles are gentiles despite their ascribed kinship with Abraham's line. The nesting of identities and the fluidity of kinship constructs made it possible to envision a single family (the people of God) composed of diverse ethnoracial people groups without dilution or supersession of any of the groups involved. The pressing question, particularly in light of all that Paul has said regarding God's people in the present, is unbelieving Israel's relationship to this newly constituted people of God.

Seen in this light, the metaphor is not as complex as modern scholarship has often made it out to be.[158] Although it is possible that Paul is drawing on the OT metaphor of Israel as an olive tree, it is equally possible that he is simply employing a ubiquitous feature of the Eastern Mediterranean landscape, a living object familiar to his audience, that provides a useful means for depicting the relationship of parts

---

158. For a brief summary of some of the positions on what the olive tree represents and a discussion of the horticultural practices described, see Wright, *Paul and the Faithfulness*, 2:1211–17; Fitzmyer, *Romans*, 610, 614–15; Jewett, *Romans*, 684–85; Moo, *Epistle to the Romans*, 702–3.

to the whole in a vivid and meaningful way. Central to this image is God as divine horticulturist. He is the one who breaks off the natural branches, unbelieving Jews, and grafts in the wild branches, believing gentiles, breaking off and regrafting existing branches according to his kindness and severity. This indicated by the divine passives ἐκκλάω and ἐγκεντρίζω (vv. 17, 19, 20) and verse 21. With this, Paul reiterates and underscores all that he has said regarding the divine origin and foundation of the people of God, which, in effect, functions to level all potential forms of group pride stemming from self-identity as the elect.

Moreover, the metaphor allows the apostle to highlight Israel's continuing temporal and hierarchical priority in two ways. First, the imagery vividly portrays gentile believers as unnatural branches taken from a wild olive tree that have been grafted into a distinctly Jewish tree with distinct Jewish roots (v. 24). The tree existed prior to this divine act of grafting and, without the tree, with its natural branches, there would be nothing to graft the unnatural branches into. Although Paul does not explicitly equate the root with the patriarchs, it is likely that this is what it represents, given Rom 4:1–2 and the reference to its fatness, πιότητος, (v. 17). The latter most likely symbolizes the blessings of the Jewish tradition, including its scriptures and promises, from which the new movement springs[159] and from which it receives sustenance. As Paul puts it, it is this root that supports the unnatural branches, and not they who support it (v. 18).[160] In essence, without the root and its sustaining sap, the new movement composed of Jew and gentile would not exist. God chose the Jewish people, Israel, as the mundane entry point for his salvific plans for humanity and this choice stands, despite majority Israel's current unbelief in the face of majority gentile acceptance. In this way, Paul sharpens his warning against gentile antagonism toward the out-group (v. 18). They and the movement with which they identify themselves receive life-sustaining nourishment from Jewish tradition, harkening back to all Paul has already said regarding the historical framework that defines and gives meaning to the present believing community.[161] The contrast the apostle makes between the natural and unnatural branches, between the cultivated tree and the wild tree is noteworthy in light of the careful argument he already has made for the ascribed kinship between gentiles and Jews. Although this kinship is no less real than physical kinship and although Paul can refer to believing Jews and gentiles as his brothers and sisters, within the historical,

---

159. That the root represents the patriarchs is also supported by 1 En. 93:5; Philo, *Her.* 279; and Jub. 21:24 (Witherington and Hyatt, *Paul's Letter to the Romans*, 271).

160. Paul uses the singular second person. Although it is possible that he has individual gentiles in mind, the use of the singular may simply serve to sharpen his warning against gentile antagonism toward the out-group. As noted above, the potential for bias against the out-group would be greater among gentiles who would not identify themselves as both Jews and members of the in-group.

161. As Wright puts it, for Paul the real anti-Jewish position would be that which maintains that "the messianic death and resurrection of Jesus . . . should be seen as a fine religious option for gentiles but off limits for Jews" (Wright, *Paul and the Faithfulness*, 1221). For the apostle, the gospel is for the Jew first.

eschatological framework of God's salvific plans for humanity, the people of Israel, as an ethnoracial entity, retain priority. This includes the members of hardened Israel, bringing us to the second point—the imagery of divine regrafting.

As noted above, the image of God as the divine horticulturalist reiterates the point that election is by grace apart from human merit, however defined, as according to the law or otherwise. The proper human response is trust or faith in this God and, more specifically, in the present, faith or trust in his work in and through Christ. Accordingly, Paul couches his warning against gentile out-group antagonism in terms of faith (vv. 20–23), with the datives ἀπιστίᾳ and πίστει indicating the cause of the divine actions of breaking off and grafting in (v. 20). Although, in this instance, Paul foregrounds the human factor in the interplay between divine and human action, he underplays its significance in God's overall scheme by pointing out that the causal effect of human choice with regard to the gospel is only possible because of prior divine elective initiative, which provides the sole context for its operation. God's elective choices, past and present, stand firm through the course of time, unlike human response which can and does vary over time. Thus, Yahweh's choice of Israel in the past is firm, since God can and will with ease regraft the hardened members of Israel back into the tree, of which they were once a part, both now and in the future, if these members should return to faith. Paul's use of "how much more" (πόσῳ μᾶλλον) language in relation to God's regrafting of formerly unbelieving members of Israel underscores their priority—they were, are, and will be the people of God, as long as they cease in their unbelief.

By way of contrast, Paul describes the relative ease with which formerly grafted-in gentiles can and will be broken off, if they should fail to continue in God's kindness, χρηστότης (vv. 21–22). Although gentiles were grafted in on the basis of belief, their continuing existence as unnatural branches on the tree is dependent not on faith per se but, explicitly, on their remaining τῇ χρηστότητι of God (v. 22c). Although gentile persistence in faith is an implicit condition of remaining grafted, it is not at the forefront here. Rather, reliance on God's kindness, most likely an equivalent for God's grace, χάρις, that is offered to undeserving humanity through a Jewish messiah (5:2), resulting in undeserved wealth (11:12), reconciliation (11:15a), life from the dead (11:15b), and access to the nourishing sap of the olive tree (11:21) is.[162] Thus, gentiles remain members of God's people by remembering and by actively engaging in attitudes and behavior that reflect the fact that their membership in the in-group, and their possession of all the resultant benefits that formerly belonged only to Israel, is a gift, in the fullest sense of the term. As former branches of the wild olive tree, they, even more than Israel, have no reason or right to boast in their present condition; such boasting, as Paul sees it, will result in removal from the fruitful, cultivated tree into which they have been graciously grafted. This is the sternest of warnings. Not only is the inclusion of gentiles the result of divine kindness that is to be mirrored in their

---

162. Jewett, *Romans*, 690.

own relationship to the out-group, their inclusion constitutes the addition of wild stock to a tree, cultivated by a divine horticulturalist who existed long before they did and who both supports and nourishes them.

5.2.2.3 Leveling Effect of God's Sovereign Mercy (Rom 11:25–32)

5.2.2.3A THE MYSTERY: FULL REVELATION OF ISRAEL'S FOUNDATION ACCOUNT

Having addressed both Jewish and gentile bias against the out-group, Paul brings his argument for Israel's priority to a climax. The argument may be divided into two sections. The first part, verses 25–29, consists of the apostle's revelation concerning the mystery of God's future plan for unbelieving Israel, the mechanism of its re-incorporation into the people of God, and an exposition of the scriptural tradition that foresaw and supports the revelation. As such, it is the concluding elaboration of the foundation account that Paul has already related in that it explicitly accounts for Israel's ultimate place among the people of God. In the second section, verses 30–36, the apostle deals the final death blow to in-group bias against the out-group by means of an extended consideration of the paradoxical operation of God's mercy that works to place both the believing community and Israel on the same level, in relation to God, while preserving the latter's priority in relation to the former.

Paul's use of the appellative mystery as a descriptor of what he is about to reveal serves, among other things, to remind his audience that their community and the one from which it springs is of divine origin. Up until this point, the apostle has hinted at Israel's ultimate salvation (11:11–12, 15, 23–24). What has heretofore been implicit is made explicit and, more importantly, is described expressly in terms of a foundation account, of divine origin, that has always maintained the irrevocability of Israel's elect status even and, especially, in the new age. Paul's warning against thinking in merely human terms (v. 25b) suggests that what he is about to convey is a prophetic insight into an eschatological event that God will bring about that he, in some way, has been made privy to.[163] As such, it represents the final chapter of the foundation account that the apostle has already related, accounting, as it does, for the ultimate fate of hardened Israel. This, as Paul points out, like the account of origins previously related, was foretold in the scriptures (vv. 26c–27), specifically, in the sense that the foundation of Israel as the people of God would ultimately involve the removal of its sin by God in fulfillment of Yahweh's covenant with his people. This harkens back to all that Paul has said regarding the final restoration and renewal of Israel as promised in the scriptures in terms of an eschatological out-pouring of the Spirit, resulting in circumcision of the heart, making obedience to God a possibility. The prophetic aspect involves the

---

163. Witherington and Hyatt, *Paul's Letter to the Romans*, 272.

precise sequence of events: rejection by the majority of Israel; acceptance by the full number of gentiles; followed by the salvation of all Israel (vv. 25–26).

These verses are controversial on a number of counts. First, there is the issue of whether the phrase ἀπὸ μέρους is adverbial or adjectival. Its use here suggests a quantitative limitation, such that, not all of Israel was hardened. Notably, believing Jews, like Paul, who are Israelites, have not been hardened and are the remaining natural branches on the olive tree (cf. vv. 5, 7, 17).[164] Second, is the similar issue of what is meant by fullness of gentiles. Given the previous warning that gentiles may be removed from the tree if they fail to continue in God's kindness, it is unlikely that Paul's use of the term πλήρωμα suggests that every individual gentile will come to accept the gospel and be grafted in. Rather, the sense is that the hardening of majority Israel will continue until the time when either all gentiles yet to accept the gospel do so or all gentiles who will be saved are saved.[165]

Third is the highly contested question of whom does all Israel refer to?[166] I take the position that the phrase πᾶς Ἰσραὴλ σωθήσεται does not suggest that every individual Israelite will be saved. Rather, the reference is communal. In light of all that Paul has said thus far, and in light of the context, it is probable that all of Israel refers to the believing remnant and the members of hardened Israel who are/will be regrafted into the olive tree when the Deliverer from Zion comes (v. 26b). It is at this point that previously hardened Israel will shed its liminal status and become fully re-integrated into the people of God, even if not every individual Israelite is restored. For Paul, there is one people of God throughout history: Israel in the past; believing Israelites, with gentiles added on, in the present; and restored Israel, with believing gentiles added on, in the future. Ethno-racial diversity is maintained among the people of God, since there is one God, who is God of both Jews and gentiles (3:29–30). How Paul sees this working within the believing community is discussed in the following chapter of this work.

Finally, there is the question of how Israel will be saved. Paul neither states explicitly that hardened Israel will accept Jesus as the messiah, resulting in a mass conversion, nor when this deliverance will occur, at the parousia or some other time, nor to whom the Deliverer refers, Yahweh or Christ.[167] I take the view that Paul cites the prophecy as a pledge that, at some point immediately before the end of history, a Deliverer will come to save Israel.[168] For Isaiah, this Deliverer was Yahweh. For Paul, Yahweh has acted in and through Christ to deliver all of humanity from its sins, including Israel.

---

164. Byrne, *Romans*, 354.

165. Also, Witherington and Hyatt, *Paul's Letter to the Romans*, 273.

166. For a summary and discussion of the various positions, see Fitzmyer, *Romans*, 619–20, 623–24; Byrne, *Romans*, 354–55; Moo, *Epistle to the Romans*, 719–26; and Witherington and Hyatt, *Paul's Letter to the Romans*, 273–76.

167. See Fitzmyer, *Romans*, 619–20, 623–25 for a full discussion of this issue.

168. Also, Byrne, *Romans*, 355.

This suggests that the apostle's audience would assume that the Deliverer is Christ, whom hardened Israel will come to accept. Paul has already made the argument that the present (and future) people of God are characterized by their faith or trust in God's work in and through Christ. The reversal of Israel's unbelief would then mean its coming to believe in Yahweh's saving work in and through Christ. Read in this way, these verses are consistent with everything the apostle has related thus far concerning God's historical dealings with humanity and, in particular, his dealings with Israel. The absence of specific details relating to precisely how and when this conversion will occur, apart from an ambiguous reference to the Deliverer banishing ungodliness from Jacob (11:26b), does not negate its consistency.

Although this sequence is a reversal of traditional Jewish expectation, where the eschatological pilgrimage of the nations to Zion occurs after the restoration of Israel,[169] the latter's priority is explicitly maintained by in verses 28–29, where Paul states that the gifts and calling of God are irrevocable. Thus, as regards the gospel, members of hardened Israel are enemies of God and are such precisely for the sake of the gentiles. Accordingly, in the present, they stand outside of the people of God. Yet, even now, they are beloved because of the fathers, a notion that harkens back to the apostle's description of unbelieving Israel as children of the promise. Verses 28–29 form an inclusio with 9:4–5 indicating that all the things Paul has said in relation to unbelieving Israel, as negative as their present condition may appear, must always be read against the larger background of God's faithfulness to his people and their priority as the recipients of his promises and as the people group founded for the purpose of providing the mundane entry point for God's salvific plans for all of humanity. As Paul once again reminds his audience, unbelieving Israel's current alienation from God serves a larger, salvific purpose—the inclusion of the gentiles, which is itself contingent on Israel's rejection of the gospel. Moreover, God's faithfulness as revealed and expressed in the mystery and as foretold in the scriptures underscores the fact that hardened Israel's liminal status is temporary. Because of God's faithfulness, all of Israel, the remnant and the rest, will count among the people of God. Its divine founder has guaranteed this and has provided an account of origins for Israel that maintains its priority over the nations.

5.2.2.3b Prisoners of Disobedience: All are Equal before God

Having unequivocally established the priority of Israel, Paul returns to the theme of inclusivity with regard to God's dealings with humanity introduced in the opening chapters of the letter. The positive identity constructed by the apostle in chapters 6–8 rests on the premise that God's election of Israel was for the purpose of the

---

169. E.g., Ps 22:27; Isa 2:2–3; 56:6–8; Mic 4:2; Zech 2:11; 14:16; Tob 13:11; 14:6–7 (Witherington and Hyatt, *Paul's Letter to the Romans*, 272; Byrne, *Romans*, 349–50).

eventual inclusion of the nations among the people of God as foretold by Israel's own scriptures. Accordingly, Paul rounds off his argument for Israel's priority by reminding his audience that despite Israel's priority with respect to the gentiles, all, τοὺς πάντας, both Jew and gentile, are equal recipients of God's grace and mercy, given that God has imprisoned each group in disobedience, for the purpose of showing each his mercy (cf. 3:9, 23).

Verses 30–31 underscore the interconnection of the two groups in a way that emphasizes their parity with respect to God. Present (νῦν) gentile experience of God's mercy is premised on Israel's disobedience, for the express purpose that the latter might also experience mercy. The dative τῇ τούτων ἀπειθείᾳ is most likely a causal dative, given that Paul has made clear that Israel's rejection made it possible for the gospel to be preached and received by the gentiles (vv. 12, 15, 17). The phrase τῷ ὑμετέρῳ ἐλέει most likely modifies the verb "disobeyed."[170] Some interpreters read τῷ ὑμετέρῳ ἐλέει in a causal sense, "so they too may now be shown mercy as a result of the mercy shown to you."[171] However, it may be understood as a dative of advantage.[172] This comports with the idea that God desires to be merciful to all, which Paul makes explicit in verse 32. The adverb νῦν (v. 31b) is missing in several major text witnesses. The difficulty of relating an original adverb understood as "now" to a future showing of mercy to Israel might be the reason for its omission.[173] However, its use may simply convey imminence, "now, at any time" or "in time."[174] The new age is juxtaposed with the old in a way that underscores the new movement's rootedness in and dependence on God's people of the past. Thus, in the new age, gentiles, who in a corporate or communal sense were disobedient to God and not counted among his people, have received mercy and are counted among God's people, because of Israel's disobedience. Although Israel is currently not experiencing God's mercy due to its disobedience, God's ultimate intention with respect to Israel is to show it mercy.[175] Israel's current disobedience works to the advantage of the in-group; a notion that harkens back to everything Paul has said regarding the new movement's history and identity. However, God's final word on the matter is that his recalcitrant people will once again experience his mercy because that has been the divine intention all along.

Appropriately, Paul concludes with a doxology celebrating God's wisdom and knowledge (vv. 33–36), in his case, as these attributes are revealed and expressed in

---

170. See, Moo, *Epistle to the Romans*, 734–35, and Fitzmyer, *Romans*, 626–29, for a complete discussion.

171. Fitzmyer, *Romans*, 627–28.

172. Byrne, *Romans*, 356.

173. Byrne, *Romans*, 356.

174. Moo, *Epistle to the Romans*, 735; Byrne, *Romans*, 356.

175. The chiastic structure of vv. 30–31 is interrupted by the purpose clause, ἵνα, drawing attention to this element of the literary construction (Byrne, *Romans*, 352).

his salvific plan for humanity.[176] Thus, underlying everything Paul has said regarding the historical legitimacy of the believing community, its identity as the people of God, and the place and role of Israel in the new age is a divine founder whose inscrutable ways and judgments work to bring mercy and grace to all people.

5.3 Conclusion

In Rom 6–11, the previously introduced motifs of God's sovereignty with regard to election, the human response of faith to this sovereignty, the provisional nature of the law, and, consequently, the ultimacy of God's present work in and through Christ, all of this in accordance with the Jewish scriptures, are recapitulated and reworked in the Paul's reinterpretation of Israel's divine filiation in light of the eschatological present. Interwoven throughout this complex, previously introduced, theological argumentation is a series of equally complex units of ethnic discourse by means of which Paul not only completes his case for the historical legitimacy of the Christ movement but also establishes a third group of humanity, unbelieving Israel, which paradoxically retains its priority despite the fact that, for the apostle, the Christ movement represents God's ultimate purpose for humankind.

In chapters 6–8, Paul constructs a positive identity for his audience as the children of God, empowered by the promised Spirit to walk before him in righteousness, apart from the Jewish law. In terms of the apostle's larger ethnographic purpose of establishing the historical legitimacy of the Christ movement, Rom 6:1—8:13 serves a dual purpose. First, by establishing precisely how the intent of the OT law can be fulfilled in believers, Paul strengthens the link between past and present, while simultaneously redefining the former in light of the latter. The righteousness that Israel could not manifest by obedience to the law in response to God's gift of election is now made possible in Christ, by the Spirit. In ethnographic terms, a legitimate people have legitimate laws. This redefinition of the law in terms of both Christ and the Spirit not only provides the necessary theological framework for Paul's reconceptualized ethic, fleshed out in the remaining chapters of the letter, but also brings to the forefront the Spirit as the agent of both the promised eschatological renewal of Israel and the creator of a new means of divine filiation that includes gentiles among the family of God. Second, with this, the apostle brings the theme of election to a climax, redefining it in terms of the Spirit, in a way that raises a host of critical questions.

More specifically, the reference to believers' divine sonship brings into sharp relief an issue, hinted at, but up until this point unvoiced, concerning the status of unbelieving Israel in the new age of the Spirit. In terms of his larger, ethnographic purposes, Paul must address this vexing question for several reasons. First, if the Christ movement, including both its founder and members, is legitimate, as Paul

---

176. Moo, *Epistle to the Romans*, 741.

claims, then why are the majority of Jews unconvinced, especially given the movement's decidedly Jewish roots? Second, for all intents and purposes, Paul's arguments strongly suggest that God has abandoned Israel, the people to whom the sonship and the promise were given in the first place. How can the apostle expect believers to trust in a God who reneges on his promises? What then is their ground for hope? This raises a third, related question concerning the precise status of Israel in relation to the Christ movement. This issue is especially poignant given the presence of Jews among both the movement's leadership and its members.

The apostle takes up these issues in chapters 9–11 skillfully laying the groundwork for a more favorable conception of the other that culminates in a portrait of Israel as not only the sustaining and nourishing root of the present believing community but also as the people group divinely commissioned to play an integral role in the process of the inclusion of gentiles within it. By carefully constructing and defining the categories of children of the promise, and the remnant as rooted in God's elective, sovereign purposes, especially as these relate to divine freedom in excluding and including people groups and reconfiguring the people of God as he sees fit, Paul not only levels in-group bias against the out-group, but also establishes Israel's continuing priority, in relation to the gentiles, in the new age.

The reintroduction of the theme of human response in the form of active faith/trust in the present work of God in and through Christ as an identity criterion of the people of God in the new age, serves to further refine the category of children of the promise in a way that underscores majority Israel's present, and temporary, liminal status in relation to God. The apostle depicts this liminal position as a nexus between the new age, in which Israel does not yet directly participate, due to its present unbelief, and the fullness of the new age to come, where its participation is divinely guaranteed. Moreover, the paradoxical operation of God's mercy works to place both the believing community and Israel on the same level, in relation to God, while preserving the latter's priority in relation to the former. This is the profound mystery that the apostle reveals to his audience. As such, it represents the final chapter of the foundation account that Paul has already related, accounting, as it does, for the ultimate fate of hardened Israel. In his incomparable and inscrutable wisdom and knowledge, God has ensured that all of Israel, the remnant and the rest, will count among the people of God. For Paul, the divine founder has guaranteed this and has provided an account of origins for Israel that maintains its priority over the nations.

In sum, throughout these six chapters, as in the prior chapters of the letter, Paul utilizes the law-faith dichotomy to connect the past to the present, drawing lines of continuity and discontinuity between God's people now and then. In this case, the dichotomy works to create a distinct place for unbelieving Israel in the new age, allowing Paul to delineate its unique role in the unfolding eschatological present. Moreover, faith in the present work of God in and through Christ opens the door to reception of the promised Spirit, in turn making possible a life of obedience that enfolds, yet supersedes, that embodied in the old written code. For the apostle, the transformative work of the Spirit creates a new, allocentric identity that characterizes the people of God in the present age constituting a people group capable of living out the full intent of the written law. As any other ethnographer worth his or her salt, Paul carefully delineates the manner of life that characterizes the people group he is describing, defining, and defending—a characterization to which we now turn.

CHAPTER SIX

The Historical Legitimacy of the Christ Movement (Part III)

The Manner of Life of the New People of God (Rom 12:1—13:14 and 14:1—15:6): Spirit-Wrought Allocentric Identity and a Transformed Ethos

GIVEN THE APOLOGETIC NATURE of ancient ethnographic texts, their authors generally not only omitted insignificant and unreliable information (i.e., information not useful to their aims), but also sought to explain a people's customs, traditions, and manner of life as a reaction to or a result of events related in the account of origins. Accordingly, Dionysius of Halicarnassus writes that he, unlike other great historians of the city of Rome and its people, has "determined not to pass over a noble period of history," the earliest events associated with the founding of Rome, for the reason that they account for the Roman peoples' present greatness (*Ant. rom.* 1.6.2–3). The Roman people are great by virtue of the fact that they spring from noble and virtuous founders. Thus, they choose "the noblest and most ambitious" lives, "when they consider that all who are sprung from illustrious origin ought to set a high value on themselves and indulge in no pursuit unworthy of their ancestors" (1.6.3–4).

This causal linkage served to strengthen (or weaken) the claim that the people group under consideration was living according to divine mandate. Recall that Strabo, in a move that shows blatant disregard for native sources, attributes the present day superstitious practices of the Jews to "superstitious men" who "were appointed to the priesthood, and then tyrannical people," who rose up after the pious Egyptian, Moses, and his immediate successors, from whom then "arose abstinence from flesh" and "circumcisions and excisions and other observances of the kind" (*Geogr.* 16.2.34–37). According to the Stoic, the Jews present spurious status as a people is the direct effect of their coming under the sway of spurious leaders. Put differently, since faithfulness to divine injunction was manifested in concrete, daily attitudes and behaviors, a given people group was legitimate precisely because it exemplified its divinely given laws in the customs, traditions, and manner of life which defined it as a distinct community. Thus, Josephus portrays the Jewish people as constituting a superior polity based on laws that are "in accordance with the will of God," "which sets God at the head of the universe," and "assigns the administration of its highest affairs to the whole body of priests," who ensure that the laws are kept in "the pursuits of everyday life" of the community (*Ag. Ap.* 2.184–87). Consequently, shared customs, including common religious beliefs, practices, and modes of worship, played a key role in defining a people group. Thus, according to Dionysius, Rome's Greekness is evidenced in its customs, temples, images of gods, and worship practices (*Ant. rom.* 1.21.1–3). In sum, a common way of life testified not only to the legitimacy of the community but also to the achieved and ascribed bonds of kinship that knit together the individuals comprising it into an ethnoracial entity. A people who claimed such ties were expected to live in a way that was an observable manifestation of them.

This comports with social identity theory, which maintains that independent group identity comes into existence through the construction of a new symbolic universe which challenges the symbolic universe as originally constituted by the parent group; that is, the original group from which it is emerging.[1] As we have seen, Paul takes on this task in the first eleven chapters of his letter where he expounds a viable worldview for the surfacing Christ movement, which while rooted in its Jewish past, looks to the present, unfolding age of the Spirit.[2] Sociologists describe the gradual emergence of a new and/or alternative community as a precarious process which entails the constant threat of group disintegration and/or assimilation.[3] Hence, the need for this ideology or worldview, which works against these leveling forces both by providing legitimacy for the emerging group's state of separation and by giving it cohesion.[4] Although a group's social identity emerges within the context of its unifying worldview, its development is also dependent on differentiation from other groups, mainly by the establishment of clearly defined group boundary markers.[5] Since identity is a social construction and depends on observable manifestations of these delineating markers, the is of a particular group takes on practical significance in light of the ought, which is expected to cohere with the former such that the group's worldview is manifested in its concrete social interactions. In cases where this coherence is lacking, the purported identity of the group will typically be called into question by critical and/or suspicious outsiders, quick to note discrepancies between who or what the group claims to be and how its members actually behave in relation to

---

1. Ukwuegbu, *Emergence of Christian Identity*, 399.

2. Accordingly, this type of social change entails the need to effect a positive reevaluation on the part of the emerging group in relation to the parent group(s). This is accomplished as the emerging group improves its actual social location by reversing the relative positions of itself and the parent group(s). In the case of religious communities, this inversion involves the claim that members of the new group are the actual upholders of the original truth and spirituality of the religion which has been either diluted and/or distorted by the community from which they are breaking loose (Ukwuegbu, *Emergence of Christian Identity*, 400). As discussed in the previous chapter, for Paul, his unbelieving kindred, according to the flesh, have a misguided zeal for God due to their unbelief.

3. Asano, *Community-Identity*, 14.

4. Ukwuegbu, *Emergence of Christian Identity*, 399.

5. Brawley, "Identity and Metaethics," 107–23.

each other and to the wider social context.⁶ In other words, a given group's legitimacy is dependent on an ethos reflective of its symbolic universe.

Thus, having established the lawful character of the believing community, albeit apart from the old, written law, Paul turns to delineating the basic contours of the allocentric or other-centered manner of communal living (12:1—13:14). This manner of life not only characterizes the people of God in the new age, but also reflects their worldview, as the apostle has described it in the account of origins. From there, he moves on to discuss how this relates specifically to the believing community's worship practices (14:1—15:6).

Since ethnoracial and/or group identity in antiquity was often deemed to be produced and indicated by religious practices, discourse on religion and ethnicity could be used to establish a variety of relationships between otherwise discrete peoples, including the forging of connections between distinctive groups in order to produce a collective identity for the new, amalgamated group. As noted above, the *Roman Antiquities* provides an excellent case in point, where the ritual practices involved in Greek sacrifice are presented as the most compelling evidence of the Roman people's true ancestry (1.20.2–3), allowing the author to claim that both Greeks and Romans stand over and against all other barbarian people groups. Moreover, the appearance of similar worship practices across different people groups could function to make claims for ethnoracial ties between these diverse peoples (cf. Strabo, *Geogr.* 10.3.10–13). In these instances, the connection between who one is and who one worships is interwoven with other criteria for defining membership in the group, including appeals to kinship and ancestry.

Accordingly, Paul's construal of the believing community's identity as other-centered has a direct bearing on the worship practices characterizing a community composed of an amalgamation of distinct ethnoracial groups, all with their own ideas of what constitutes proper worship of the one God. As we will see, the apostle skillfully negotiates the thorny shoals of ethnic diversity in a manner that makes room for such diversity, while preserving a unified group-identity consistent with its spirit-wrought allocentric character. As discussed below, all of this functions to further strengthen the legitimacy of the new movement. In terms of Paul's larger ethnographic purposes, the elaboration of the community's ethos serves to fortify his audience's resolve to remain faithful to the gospel within an environment that continually exerts pressures toward social and cultural conformity both by establishing the divine origins of its ethos and by providing viable boundary markers that work to maintain both group cohesion and group differentiation, while simultaneously allowing for incorporation of the other.

---

6. David G. Horrell discusses the relationship between a community's ethos and its symbolic universe in detail in Horrell, *Solidarity and Difference*, 98.

6.1 Constructing an Allocentric Identity: Renewed Mind, Living Sacrifice, and a Transformed View of Self in Relation to the Other (Rom 12:1—13:14)

Recall that an allocentric identity is characterized by interest focused on the other, rather than on the self. As such, this identity entails the ability to resist the common inter-group identity processes by means of which positive group identity is maintained through negative evaluations of the other. Paul's involved discussion of the unique place and role of the Jewish people in the dawning new age of the Spirit in chapters 9–11, is premised on the assumption that the members of his audience, especially its gentile members, have the Spirit-given capacity to resist these normal, negative out-group evaluative processes. His task of making them cognizant of this reality and its practical implications is carried forward in 12:1—13:14. According to the apostle, the Spirit creates an allocentric identity for the believing community that is characterized by the ability of its members to love both insiders/in-group and outsiders/out-group.[7] This is the identity that Paul fleshes out in 12:1—13:14; an identity whose basic contours have already been sketched in the preceding chapters of the letter.

Specifically, the apostle has already established that faith, manifested in both attitude and conduct, in the present work of God in and through Christ (i.e., faith in the gospel) is what characterizes the new people of God. However, in the present, new age, this faith entails reception of the promised Spirit, who makes obedience to God a real possibility, resulting in the manifestation of attitudes and behaviors commensurate with that faith. As such, the Spirit functions in tandem with faith as the primary indicator of membership within the believing community. Put differently, faith in the gospel and possession of the Spirit are the primary markers of identity of the people of God in the present age. They are the people who have been freed from the power of sin, to walk according to the Spirit, united with Christ, as the servants of God. The social identity of the believing community is rooted in this reality, making believers, Jew and gentile alike, the sons and daughters of God, who bear a family resemblance to their divine Father. Accordingly, this identity may be described as "superordinate," in that it transcends the existing, traditional ethnoracial categories of Jew-gentile, incorporating diverse peoples under a common identity.[8]

However, as I have already pointed out, this supraordinate identity involves more than a simple change in thinking with regard to one's attitude and behavior toward the ethnic other. In this regard, we may recall the example provided by Thucydides, discussed in chapter four of this work. That is, as Paul will make clear, it entails more than a call to temporarily subsume subgroup identities, such as Dorian, Ionian, and Chalcidians under the the overarching ethnoracial identity, Sicilian, for political

---

7. Kuecker, *Spirit and the 'Other,'* 48–49.

8. Kuecker, *Spirit and the 'Other,'* 50. This new social identity does not mean that ethnic identity is negated (Kuecker, *Spirit and the 'Other,'* 19). I will return to this point in my examination of Rom 14:1—15:6.

expediency (Thucydides, *Hist.* 4.59.1—4.64.5). Unlike Thucydides's construction of a supraordinate identity, the creation of an in-Christ identity involves a profound, Spirit-wrought transformation of believers that allows subgroup identities to continue at the penultimate level. Moreover, the identity the apostle constructs is viable precisely because it works to directly shape the ethos of the community it characterizes.

Foundation narratives, such as the one Paul has presented, in their capacity to provide a viable symbolic universe for the communities that embrace them are identity and community forming. This means that they necessarily shape relationships both within the group and without. As noted above, it is the the ethos of the group, the ought, that directs the community in enacting or making concrete its symbolic universe, which is largely conceptual. It is these relationships that are the focus of Rom 12:1—13:4. As we have seen, Paul applies the OT appellation "servants of God" to the ethnically diverse believing community, suggesting that their affiliation and relationship with the one God is what unites them as a single people with the single purpose of walking righteously before their Lord. Thus, according to the apostle, the concrete manifestation, or living into and living out, of this identity entails the proper worship of God (12:1–2) as the beginning point. This, in turn, calls for a due assessment of the self in relation to others within the community (12:3–8), which itself necessitates a proper view of the other, both within and without the believing community (12:9—13:10). In other words, this common identity results in a common way of life that testifies to and exemplifies its divine origins/foundation and its ability to form a distinct people group among whom the beginning of new age finds expression (13:11–14).

6.1.1 Establishing the Foundations for a Transformed Communal Identity and Ethos

6.1.1.1 *Rational Worship of God (Rom 12:1–2)*

The parenetic character of this portion of the letter is duly noted by its interpreters. Although elements of exhortation appear in earlier portions of the missive (e.g., 6:12–14; 8:5–13; 11:17–24), there is a distinct shift in tenor and focus beginning with 12:1, as the apostle moves from what is primarily an exposition of the content of the gospel to its ramifications for daily life. In light of Paul's ethnographic purposes, the causal οὖν (v. 1) suggests that the manner of life that the apostle is about to expound for his audience is premised upon and results from the account of origins presented thus far. The reference to God's mercies (οἰκτιρμῶν) as the grounds (διὰ) for the first exhortation specifically evokes the experience of divine mercy by both Jews and gentiles presented in 11:30–32. However, other elements in these two verses harken back to even earlier passages.

The reference to believers' bodies as living sacrifices offered to God stands in sharp contrast to the degrading form of bodily life portrayed in 1:24, 26–27. As the latter mode of existence was the result of futile thinking (1:21), leading to idolatry (1:23, 28), so the renewal of the mind (v. 2) leads to a new mode of existence that allows for nonconformity to the world, including its patterns of idolatry and immorality, and the proper worship of God as Lord and Creator. According to Paul, acceptable worship of God, the giving to him of due honor and gratitude (1:21), entails the offering of one's entire self to him. Here, σώματα refers to the physical or material bodies of believers. The renewal of the mind, τῇ ἀνακαινώσεε τοῦ νοὸς, most likely refers to the liberation of the thinking and discerning faculty of believers from the dominion of sin.[9] As a result, believers are enabled to think and to comprehend reality in a way that leads them to making decisions in keeping with the unfolding of a life that is pleasing to God. The present imperatives, συσχηματίζεσθε and μεταμορφοῦσθε, suggest an ongoing act. Although it is possible that Paul has outward conformity in view here, given the verbs he uses, it is just as likely that he is using a concept from Stoicism, which speaks of moral or inward transformation (e.g., Seneca, *Ep.* 6.1).[10] Accordingly, they, unlike unbelieving humanity, are not compelled to conform to the pattern of the world, which is characterized by its inability to please God, bound as it is to the power of sin. Paul has already argued that this liberation from the power of sin and, consequently, liberation from futile thinking, is the result of the reception of the Spirit in and through Christ. It is this Spirit-transformed mind that enables believers to make the choices commensurate with walking righteously before God. The exhortation to offer one's body as a living sacrifice and to be transformed, in the sense that one no longer lives according to the pattern of the world, presupposes that believers, as persons free from the power of sin and empowered by the Spirit, are capable of carrying out the apostle's injunction, harkening back to the 6:12–23 and 8:5–13. Finally, Paul's insistence that believers are capable of discerning God's will (v. 2), implicitly apart from the old, written code, evokes both the Spirit-led obedience that believers experience, discussed in 8:5–13, and the provisional nature of the law treated in 7:4–6.

Three things emerge from this that are particularly salient for the Spirit-wrought allocentric identity that Paul is constructing. First, possession of the Spirit (which accompanies faith in the gospel), evidenced in a transformed mind, is the primary identifying mark of those who belong to the believing community. However, in this regard, it is important to keep in mind that, without faith, the believing community would not have the Spirit. Thus, when I speak of the Spirit as the primary marker of identity, I am assuming the presence of faith. Accordingly, Spirit and faith, operating

---

9. As Jewett notes, the term ἀνακαινωσίς in light of the prominence of the term "newness" in Rom 6:4 and 7:6 as denoting humanity's restoration through the power of Christ, suggests that Paul has in mind the recovery of righteousness and right thinking through faith in the gospel (Jewett, *Romans*, 733).

10. Witherington and Hyatt, *Paul's Letter to the Romans*, 286.

in tandem, function as the primary identifying mark of those who belong to the believing community; a two-sided descriptor that may be denoted by the word, "Spirit," for the sake of simplicity. It is the Spirit (which is present by/in/through faith in the gospel) that enables each individual member of the in-group to live sacrificially to God; that is, in a manner that is good, pleasing, and perfect. The Spirit not only identifies those who have faith in the gospel, but also fashions these transformed individuals into a community. In this regard, it is noteworthy that Paul begins his appeal by addressing his audience as ἀδελφοί. The use of this kinship term harkens back to believers' Spirit-wrought identity as the children of God in 8:14–17. Thus, believers, Jews and all manner of gentiles, are unified not only on the basis of this status, that is, as together constituting the new people of God, but also on the more intimate basis of shared blood via the Spirit. This picture of a singular people, united by blood, allows for the recognition of a common social identity, whereby ethnoracial identities, similarly based on blood ties, are nested within and under the terminal Spirit-wrought identity, a matter Paul will take-up more specifically beginning in 14:1.[11]

Second, the worship that characterizes and defines this singular people is similarly Spirit based. As such, it is not recognized by a clearly defined set of rites and rituals. Paul refers to this worship as being τὴν λογικὴν (v. 1). As regards this adjective, the meaning "spiritual," in the sense of inward as opposed to the material or physical, does not agree with his instance that believers offer their material bodies as an act of worship. Thus, it is more likely that the apostle is describing worship that is rational, in the sense of that which is distinctive of humans as rational, reflective creatures.[12] However, given the allusions to earlier portions of the letter noted above, it is highly probable that this worship is rational also in the sense that it reflects the community's account of origins as it has been presented by Paul.[13] In other words, it is the type of worship reflective of a Spirit-infused and transformed people living in the in-breaking new age of the Spirit. As such, it entails the offering of the entire self, mind and body, by each member of the community, to God as a living sacrifice, θυσίαν ζῶσαν. Rather than being a people characterized by the type(s) of objects they bring to sacrifice to their god(s)/God and by the rules and rituals associated with these sacrificial offerings, believers are a people who offer themselves to God, not in death but in life. This brings us to the third observation.

---

11. As Kuecker points out, evidence and appreciation of the full incorporation of non-Jews into the believing community is what allows for a common social identity, which in turn allows for an ethnically diverse group to be recognized in a meaningful way. Moreover, ethnic identity is not obliterated, since Jews can speak of themselves as the ethnic brothers of other Jews (Kuecker, *Spirit and the 'Other,'* 215). As we have seen, Paul does this very thing in Rom 9:3.

12. Byrne, *Romans*, 365–66. The latter connotation is found among the Stoics (e.g., Epictetus, *Dis.* 1.16.20–21; 2.9.2; Philo, *Spec.* 1.277).

13. Wright makes a similar point, maintaining that Paul is referring to worship, which his logic or arguments point to (Wright, *Romans*, 705).

The terms παραστῆσαι and θυσίαν are generally acknowledged by interpreters as technical language drawn from Greco-Roman sacrificial language.[14] However, not only are any references to particular sacrificial rituals and rites absent, with the sacrificial object being believers themselves, but also the term denoting "sacrifice" is explicitly qualified by the term "living," further differentiating this community's practice from any other contemporary customs. Sacrificial offerings in antiquity were often bloody, requiring the death of the live animal offering. With respect to Jewish sacrificial practices, although certain rites called for the slaughter of a living animal, the prophetic critique of sacrifices unaccompanied by true devotion to God (e.g., 1 Sam 15:22; Isa 1:10–20; Jer 6:20; Hos 8:11–13; Amos 5:21–27), likely provides a line of continuity between the new movement and its Jewish past. That is, Paul appears to stand within the broad flow of this tradition in that, for him, like for the prophets, adherence to ritual and rites alone, unaccompanied by the devotion of one's entire self to God, does not qualify as acceptable worship of God.[15] In the new age, with the coming of the Spirit, God's people are enabled to worship God in a way and to a degree that his people in the past were not capable of. Once again, past and present converge in Paul's reinterpretation of Israel's scriptural tradition. Here, obedience to God is made possible by the Spirit, with this radical obedience constituting the heart of his people's worship. In other words, ceremonial traditions, rites, and rituals are no longer necessary and, if they exist at all, are, at best, penultimate markers of the people of God.[16] The present people of God worship in and by the Spirit. This accords with all that Paul has said with regard to the provisional nature of the law and, in this instance, specifically, to the ritualistic laws regarding sacrifice.

Moreover, the allusions in verses 1–2 to the first part of the letter suggest that Paul has Christ's sacrificial pattern of obedience in mind as that which is to be exemplified by the believing community. The injunction to offer one's body as a living sacrifice harkens back to the apostle's exhortation to believers to offer their members to God in 6:13. In the case of the latter, the ability to heed is explicitly premised on believers' unity with Christ (6:5–7), who himself lives for God (6:10b). Thus, in similar fashion, believers are to consider themselves dead to sin and alive to God (6:11), living according to the τύπος of Christ (6:17)[17] and not according to fleshy passions and desires. In accordance with how Paul characterizes the worship of the believing community, the obedience constituting this worship is likewise not circumscribed by a written body of rules and regulations, as in the past. Rather, the community is to discern what is good and acceptable and perfect to God, with the second person plural suggesting that communal rather than individual discernment is in view.[18] The

14. Jewett, *Romans*, 727–28.
15. Byrne, *Romans*, 363.
16. Paul will return to this beginning in 14:1.
17. This verse and the term τύπος were discussed in the previous chapter of this work.
18. Byrne, *Romans*, 364.

Spirit-transformed mind of its members gives the community the ability to discern what is required to live according to God's will, while the obedience flowing from that discernment makes its life a continual sacrifice pleasing to God,[19] as members resist conformation to the moral, ethical, and behavioral patterns of the world.[20]

Thus, the new movement's social identity, as characterized by its worship, is at its core allocentric, since the Spirit-derived impetus that guides its thinking and actions is focused on God, the divine other, rather than on its own will or that of the world. Put differently, the community lives to God, continually putting his will above their own, according to the pattern of Christ. In this people group there is no room for boasting, apart from boasting in God, or self-glorification (1:30; 2:17, 23, 29; 3:27; 4:2; 5:2, 11; 11:20, 25). In terms of Paul's larger ethnographic purposes, the appeal to God-focused rather than self-focused living evokes the reference to the community's suffering in 8:17–18, which itself is grounded in Christ's own suffering and glorification (v. 17). In other words, the sacrificial worship/life (the two are inseparable) of the community includes its remaining faithful to the gospel in the face of social pressures to do otherwise. As Paul has already affirmed, the believing community's hope resides in its trust in the God, who is true to his promises, including the promise of both believers' and creation's final redemption.

In sum, it is Spirit-wrought worship, which is made possible through faith in the gospel, which identifies this new people, forming the subgroups of Jew and gentile into a unified family, which at its heart is God-focused. It is God, through Christ and the Spirit, who unites them as a singular people with a singular purpose—to worship the Creator by living sacrificially (i.e., by adopting an allocentric posture) to him. In other words, the community's terminal identity is Spirit-wrought and is manifested in Spirit-led worship/life that has God's will as its center. This suggests that any and all traditions, rites, and customs associated with communal worship and/or life function as penultimate markers of the group's identity. This differs markedly from the ancient belief that membership within a given people group is evidenced mainly by "the structure of their temples, the images of their gods, their purifications and sacrifices and many other things of that nature" (Dionysius, *Ant. Rom.* 1.21.1–2). The believing community's ethos is essentially other-focused in that it is grounded in and receives its impetus from what God desires and wills for his people, rather than on what any individual member or circle within the community may deem as good for the group as a whole.

This is not to say that traditions, rituals, and rites have no place in the believing community. For example, it is clear that members of the new movement participated in the Lord's Supper and that this rite, properly performed, was central to communal

---

19. Byrne, *Romans*, 364.

20. As noted in the previous chapter of this work, the teachings and example of Christ and the Spirit work in tandem to guide and direct believers in living a life that is morally and ethically pleasing to God.

worship (1 Cor 11:10–34; Rom 14:13–23). Moreover, this particular rite distinguished the believing community from all other worshipping communities and, as such, was a means of constructing and sustaining group self-identity. Paul's point appears to be that identity forming rites and rituals are valid in so far as they are performed and executed in the Spirit. That is, they are valid forms of worship when they are allocentric, in that they provide a means of worshipping God that is pleasing to him, in the fullest sense. This, as we will see, necessarily includes an allocentric concern for fellow worshippers (cf. 1 Cor 11:21–22).

As we have seen, the transformative power of the Spirit creates an ethnically diverse family characterized by Spirit-renewed minds. For this kinship bond to be viable there must necessarily be concern for the human other expressed specifically by the willingness to subordinate privileged identity, in this case, ethnoracial identity, for the sake of individuals not of one's ethnicity. This is a defining characteristic for the kind of persons capable of participation in an ethnically diverse social group.[21] Consequently, Paul turns to delineating a more detailed picture of how members of the believing community are to relate to one another within the context of their communal, sacrificial worship of God, as the apostle has just described it. As we will see, for Paul, a God-focused social identity and communal life are viable only if members of the group see themselves in relation to the other and as a consequence, live for each other.

6.1.1.2 *Due Assessment of Self (Rom 12:3–8)*

That the Spirit-wrought, allocentric identity ought to be the terminal identity of every member of the believing community is made explicit in this passage, with the γάρ closely linking these verses with the previous two. The communal discernment of God's will includes the proper assessment of who one is in this multiethnic family of God. For Paul, who one is within this diverse community is primarily defined by the spiritual gift that each member has been given by God. Moreover, these gifts are given expressly for the benefit of the community as a whole. Thus, identity and role are integrally linked and Spirit-determined. As such, no individual can claim special privilege, since each individual spiritual gift is freely bestowed, apart from human merit, achieved, ascribed, or otherwise. However, since these gifts are diverse, uniformity of social identity and purpose is manifested in a plurality of roles or functions, each organically linked to the other in a way that defies human derived standards of ranking and status. Put simply, one is not primarily a Jew, a Roman, a Greek, or a Scythian, man-woman, slave-free, merchant, aristocrat, or peasant. Rather, one is first and foremost a member of the body of Christ with a specific, divinely mandated function within that body that derives from one Spirit. All other social identities are subsumed and transformed by this reality and, as such, are penultimate.

---

21. Kuecker, *Spirit and the 'Other,'* 217–18.

6.1.1.2A The Divinely Given Standard of Measurement

In antiquity, a person's genealogy, gender, and place of origin were several key factors that worked together in a complex, integrated way to determine one's identity and role in society. For example, Paul identifies himself as Saul of Tarsus, a city of considerable renown (Acts 22:3).[22] The apostle's charge to a sober assessment of one's self (v. 3) signals that he is about to call this human derived method of self-assessment into question. Moreover, any individual who continues to evaluate him or herself according to these human patterns of appraisal is in danger of thinking too highly of oneself, given that all believers are members of one another, while together forming the one body in Christ (v. 5). With this image, Paul sets the groundwork for a different way of assessing the self that finds its point of departure in the ontological reality of being ἐν Χριστῷ. This state of existence has the effect of not only leveling all forms of self-promotion or self-glorification based on either the above-mentioned factors or any other humanly determined criteria, but also mandates an other-focused ethos that has no place for such thinking.

The basis for Paul's injunction to adopt a sober mindset with regard to the self is the cryptic and controversial clause ὡς ὁ Θεὸς ἐμέρισεν μέτρον πίστεως (12:3).[23] Since its meaning cannot be determined solely on grammatical and syntactical grounds, the immediate context must be considered. In this case, the body metaphor and spiritual gifts and their exercise within that one body are the topics the apostle turns his attention to. That he makes reference to his own gift as the authoritative basis for the injunction he is about to give (v. 3a) further suggests that these topics and the necessity for sober self-appraisal, in light of them, are in view in verse 3c. Accordingly, interpretation of the above mentioned phrase must allow for a logical connection between verse 3 and the verses immediately following and must agree with the apostle's call for believers to eschew competitive comparisons with each other based on either penultimate social identities or other criteria.

Thus, in light of the latter consideration, it is unlikely that Paul is making the case that self-assessment should be in accordance with the amount, in a quantitative sense, of faith an individual possesses in relation to others. The context suggests that the apostle is discouraging such comparisons among believers.[24] Furthermore, the idea that God would give different amounts or degrees (in a quantitative sense) of

---

22. Witherington, *Paul Quest*, 32.

23. See Moo, *Epistle to the Romans*, 761, for a discussion of the two main positions. Exegetes also tend to associate this clause with the equally difficult phrase, κατὰ τὴν ἀναλογίαν τῆς πίστεως, in verse 6b. However, although there is some overlap in meaning between μέτρον and ἀναλογία, they need not necessarily be equivalents. In the following sequence of gifts, the mention of each gift is followed by a reference to its fruitful exercise. Thus, it is likely that the phrase qualifying the gift of prophecy serves the same function. Accordingly, the value of a given prophecy is shown in direct proportion to its ability to build up the faith of the community, which is the primary task of the prophet (cf., 1 Cor 14:3–4, 22) (Byrne, *Romans*, 371–73).

24. Byrne, *Romans*, 371.

faith to believers is a difficult one and suggests that faith, in this context, refers to something other than basic Christian belief.²⁵ It is clear that believers themselves may have different degrees of faith. For example, Jesus refers to his disciples as those with little faith (e.g., Matt 8:26; Mark 4:40). However, this does not mean that it is God who gave them this level of faith, and no more. Rather, Jesus's rebuke stems from the disciple's own obtuseness with respect to their master's true identity. Likewise, the phrase "weak in faith," (discussed below) need not imply that it is God who has caused these persons to be such by apportioning to them a lesser degree of faith than that given to the strong. Moreover, in 1 Cor 13:2, Paul speaks of miracle-working faith, or a special strength of faith, that certain persons possess as a spiritual gift. In this case, faith is directly linked to a particular charismatic gift and clearly does not refer to belief in the sense of belief in fundamental Christian truth. Accordingly, it is likely that the faith that Paul refers to is related in some way to the different spiritual gifts that God gives to his people for the benefit of the community. Thus, μέτρον πίστεως refers to faith in relation to a particular spiritual gift,²⁶ perhaps in the sense that one has properly discerned one's gift(s) and is using it (them) appropriately within the body; that is, not for one's own benefit or self-glorification but in the service of the community. In this case, μέτρον is understood as denoting "criterion" or "standard," with faith functioning as an attributed genitive, faithful standard of self-assessment, and it may well be that Paul is engaged in wordplay here. In other words, believers are to assess themselves according to the trustworthy standard that God himself has provided; that is, according to the fact that each has been given a spiritual gift that one must discern and then use appropriately (i.e., in a faithful way, according to God's will) within the community for the benefit of its members. It is by this means by which every believer both answers the question "Who am I?" and determines his or her role within the body of Christ. This interpretation not only comports with the thrust of both the immediate and broader context, but also preserves the distributive sense of the verb μερίζω, in the sense that God apportions to each believer a distinct gift through the Spirit.

Thus, this is the only standard of self-assessment that can lead to a sober judgment of oneself, since it entails acknowledgement that one's essential identity, a member of the family of God with a distinctive gift to contribute, comes freely from God through the Spirit and is not determined by such things as ancestry, gender, place of origin, education, etc. All other human standards of assessment fail presumably because they inevitably result in raising penultimate social identities over the terminal, Spirit-wrought, allocentric identity that defines the community in Christ. Although believers could conceivably fail to recognize their gifts(s) and/or usurp roles for which they are not gifted, comparison of gifts is ruled out *de facto* on the grounds that all *charisma* come from God through the Spirit and, as Paul will make clear in verses 4–5,

---

25. Byrne, *Romans*, 371.
26. Keener, *Romans*, 145.

all exist for the benefit of the community. That is, they stem from one, common grace, and they have a unity of purpose and function, despite the fact that they exist in a diversity of forms. The ontological reality of being in Christ as the body of Christ, with each member interrelated with every other, overrides humanly conceived hierarchical rankings of individuals. As discussed below, although Paul does not exclude the ranking of gifts (cf. 1 Cor 14:5) where practical needs dictate such an ordering, hierarchy cannot be said to be constitutive of the body of Christ.[27]

Rather, recognition of *charisma* and their proper use entails a focus on the other, given the ontological framework within which the divine act of gifting is to be understood.

6.1.1.2B MEMBERS OF ONE ANOTHER IN THE BODY OF CHRIST

The image of a city or state as a human body was widely used by writers in the ancient world to illustrate the unity of purpose needed for the ideal functioning of these sociopolitical groups, in some cases, using the image to reinforce the hierarchical structure inherent in these entities.[28] Although the theme of unity in diversity within the body of Christ for the common good of the community is evident in Paul's writings (e.g., 1 Cor 12:4–11), the apostle's rendition of this common political/sociological figure of speech extends its meaning well beyond the mundane to include the description of the ontological reality that underlies it and gives it substance. In this case, he does this by explicitly linking the body metaphor to Christ by means of the prepositional phrase, "ἐν Χριστῷ," (v. 5a).[29] Moreover, Paul uses the metaphor to emphasize the interdependence and interrelatedness of believers.

There is no consensus as to what Paul actually means when he refers to the believing community as the body of Christ; that is, whether the phrase is best understood in a metaphorical sense or as making a literal statement.[30] However, given that the effectiveness of metaphorical language resides in its ability to preserve the literal meaning of the symbol, while simultaneously intending an analogical secondary meaning, suggests that these figures of speech are meant to convey profound truths about reality.[31]

---

27. Käsemann, *Commentary on Romans*, 339. Also, Dunn, *Romans*, 2:724.

28. Field, "Discourses behind the Metaphor," 88–107. Also, McVay, "Human Body," 135–47; and Lee, *Paul, the Stoics*, 50, 54.

29. Minear, *Images of the Church*, 247. Paul's use of similar prepositions (with, through, of, into) serve the same purpose.

30. Pelser, "Once More," 525–45. Also, Carter, "Looking at the Metaphor," 93–115. The traditional or metaphorical view is that the body of Christ refers to the church as a fellowship constituted as such by either the Holy Spirit or through participation in the Eucharist (Ridderbos, *Paul*, 3643–64). The literal view is well represented by Ernst Käsemann who writes: "The exalted Christ really has an earthly body, and believers with their whole being are actually incorporated into it and have therefore to behave accordingly" (cited in Carter, "Looking at the Metaphor," 93). Similarly, see Conzelmann, *Commentary on the First Epistle*, 212–13; Field, "Discourses behind the Metaphor," 91.

31. Ricoeur, *Conflict of Interpretations*, 288, 290, 299. Also, Field, "Discourses behind the

Accordingly, the metaphor of the believing community as the body of Christ is best viewed as describing a real, although not literal, relationship that exists between it and Christ.[32] This in turn suggests that the metaphor is not simply illustrating unity and diversity in the believing community, although that meaning is present. Rather, the community is the body of Christ in the sense that it is constituted by Christ and is given impetus by his indwelling, such that the community belongs to Christ and is ruled by him.[33] Thus, the metaphor suggests that believers, as members of Christ's body, are called to participate in this reality by living in a manner that reflects the lordship of Christ, both in the relationships among its own members and those which it has with larger society.[34]

Metaphors not only describe reality, but also construct it. As noted above, Paul accomplishes this by explicitly linking the body metaphor to Christ through the use of the prepositional phrase, "in/with Christ," thereby incorporating believers into the ontological reality of Christ.[35] For Paul, whether or not one is in Christ determines whether or not one is part of the body. Conversely, to be in Christ is to be part of the body of Christ. Consequently, both images must be held together in order to adequately understand Paul's metaphorical language.

Taken in tandem, these two images suggest both an individual and a corporate dimension. On one level, the body-as-self actualizes the meaning of the body as a corporate entity, and vice versa, since such symbolism is intelligible only in the personal experience of embodiedness.[36] On another level, the faith that unites a person to Christ also unites him or her to other believers. Believers exist in Christ with other believers. By the same token, reception of the grace-gift(s) on the part of each individual is primarily for the benefit of the other. Although the relationship between Christ and the individual is direct (cf. 1 Cor 6:16–17), one's identity as a believer has a communal aspect, in that each individual, as well as the community as a whole, must submit to Christ's authority, thereby allowing Christ's power to be manifest in the body.[37] Accordingly, those who demonstrate Christlikeness in their conduct and relationships with others show that they are in Christ (and he in them) and that they are members of his body; that is, that they are members of the believing community.[38] Put differ-

---

Metaphor," 93.

32. Carter, "Looking at the Metaphor," 96.

33. Field, "Discourses behind the Metaphor," 93. See also, Barrett, *First Epistle to the Corinthians*, 292.

34. Kim, *Christ's Body in Corinth*, 65–66.

35. Minear, *Images of the Church*, 247. Paul's use of similar prepositions (with, through, of, into) serve the same purpose.

36. Gupta, "Which 'Body' Is a Temple?," 518–36.

37. Gupta, "Which 'Body' Is a Temple?," 51.

38. Barclay, "*Christ in You*," 114. For example, in 1 Cor 6:15–20, Paul makes clear that what believers do with or in their physical bodies has ramifications for their spiritual lives, since their bodies belong to Christ. Moreover, what an individual does with his or her body affects the community as a

ently, as slaves of God in Christ, believers become slaves of one another, each member serving the body by serving others.³⁹ This singular grounding makes it problematic to speak of the individual and the community as polarized entities. Rather, each is understood in relation to the other, since both aspects of embodiedness receive their meaning from a common reality —participation/incorporation in Christ.

Thus, the metaphor of the community as the body of Christ, by virtue of the fact that it is in Christ, harkens back to Paul's description of the believing community as a people who live to God, continually putting his will above their own, according to the pattern of Christ, with all of this made possible through the Spirit. This suggests that unity in diversity is maintained by the active choice on the part of believers to view themselves not only in terms of their specific function within the body as determined by their gifts(s) but, more importantly, to see this identity and role as one that is organically linked to that of every other member in the community, such that one's gift(s) and its/their exercise is realized expressly within the context of the body as a whole. As 12:4 indicates (γάρ), those who do assess themselves in the way Paul commends (v. 3) are able to discern the one body. That is, they recognize that they do not exist for themselves, and that their fellow believers, whatever their gifts, and however impressive these may be, are equally with themselves members of one body.⁴⁰ That this is the case is suggested by the phrase καθ᾽ εἷς ἀλλήλων μέλη (v. 5), which places emphasis on the interrelatedness of individuals within the body rather than on the overall unity of the body.⁴¹ Each of the gifts exists for the benefit of the members comprising the body. Moreover, the community worships God, in the sense described in verses 1–2, by embracing its gifts, in all their diverse forms, and using them in the manner intended by him (vv. 6–8).⁴² Accordingly, the Spirit-wrought allocentric social identity that characterizes this people group is manifested when each individual member sees him or herself as living/belonging not only to Christ but also to his or her siblings in Christ, such that each uses his or her gift(s) in service to the other. From this it may be inferred that the body would fail to function properly if its members should fail to recognize and use their gifts and/or choose to use them inappropriately; that is, for self-promotion or self-glorification;⁴³ hence, Paul's injunction to love one another, to which we now turn.

---

whole (1 Cor 4:6-8, 11–13). This is so because the body, both individual and corporate, participates in the resurrected Christ (1 Cor 6:15) and belongs to him exclusively (Sandnes, *Belly and Body*, 213).

39. Minear, *Images of the Church*, 244–45.

40. Cranfield, *Epistle to the Romans*, 2:616–17. Also, Witherington and Hyatt, *Paul's Letter to the Romans*, 289.

41. Byrne, *Romans*, 372.

42. It is likely that the seven gifts that Paul lists are meant to be descriptive and exemplary, rather than exhaustive (cf. 1 Cor 12:7–10 and 28–29), with verses 6–8 continuing the body metaphor. Moreover, the list in Romans lacks the hierarchical structure of 1 Cor 12–14. (Jewett, *Romans*, 744). This accords with Paul's aims in this section of the letter.

43. Keener, *Romans*, 146.

6.1.2 Executing the New Communal Identity

6.1.2.1 Genuine Love for the Other (Rom 12:9—13:10)

From the discussion above, it may be inferred that unlike most social groups, the boundaries of the believing community are not primarily enforced through intragroup processes of inter-group differentiation.[44] According to Paul, the Spirit (faith), and not a particular set of group-specific ethnoracial criteria, however these are defined, is the primary identity marker for those rightly related to God through Christ.[45] Thus, this people's worship cannot *primarily* be described with a specific set of rituals and rites, although these need not be completely absent. At best, its uniqueness resides not in a set of definitive criteria, but rather in the lack of a generic, prescribed set of rites and rituals applicable to each and every believing community.[46] Moreover, it is the Spirit who directs the intragroup relationships between the ethnoracial other comprising the membership of the body of Christ, such that each exercises his or her gift for the benefit of the other, regardless of ethnoracial affiliation, gender, socioeconomic standing, or any other humanly conceived ranking. Apart from the Spirit, ethnoracial boundaries tend to be particularly unyielding.[47] Yet, by virtue of a renewed mind, able to yield to the will of God, believers are enjoined to do just that, in addition to breaking other common boundaries that work to categorically separate humans, one from another. An excellent case in point of intractable boundaries is Hermocrates's appeal to the Sicilians to set aside their ethnoracial differences in order to resist a common enemy. He urges this, while simultaneously acknowledging that these various ethnic groups would, in all likelihood, engage in war with each other in the future (Thucydides, *Hist.* 4.59.1—4.64.5), indicating his experience with the all-to-human, temporary nature of deference toward the ethnoracial other. For Paul, the breaking of such boundaries can only be accomplished by the transformative power of the Spirit, who makes the taking of an allocentric posture toward the ethnic other a real possibility.

44. Kuecker, *Spirit and the 'Other,'* 218–19.

45. This does not mean that outsiders would not attach group-identifying criteria to the believing community. There is historical evidence that they did just that thing. For example, associating believers with the rite of infant cannibalism.

46. In ancient religions, it was imperative that worshippers carry out all of the rites and rituals in a clearly specified order and manner, so as to garner the favor of the god(s) to whom homage was being given. As noted in the previous chapter of this work, the OT prophets excoriated Israel for engaging in such practices, while lacking true devotion to God, as evidenced in its people's unrighteous attitudes and behaviors. This suggests that rites and rituals have their place within believer communities, as long as worship is done in the Spirit and, thus, in true devotion to God. Accordingly, this would allow for regional diversity, since it is difficult, if not impossible, to separate ethnoracial and cultural modes of expression from a given people's worship. Worship is always embodied and that embodiedness will always be dependent to some degree on a given people group's ethnic identity. This introduces the issue of syncretism, something Paul does not address in Romans. Rather, the presumption in this case is that the issue of eating, drinking, and keeping of days does not go to the heart of orthodox Christian belief.

47. Kuecker, *Spirit and the 'Other,'* 218–19.

With all of this in place, Paul sets forth the basic principle that is to guide the life of the community (12:9–13). This principle flows directly from the Spirit-wrought, allocentric identity he has constructed in the previous section. As we will see, ἀγάπη leads and governs the entire sequence of instructions that the apostle gives,[48] forming an inclusio (12:9a, 13:10). Moreover, for the apostle, the renewal of the mind by the Spirit includes the transformed ability to look beyond the interests of the in-group and to extend in-group benefits to all manner of outsider (12:14—13:7).[49] It is this Spirit-wrought, allocentric identity, manifested in an other-focused disposition that fulfills the law (13:8–10). Furthermore, it is this identity, whose historical legitimacy Paul has so fervently argued for, that empowers the community and ensures the coherence of the group's is and ought; a consistency necessary for its legitimacy in the present age (13:11–14).

6.1.2.1A Defining Sincere Love

The principle that is to guide the believing community in members' relations with one another is that of genuine, ἀνυπόκριτος, love (12:9a); that is, love without pretense or dissimulation. Thus far, the only references to love have been to God's own love (5:5, 8; 8:35, 37, 39),[50] which has been poured into believers' heart through the Spirit (5:5), and is completely unmerited and freely given to sinful, undeserving humanity by means of Christ's death (5:8), who himself ensures that God's people remain in both his and the Father's love through and despite all of life's perils (8:35, 37, 39). This then is the type of love, a completely other-focused concern for the neighbor, broadly defined, that provides the pattern (cf. Rom 6:17) for how believers are to conduct themselves in relation to both each other and outsiders. Such love ought to both accompany the reciprocation of spiritual gifts in the life of the believing community[51] and guide its relations with outsiders. As such, it flows from the ontological reality of the community's existence as the body of Christ in Christ; that is, it flows from their Spirit-wrought, allocentric identity.

As I noted in chapter 3, the inclusio, 12:9 and 13:8–10, explicitly links genuine love to love of neighbor, which includes both fellow believers and outsiders, with the latter encompassing both friendly and hostile persons. Thus, although 12:9–21 appears, on the surface, to lack a tight structure and flow of thought, composed as it is of a variety of source material,[52] there are several previously introduced motifs in this

---

48. Byrne, *Romans*, 375.

49. Kuecker, *Spirit and the 'Other,'* 95.

50. Byrne, *Romans*, 375.

51. This is similar to 1 Cor 12:1–31, and the exposition on love in 1 Cor 13:1–13 (Fitzmyer, *Romans*, 653).

52. Many commentators maintain that 12:9–21 contains echoes of the Jesus tradition (e.g., vv. 14, 17a, 18, 19a). Others believe that Paul is using a Semitic source originating in primitive Christian

passage that directly connect it to the larger picture of the community's self-identity that the apostle is constructing. Moreover, the tight link Paul establishes between intragroup relations and inter-group interaction describes an identity that is allocentric in the fullest sense of the term. That is, it is able to maintain in-group love and privilege while simultaneously extending those benefits to all manner of outsiders. Thus, bias for the in-group is established apart from the normal processes involved in constructing a favorable in-group identity, that is, apart from negative evaluations and responses to the out-group other. Like the love that characterizes God's action in and through Christ, this love embraces the outsider and the enemy (vv. 14, 17, 20) and, thus, overcomes evil with good (v. 21). Paul's exhortation to hate what is evil (πονηρόν) (v. 12:9b) and to hold fast to what is good (τῷ ἀγαθῳ) (v. 12:9c), which is sandwiched between the exhortations to genuine love (12:9a) and to love for one another (12:10a), including the showing of proper honor (12:10b, τῇ τιμῇ), links to 13:1–7, specifically verses 3–4 and verse 7. Thus, genuine love is doing good (and shunning evil) with respect to others, which includes persecutors and enemies, and showing due honor, to civic authorities, which, as discussed in chapter one of this work, has as its ultimate goal, the benefit of the believing community.

The stark choice between doing good or evil to the other applies first to relationships within the community. The term φιλαδελφίᾳ in its strict sense refers to love between siblings, while the noun φιλόστοργος similarly expresses family love, especially that of parents for children (v. 10).[53] Ancient Mediterranean families traditionally worked as a unit, each member defending the honor of the other.[54] Thus, in line with Paul's conception of the community's terminal social identity as the Spirit-transformed children of God, each is to view the other, including the ethnoracial other, as the closest of kin, eschewing competitiveness in favor of actively seeking to show respect for him or her. The following verse expresses the vigor and enthusiasm of this active love. Believers are to be zealous in showing this love, being, as they are "on fire" or "boiling over" (ζέοντες) with the Spirit (v. 11a–b).[55] It is in this way that they serve the Lord (v. 11c). Moreover, believers are to conduct themselves in this fashion surrounded as they are by a larger, suspicious community of outsiders in a world where

---

circles, suggesting that the list represents a list of instructions commonly used among early Christian preachers (Fitzmyer, *Romans*, 652). The content suggests that the passage taps a variety of source material: the OT prophetic and wisdom traditions; the Jesus tradition; and ethical reflections and maxims of Greco-Roman philosophy. Moreover, there are close parallels with similar sequences in 1 Thess 5:12–22 and 1 Pet 3:8–12, suggesting that the present sequence reflects early Christian parenetical tradition (Byrne, *Romans*, 375).

53. Byrne, *Romans*, 379.

54. Byrne, *Romans*, 376, 379.

55. Byrne, *Romans*, 376. There is some debate as to whether Paul is referring to the human spirit or to the Spirit. Thus far, the emphasis in Romans has been on God's Spirit. The immediate context also deals with spiritual gifts given by the Spirit. Given this, it is quite likely that the Spirit is in view here and empowers believers to actively love the other. Similarly, see Keener, *Romans*, 148, and Byrne, *Romans*, 376–77, who argues that this passage has distinct eschatological overtones.

self-promotion, competitiveness, and the seeking of honor is the norm (v. 12). They are to show their trust in God in such adverse conditions by rejoicing in hope and persevering in prayer (v. 12). Moreover, the definition of the other is expanded to include believers outside of the house churches comprising the community in Rome, as Paul exhorts his audience to contribute to the needs of the saints, including those in Jerusalem (15:26–27, 31) and to show hospitality, φιλοξενία, (v. 13), presumably to believers from other communities traveling to/through Rome.

With verse 14, the apostle expands the definition of the other even further, to include those outside of the believing community at large, with an exhortation that goes against the norms of an honor-shame culture, turning them upside-down. The two-fold repetition of the injunction, first positively (v. 13a), then negatively (13b) suggests the difficulty of doing what is enjoined and indicates that the love required of believers reflects that which they have received from God in Christ, who died for those who were still enemies (5:10).[56] Thus, the Spirit-wrought identity that characterizes the new movement is other-focused in the most extreme sense of the term, including not only outsiders, but also outsiders who actively seek to injure and/or oppress the in-group. The benefits that members of the in-group experience, unity, good, peace, compassion and mercy are to be extended, as far as practicable, to all manner of out-group other.

Although it is possible that Paul turns his attention back to the believing community in verses 15–16, it is more likely that outsiders are in view in verses 15–21 for several reasons. First, with this reading, unity and coherence of the sequence is maintained, since it begins (v. 14) and ends with references to doing good to the enemy (v. 20), where that behavior is equated with overcoming evil with good (v. 21). If verses 15–16 are taken as applying to the in-group, the sequence becomes disjointed, moving from outsiders (v. 14) to insiders (vv. 15–16) and back to outsiders (vv. 17–21). Given that Paul explicitly addresses members of the believing community in verses 9–13, suggests that if the exhortations in verses 15–16 were meant for insiders, the apostle, careful and skilled rhetor that he is, would have expressed them prior to giving the injunction in verse 14. Second, the tenor of the sequence, when taken as applying to outsiders, comports with Paul's particular telling of the gospel in two ways.

First, the emphasis on humanity's godlessness and its captivity to sin and, thus, its total dependency on God's radically allocentric love, his mercy, and act of salvation parallels the type of love, mercy, and compassion that believers are to show toward outsiders, irrespective of their ethnicity, rank, status, or designation as foe. Second, the pronounced emphasis on nonretaliation and reliance on a God, who is just, righteous, and trustworthy, in the face of adversity caused by uncomprehending, suspicious, nonbelieving neighbors in this section (vv. 14, 19–20) accords with everything Paul has said regarding hope. That is, the community's strength in adversity comes from their legitimate identity as the children of God and all of

---

56. Byrne, *Romans*, 377.

what that entails. That is, its members need not be afraid to extend love to the larger, outside community within which they live. The exhortation to leave vengeance to God (v. 19) (Deut 32:35) underscores that believers can trust that God will restore justice on his own terms, at the right time, presumably at the eschaton.[57] Moreover, the active implementation of this radically allocentric love ensures the equally radical coherence between the new movement's is and ought, in a way that simultaneously demonstrates the efficacy of the gospel in both constituting and maintaining a heretofore unprecedented, transformed community that serves as a signpost of God's intent for all of humanity. Thus, the gospel legitimates the community and the community, in turn, reflects the gospel's intent by extending God's love in Christ to all and, in so doing, overcomes evil with good (v. 21b).

Accordingly, relations with outsiders are preserved at the highest level by members of the in-group seeking to do good to those who are actively opposed to it (vv. 15, 17a, 19, 20). Apart from and in addition to this, believers are to actively seek unity with outsiders, not in the sense of conforming to the worldly, sociocultural norms they espouse, but in the sense of extending the benefits of the gospel to those who have not yet received it. That this is likely is suggested by the phrase, "pouring burning coals upon (the enemy's) head" (v. 20b) (Prov 25:22a). Although its meaning is obscure in both Proverbs and here, in keeping with the tenor of the entire passage, it most likely refers to acts of kindness overcoming enmity, in the sense that the adversary is led to repent, accept the gospel, and enter into the very community that has demonstrated such mercy and compassion toward him or her. This purpose is also suggested by the injunction that echoes Jewish wisdom tradition (cf. esp. Sir 7:34),[58] where Paul exhorts believers to eschew feelings of envy and jealousy over the good fortune or successes of outsiders and feelings of smugness or triumph when those outside of the in-group fail or experience set-backs (v. 15). Such a mindset promotes concord by producing behavior that accords with what the out-group neighbor is experiencing; hence, the appeal not to repay anyone evil with evil (v. 17a). Rather than preoccupying itself with thoughts of revenge, the community is to give careful thought (προνέω) to what is good or honorable in the sight of all (v. 17b). Most likely this means that the believing community is to live in a manner worthy of the gospel (Phil 1:27–28; 2:15), such that outsiders would find its message and transformative effects appealing. The following injunction to live peaceably with all, as far as possible (v. 18), underscores the importance of cultivating positive relations with all manner of outsiders for the sake of both the legitimacy of group self-identity and for the gospel that constructs, maintains, and empowers the community which embraces it as the truth for all of humanity.

This appeal for concord and positive relations is underscored by the exhortation to think, φρονέω, in harmony with one another; that is, have the same regard for one another (v. 16a). What this means is spelled out in verses 16b and 16c and suggests

---

57. Similarly, Byrne, *Romans*, 382.
58. Fitzmyer, *Romans*, 655.

that in-group bias is not to be maintained by the normal means of negative evaluations of the out-group. Thus, Paul cautions the in-group against the type of lofty or prideful thinking (ὑψηλὰ φρονοῦντες) that views in-group benefits as conferring a privileged status to the group over and against outsiders. Rather, right thinking corresponds with right action. Thus, believers are to associate with the lowly, and/or give themselves over to humble tasks, such as providing food and drink to hostile outsiders in need.[59] Such behavior works to dispel feelings of in-group privilege and pride and is in service to the gospel; that is, in service to Christ (v. 11c). The appeal against becoming wise in one's thoughts (v. 16c) harkens back to the theme of prideful human self-assessment, which ultimately has no place for God as sovereign Lord and Creator (1:22). Believers, by way of contrast, are to accept God's way of dealing with sinful, hostile humanity. In other words, they are to live in a way that demonstrates God's love as revealed in and through the gospel. Paul's point is that in-group benefits are given by God through the gospel not for the purpose of conferring privilege to the in-group. Rather, these benefits, like the gifts given by the Spirit to every believer, are for the benefit of the other, whether insider or outsider.

6.1.2.1B Love Fulfills the Law

Paul has already made the case that believers are removed from the requirements of the old, written law in the sense that they now walk according to the Spirit, who empowers them to fulfill what the OT law, in its totality, required of God's people; that is, living righteously before him (3:21—4:25; 7:1—8:4). Given this, it is interesting that he links love of the other, more specifically, the neighbor, which, for the apostle, includes members of the in-group and outsiders, with fulfillment of the Jewish law (13:8, 10). However, in light of Paul's ethnographic purposes, this linkage serves as an adumbration of the lines of continuity and discontinuity he has already drawn between God's people in the past and in the present in terms of faith and law. More specifically, the recapitulation of this major theme at this point in the argument, serves to underscore the ultimacy of the identity that he has thus far constructed.

Recall that the Mosaic or written law served as a primary marker of identity for God's people in the past; in that, faith in God was demonstrated by keeping its precepts. As such, it functioned as the key boundary marker, separating God's people, primarily ethnoracial Jews, from all other people groups. Consequently, the law also provided an essential set of salient criteria for identifying the Jewish people as an ethnoracial group. In this regard, it is important to note that Paul does not make an explicit distinction between the ethical content of the law and its more ritualistic aspects. The fact that the apostle makes explicit reference to the decalogue in this passage, specifically referring to the portion of the decalogue listing the commandments

---

59. Ταπεινός, understood as masculine, is usually translated as "lowly people." However, in view of the neuter "lofty thoughts," it could mean "give yourselves to lowly tasks" (Fitzmyer, *Romans*, 656).

governing conduct towards fellow human beings (v. 9), does not necessarily indicate that he has only the ethical aspects of the law in mind. First, the phrase εἴ τις ἑτέρα ἐντολή which can be taken as referring to any other commandment in the decalogue, could also have a more remote sense, extending what Paul has to say about love to the entirety of the law.[60] Second, for the apostle, the written code, in its entirety, is provisional, finding its ultimate expression and fulfillment in Christ through whom believers are empowered by the Spirit to worship God and to live in obedience to him in a radically new way as promised in the Scriptures (Jer 31:33 and Ezek 36:26). Moreover, this worship, like this new life, is not associated with a specific set of rites, rituals, or rules. Rather, since love is the working out of faith (cf. Gal 5:6), a faith that works through love actively pursues all that is good for the other[61] and, thus, results in the proper worship of God as Paul has defined it.

For Paul, the Spirit is central and both directs intergroup contact, according to the principle of allocentric love, and marks believers as those who share a common identity, allowing for the incorporation of all manner of the other into the community.[62] As such, the Spirit replaces the written law as the primary marker of identity of the people of God in the present, directing the group's self-identity as it is manifested in its manner of life, including its worship. It is in this sense that the OT law, both its ethical and more ritualistic aspects, no longer applies to the community. The group's identity is expressed rightly not by virtue of adherence to the law, but when members of the community exist in an allocentric posture toward the other. Moreover, the boundaries of this new identity are maintained by the Spirit,[63] not the old, written law. However, although participation in this allocentric group requires a new social identity that recognizes that ethnic identities are not ultimate, old identities continue to be affirmed, as long as they are nested and exist at a penultimate level.[64] This suggests that the OT law, particularly its more ritualistic aspects, retains salience as providing the criteria for identifying Jews as an ethnoracial group. Paul will make this clear beginning in 14:1, where he addresses the issue of a trans-ethnic group comprised of a variety of people groups all intent on preserving their ethnic identity, which, in antiquity, was more often than not tied to discreet worship practices. As we will see, such identity-constructing practices are penultimate and are to be understood in light of the community's terminal Spirit-wrought, allocentric identity that is grounded in faith, not the old, written law.

In sum, Paul's statement that love fulfills the law brings the discussion back once again to the provisional nature of the law and the culmination of God's intent for it

---

60. Fitzmyer, *Romans*, 679.

61. Fitzmyer, *Romans*, 679. This is what Paul means when he writes that "love does no wrong to a neighbor (v. 10)."

62. Kuecker, *Spirit and the 'Other,'* 179–80.

63. Kuecker, *Spirit and the 'Other,'* 179–80.

64. Kuecker, *Spirit and the 'Other,'* 179–80.

in the circumcision of believers' hearts by the Spirit. The law that first, in its written form, acted to divide Jews from all manner of non-Jewish people groups, now under the aegis of the Spirit, acts as the inner, creative agent of unity, uniting all manner of people groups into the one body of Christ by means of radical love of the other made possible by the empowering presence of that same Spirit, who views everyone as the neighbor to whom the benefits of the community apply. In the present, unfolding new age, the Spirit (and Christ) replaces the OT law by transcending it, while at the same time bringing it to its fulfillment, all in accord with Scripture. The Spirit marks and maintains the boundaries of community, making them permeable, so that all are invited to enter in and to be transformed.

6.1.2.2 *Standing Firm in the New Age (Rom 13:11–14)*

Thus, Paul rounds out his discussion by reminding his audience of where they stand in relation to the past and the in-breaking new age of the Spirit. The apostle has just intimated that the age of the OT law has ended and the age of the Spirit has come. He now returns to the theme of nonconformity to the pattern of this world, the old age (12:2), urging believers to live in a way that looks to the day of final salvation (13:11). Thus far, Paul has explicitly touched on the topic of the eschaton only once, in 2:5–11, where he reminded his audience that on the last day all of them will have to reckon with God's just judgment, which will proceed according to each individual's deeds.[65] His focus has remained largely on the implications of the gospel for the believing community's identity and life in the often hostile environment of the present world, although, implicitly, with an eye consistently cast on the horizon of the promised eschaton. The fact that he not only returns to this theme but also brings his parenesis to close on an explicitly eschatological note suggests that Paul wishes his audience to see the gravity of the choice to embrace or not to embrace their identity and live accordingly. By implication, this also entails the implications of the choice to actively embrace or not their mission as a community that invites all manner of other to enter in and experience the transformative power of the gospel.

By calling attention to the time, τον καιρόν, of the overlap of the old age and the new, Paul underscores the necessity for believers to take direct, decisive action in discerning the reality of the Spirit's transformation of the community's relationship with God and fellow human beings and to pattern their lives according to God's will, rather than that of the world. The images of waking from sleep, embracing the day/light and laying aside the night/works of darkness, so as to live honorably, making no provision for the flesh, by putting on the armor of light/Christ and, implicitly, taking off the old self/old clothes (vv. 12–14) places the previous exhortations to allocentric living at the center of what constitutes walking righteously before God, particularly as this will play out on the Last Day. The warnings against drunken revelry, sexual debauchery,

---

65. Fitzmyer, *Romans*, 681.

and quarreling stemming from envy serve as an antithesis to the positive injunction to live decently as in the day; that is, as a people who know that they live in the dawn of the new age of the Spirit.[66] Such people eschew the type of conduct that often occurs under the cover of darkness; that is, behavior that is focused on the self and the gratification of its desires, with the final warning of the three providing a segue to the discussion concerning worship practices within a multiethnic community.

6.2 Intracommunal Allocentric Identity in Action: Mutual Acceptance, Nested Ethnic Identities, and Communal Worship Practices (Rom 14:1—15:13)

Up to this point, Paul's has been concerned, more generally, with establishing the legitimacy of the believing community's Spirit-wrought, allocentric identity on the grounds that it both provides the central point of coherence between the group's symbolic universe and ethos and represents the culmination of the old, written law's intent. Ultimately, its legitimacy is grounded in its transformative power. However, the successful incorporation of the other into the community necessitates a second type of identity transformation that challenges the in-group, as a whole, to transform its own group identity.[67] As a trans-ethnic group, the community must be able to embrace diverse ethnicities, Jew and all manner of gentile, in a way that preserves the terminal identity of the group, as the apostle has defined it, without leveling ethnic differences into a generic whole. Conversely, no one ethnoracial criterion or set of criteria can be allowed to attain to a level where it functions as the primary marker of identity. Rather, lesser identities must be embraced and integrated, or nested, in a way that maintains the primacy of the terminal identity.[68] This suggests a dynamic process, requiring ongoing negotiation between diverse parties within the group.

As Paul has made clear, for both Jewish and non-Jewish believers, the believing community, understood as the family of God, constituted in and by Christ and the Spirit, is the source of their terminal identity and, as such, circumscribes how ethnic differences are both preserved and lived out in a ethnoracially diverse social group claiming unity and cohesion on the basis of Spirit-wrought kinship. As previously noted, ethnoracial identity, more than any other group identity, has historically been the most intractable source of strife within the human community, usually resulting in hatred and/or violence toward and oppression of one ethnic group against another.[69] The apostle is aware of this harsh reality and turns to address the potentially deci-

---

66. Byrne, *Romans*, 399–400, 402. Each pair within the three-line block represents a hendiadys. Four of the six items also appear in Gal 5:19–21, suggesting that Paul is working from a standardized list.

67. Kuecker, *Spirit and the 'Other,'* 50, 179–80.

68. Kuecker, *Spirit and the 'Other,'* 50.

69. Kuecker, *Spirit and the 'Other,'* 1, 183–84.

sive issue of worship practices, specifically those related to eating, drinking, and the keeping of holy days within the ethnoracially diverse believing community.

As noted above, persons who receive the Spirit do not have to renounce their ethnic identities or any of the markers of identity that compete with other ethnic identities (e.g., Rom 9:3). While the believing community remains, at one level, composed of Jews and all manner of gentiles, the group functions properly only when the ethnically diverse subgroups comprising it see themselves as co-members of an in-Christ community marked by the Spirit (faith).[70] The Spirit marks a new identity that relegates ethnic identity to a penultimate level.[71] Although 14:1—15:13 raises a variety of interpretative questions, such as the precise identity of the weak and the strong and the exact issue at stake, it does provide a clear picture of intracommunal allocentricism in action as the apostle negotiates the vicissitudes associated with the worship of the one God by all manner of people groups. This is the one God, whom the apostle has already argued continues to maintain the primacy of his people of the past. The theme of welcome/acceptance of the other appears both at the beginning (14:1) and the end (15:7) of this portion of the letter, with 15:8–13 filling out the picture of unified, trans-ethnic worship of the one God. Within this inclusio, Paul appeals for mutual tolerance (14:1–12), on the basis of the principle of Spirit-wrought allocentricism which works to bind all subgroups into a unified worshipping community (14:13–23), such that the worshipping community as a whole worships God according to the pattern of Christ (15:1–13). As we will see, in addressing the contentious issue of what constitutes the proper worship of God, Paul maintains a delicate balance between the primacy of worship in/by the Spirit, in faith, that marks the new, ethnoracially diverse people of God and the continuing salience, at the penultimate level, of particular ethnic expressions of worship.

This balance is difficult to maintain due to the fact that, generally speaking, ancients deemed ethnoracial identity as produced and indicated by religious practices. For example, the Romans reconstructed a range of Greek and Etruscan cults, rituals, and rites to bring them under the umbrella of a distinctly Roman religion, incorporating aspects of foreign culture deemed desirable, while preserving clear Roman identity by defining specific styles of Roman worship.[72] Similarly, the author of Judith describes the Israelites as descendants of the Chaldeans, who abandoned the ways of their ancestors to worship the God of heaven (Jdt 5:6–8), suggesting that they ceased to be Chaldeans by changing their religious allegiances and practices. Likewise, the non-barbarian ancestry of the Roman people is indicated by the Greekness of their

---

70. Kuecker, *Spirit and the 'Other,'* 163.

71. Kuecker, *Spirit and the 'Other,'* 163, 183–84. As Kuecker notes, the creation of a superordinate identity with simultaneous retention of subgroup salience has been proven to be an effective strategy for intergroup reconciliation. This requires that subgroup identities remain valid, but penultimate.

72. Gruen, *Rethinking the Other in Antiquity,* 348–57; Orlin, "Urban Religion in the Middle," 58–70.

religious customs and practices (Dionysius, *Ant. rom.* 1.21.1–2). For Paul, as I have pointed out, the gospel mandates that ethnic particularity be retained among the present people of God, since God's work in and through Christ marks the coming in of the nations to Israel for the purpose of worshiping the one God (Rom 3:29–30). Thus, gentiles are not required to take on Jewish forms of worship as these are spelled out in the law, since, by doing so, they would in effect become Jews. Moreover, as discussed in more detail below, the christocentric, Spirit wrought identity that Paul constructs, which calls believers to live in a way that exemplifies Jesus's teachings and allocentric postures calls on them to welcome the ethnic other as Christ has welcomed both Jew and gentile (Rom 14:1; 15:7).

In terms of the apostle's larger ethnographic purposes, unity in worship is important for several reasons. Since group-identity and patterns of worship are interlinked and mutually constituting, the integrity of the community's identity is dependent on the group's acceptance of an understanding of worship that is group-identity constructing. In dealing with a trans-ethnic community it is essential for Paul to delineate a primary mode of worship that is commensurate with the group's worldview and that allows for the incorporation of diverse penultimate expressions. In addition, in more practical terms, factious attitudes and behaviors associated with subgroups advocating for unilateral adoption of their own specific customs and traditions destroys intragroup cohesion, making the group less appealing to both members and outsiders. This would become especially problematic in a social environment that is already hostile to and suspicious of the new movement, since a group in disunity would not be capable of supplying satisfactory aspects of individual members' social identity. Where such satisfaction is lacking, a decrease with or even alienation from the group is inevitable. These feelings of satisfaction would need to be particularly strong in cases where members are already under scrutiny by and are experiencing pressure from out-group neighbors. Furthermore, as noted above, the allocentricism that lies at the heart of the group's self-identity is expressed not only in the stance its members take toward one another, but also in the group's relations with outsiders. Suspicious, hostile, and/or unbelieving others would find little reason to join a group that displays a lack of tolerance among its members for each other. The lack of cohesion between what the community professes and what it actually does would seriously compromise the community's mission of reflecting the power of the gospel, which it professes to be at work among it, to the outside world.

Thus, for Paul, intragroup acrimony and disunity has serious repercussions for both the group's self-identity and its legitimacy as a valid subgroup among the variety of subgroups comprising the larger sociocultural context. Moreover, as the divinely constituted subgroup that uniquely reflects the one God's intent for all of humankind, in all of its diversity, its legitimacy has import on a scale unequaled by any other group.

6.2.1 Intragroup Love for the Ethnoracial Other (Rom 14:1–12)

6.2.1.1 *The Weak, the Strong, and Social Identity Theory*

Although some have suggested that Rom 14:1—15:13 has no specific referent within the Roman community in the sense that it addresses the problem of unity in diversity and is an issue that may arise in any group,[73] the opening exhortation to welcome the weak without quarreling (14:1) strongly suggests that some kind of falling-out had actually occurred between this subgroup and a second subgroup, composed of individuals whom Paul identifies with and refers to as the strong. What this falling-out was actually about and precisely who was involved, and on what scale, remain points of debate, given that Paul seems to assume that his audience knows exactly who is involved and what he is talking about. Specifics are sorely lacking, and interpretations based on detailed reconstructions not only extract too much from the limited textual evidence,[74] but also rest on the presupposition that the apostle's main purpose for writing to the community in Rome is to achieve Jewish-gentile reconciliation.

This interpretation of the letter's purpose is linked to a particular historical reconstruction based on the expulsion of the Jews from Rome by Claudius. During the first century CE, Roman authorities took a definite stand against the Jewish community in Rome in the form of expulsions by Tiberius (19 CE) and Claudius (c. 49 CE). What is not so clear is the number of Jews expelled during the latter edict (perhaps only those directly involved in the *Chrestus* related disturbances, perhaps more) and what percentage of the people forced out were Jewish Christian leaders. That some Jewish believers/leaders were expelled is known (Acts 18:2). This historical situation has prompted a plausible historical reconstruction of the relationship between gentile and Jewish believers in the Roman house churches. According to this reconstruction, at the time Paul penned his letter to the Romans, after Claudius's death, Jewish believers, including their leadership, were just beginning to return to Rome and to reestablish themselves among the majority gentile believers, who had remained there during the expulsion. Thus, Paul's concern is with addressing the issue of Jewish marginalization by gentile fellow believers, who currently outnumber them and who have developed erroneous beliefs about Judaism and Jewish believers.

Although there may be some truth in this reconstruction (irrespective of the fact that it assumes that quite a number of Jewish believers/leaders were expelled, thus creating a gentile believer majority), the thesis of this work is not dependent on it. In other words, the validity of the argument for the ethnographic character of Romans does not rest on the idea of Jewish believer marginalization. Rather, Paul's writes to encourage all manner of believers to persevere in obedience to the gospel in the face of general social persecution from *outsiders*. As I will demonstrate below,

---

73. E.g., Karris, "Romans 14:1—15:13," 65–84.
74. Keener, *Romans*, 160.

although there is tension between Jewish and gentile believers, this tension is part of a larger context of insider tension created by in-group ethnoracial differences related to specific acts of worship. The ratio between Jews and gentiles is immaterial to this argument. Moreover, as shown below, resolution of this insider tension is directly related to the apostle's larger ethnographic aims of both providing legitimacy for the new movement and creating a positive group self-identity in order to bolster group cohesion. Thus, Jewish marginalization by gentiles is, at best, a matter of peripheral concern to my argument, if it is of concern at all. The strength of the sociohistorical reconstruction presented in this work resides in its dependence on textual evidence of outsider hostility toward the Roman believing community and not on a relatively general reference to expulsion that contains little detail as to the number of Jews expelled and their primary group affiliation.

As demonstrated below, the textual evidence suggests that, although the subgroup referred to as the weak most likely includes law observant Jewish believers and former gentile proselytes, who may have considered themselves Jews in the ethnoracial sense, the category is, in actuality, broader. That is, the weak appear to consist of diverse believers, from a variety of ethnic groups, who are not fully convinced that certain worship customs from their past are no longer necessary for the worship of God in the new age of the Spirit. However, before turning to the exegetical evidence that points to this conclusion, some clarity may be achieved by considering the passage as a whole in light of social identity theory. If we accept that Paul is writing as an ethnographer and, as such, is concerned with the issue of group self-identity, then this theory serves as a useful heuristic tool in shedding some light on this intragroup conflict. Any insights gained through this process may then be tested against the textual evidence.

Briefly, in terms of social identity theory, the weak believe that their identity as members of the in-Christ movement is necessarily bound-up with certain, specific worship practices; that is, particular patterns of eating and drinking and the keeping of special days. This may seem peculiar to modern persons, who readily separate ethnoracial from religious identity. However, in antiquity, worship practices and customs were inextricably linked with a person's most essential identity; that is, his or her ethnicity. Thus, the temple of Helios in Egypt is described by Strabo as "constructed in the Egyptian manner" and as housing the "οξ Μνευϊς" thought to be a god by the Egyptians (*Geogr.* 17.1.27–28). Here, the Egyptian priests "explained to strangers what pertained to the sacred rites," performed there and understood only by native Egyptians (*Georg.* 17.1.29). Moreover, the Stoic notes that, "certain animals are worshipped by all Egyptians in common," while "other animals" are associated with and worshipped by various Egyptian subgroups, with each animal identifying its respective ethnoracial subgroup and its distinctive worship customs (*Geogr.* 17.1.40). To ask an ancient person to give-up all past worship practices was essentially to ask him or her to give-up his or her ethnic identity. This would necessarily be the case, unless that person was fully convinced that certain practices were no longer required and, thus, no longer functioned as salient criteria of ethnoracial identity.

The strong, on the other hand, are those who are fully convinced that matters of eating and drinking and the keeping of special days are no longer necessary for the proper worship of God. This in turn indicates that these individuals do not see their identity as members of the new movement as bound-up in any way with these particular practices. Moreover, this further suggests, that they are able to define their ethnoracial identity by other, alternative, salient criteria; for example, by circumcision, in the case of a strong Jewish believer, like Paul. Presumably, strong believers, like the apostle, but of other ethnoracial affiliations, would be equally capable of defining themselves as Greek, Roman, or Syrian, etc., based on alternative criteria such as the type of education they received, their native or childhood language, and/or region of birth. These, rather than a set of defined worship practices related to food, drink, and the keeping of days would function as the criteria for ethnoracial identification for such persons.

As an ancient person, Paul is aware of the importance of worship practices to ethnoracial identity. Thus, he knows, that if he were to insist or demand that the weak adopt an attitude of indifference toward matters of eating and drinking and the keeping of days, then he would only, in all likelihood, end-up drawing a line in the sand, escalating the conflict to an even higher level. It is to be expected, that persons who feel that their ethnic identity is being threatened will dig their heels in deeper, stridently judging and denouncing the practices of the strong other, in an effort to maintain the salience of these criteria for the self-identity of the group as a whole. Alternatively, if the weak were pressured by either Paul or the strong, on any other basis than personal conviction, to adopt an indifferent attitude toward these things, then there is the risk of leveling ethnic differences, as far as these persons are concerned, into a generic whole. For the weak to take-up an attitude of indifference regarding these matters would be tantamount to giving-up their ethnic particularity. Moreover, capitulation to the practices of the strong and, presumably, vice versa, based on anything other than belief that God has indeed made certain worship practices nonobligatory/obligatory is, according to the apostle, an act of unbelief since it does not have faith in what God has determined to be unnecessary/necessary at its base. Rather, it represents a decision stemming from some perceived need to respond in some fashion to human preference. Consequently, Paul articulates the principle of "living to the Lord" that allows for diversity in unity by establishing worship by the Spirit (in faith) as the primary marker/practice that defines the allocentric, believing community. It is Spirit-wrought allocentricism that not only establishes the order of nesting of self-identities, placing ethnoracial identity at the penultimate level, but also empowers both the weak and the strong to mutual acceptance of each other, in all of the other's diversity.

6.2.1.2 Diversity: A Matter of Conviction

6.2.1.2A ALL MANNER OF ETHNORACIAL OTHER

The use of κοινὸν in the technical, Jewish sense of unclean in 14:14 and καθαρά in 14:20, as well as, the implied contrast between Jews and gentiles in 15:7–13 has led interpreters to conclude that the weak consist of like-minded, believing Jews, a loosely knit group, lacking formal organization, who believe that members of the new movement ought to keep the Jewish food laws, sabbaths, and feast/fast days as part of the community's worship practices.[75] However, this conclusion appears to be premised on the assumption that Romans is meant to primarily address the issue of Jew-gentile reconciliation. Although Jew-gentile reconciliation is in all probability one issue of concern to the apostle, it is but one aspect in the larger attempt to reconcile diverse practices within a multiethnic community.

In this regard, it is important to note that the Jews were not the only people group in the ancient Mediterranean who maintained special food customs. Like Jews, some other people groups also avoided pork, including Phoenicians, Syrians, and Egyptian priests. Orphics, Dionysiac mystics and Pythagoreans abstained from eating meat and also from wine.[76] Strictly speaking, the law did not restrict Jews to eating vegetables (14:2), nor did it prohibit them from drinking wine (14:21). Granted, it is conceivable that in the absence of kosher or clean food, Jews might resort to vegetarianism.[77] However, in view of Greco-Roman ascetic ideals present in Rome, it is possible that the weak also included believing ascetics from a pagan background.[78] The sociocultural evidence concerning the keeping of holy or sacred days (14:5–6) is equally ambiguous in terms of an explicit ethnoracial referent. It is also important to note that there is no explicit mention of the Jewish sabbath in verses 5–6. Thus, although it is conceivable that Paul is speaking to the Jewish sabbath, and/or Jewish festival/fast days, it is possible that propitious days of Greco-Roman astrological calculation or Roman feast days are also in view.[79] Paul mentions pagan holy days in Gal 4:9–10, where he seems to slight such practices among believers.[80] However, the situation in Galatians is different than in Romans. There the apostle is attempting to dissuade his audience from taking on the markers of Jewish ethnoracial identity in the erroneous belief that this particular identity is necessary for membership in the new movement. The point in Galatians is that the keeping of any kind of days, pagan or Jewish, is no longer necessary. In

---

75. E.g., Fitzmyer, *Romans*, 688.
76. Keener, *Romans*, 161, and Fitzmyer, *Romans*, 687.
77. Keener, *Romans*, 162.
78. Jewett, *Romans*, 835.
79. Jewett, *Romans*, 844. Also, Keener, *Romans*, 165, who notes that Romans also took off regular market days.
80. Byrne makes the case that this suggests that Paul does not have pagan practices in view in Romans (Byrne, *Romans*, 412).

Romans, the concern is with maintaining ethnic diversity within a trans-ethnic community whose membership includes persons who continue to believe in the saliency of particular worship practices for both the appropriate honoring of the one God and for ethnoracial identity. As noted above, in antiquity these two prongs of self-identity were inextricably linked making it very difficult to invalidate specific aspects of one without invalidating the other. Hence, Paul must walk a fine line.

That the categories the strong and the weak do not have a one to one correspondence to gentiles and Jews, with the second group, perhaps including, former gentile proselytes, is further evidenced by the terms Paul uses to describe each group. In v. 2, the weak, who are said to eat λάχανα, are contrasted to the those who eat everything, πάντα. In both cases, the descriptive terms are broadly drawn, on the one hand, describing persons who eat only garden herbs or vegetables and, on the other hand, referring to those who essentially eat anything and everything.[81] However, ancient vegetarians did not restrict their diet to leafy vegetables and herbs, nor was it likely that any person in Rome ate everything that might be deemed edible by one group or another occupying its environs. These hyperboles are just that and are not meant to describe a discreet ethnoracial group.[82] Rather, the language invites all the ethnoracial subgroups present in the Roman community to find their place somewhere along the line between the two poles, such that the full diversity of food customs represented within it are incorporated, including those who believe that all types of food customs and sacred days no longer have any significance for the proper worship of God.[83]

The fact that Paul later equates the strong with those who eat meat and drink wine (14:21) does not negate the conclusion that both this group and the weak include a variety of ethnoracial subgroups. In this instance, he is addressing ascetic practices that some within the community are advocating as salient markers of group-identity for the new movement and, as such, applicable to all its members, as 14:3b indicates. Eating meat was a purview of the wealthy elite in antiquity. Most persons ate meat only rarely, in most cases, in connection with state festivals in honor of the gods. Similarly, most meat sold at the markets had at some point in time been sacrificed to the gods.[84] This suggests that the issue of whether or not to eat meat in the context of worship is related to the issue of the source of that meat, as the rare instances of Jewish advocacy of total abstinence from meat and wine similarly indicate.[85]

Thus, cases involving both Jewish and non-Jewish abstinence by believers most likely reflects a fear of involvement with and, perhaps, inadvertent condoning of pagan practices. As in the case of eating meat, given wine's sacred significance in

---

81. Jewett, *Romans*, 838.
82. Jewett, *Romans*, 838.
83. Jewett, *Romans*, 838.
84. Jewett, *Romans*, 868.
85. Jewett, *Romans*, 869.

Greco-Roman culture,[86] it is also conceivable that non-Jewish persons might conclude that drinking it no longer has a place in their worship of the one, true God. This suggests that the weak would include those Jews and persons of other ethnoracial backgrounds who explicitly associate meat and wine with pagan practices and, thus, would not eat or drink on those grounds. Abstinence, in this case, for these persons, would function as a salient marker of identity for membership in the believing community, demarcating it from all the other pagan worshiping communities. Jewish believers abstain on the basis of the law, while their non-Jewish counterparts abstain in order not to serve pagan gods. Conversely, it is equally conceivable that other, Jewish and non-Jewish believers, including Paul (14:14), would maintain that eating meat and drinking wine in honor of the one God essentially nullifies both the gods and idol worship, possible pagan sources and practices associated with these edibles and potables notwithstanding.[87] As in the case of ethnic food traditions, the apostle is aware that a variety of opinions exist regarding the potentially tainted nature of meat and wine and whether such contamination holds any significance in relation to one's identity as a believer.

Moreover, that Paul offers himself as an example of one of the Jewish strong, couching his reason for eschewing these ascetic practices explicitly in terms of clean and unclean and Jesus's declaration that nothing is unclean in itself (14:14), does not necessarily mean that the weak exclusively represent believers of Jewish descent. As an ethnographer, Paul has been building his case for the historical legitimacy of the believing community on the grounds that its existence was foretold in the scriptures, with this written tradition providing the only valid historical framework within which all of humanity finds its identity, meaning, and significance. Within this global perspective, Jesus's declaration concerning Jewish food laws, though initially directed toward his own people, has a wider significance in that it affirms that matters of food and drink no longer function as a salient marker identifying the people of God, as they did in the past. As Paul will make clear, in God's eyes and in terms of his people's worship of him, these practices no longer have the significance they had in the past where they served as primary markers of identity as God's elect. However, they do retain their significance as markers of ethnoracial identity, at least for some, allowing for diversity in worship practices, but only with the caveat that they remain penultimate markers of God's people in the present.

86. Jewett, *Romans*, 868.

87. Paul deals with a similar situation in 1 Corinthians. In this case, *some* of the Corinthian believers abstain from food not because of Jewish proscriptions (as others among the Corinthians do) but rather because of pre-Christian involvement in pagan worship (Gäckle, *Die Starken und die Schwachen*, 216–17, 276–79). It is Paul's identity in Christ that allows him to be free with respect to how he deals with questions of idol meat. However, aside from the fact that in 1 Cor 8 and 10, Paul deals explicitly with the issue of idol meat, there is no mention of "the strong." Moreover, 1 Cor 10:23—11:1 does not mention "the weak." When the term "weak" does appear in 1 Cor 8, it refers three times out of five to a weak conscience (8:7, 10, 12; cf. 8:9, 11) (Karris, "Romans 14:1—15:13," 73). Thus, it is not entirely clear that Paul has imported the categories of "weak" and "strong" from 1 Corinthians into Romans.

Similarly, as noted above, 15:7–13 is often invoked by interpreters as signifying that the weak and the strong have a one to one correspondence with Jewish, perhaps including non-Jewish sympathizers, and gentile believers. However, as he does throughout Romans, Paul invokes scripture in support of what he is arguing. In this case, the string of quotations (vv. 9–12) speaks in terms of the traditional Jewish binary categories that were used to divide all of humanity. Recall that the term ἔθνη, translated as "gentiles," was an exclusively Jewish designation. Gentiles would never have identified themselves as such. For these scriptures to apply to them, the non-Jewish members of Paul's audience would have understood that term as speaking to and/or encompassing their own ethnic particularity, including their own unique worship practices. In other words, the fact that the apostle makes use of Jewish scripture to support his claims does not necessarily mean that he means to reduce the tensions created by diverse ethnic subgroups participating and worshipping in a trans-ethnic community to a purely Jewish versus non-Jewish issue. Nor does it prove that the issue Paul is addressing in 14:1—15:3 must be understood as an exclusively Jewish one, precipitated by a Jewish minority bent on keeping the law and a gentile majority bent on shaming them. Rather, the evidence above suggests that Jewish-gentile tension is but one aspect of a multifaceted point of friction that is to be expected when persons of diverse ethnoracial backgrounds come together to form one worshipping community, the body of Christ.

Similarly, the exhortation to welcome one another on the grounds that God has accepted gentiles into the people of God through Christ, also need not be read as indicating that Paul has only Jew-gentile reconciliation in mind. Rather, it is implicit that not only will Jews accept non-Jews and vice versa, but that specific non-Jewish ethnic groups will accept each other. As discussed in more detail below, 15:1–6 and 7–13 are not related via the link the weak equals Jewish believers and the strong equals gentiles. Rather, the link is via love that should not please itself (15:1–3).[88] This love is patterned on the divine love that goes out to save all and to welcome all, despite ethnoracial distinctions (15:7–13).[89]

In sum, the designations weak and strong appear to represent two loosely knit groups of people within the Roman community, taken as a whole, each comprised of individuals of a variety of ethnoracial backgrounds. There is no evidence in the text to determine with certainty whether the terms weak and strong are Paul's own or whether they were in use among the Romans, with the former used by the latter for the purpose of shaming. However, the verb ἀσθενέω clearly denotes powerlessness of any kind, including physical illness and social or economic inferiority. In light of this, it is difficult to imagine that any group would have either embraced the epithet, the weak, or coined and attached it to themselves. Accordingly, it is likely that its source is the strong, with Paul adopting it for the express purpose of countering the

---

88. Karris, "Romans 14:1—15:13," 81.
89. Karris, "Romans 14:1—15:13," 80–81.

kind of prejudicial assessment that the expression implies.⁹⁰ Given that the bulk of Paul's exhortations are directed at the strong suggests that this group is the dominant one, although it is not clear from the text whether this dominance stems from their being in the majority or from some other factor. Regardless, it is likely that a dominant group would seek to shame and/or convince the weaker other into agreement with its point of view (4:1b).⁹¹

The factor determining membership in one or the other of these subgroups seems to be whether or not one believes that food traditions and/or the keeping of sacred days continue to have saliency as markers of identity for the believing community. The strong, with whom Paul identifies, are convinced that matters or food and drink and the keeping of days no longer have saliency when it comes to the worship practices characterizing the people of God in the new age. Conversely, the weak believe either that certain ethnic food/calendar traditions or that ascetic practices related to meat and/or wine continue to have salience for the self-identity of the believing community. For Jewish believers among the weak, abstinence, in all probability, is also linked to their ethnic-identity as Jews who continue to practice the dietary regulations in the law, while for non-Jewish believers abstinence appears to reflect the conviction that all former religious practices involving meat and/or wine should no longer have ethnoracial saliency and should not be consumed by believers in the context of worship. What emerges from this is a diversity of opinion regarding the place and manner of food and drink and the significance of keeping one or more days as markers of both ethnoracial identity and the group-identity of the new movement. For Paul, all of these opinions have validity if they are based on faith and if they are viewed as being penultimate in regard to group self-identity.

6.2.1.2B Everything in Faith

The clause τὸν δὲ ἀσθενοῦντα τῇ πίστει προσλαμβάνεσθε (14:1a) is problematic since it seems to imply that the weak suffer from some deficiency in their trust in God and/or his work in and through Christ. Interpreters have attempted to alleviate the implications of qualifying the participle ἀσθενοῦντα with τῇ πίστει by maintaining that, given the meaning of faith as it appears in verses 2, 22, and 23, Paul cannot be referring to belief in the sense of the essentials of Christianity; that is, belief in the gospel or in Christ as Lord.⁹² Rather, the apostle is talking about conscience. That is, although he does not use the word for conscience here, using instead the term for "conviction" (πληροφορέω), that is the implied meaning.⁹³ Hence, given that

---

90. Jewett, *Romans*, 834, 836.

91. Similarly, Jewett maintains that Paul flatly repudiates the ulterior motive of welcoming for purpose of persuading the "weak" to adopt the opinions of the "strong" (Jewett, *Romans*, 836).

92. E.g., Fitzmyer, *Romans*, 689.

93. Fitzmyer, *Romans*, 687.

faith for Paul is always faith in God and his work in and through Christ, so as to live according to that reality, suggests that the weak are those who have not allowed their faith to permeate all aspects of life.[94] Put differently, the basic sense of "weak in faith" seems to involve a failure to trust in God without reservation.[95] More specifically, the weak cannot, in all good conscience, believe or trust that God has indeed made specific worship practices nonobligatory for his people, who live in the age of the Spirit. In other words, these individuals are weak in the sense that they are not fully convinced of this reality and continue to see their identity as believers as bound-up in some way with these customs.

On the one hand, there is some truth in this assessment. Paul does maintain that the primary marker of identity for the believing community is the Spirit (faith). On the other hand, the apostle equally maintains the significance of ethnoracial diversity within the community marked by the one Spirit. The notion that the weak have some sort of deficiency with respect to their faith, however this deficiency is described, suggests that ultimately it is a deficiency that can and will be overcome. The notion that the "community must tolerate gradations in the working out of faith implications,"[96] implies that the hope someday is that believers who continue to maintain the saliency of particular worship practices will eventually come to see the error of their ways. Taken to its logical conclusion, this in turn suggests that ethnic worship practices ultimately do not matter at all, since all expressions of worship will be leveled into one expression (however, this is conceived and defined) as individual believers come to realize that ethnically particular practices no longer have any salience. Of especial note in this regard is that Paul never urges the weak to give-up their practices related to food, drink, and/or the keeping of days.[97] Rather, his exhortations are directed at correcting judgmental and disdaining attitudes and behaviors directed toward persons holding a viewpoint that is different from one's own (14:3).

Moreover, it is grammatically possible that in faith modifies the main verb, προσλαμβάνεσθε, rather than the participle: "Welcome, in/by faith, those who are weak." That is, if in faith were attributive in connection with the substantive use of the participle, then one would expect repetition of the article, which is absent here. The same prepositional phrase occurs in Rom 4:19 and modifies a participle of the same verb. However, in this case, the participle is circumstantial.[98] Accordingly, instead of describing the weakness of the weak in terms of faith, Paul is urging the members of

---

94. Byrne, *Romans*, 408.

95. Dunn, *Romans*, 2:9–16.

96. Byrne, *Romans*, 408.

97. Jae Won Lee points out that the conclusion that Paul judged one form of behavior to be wrong, living according to the law, contradicts the fact that he asks "the weak" to change their attitude but not their practice (Lee, "Paul and Ethnic Difference," 141–57).

98. Lee, "Paul and Ethnic Difference," 150.

his audience to receive the one who is weak as part of their faith.[99] This makes sense in light of the mildly contrastive clause that follows. That is, instead of welcoming the weak for the purpose of trying to convince them of their erroneous ways, Paul urges those of differing opinion to accept them in a way that accords with the allocentricism that is expected of all believers as part of their faith in God and his work in and through Christ. Exactly what this looks like is spelled out in greater detail in the exhortations that follow. Accordingly, although the weak, designated as such by those of differing viewpoint, do not believe or are not convinced that God has made certain aspects of worship nonobligatory, Paul's point is that there is no shame in this, the attitude of disdain by the strong notwithstanding, as long these things are seen as penultimate markers of identity. That is, these customs are acceptable as long as the weak do not try to impose their practices onto the community by judging those who disagree. That is, the apostle's correction does not have as its ultimate goal the rectifying of a deficiency in faith but rather it is aimed at both providing a hierarchical framework for the nesting of identities and putting to an end nonallocentric attitudes toward the other.

6.2.1.3 Unity: Living to the Lord

The basis for unity within the community is God, who has welcomed all (14:3) into his household as his house slaves/servants (v. 4). This powerful metaphor draws together several strands of the community's identity that Paul has already developed, grounding the exhortation to accept the other in the ontological reality of the group's divine origins. In antiquity, the οἰκέτης was a domestic slave, whose mere presence and membership in the household guaranteed a more immediate relationship with the master than that enjoyed by the slave employed outside of the domicile.[100] Moreover, membership in the household, which also included children, freed persons, clients, and spouses, lent a familial connotation to the term οἰκέτης that was lacking in the term δοῦλος.[101] As such, the apostle's use of this term harkens back to the identity of the community as the family or children of God (8:16; 9:8), joint heirs with Christ (8:17), and the one body in Christ (12:5); a connotation that is further strengthened by the fact that masters did not welcome slaves, regardless of whether they were household slaves or not.[102] Furthermore, Paul's choice to refer to believers as domestic slaves also echoes the community's identity as the slaves of God/righteousness who serve God by the Spirit (6:15–22; 7:5–6; 8:3–9). As I noted in the previous chapter, this OT title lacked the negative connotations associated with slavery in the Greco-Roman context and was used to denote the privileged status of Israel in relation to God. Thus, Paul's

---

99. Lee, "Paul and Ethnic Difference," 148.
100. Jewett, *Romans*, 841–42.
101. Jewett, *Romans*, 841–42.
102. Jewett, *Romans*, 841–42.

use of this complex image allows him to draw the familial and worshipping strands of identity together; an identity whose nexus is the Spirit, who both creates the kinship ties and transforms and empowers believers so that they are enabled to worship God in a manner commensurate with the in-breaking of the new age (12:1–2).

The third strand that the apostle weaves into the cord is believers' identity as those welcomed, προσλαμβάνω, by God. Specifically, each has been welcomed as a domestic slave into the master's household. The verb προσλαμβάνω carries the basic sense of taking the other to oneself as one's helper or partner in a common enterprise or for a common purpose.[103] In a more technical sense, it refers to welcoming another into one's home or social space.[104] In light of the full meaning of the verb, individual believers are to consider themselves members of God's household solely by virtue of the fact that their master has put them there and that they are all there for a common purpose, presumably to work in accord with the master in pursuing what is best for the household. This harkens back to everything Paul has said concerning the sovereignty of God in both establishing and maintaining his community and in determining its ethnic composition both in the past and in the present. In effect, although every believer enters the community with his or her own particularity in terms of both identity, ethnoracial identity included, and spiritual gifts, all stand equally before God, in their status as domestic slaves, whose purpose is to serve him and the interests of his household. Thus, believers' identity as members of the household of God through the Spirit, who worship him by the Spirit, is primary. Since the master's affairs are paramount and the household, as a unit, is obliged to function in tandem to meet these interests, any specific acts of service/worship, recall that for Paul all of the believer's life is offered as an act of service/worship (12:1), including those governed by ethnically determined custom, are penultimate. In terms of believers' identity they are nested under the primary marker of identity, the Spirit (faith).

It is telling that Paul's elaboration and explanation of why believers are to welcome each other is bracketed by the theme of judging (14:4; 14:10–12). The inclusio suggests that various subgroups within the community had determined that their particular worship customs were of primary importance, such that those who were of a differing viewpoint were considered as either substandard members of the people of God or as nonmembers, no better than outsider nonbelievers. The apostle's response to this assessment addresses the issue at two related levels: the ability of individual believers to discern which customs and practices constitute the proper worship of God as a consequence of their Spirit-wrought primary identity; and the determination of membership in the people of God as the sole prerogative of God. Both prongs of the two-pronged argument have at their center the idea of judging, κρινέω.

With regard to the first prong, Paul states in a rather matter of fact way that varying opinions regarding the keeping of days, and implicitly the eating of meat

---

103. Jewett, *Romans*, 835–36; Lee, "Paul and Ethnic Difference," 150.
104. Jewett, *Romans*, 835.

and drinking of wine, are the result of equally valid judgments concerning these matters (14:5–6). They are equally valid because they stem from a conviction of the mind of each individual involved, ἕκαστος ἐν τῷ ἰδίῳ νοΐ πληροφορείσθω. The term νοΐ harkens back to the renewal of the mind in 12:2 by the Spirit, who enables believers to discern the will of God in terms of determining what is pleasing, acceptable and perfect in his eyes. Furthermore, there is some evidence that the passive form of πληροφορέω, at the time Paul penned his missive, was on its way to becoming a technical term for charismatic assurance.[105] That this was the case is evidenced by its use in pre-Christian sources in the context of religious certainty.[106] In light of this, and given the broader context of the letter, it is quite plausible that Paul is arguing that all believers, whether weak or strong have the Spirit-wrought ability to discern what are acceptable worship customs in light of their own past practices and ethnic affiliations. This gives the community the "charismatic freedom that sanctions different attitudes and legitimates an infinite breadth of possibilities for cultural variation in belief and practice."[107] This is a work of the Spirit, who both marks and maintains individuals as members of a trans-ethnic community. In other words, the varying opinions within the community are a result of careful judgment by minds renewed by the Spirit of God. To judge the other, who is fully convinced in this charismatic sense of his or her viewpoint regarding customs related to worship, is tantamount to judging the work of the Spirit.

That decisions related to worship customs are a result of the working of the Spirit is further suggested by Paul's statement that those who eat, and those who keep the day, and those who abstain all do so in honor of God, in thankfulness to him (14:6). To honor and thank God is to worship him as Creator (1:21, 25), an act made possible by the Spirit, such that all of one's life becomes a living sacrifice to him (12:1) Thus, not only are all believers, regardless of individual opinions concerning worship practices, on equal footing by virtue of their being the domestic slaves of God, but also because of their primary identity as those marked by the Spirit (faith). Although each individual sacrificial life may look different due to differing spiritual gifts, convictions regarding worship, and ethnicities, all these ways of living are equally valid in so far as they have as their source the power and leading of the Spirit. It is the believer's primary identity that validates and orders all other, penultimate identities.

The gravity of judging or disdaining the work of the Spirit as it is manifested in its diversity within the worshipping community is underscored by the reminder that the judging of believers is the sole prerogative of God, who has welcomed all, as he has seen fit. As noted above, each is a domestic slave within the household of God by virtue of the fact that God has put him or her in that position. Moreover, as slaves, each is accountable to the master (14:4). The phrase, στήκει ἤ πίπτει appears to have

---

105. Jewett, *Romans*, 845.
106. Jewett, *Romans*, 845.
107. Jewett, *Romans*, 845.

a multivalent referent, referring both to the social relationship between the head of household and its members, who determines the acceptability or unacceptability of his or her slave's conduct, and to the eschatological situation of believers in relation to the Lord as divine judge.[108] Paul's use of the term κύριος moves the metaphor clearly into the divine realm where it is God/Christ who both welcomes the other and empowers him or her to stand, presumably as a member of God's household. In other words, matters of food and drink and the keeping of days are not salient criteria for determining membership within the community, on the grounds that God has not made them such. Those who judge and disdain the other based on these criteria in essence attempt to usurp the sovereign power and authority of God, who alone determines who and on what grounds each one stands as a member of his household.

In addition, the lives of believers, in their entirety, belong to the Lord, in service to him (14:7–8). In life and death, believers' existence is circumscribed by the lordship of Christ, who is Lord over both the living and the dead (14:9). This is a truth that is to be assumed about every believer, regardless of his or her viewpoint on matters of eating, drinking, and the keeping of days. According to Paul, the ultimate determination of who belongs to the people of God lies in the future, before the judgment seat of God, where each will give account of his or her life (vv. 10c–12). Verse 12 harkens back to 2:6, suggesting that it is believers' life of service to God that will be a determining factor. Implicitly, this includes one's attitude and conduct toward the other, which, according to the apostle, should be characterized by allocentricism, particularly in the case of those who consider themselves the strong.

6.2.2 Believer's Freedom and Allocentric Concern for the Other (Rom 14:13–23)

In the preceding section, the warning against disdaining and/or judging the other was aimed at both the weak and the strong. In this section, Paul's focus shifts to the strong. The exhortations are introduced with the familiar warning against judging (v. 13), conduct, which in the previous pericope, had been associated more explicitly with the weak (v. 3b). However, the act of disdaining implicitly includes the aspect of judging the other as worthy of disdain, while critical judgment of the sort Paul censures almost inevitably leads to disdain of the one being judged. Thus, in all likelihood, both groups are engaging to some degree in both types of conduct toward the other, with the one to one correspondence in verse 3 reflecting stylistic choice. It is not evident from the text why the strong are in a position to make the weak stumble, even though the latter appear to be as firm in their convictions as the former.

However, the broader context suggests that a community worship setting and, more specifically, the fellowship meal, is in view. This in turn implies a specific scenario

---

108. Jewett, *Romans*, 843.

where either the only edible and potable items available are either meat and/or wine of unknown origin, and/or only meat or wine are present, nothing else, and/or the gathering fails to fall on a designated sacred day. In any or all of these situations, the weak might be tempted to partake either on the grounds that participation in this pattern of worship is better than nonparticipation or as the result of some other social pressure to conform. What is clear is that the strong have the ability to injure the weak (v. 15) to the point of destroying the work of God (v. 20). Given the gravity of the latter, it is unlikely that λυπέω merely signifies "hurt feelings" or "emotional pain," on the part of the weak. For the apostle, strongly held convictions that cause the other to stumble defy the Spirit, since they stem from self-interest, rather than from the allocentric stance expected of all believers. This type of attitude and associated conduct has the potential to cause spiritual harm to the other and, if allowed to reign unchecked, has the capacity to destroy the community.

Of note in this regard is that, although Paul acknowledges the claim of the strong that all forms of food and drink may be consumed by the present people of God on the grounds that they are all now clean, he does not make that the issue.[109] The more important matter is the wrong committed when one's freedom to eat and drink causes the other to stumble.[110] Accordingly, the apostle exhorts the strong to be determined (κρίνατε) in ensuring that they do not put a stumbling block in the way of a brother or sister (v. 13). To do otherwise, signifies that one is no longer walking in love (v. 15). The verb περιπατέω harkens back to the notion of believers' ability, by virtue of the Spirit, to walk in righteousness before God as manifested in love for the neighbor as fulfillment of the law (13:8–10). The decision to eat and drink; that is, to live according to one's strongly held convictions, irrespective of the effect this decision might have on the other, is a decision not to walk according to the Spirit. It is a decision to deny one's primary identity by making the penultimate, the ultimate. That is, one's convictions about food and drink, despite God's declaration that these things are good, are nevertheless penultimate, since allocentric concern for the other is the manifestation of the Spirit-wrought identity that marks all believers.

According to Paul, allocentric concern for the other is denied when one's actions, irrespective of their objective correctness, serve to entice or pressure an individual holding religious prohibitions to act in a way that goes against his or her own conscience. The person who acts without self-condemnation, ὁ μὴ κρίνων ἑαυτὸν, (v. 22b) according to what he or she has discerned to be right or good, ἐν ᾧ δοκιμάζει, is blessed, in the sense that he or she has God's approval. This reflects Paul's basically high view of human conscience, both his own (1 Cor 4:3–4; 10:28–29) and other believers (2 Cor 4:2).[111] The apostle has already established that believers have a mind renewed by the Spirit that allows them to discern what is pleasing to God and approved

---

109. Lee, "Paul and Ethnic Difference," 154.
110. Lee, "Paul and Ethnic Difference," 154.
111. Byrne, *Romans*, 419.

by him. This is true of both the weak and the strong. As long as each acts according to conviction, or faith, in matters of food and drink, each is also blessed by God. What one approves, either abstinence or nonabstinence is valid as long as it is done according to good conscience. However, when an abstaining believer is pressured or enticed to eat or drink something that he or she believes to be prohibited, that person's actions no longer flow from what he or she believes to be acceptable to God but rather from some sense of need to placate or please the strong (v. 23a).

In essence, given such a scenario, these individuals are induced to choose pleasing others over pleasing God. For Paul, love of neighbor, which may or may not involve pleasing him or her, is fundamentally grounded in serving God and, hence, does not and cannot involve a choice between serving him or serving a fellow human being. If the strong should insist on the presence of certain food items at communal worship, the choice to please the human-other over God becomes a viable reality for the weak; thus, creating the potential for sin, on the part of the latter should they choose to act against what they believe is acceptable to God (v. 23b). Paul has already underscored the gravity of such a choice, linking it to final eschatological judgment (v. 15b).[112] How this stumbling on the part of the weak operates in leading to their final, eschatological destruction Paul does not explain. What is clear, is that the potential for this kind of choice for the strong simply does not exist, since, for them, food and drink are nonissues. Consequently, allocentric concern for the other means that believers' legitimate freedom must be subsumed under the more important responsibility of ensuring that the other is not enticed to act in a way that destroys his or her integrity in the present and which might very well lead to final destruction.

The actions of the strong not only have consequences for the spiritual well being and ultimate fate of individual, weak members of the community, but also have important ramifications for the spiritual health and, thus, legitimacy of the group as a whole. The idea of the community as something in the process of being built (14:19) is common to Paul (cf. 1 Cor 3:9–17).[113] Although it is sometimes applied to the individual (e.g., 1 Cor 8:10; 14:7), in Romans, the primary reference seems to be the community.[114] The warning that insistence on exercising complete freedom with regard to food and drink could lead to misconstruing and labeling something that is good in itself as evil (v. 16), suggests that the actions of the strong also have the potential to jeopardize the legitimacy and standing of the community in relation to its wider sociocultural context. Although it is possible that this misapprehension applies to the weak, the reference to human approval in verse 18 indicates that outsiders may be in view here.

---

112. The verb ἀπόλλυμι introduces the notion of final, eschatological ruin (cf. 1 Cor 8:11a) (Byrne, *Romans*, 420). In this case, the freedom of believers to eat and drink, which in itself is good, might rightly be criticized for being evil (v. 16).

113. Byrne, *Romans*, 417, 421.

114. Byrne, *Romans*, 417, 421.

In this regard, it is important to note that Paul mentions the kingdom of God in the preceding verse. Implicitly, it is a present reality among believers, manifesting itself within the community as righteousness, peace, and joy in the Spirit (v. 17). It is the fruit of the Spirit (cf. Gal 6:22–23) that both marks the believing community as distinct from all other communities and establishes it as the legitimate community for all people, reflecting, as it is meant to do, God's intent for all humanity. Its validity as the signpost of God's kingdom resides, to a great degree, in the extent to which it embodies the transformative work of the Spirit in the relations of is members to each other. If the strong should choose to exercise their freedom indiscriminately the result would, in all likelihood, either be greater acrimony and group discord, rather than peace or joy, or an increase in sinful choices, unrighteousness, among the weak, or both. In either case, this would destroy both the work of the Spirit and any appeal or good standing the community might have in the eyes of outsiders. However, if the strong should choose to take an allocentric stance and implement the higher principle of pursuing what makes for peace and for mutual upbuilding over their rightful exercise of freedom, then they would not only serve Christ but also gain the approval of watchful, often suspicious, outsiders (vv. 18–19). The spiritual well being of the community and its legitimacy are inseparable. In this case, the valid exercise of believer freedom must give way to allocentric concern for the in-group other. Love of neighbor fulfills the law and, thus, establishes the community's legitimacy, maintains its spiritual robustness, and actualizes its mandate to welcome all persons with the good news that God has welcomed all into his kingdom.

6.2.3 According to the Pattern of Christ (Rom 15:1–13)

In this section, Paul carries forward the appeal he has just made both by providing the christological grounds for deference by the strong to the weak (vv. 1–6) and by reminding the community that it exists, as the scriptures themselves affirm, for the purpose of worshipping God (vv. 7–12). The concluding prayer (v. 13) ties the appeal for unity to Paul's larger purpose of encouraging the beleaguered community to persevere in hope. In this way, the apostle rounds out his ethnography by linking the group's identity and its legitimacy, which is manifested in its Spirit-crafted unity in diversity, to the hope believers have in God, who both established them as his people and who will maintain them to the end.

As Paul has already demonstrated, the formation of a trans-ethnic social identity not only requires allocentric individuals transformed by the Spirit, but also calls for a group capable of incorporating the other.[115] Verses 1–2 recap, in summary fashion, the group dynamics necessary for this to occur. A group capable of incorporating the other is characterized by the ability of its strong members to discern a course of action

---

115. Kuecker, *Spirit and the 'Other,'* 218.

that pleases the other for the purpose of establishing the good (εἰς τὸ ἀγαθόν); the building-up of the community (πρὸς οἰκοδομήν)(v. 2). The strong do this by bearing the weaknesses of those unable to bear them (v. 1). The phrase, τὰ ἀσθενήματα τῶν ἀδυνάτων βαστάζειν, reinforces Paul's point that it is the weak, and not the strong who are uniquely vulnerable to sin. The proscriptions regarding food and drink that the former hold, that is, their weaknesses, ought to be borne by the strong, who are able to bear them in the sense that they are not vulnerable to the temptation to act against their convictions. The quote of Ps 69:9 (LXX 68:10) in relation to Christ (v. 3) gives this exhortation a christological basis and harkens back to the idea that believers are to walk according to the pattern of Christ, empowered as they are by the Spirit to do so (6:17). In the original context, the psalmist bears the insults against God by the ungodly for the sake of God and his purposes. The idea appears to be that Christ, in like fashion, bore the insults of iniquitous persons in his commitment and obedience to God's plan of salvation, which has at its heart love for sinful humanity (5:6–8). Consequently, the strong, who walk according to the pattern of Christ, are to exhibit the same kind of allocentric love toward the weak by bearing their weaknesses, specifically, by ensuring that they are not put in a vulnerable position where they may act against their convictions. The choice to relinquish one's freedom out of concern for the other's spiritual well-being results in the building up of the community that God originated and established and, thus, serves his purposes.

Although the strong are to bear the weaknesses of the weak in a way that is analogous to Christ's choice to humble himself and take up humanity's burdens, it is not immediately clear what type of injury the strong are expected to suffer. It is possible that these sufferings relate to the act of self-denial in freely choosing to give-up the right to eat and drink in good conscience. However, the references to steadfastness, encouragement, and hope (vv. 4–5) suggest that this existential suffering is tied to a larger purpose. As Paul has already made clear, the community does not exist only for itself. Rather, it exists also for the sake of the outsider-other, as a signpost of God's intent for all of humanity. Accordingly, the choice to curtail one's legitimate freedom in deference to the weak not only serves to protect the latter but also strengthens the community by unifying it so that it can remain a faithful witness to the good news that God has now included all peoples among his people. Thus, the apostle prays that the God who is the source of steadfastness, encouragement, and perseverance in faith would grant the community to be of one mind according to Christ Jesus (v. 5); that is, that they would take on the attitude of Christ. By seeking to please the neighbor, rather than the self, both the weak and the strong ensure that opinions regarding food and drink will not destroy the unity of their trans-ethnic community—a solidarity that lies at the heart of its witness to a hostile world, manifested in its unified worship of the one God (v. 6).

This notion is carried forward in 15:7–13, with verse 7 forming an inclusio with 14:1, explicitly linking welcome of the other as an act patterned on Christ's act of welcoming sinful humanity for the express purpose of bringing glory to God. According to Paul, it is precisely when the believing community in all its ethnoracial diversity is able to glorify God with one voice (v. 6) that it stands as a faithful witness to the gospel (cf. 3:29). The gospel stands as God's confirmation of the promise of the incoming of the gentiles into the people of God. It is in this sense, that both trans-ethnic unity and ongoing subgroup particularity are necessary in light of the new eschatological situation in Christ. As at every key juncture of his ethnography, the apostle presents Christ as the nexus between past and present. Whereas in the preceding passages Paul spoke in terms of the strong and the weak, here his focus shifts to the traditional binary categories of Jew (περιτομῆς) and gentile. As noted above, the apostle's recourse to Scripture and its traditional binary categories does not necessarily mean that he is exclusively concerned with Jew-gentile relations. Moreover, verses 7–13 are linked to verses 1–3 via the idea of allocentric love that does not please itself, a love patterned on the divine love of God/Christ that goes out to all and welcomes all.

Thus, Christ, on whom the believing community ought to be patterned, in his allocentric love has become a servant to the circumcision, in the sense that he acts as God's agent to establish God's truth and confirm the promises given to the patriarchs (v. 8). Likewise, in his capacity as a servant to Israel, he opened the door to God's mercy for the gentiles (v. 9). Christ humbled himself on behalf of both the Jewish and non-Jewish other in order to bring glory to God by forming Jews and all manner of non-Jews into the one, present people of God. Accordingly, believers are to humble themselves on behalf of the other in order to bring glory to God by worshipping God as one, unified people. The chain of scriptural citations (vv. 9b–12) (Deut 32:43; Isa 11:10; Pss 18:49, 117:1) underscores the unity of all people groups as the people of God as something promised and foretold by God. In the original context, the reason for the gentile nations' praise of God is the love God manifested toward Israel (Pss 18 and 117), such that the nations praise him in union with his chosen people (Deut 32:43 LXX, Isa 11:10–12). It is in and through Christ that God confirms the promises given to Israel and brings them to fruition. Moreover, it is the community in Christ that stands as a witness to what God has done. Thus, the allocentric love of God/Christ that stands at the heart of these promises foretold in the scriptures is reflected in the allocentric love that stands at the heart of a trans-ethnic community that is empowered to embrace and incorporate the other.

In sum, continuing ethnoracial subgroup salience is a good that Paul sees as necessary in light of the new eschatological situation in Christ for two reasons. First, when the present people of God, composed of Jews and all manner of non-Jews, worships the one God and Lord of all the world, in one Spirit-wrought, trans-ethnic voice this serves as a confirmation that the promises given to Israel have been brought to fruition in and through Christ. This is because Christ has welcomed all people groups, in all of their diversity, into the family of God through his death and resurrection. Second, since Christ's teaching and example have replaced the Jewish law as that which circumscribes the worship of the people of God, with worship broadly defined as living one's life entirely to God, believers are to welcome the ethnic other, as the ethnic other, just as Christ has.

This suggests that the reason that Paul never uses the term "γενός" in relation to the new or present people of God is because the scriptures envision the eschatological people of God as ethnically diverse (cf. Rev 5:9–10). In other words, unlike the author of Judith, who portrays the decision to worship the God of Heaven as a change in ethnoracial identity (Jdt 5:6–8; 14:10), Paul pictures entrance into the believing community as becoming a member of an ethnically diverse family. Moreover, it is a family whose members are united by the Spirit who empowers believers to preserve particularity without allowing any of the basic categories of human difference to assume a primary place in the group's self-identity. Thus, although Jews and Greeks, slaves and free, and male and female continue to exist within the people of God, this identity is secondary to that which defines the children of God, who are one in Christ, who himself has presently welcomed all humanity, in all of its diversity (Gal 3:26 –28).

6.3 Conclusion

The emergence of a new and/or alternative community is a precarious process that entails the constant threat of group disintegration and/or assimilation. In Rom 1–11, Paul carefully constructed a worldview for his audience designed to work against these leveling forces both by providing legitimacy for the emerging in-Christ movement's state of separation and by giving it cohesion. In chapters 12–15, the apostle carries his ethnographic purposes forward by providing the Roman community with an ethos that coheres with its symbolic universe in order to fortify his audience's resolve to remain faithful to the gospel within an environment that continually exerts pressures toward social and cultural conformity. He accomplishes this both by establishing a causal link between the community's ethos and its account of origins and by providing viable boundary markers that work to maintain both group cohesion and group differentiation, while simultaneously allowing for the incorporation of the other. This dynamic interplay between group boundary markers, group cohesion and differentiation, and Spirit-wrought allocentricism that Paul explicates is then brought to bear on the specific issue of worship in a community composed of an amalgamation of distinct ethnoracial groups. Here, Paul skillfully navigates the thorny subject of ethnic diversity within a unified community in a way that makes room for differences in worship customs and traditions, while preserving a unified, Spirit-wrought group-identity consistent with its other-centered character.

In 12:1—13:14, Paul delineates the basic contours of the allocentric or other-centered manner of communal living that characterizes the people of God in the new age. This common way of life reflects the community's worldview as the apostle has described it in the account of origins where he established that faith in the gospel and possession of the Spirit are the primary indicators of membership within the believing community. Believers are the people who have been freed from the power of sin, to walk according to the Spirit, united with Christ, as the servants of God. The social identity of the believing community is rooted in this reality, making believers, Jew and gentile alike, the sons and daughters of God, who bear a family resemblance to their divine Father. According to the apostle, the concrete manifestation, or living into and living out, of this identity entails the proper worship of God as its beginning point. This, in turn, calls for a due assessment of the self in relation to others within the community, which itself necessitates a proper view of the other, both within and without the believing community. In other words, this common identity results in a common way of life that testifies to and exemplifies its divine origins/foundation and its existence as a distinct people group among whom the beginning of new age finds expression.

Moreover, this identity may be described as superordinate, in that it transcends the traditional binary categories of Jew-gentile, incorporating diverse peoples under a common identity. It is God, through Christ and the Spirit, who unites believers as a singular people with a singular purpose—to worship the Creator by living sacrificially to him. In other words, the community's terminal identity is Spirit-wrought and is manifested in Spirit-led worship/life, the two being inseparable. The community's ethos is essentially other-focused in that it is both grounded in and receives its impetus from God and calls for a concern for the human-other expressed specifically by the willingness to subordinate privileged identity for the sake of the neighbor, both insider and outsider. Within the in-group, privileged identity is subordinated when members of the community properly assess themselves in terms of their spiritual gift(s), given to each, by God, for the benefit of the community. Given the diversity of spiritual gifts, uniformity of social identity and purpose is manifested in a plurality of roles or functions, each organically linked to the other in a way that defies human derived standards of ranking and status. In this way, all other social identities are subsumed, transformed, and rendered penultimate. Moreover, since renewal of the mind by the Spirit includes the transformed ability to look beyond the interests of the in-group and to extend in-group benefits to outsiders, the community's ethos reflects the gospel's intent by extending God's love in Christ to all.

It is this Spirit-wrought, allocentric identity, manifested in a radically other-focused disposition that fulfills the law. The link Paul makes between the community's identity and ethos and the fulfillment of the written code serves as an adumbration of the lines of continuity and discontinuity between God's people in the past and in the present, in terms of faith and law, that he drew in the previous chapters. In the past, the Mosaic or written law served as a primary marker of identity for God's people, separating God's people, primarily ethnoracial Jews, from all other people groups. In the present, it finds its ultimate expression and fulfillment in Christ through whom believers are empowered by the Spirit to worship God and to live in obedience to him in a radically new way. Thus, for Paul, the Spirit is central and both directs intergroup contact, according to the principle of allocentric love, and gives believers a common identity, allowing for the incorporation of outsiders into the community. As such, the Spirit replaces the law as the primary marker of identity of the people of God in the present, directing the formation of the group's self-identity as it is manifested in its manner of life. Moreover, the Spirit maintains the boundaries of community, making them permeable, so that all are invited to enter in and to be transformed.

However, although participation in this allocentric group requires a new social identity capable of subordinating and transcending ethnic identity, all forms of ethnoracial identity that do not contradict the gospel and the teaching and example of Christ continue at a penultimate level. This suggests that the Jewish law, particularly its more ritualistic aspects, retains salience as providing the criteria for identifying Jews as an ethnoracial group. Nevertheless, these identity-constructing practices are penultimate and are to be understood in light of the community's terminal Spirit-wrought, allocentric identity that is grounded in faith, not the law. Thus, this people's worship practices, which in antiquity were inextricably linked to ethnoracial identity, cannot be *primarily* described with any specific set of rituals and rites. Rather, as a trans-ethnic group, the new movement must be able to embrace diverse ethnicities, with their varied customs and traditions, in a way that preserves the terminal identity of the group without leveling ethnic differences into a generic whole. This suggests a dynamic process, requiring ongoing negotiation between diverse parties within the group; a process Paul makes explicit in 14:1—15:6.

In these chapters, the apostle maintains a delicate balance between the primacy of worship in/by the Spirit, in faith, that marks the new, ethnoracially diverse people of God and the continuing salience, at the penultimate level, of particular ethnic expressions of worship. Unity in worship is important in terms of the apostle's larger ethnographic purpose. A current lack of unity in worship among the Roman believers is suggested by the context. Rather than worshipping together, they are preoccupied with disputes, judging those who disagree, and maintaining their own specific set of practices. This may be the reason why Paul does not refer to the Roman believers as an ἐκκλεσία. In this sense, his ethnographic account of the present people of God serves as an attempt to remedy the situation before his arrival. Since group-identity and patterns of worship are interlinked and mutually constituting, the integrity of the community's identity is dependent on the group's acceptance of an understanding of worship that is group-identity constructing. In addition, the allocentricism that lies at the heart of the group's self-identity is expressed not only in the stance its members take toward one another, but also in the group's relations with outsiders. Outsiders would find little reason to join a group that displays a lack of tolerance among its members for each other. Moreover, the lack of cohesion between what the community professes and what it actually does would seriously compromise the community's mission of reflecting the power of the gospel, which it professes to be at work among it, to the outside world.

Accordingly, recognizing the diversity of opinions regarding the place and manner of food and drink and the significance of keeping one or more days as markers of both ethnoracial identity and the group-identity of the new movement, Paul argues that all of these opinions have validity if they are based on faith, that is, if they are according to conviction, and if they are viewed as penultimate in regard to group self-identity. Decisions about whether or not to maintain specific forms of worship practices are, according to Paul, a result of the working of the Spirit, who enables believers to discern the will of God, what is pleasing and acceptable to him. To judge the other, who is fully convinced, in this charismatic sense, is essentially to judge the working of the Spirit and to usurp the sovereignty of God, who has welcomed all believers. Thus, although each individual sacrificial life may look different due to differing spiritual gifts, convictions regarding worship, and ethnic-racial identities, all these ways of living are equally valid in so far as they have as their source the power and leading of the Spirit. It this primary, Spirit-wrought identity, that validates and orders all other, penultimate identities.

Although Paul acknowledges the claim of the strong that all forms of food and drink may be consumed by the present people of God on the grounds that they are all now clean, he does not ask the weak to give-up their ascetic practices. Rather, according to the apostle, the essential matter is the wrong committed when one's freedom to eat and drink causes the abstaining-other to stumble. Allocentric concern for the other is denied when one's actions, irrespective of their objective truth, serve to entice or pressure an individual holding certain convictions regarding proper worship practices to act in a way that goes against his or her own conscience. In essence, given such a scenario, these individuals are induced to choose pleasing others, namely the strong, over pleasing God. The decision to eat and drink; that is, to live according to one's strongly held convictions, irrespective of the effect this decision might have on the other, is a decision not to walk according to the Spirit. It is a decision to deny one's primary identity by making the penultimate, the ultimate. Since the potential for stumbling does not exist for the strong, given that for them food and drink are nonissues, allocentric concern for the weaker-other means that believers' legitimate freedom must be subsumed under the more important responsibility of ensuring that one's brother or sister is not enticed to act in a way that destroys his or her integrity. Moreover, since the community's validity as the signpost of God's Kingdom resides in the extent to which it embodies the transformative work of the Spirit in the relations of its members to each other, indiscriminate exercise of legitimate freedom in this situation would not only destroy the work of the Spirit but would be detrimental to the new movement's standing in the eyes of suspicious outsiders. Since the spiritual well being of the community and its legitimacy are inseparable, the choice to take an allocentric stance and to implement the higher principle of pursuing what makes for peace and for mutual upbuilding establishes the community's legitimacy, maintains its spiritual robustness, and actualizes its mandate to welcome all persons with the good news that God has welcomed all into his kingdom.

Drawing all these strands together, Paul rounds out his ethnography by linking the group's identity and its legitimacy, which is manifested in its Spirit-crafted unity in diversity, to Christ. As at every key juncture of his ethnography, the apostle presents Christ as the nexus between past and present. In this instance, he explicitly associates welcome of the other with Christ's act of welcoming sinful humanity for the express purpose of bringing glory to God. As Christ humbled himself on behalf of both the Jewish and non-Jewish other in order to bring glory to God, forming Jews and all manner of non-Jews into the one, present people of God, believers are to humble themselves on behalf of the other in order to bring glory to God by worshipping God as one, unified people. According to Paul, the unity of all people groups as the people of God is something promised and foretold by him in the scriptures. It is in and through Christ that God confirms the promises given to Israel and brings them to fruition. Moreover, it is the community in Christ that stands as a witness to what God has done.

Consequently, continuing ethnoracial subgroup salience is a good that Paul sees as necessary in light of the new eschatological situation in Christ. Since Christ's teaching and example has replaced the Jewish law as that which circumscribes the worship of the people of God, with worship broadly defined as living one's life entirely to God, believers are to welcome the ethnic other, as the ethnic other, just as Christ has. Paul never ascribes the term "γενός" in relation to the new or present people of God, since the scriptures envision the eschatological people of God as ethnically diverse. Rather, entrance into the believing community is described in terms of becoming a member of an ethnically diverse family, whose members are enabled by the Spirit to preserve particularity without allowing any of the basic categories of human difference to assume a primary place in the group's self-identity.

It is the allocentric love of God/Christ that both stands at the heart of these promises foretold in the scriptures and is reflected in the allocentric love that stands at the heart of a trans-ethnic community that is empowered to embrace and incorporate the other. It is precisely when the believing community in all its ethnoracial diversity is able to glorify God with one voice that it stands as a faithful witness to the gospel. By seeking to please the neighbor, rather than the self, both the weak and the strong ensure that opinions regarding food and drink will not destroy the unity of their trans-ethnic community—a solidarity that lies at the heart of its witness to a hostile world, manifested in its unified worship of the one God.

CHAPTER SEVEN

Conclusion

ONCE ASKED BY A Jewish Christian as to how modern day Christian-Jews were to retain any meaningful ethnoracial particularity in light of both Paul's seemingly unconditional negative appraisal of the law and the church's apparently unequivocal claim to universality, I was unable to provide a satisfactory answer. This question brought me face-to-face with both my own failure to think deeply on the matter and with the impoverished state of Pauline scholarship as it relates to this issue. Moreover, I realized that my own understanding of the subject was largely determined by a particular reading of Romans which, although not based on an interpretation of the so-called law-faith (works-grace) dichotomy as representing two antithetical paths to salvation, nevertheless posited Christianity as superior to Judaism precisely because it is seen as transcending the ethnic particularity of the latter. Taken to its logical conclusion, this view quickly spirals into a portrayal of Christianity as a nonethnic, supra-cultural, and, essentially, disembodied phenomenon; hence, the pointed nature of my colleague's question.

His question is a fitting critique of the current state of scholarship on Paul and, in particular, on his letter to the Romans in several respects. Although there is a consensus that Romans deals with both the respective roles of the law and faith in light of Christ and the relationship between Jews and gentiles in Christ, the purpose of the law-faith (grace-works) dichotomy(s) continues to be understood as Paul's way of referring either to two alternative paths of salvation and/or religious systems. Consequently, despite the recognition that Romans deals concretely with the issue of gentile inclusion, interpreters, on both sides of the justification issue, Traditional and New Perspective, nevertheless maintain that justification by faith is the apostle's fundamental premise from which all of his arguments flow. Thus, Romans continues to be read as a kind of manifesto on Pauline soteriology, in spite of assertions to the contrary. Moreover, since the third dichotomy is rooted in and entangled with the first two, the Pauline Christ movement is generally interpreted as antithetical to Judaism and gentile inclusion occurs at the expense of any meaningful retention of Jewish ethnic identity.

Furthermore, although investigations of Paul's formation of in-Christ identity in Romans have provided a useful corrective to the tendency to overly distance the apostle and his converts from their Jewish roots, the perceived need to firmly establish that Paul upheld ethnic diversity in unity has led to a selective focus on certain portions of the letter without adequate consideration of how these sections relate to the larger whole. As a consequence, in-Christ identity resolves into an essentially Jewish identity, with Jewish believers remaining exempt from the work of the Spirit. Conversely, gentile in-Christ identity is reduced to a kind of liminal identity which, although dependent on a Jewish symbolic universe, is antithetical to Jewish in-Christ identity. Apart from faith at the cognitive level, it is unclear what unites Jewish and gentile believers and what characterizes the Christ movement as an integral social group distinct from both Judaism and all other pagan religious groups.

In sum, both views are limited in their interpretative potential. The view that Romans is primarily about soteriology, regardless of whether one begins with justification by faith, moving to Jew-gentile reconciliation or vice versa, naturally assumes a soteriological polarity between law and faith and proceeds from there. This precludes any meaningful exploration of the possibility that the law-faith dichotomy may play a different, equally important role in the apostle's attempts to either define some continuing, historical and/or theological relationship between Judaism and the new movement, or to explain how ethnic diversity is maintained in the context of in-Christ unity. The studies concerned with Paul's construction of in-Christ identity, which seek to preserve the essential Jewishness of the new movement as a backlash against the Jew-gentile dichotomy created by scholarship, fail to consider the eschatological framework that structures Paul's theological and ethnic discourse and within which he constructs in-Christ identity. The identity the apostle establishes can only be understood within the context of what he says regarding the role of the Spirit in the new age and how he conceives of this in relation to the Jewish past. The fact that he makes copious recourse to Jewish Scripture indicates that he is deliberately working within an assumed narrative, which he believes is basic to the lived reality of his audience. Accordingly, an adequate understanding of an ethnically diverse in-Christ identity must explain: how and why Paul reworks the basic Jewish narrative in the way he does; how does the law-faith dichotomy fit into this and what bearing does it have in the construction of in-Christ identity; and, finally, how does the new age of the Spirit make a difference in the concrete, embodied life of an ethnically diverse community composed of Jew and gentile united in Christ. In other words, the issue of identity can only be understood within the larger framework of the letter's purpose and generic characteristics. Thus, apart from a major shift in our understanding of the generic framework (which necessarily entails reconsideration of the letter's primary purpose) within which Paul constructs his letter to the Romans, the current interpretational stand-off will continue. As a consequence, a satisfactory answer to the question of how modern Jewish Christians are to maintain any meaningful ethnoracial particularity in a trans-ethnic, law-free community will remain elusive.

7.1 A Summary of Reading the Dichotomies of Law-Faith and Jew-Gentile in Light of Ancient Greco-Roman and Hellenistic Jewish Ethnography and Social Identity Theory

If the general consensus is correct that, in Romans, Paul is addressing the respective roles of law and faith in light of the Christ event, elucidating the relationship between Jews and gentiles in Christ, and as a result, constructing in-Christ identity for a trans-ethnic community, this then raises the question of whether there existed at that time a literary mode concerned with the construction and legitimization of social identity which might shed light on the textual integrity of Paul's argumentation. A literary model that could make sense of all the textual data would, in turn, bring clarity to the apostle's use of the so-called law-faith dichotomy and his purpose for writing. Carrying forward Hodges's insights regarding the ethnographic aspects of Romans, I have argued that the letter, taken as a whole, represents an example of early Christian ethnography patterned on Greco-Roman ethnographic works and related indigenous, Hellenistic Jewish pieces. This contemporary genre exhibits the most points of continuity, in terms of motifs and type of discourse, with the epistle, providing a framework for its interpretation, allowing us to place the various pieces of the puzzle, the letter's theology, ethnic and kinship language, and its sociological elements into a meaningful whole. Put differently, the multifaceted nature of this literary genre provides a central interpretational point where the main purpose of the letter and the meaning of the law-faith dichotomy and its siblings intersect, whereby each element is illumined by and illumines the others. That is, attention to the ethnographic characteristics of Romans provides a clearer understanding of its purpose, shedding greater light on the meaning of the three, related dichotomies.

Ancient ethnographic texts were concerned with far more than providing a description of foreign peoples and their lands. Flexible in both form and content, these works satisfied a variety of political and apologetic agendas, including relating the story of a people for the purpose of defining and legitimizing them within the vast network of a new world order. The ethnoracial discourse present within them reflects this purpose. Ethnicity-race, including the notion of kinship upon which this construction rests, although often presented in these works as natural and fixed, was equally open to negotiation and reworking through the selective choice of varying ethnoracial criteria and attributes, making these constructs particularly useful to writers writing with an apologetic intent. Similarly, through the proclamation of the gospel of hope, Paul presents the believers in Rome with a positive group self-identity that legitimates their standing vis-à-vis the broader culture so as to strengthen and encourage them to continued faithful obedience to its message. By portraying the believing community as a distinct people group related by the shared worship of the one, true God, a common way of life, and shared ancestry, Paul joins the ranks of contemporary Greco-Roman and Hellenistic-Jewish ethnographers in telling the story of a particular people in an attempt to situate and legitimate that people within the context of a new age.

Indigenous ancient ethnographers, like the apostle, wrote for the purpose of defining and legitimizing a particular people group with its unique laws, customs, and way of life, within the larger context of a new world order that claimed cultural, political, and economic superiority. As a result, it was imperative for these writers to buttress group affiliation, mainly by providing a positive identity for their people, against the pressures of cultural and social assimilation. This was especially important for groups like the Christ movement, which existed on the fringes of Greco-Roman society and culture. In these indigenous writings, the integrity of the group in question is a presupposition. Its legitimacy is not, and it is with this issue that these authors are concerned. As I have demonstrated, careful examination of the text of Romans suggests that Paul sought to defend the legitimacy of the community in Rome in order to increase in-group affiliation, bolstering believers against possible assimilation in the face of social ostracism and general persecution perpetrated by nonbelieving friends, neighbors, business associates, and family, including nonbelieving Jews.

In addition to the evidence that points to letter's purpose, there are other textual clues which indicate Paul's ethnographic aims. As I have noted, similar to contemporary indigenous writers, the apostle establishes his credibility as a native ethnographer, whose authority is rooted in the fact that he is an accurate and reliable interpreter of his ancestral traditions, in several ways. He casts his apostolic mission in terms of a divinely ordained charge to proclaim and elucidate both the gospel and Israel's scriptural traditions. A prophet, standing in the line of Israel's greatest seers, he views his ministry as a call to reinterpret righteousness in light of Christ. Accordingly, his ministry surpasses the tradition in which he is rooted, in that, the content of the divine revelation given to him represents the culmination of God's hidden plan for all of humanity. Made privy to the divinely revealed future, while simultaneously viewing the past as a credible interpreter of it, Paul perceives how both perspectives converge on the present and brings to light the ramifications of this insight, for his audience. Moreover, as a priest of the new, eschatological community, Paul presents himself as uniquely qualified to provide his people with the teaching and praxis necessary for their sanctification. Accordingly, the ethnography he provides for his audience, in which he establishes both the identity of the present people of God and the customs and way of life by which that identity is embodied, can be trusted as an accurate reflection of who the people of God are. Moreover, in experiential terms, the apostle has not only personally encountered divine power but has also successfully carried the gospel across the entire Eastern Mediterranean. Thus, he presents himself as the locus of divine activity through whom God works to establish and maintain believing communities. As a travel-seasoned man, operating under divine mandate, his wisdom is as broad as the extent of his sojourns.

Consequently, Paul's own knowledge and wisdom and his personal witness of God's creative power operative in and through the gospel in inaugurating and sustaining believing communities makes him particularly suited for the task of providing his audience with an account of origins of the new movement. For ancient ethnographers, etiological accounts, establishing the antiquity and historical legitimacy of a given people group, played a central role in constructing a positive identity for the ethnoracial groups for which they were advocating. As social identity theorists point out, individuals will seek to identify with groups that are defined by what are perceived to be positive rather than negative characteristics. In cases where the in-group is seen to lack positive distinctiveness, a decrease in affiliation with or even alienation from the group is inevitable. Historically, the Jewish people perceived themselves as the elect of God. They identified themselves as Yahweh's chosen people, with the covenant and the law standing as the major attestation to this unique divine-human relationship. Accordingly, in his effort to strengthen group affiliation among the believers in Rome, Paul seeks to present the Christ movement as representative of the people of God in a way that stands in some continuity with this revered Jewish self-perception, yet acknowledges the reality of the new age where the past is reinterpreted in light of the present.

For the ancients, the new was acceptable as long as it proved to have ties with the esteemed past. Accordingly, what was needed was an interpretation of God's historical dealings with Israel that finds its climax in Jesus. Thus, beginning with the assumption that the Jewish scriptures provide the only valid frame of reference for the world's history, Paul finds in them both an account of the universal human condition and God's work in rectifying that condition as promised and foretold through the Jewish prophets. Utilizing this frame of reference and drawing upon common ethnographic motifs and strategies of discourse, the apostle not only establishes the antiquity but also the world embracing quality of the Christ movement. He does this in two ways: by providing an interpretation of a prior, Jewish history that finds its climax in the eschatological present and by presenting an account of the new movement's two divinely instituted founding figures—Abraham and, ultimately, Christ.

In keeping with the ethnographic tradition of his time, Paul reinterprets Israel's history in light of the gospel, carefully working through the intricacies of the relationship between the Jewish people and their particular and distinct role in history, and believing gentiles, who stand both in continuity with and in discontinuity from Israel. Although this task will occupy the better part of the letter, he lays the groundwork in chapters 1–5. According to Paul, the sin, alienation, and enmity that characterizes humanity's relationship with God is decisively dealt with in and through Christ, as God works to renew and restore Israel, along with all gentiles who acknowledge his sovereignty. This redrawing of the boundaries of the people of God to include all who acknowledge him inevitably collides with the historical reality of Israel's election. Consequently, the apostle establishes a scriptural basis for universal inclusion that points to an active faith or trust in God, manifested as obedience to him, as the primary identifying characteristic of his people, both in the past and in the present—thus, drawing a historical line of continuity between Judaism and the Christ movement. The place of the law in this scheme and, by the same token, the unique role of the Jewish people raises the issue of discontinuity.

Analysis of the ethnic discourse present in these first, five chapters indicates that the apostle's primary strategy for establishing points of historical continuity and discontinuity, resides in an effective dismantling of a particular Jewish intragroup stereotype of election. According to Paul, this intragroup self-conception is no longer valid, since it is based on a failure to recognize the provisional role of the law in defining the people of God. In this way, Paul maintains the law's saliency as providing a source of valid ethnoracial identifiers, while simultaneously reinterpreting its past, historical role in defining the people of God, in light of the present. As in ancient ethnographic works in general, the past (the decline of humanity), the present (the revelation of the righteous wrath of God against the consequent wickedness and impiety of humanity), and the future (the Last Judgment) are reinterpreted in light of the present eschatological reality of the gospel. Paul's main point in this rehearsal of the basic premises of the gospel is to underscore the Jewish roots of the new movement, while simultaneously deconstructing traditional oppositional categories premised on a common, Jewish construal of Israel's election. Both of these aims come to a head as the apostle redefines this self-identity according to the prophetic tradition as reinterpreted in light of the Christ event. In doing so, he reconfigures and expands Jewish self-understanding as the elect people of God in a way that allows for the inclusion of non-Jewish ethnic groups.

Paul begins with an indictment of the ethnic pretentiousness characteristic of humanity in general; that is, the basic human propensity to stereotype the other as inferior. This is followed by a specific indictment of Jewish ethnic pretension premised on the belief that possession of and instruction in the law is what defines Israel's unique, and hence, superior, relationship to God, and their knowledge of him and of what he expects and desires from his people. The issue, as Paul sees it, is not Jewish ethnic superiority rooted in certain observable markers found in the law, such as circumcision, Sabbath and dietary prescriptions, but about insider understanding of the precise relationship between Israel's status as the elect and its possession of the law. According to the apostle, this particular construal of self-identity is problematic because it fails to take into account both Israel's and the law's place on the timeline of God's dealings with humanity.

In this regard, Paul draws a careful distinction between physical and spiritual circumcision based on the distinction drawn in the prophetic tradition, which is itself reinterpreted in light of the present, unfolding eschatological reality. He does not argue about the saliency of physical circumcision as an ethnic identity marker. Rather, the point he makes is that it is God who not only initiates election, but, more importantly, defines and sustains it; and it is he who determines who will be included among the elect. In other words, it is not the law that ultimately confers and sustains Jewish self-identity as the elect, but rather God himself, who is the only one able to confer inward circumcision by the Spirit. This is in contrast to the law, which only mandates physical circumcision and which, accordingly, is a penultimate marker of Jewish election. Consequently, the circumcised heart is the ultimate marker of the Jewish (and the gentile) people of God in the eschatological present, as foretold and promised in the scriptures.

Thus, the historic, Jewish people of God are not replaced with righteous and/or believing gentiles. Paul neither redefines the term "Jew" to include gentiles (righteous/law-keeping gentile = true Jew), nor does he annihilate Jewish ethnic identity (true Jew = nonethnic/universal believer). Nor does he suggest that Israel's election has been revoked and/or that the Jewish people have been replaced by another group on the grounds that Jewish election is based either on a condition impossible to fulfill and/or on a faulty understanding of what it actually consists of. Rather, what is implied is that Jewish self-identity is misconstrued because it fails to recognize that the divine promise of future forgiveness of Israel's sins of idolatry and disobedience and the cleansing and renewal of its people has become a present reality in God's work through Christ. Jewish self-identity, including Israel's unique position among the nations stems from the fact that it is through this people group that God's salvation would be accomplished.

Thus, although circumcision retains its saliency as an ethnic marker of identity, it is not instrumental in establishing Israel's self-identity as the chosen people of God. Moreover, the purpose of the law was not to confer a special status upon Israel as an authority over the nations concerning the truth about God. Rather, its purpose is much more narrow, both in terms of what it actually accomplishes, bringing knowledge of sin, and with respect to its limited temporal span in the history of God's dealings with humanity. It is through the Jewish people that God made and makes humanity's sinfulness plain. However, God has revealed through his prophets that the ultimate resolution of the crisis of universal disobedience of his precepts lies in an inward renewal of the heart, wrought by the Spirit—a transformative renewal that makes possible the fulfillment of the requirements of the law. Thus, Paul does not censure keeping the law as a means of establishing Jewish, ethnic identity and of maintaining covenantal responsibilities. Rather, his point is that a new age has dawned, with a new covenant of the Spirit, which not only makes obedience to the intent of the law possible, in a radically new way, but also guarantees the Jewish people's continued existence as an ethnic group and their continued primacy as the people of God.

Thus, Paul brings his recitation of human history to a climax, achieving his ethnographic aim of linking the Christ event to an event described in the prophetic tradition. Moreover, acknowledgment of the fulfillment of these scriptural promises calls for the human response of faith in God's present work. In this sense, Israel's past faithfulness to Yahweh and the covenant is linked to believers' faithfulness to Christ in the present, since faith in God, wherever one may stand on the salvation timeline, marks the people of God. However, by relegating the law to a penultimate position, and positing faith in God's present eschatological dealings with humanity, including the reception of the Spirit, Paul provides a point of discontinuity, opening the door wide to the inclusion of non-Jewish people groups. Furthermore, by introducing faith as a point of continuity between past and present, in opposition to the time-bound, written code, he lays the foundation for an oppositional strategy that will allow him to categorize humanity into three essential groups, while maintaining ethnic distinctions. These are: the people of God, those under the Spirit, consisting of both believing ethnic Jews and gentiles; the unbelieving people of God, those under the written law, a liminal category composed largely, but not exclusively, of ethnic Jews; and unbelieving, non-Jewish persons.

Therefore, attention to the motifs and discourse that characterize ancient accounts of origin suggests that the law-faith dichotomy, as Paul uses it in Rom 1–5, does not function primarily as a shorthand form of describing two diametrically opposed paths to salvation. According to Paul, judgment will be according to deeds; a point which is underscored by his insistence that the law is not overthrown by faith, but, on the contrary, is upheld. Rather, when examined in light of Paul's ethnic discourse, these terms signify both the Christ movement's continuity with its Jewish roots, faith in Yahweh and in his dealings with humanity, and its discontinuity with it, in terms of the law's provisional nature with respect to God's salvific actions.

With this in place, the apostle turns to the new movement's divinely instituted founding figures—Abraham and Christ. Divinely appointed founding figures figure prominently in foundation accounts, where the founder functions as the locus of divine activity through whom the intentions and purposes of the god(s) are accomplished. Appeal to such figures lent credence to a given community's social, cultural, and political arrangements, especially, and including, its religious practices and observances. Like other contemporary, indigenous ethnographers, Paul draws on key biblical figures, Abraham, David, and Adam, because these scriptural persons point to moments of foundation and transformation that have import for the present life of the believing community.

In essence, in chapters 4–5, the apostle recapitulates the etiological account given in Rom 1–3. However, in this instance, he draws in the founding figure and patriarch, Abraham, in order to show that it is God alone who establishes that the line of descent will be reckoned via faith or trust in him, both in the past and in the present. Rather than portraying Christ as the promised seed of Abraham, as he does in Gal 3:15–16, Paul highlights Christ's role as God's established means of setting right the unrighteous in the present time. Thus, he presents Christ as the divinely ordained founder of a new community of people, who stand in both continuity (descendants of Abraham) and discontinuity (joint heirs with Christ) with the historical people of

God. By deemphasizing the ancestral line of descent between Abraham and Christ, Paul, in effect, places the emphasis on God, who himself is the link between the new movement and its Jewish past. There is no stronger link than this, given that the same God, in effect, founds both movements. In this way, Paul simultaneously constructs a venerable ancestry for the members of the new movement that links them to their Jewish past and provides divine legitimation for its founding figure, Jesus. Moreover, by introducing the figure of Adam as the counterpoint to Christ, the apostle maintains a universal perspective both in terms of humanity's universal condition and God's universal solution to the problem of sin and death.

The introduction of Abraham serves a dual purpose in the apostle's ethnography. The first capitalizes on the usefulness of aggregative discourse in constructing kinship ties between Jews and gentiles in a way that allows Paul to think and argue in terms of family resemblances between believing Jews and gentiles, in effect, tightening the link between the Christ movement and its Jewish roots. The second, although related to the first, pertains more specifically to the apostle's task of constructing a respectable, principle or primary identity for the believers in Rome.

With reference to the first aim, and in light of the larger argument he is making, Paul establishes the temporal primacy of Abraham's act of faith, relegating his obedience to the law, as evidenced in his acceptance of circumcision, to a secondary position; thereby, introducing faith as the prime criterion defining the people of God. He then links Abraham to Christ in a way that guarantees the preeminence of the latter as a divinely appointed founding figure of a movement firmly rooted in the promises given to Israel in the past. According to Paul, Abraham became a chosen person of God, prior to any act of obedience with respect to the law. God's pre-circumcision reckoning of righteousness was to make Abraham the ancestor of the gentile who has been set right by God and does not bear the physical sign; and of the Jew who has also been made righteous by God but bears the physical mark. The common denominator in both cases is God, who reckons his people as righteous based on their trust or faith in him. Accordingly, the above mentioned, Jewish intragroup stereotype is invalid at an even more profoundly fundamental level in the sense that God never intended the law to function as the ultimate criterion defining his people, as evidenced by his dealings with Abraham. Moreover, as Abraham was reckoned righteous based on his trust in God's promises, David was also, similarly reckoned righteous due to his trust that God forgives the repentant sinner—even one, for whom, given the gravity of his transgressions, there is no recourse under law. In this way, Paul draws a line from Abraham to David and, ultimately, to Christ via faith or trust in God as the one who both establishes and restores his people.

Thus, faith or trust in God is the trans-historical criterion identifying the people of God. By redefining Abrahamic descent as based on faith, thereby, disengaging the traditional link between such descent and physical circumcision, Paul simultaneously redefines Abraham's trans-historical ancestral role, broadening it, so that his dealings with God remain determinative not only for the Jewish people as a whole, but also for the gentiles. However, although Abraham's faithfulness is the means by which God's promise is mediated to both Jews and gentiles, Jesus's faithfulness is that which confirms this promise and makes it certain for those who trust in God. Thus, both temporally and hierarchically, Christ stands as the preeminent founding figure.

As a skilled ethnographer, the apostle makes recourse to Adam in order to draw his audience back to humanity's mythological origins and the intrusion of death and sin into the world so as to highlight Christ's unique standing as the only one through whom the basic human condition of sinfulness and unrighteousness is rectified. According to both Paul and the Jewish prophets of old, the problem of human sin finds its ultimate solution in God. Moreover, for the apostle, God has provided this remedy in Christ, who reestablishes humanity's rightful dominion over creation, which Adam relinquished, by his transgression, to the destructive powers of sin and death. The community that Adam established, which encompasses all peoples throughout history, up until the present time, is characterized by its submission to these two rulers who, as ruling powers, prescribe the laws and customs, or way of life, that define this universal community. Moreover, according to Paul, the law, rather than overturning this destructive, subversive reign, serves only to reveal its true nature. The reference to Adam's abdication of the rule originally given to humanity stands in contrast to Christ as the founder of a new community through whom God reestablishes humanity's rightful dominion.

Thus, Christ is greater than Abraham not only in the sense that it is through his faithfulness that God conquers the ubiquitous power of sin and death but, more importantly, in the sense that he stands as the head of a newly created community composed of diverse peoples who are characterized by their faith in a God who delivers on his promises. Christ not only confirms the promises made to Abraham but also brings them to fruition by establishing a community, appointed by God, to exercise its rightful rule over his creation. Thus, the Roman believers are reminded not only of their ties to an ancient, venerable religion and its preeminent founder, Abraham, but also, and more importantly, of their royal status in Christ, God's ultimate and preeminent founder. In ethnographic terms, their preeminent status as a people group is grounded in God himself.

Thus, with respect to the task of constructing a principle or primary identity for his audience in Rome, Paul maintains that believers, because they are united with Christ, ultimately represent the progeny of God, not Abraham, who is a penultimate ancestor—a theme he develops in the ensuing arguments. Moreover, unbelieving Jews, although they are able to claim physical descent from Abraham, are not his true descendants, in the sense that, in their failure to trust God in his present work in and through Christ they lack the characteristic of faith (and the Spirit) that is the stamp of the present family of God. Taking the basic idea that kinship depends on blood or seed (fixity), while simultaneously introducing a criterion (faith or trust in

God) that functions to give fluidity to his construction, the apostle incorporates both believing non-Jewish peoples and believing Jews into one family via Christ through faith and the Spirit. Central to Paul's logic is the affirmation that there is one God who acts in a manner consistent with past promises. Thus, the faithfulness of God guarantees that what was true for Abraham, his being reckoned righteous through faith, is also true for his descendants. This then becomes the basis of believers' hope as they struggle to live faithfully in a hostile world.

In sum, in light of Paul's broader ethnographic aims, the new movement finds its legitimacy in the fact that it is established by the God, himself, who not only revealed his design for humanity to his people in the past, but who himself established its founding figures according to his own plan and purposes. Moreover, the new movement's self-identity as the people of God is secure, since it is established and maintained by a righteous God, faithful to his promises. However, the apostle's insistence on the provisional nature of the law raises an acute issue. A legitimate people were thought to have divinely mandated laws that functioned to circumscribe and define the group by spelling out the worship practices, norms, customs, and way of life that made it a distinct community, giving it its identity. If the Jewish law is provisional, then what is to guide the emerging community in its religious, communal, moral, and ethical self-definition?

It is this question that guides Paul's continuing construction of believers' identity in Rom 6–8 and, to some degree, his refinement of that identity vis-à-vis that of unbelieving Israel in chapters 9–11. These two sets of chapters work in tandem, each addressing one side of the self-identity coin. In the first three, the apostle concerns himself with constructing a favorable in-group bias for his audience, while in the second set, his interest lies in dispelling the out-group antagonism that normally accompanies the evaluative processes associated with the former.

With respect to establishing favorable in-group bias, Paul maintains that, in the new age, the pattern of Christ, his teachings and example, and the Spirit not only replaces the old, written law as a moral and ethical guide, but more importantly, frees believers to live the life of righteousness envisioned in the written code but never attained by Israel. As in Rom 1–5, the apostle reinterprets the past in light of Christ, reframing the identity of God's people in terms of his death and resurrection. As in the first chapters of the letter, Christ stands at the nexus of past and present, continuity and discontinuity. The coming of the Messiah brings the outpouring of the Spirit, promised and foretold in the Scriptures, two events which result in a complete reconfiguration of the law from a written code associated with death to a life-giving mode of existence in the Spirit, who enables a life of righteousness. In the new age of the Spirit, believers' union with Christ in his death and resurrection opens the door to the possibility of radical obedience to God that not only fulfills the intent of the law but also represents an inner transformation of believers, such that they bear a family resemblance to Christ in their orientation to and actions within the world. They are the children of God in a sense that was never possible for God's people in the past, who lived under the old written code.

In his bid to establish favorable in-group bias, Paul utilizes the images of dominion/rule, slavery, and marriage in a highly creative way, defining freedom from the law as subjugation/bondage to God. The rule of sin is linked with existence under the rule of the law and contrasted with that of grace, which is associated with the rule of God; thereby emphasizing the superiority of the present situation, within which believers are active participants. In ethnographic fashion, the apostle ties the believing community's identity as the subjects of God to its christological basis by recourse to its founding experience, which is defined in terms of the events of Jesus's death, burial, and resurrection. These events are appropriated by believers in their participation in them, signaling a change in the old self and the body of sin, such that, union with Christ's death becomes a gateway to life; a new life that begins in the present and culminates in the future. Accordingly, freedom from the rule of sin via union with Christ, which manifests faith in the gospel, becomes the identity criterion that distinguishes the believing community from all other people groups. The master-slave metaphor further elaborates on this identity by evoking a powerful image from the scriptures—that of Israel as the slave of Yahweh. Appropriating this traditional, honorific title for his audience, the apostle redefines this bondage in terms of Christ. In the present age, those persons united with Christ's death are enabled to live a life reflective of the life of Christ, with Christ replacing the written law as a pattern to be emulated. Thus, although the nature of the law is radically different from that of God's people in the past, the community's identity, like Israel's, stems from its relationship with God; an identity which is manifested in a righteous and holy life.

In ethnographic terms, the new movement's identity as the subjects/slaves of God implies that believing communities operate in accordance with divine norms, customs, and laws. In other words, it implies that God's people in the present are a legitimate people group. They, like God's historic people, are his slaves, who walk in righteousness before him. Yet, unlike Israel in the past, they are no longer slaves under the old written law, but under the Spirit. The present people of God are a renewed and restored people, who have experienced the promised, eschatological circumcision of the heart through the life, death, and resurrection of Christ. Accordingly, faith is presupposed, in that all who have faith in the present work of God enter into this new reality through Christ, such that their identity as citizens or subjects of sin's realm is exchanged for a new identity characterized by the rule of God. Moreover, Paul uses the law-faith dichotomy, once again, to illustrate the lines of continuity and discontinuity between the past and the present, while, in this instance, he utilizes the law as a foil to the Spirit. However, obedience to God as a direct manifestation of self-identity, whether under the old written code (in the past) or under the Spirit (in the present), remains of prime importance. Thus, believers are exhorted to remain enslaved to God, since, as the apostle has already clearly stated, they will be repaid according to their deeds. Yet, it is the Spirit who enables their fulfillment of the intent of the law and it is in this sense that their righteousness is radically new, surpassing the tradition it springs from, as it fulfills it.

With these first two metaphors, Paul's focus remains on the fluid end of the identity spectrum, where identification with the believing community is viewed as attainable through a common way of life of walking righteously before God. This achieved identity is given substance by his appeal to the third metaphor. Following certain Jewish traditions that portray Israel's identity as the people of God as stemming from its union with the law, Paul's depicts believers as widowed wives, who have died through Christ, to their husband, the law, freeing them for union with Christ in marriage. This compellingly intimate, kinship image of the one flesh union of husband and wife, more powerful than the image of shared blood, gives substance to the community's identity as the subjects/slaves of God, with the image of the marriage of believers to Christ standing at the core of their transformed identity. Accordingly, believers are said to bear offspring to God, where these offspring are understood as acts of obedience, which flow from their identity in Christ.

Moreover, as an ethnographer, Paul is aware of the important role foundation narratives play in an emerging community's self-understanding and self-definition. Accordingly, he rounds off his exposition of the new movement's self-identity by recounting the foundation narratives introduced in chapters 4 and 5. In light of his aim to establish favorable in-group bias, he draws on both Israel's/humanity's and the new movement's origins not only for the purpose of defining the lines of continuity and discontinuity between past and present, but, more importantly, for the purpose of underscoring the superiority of the present situation. By linking Adam's experience of the law with Israel's, Paul draws all of humanity under the rubric of sin's hijacking of God's law for its own evil purposes. It is this experience that is common to both Jewish and gentile human families and it is this history of origins that defines and identifies all persons who lived prior to Christ. Accordingly, all of humanity outside of Christ is portrayed as bearing a family resemblance to Adam and, as such, as a people whose identity is wrapped-up with sin, death, and the law. At its core, their identity is constituted by the fact that they are enslaved to sin and, as such, unable to be obedient to the law, even though they know that what the law demands is good. Paul's gripping account of personal struggle drives home the point of the inferior quality of life under the law both in terms of ethical and moral impossibility and in terms of the present eschatological reality of the giving of the Spirit. The only means of release for Adamic humanity from enslavement to sin and moral and ethical impossibility is through the means that God has provided—that is, through faith and trust in his work in and through Christ.

Paul underscores the superiority of present state within which believers exist by emphasizing the transformative effect that the new community's foundation account has on its members. Accounts of origin are both community-defining and community-constructing. God's condemnation of sin through his Son provides the entry point into the transformation of identity which occurs at believers' manumission from slavery to sin. It is by virtue of their existence in the founder of this new, transformed community that they take on the characteristics of their family of origin. Paul sets the primary characteristic of this new identity in contrast to the σάρκινός identity of those enslaved to sin. The fact that believers walk according to the Spirit means not only that they are divinely enabled to live righteously before God, but also that their minds are renewed in a transformative way that allows for ethical and moral possibility.

This richly evocative, multifaceted presentation of the community's self-identity reaches its climax in Paul's identification of believers as the sons (and daughters) of God. By applying the OT image of Israel as God's child to the new community, Paul redefines election in terms of the Spirit and faith in God's work in and through Christ. Accordingly, the law-faith dichotomy is implicitly at work here as the apostle casts favorable in-group bias in terms of righteousness and divine filiation by the Spirit, in contrast to that by the law, seen as the fulfillment of the promises given to Israel. This promise is seen as fulfilled in the believing community both in terms of its conduct, the ability to walk righteously before God, and in terms of ancestral descent, by which its members bear a family resemblance to the righteous and holy God.

God's fatherhood of Israel, although relatively limited in the OT was, nevertheless, a distinctive and defining feature of Israel's identity. Moreover, this feature was foundational in the sense that it was seen as undergirding Israel's covenantal relationship with God. Similarly, for Paul, this filial relationship is not only the basis for the formation of a new people (election) but also functions as the underlying narrative that creates and legitimates their customs and manner of life as a distinct people group or community. In other words, by appealing to the father-son (daughter) relationship, the apostle gives substance to the ascribed pole of his kinship discourse, grounding it in formative discourse that appeals to shared blood via filial kinship ties. By appropriating a self-identity and an understanding of election that reaches back, before the covenant and the law, Paul tightens the link between the past and the present, drawing a line of continuity between the believing community and its Jewish roots. Furthermore, by applying this self-understanding within the context of an unfolding eschatological present defined by the Spirit's construction of divine-human kinship, Paul pushes past the particularizing effect of the traditional understanding of the family of Israel, expanding its boundaries so as to include all members of humanity who respond in trust to God's new work in and through Christ. The casting of believers' identity in terms of divine filiation also creates a new unity among ethnoracially diverse people groups in the form of Spirit-wrought, material kinship ties, in a way analogous to shared blood. As a result, and in contrast to the traditional, Jewish binary categories, Jews and gentiles are now ἀδελφοί members of the same household, whose head is God.

Emerging from this divinely constituted and reconfigured family of God is a new set of boundaries that essentially operate to divide humanity into three categories: Jewish and gentile believers; gentile unbelievers; and Jewish unbelievers. The eschatological frame of reference within which Paul operates, based as it is on the traditional sacred texts, points to a reality where unbelieving Jews stand apart both from believing Jews (and believing gentiles) and unbelieving gentiles. This raises the issue of Israel's past, present, and future identity as the children of God. This group, from which the Messiah springs and to whom the adoption and the promises belong, stands in a unique position at the border between past and present—a distinct, divinely constituted people group whose liminal status Paul must address. He takes this and related issues on in chapters 9–11, skillfully laying the groundwork for a favorable conception of the other. By carefully constructing and defining the categories of children of the promise, and the remnant as rooted in God's elective, sovereign purposes, the apostle not only levels in-group bias against the out-group, but also establishes Israel's continuing priority.

Here, as in chapters 2–4, Paul challenges the traditional Jewish understanding of election, in this case, by virtue of biological descent from Israel's patriarchs. As in the former case, it is God, who initiates, defines, and maintains election according to his will, by determining which of the biological descendants of Israel's primary patriarchs would provide the seed from which this elect people would descend. Utilizing oppositional and aggregative discourse in a complex, creative way he drives home the point that human reckoning of lines of descent is trumped by divine choice. What matters and has always mattered in the divine economy of things is the category of kinship according to the promise, with kinship according to the flesh secondary to the former.

Accordingly, the children of the promise include: nonbelieving Jews, believing Jews and, finally, believing gentiles, insofar as the gentiles represent the offspring of Abraham, who was given the promise that he would be the father of many nations. However, the children of the promise, who are also currently vessels made for destruction, due to their unbelief (i.e., unbelieving Jews), essentially form a third category of humanity that exists in a liminal state. They are temporarily cut-off from the present people of God, yet remain the people of God in the sense that their restoration lies in the future. This restoration is guaranteed, since the historical facts of Yahweh's dealings with Israel indicate that God has consistently preserved a remnant of his people as a sign of his unerring faithfulness to Israel, as a whole. This is no less true in the present where the Jewish members of the believing community represent God's remnant. It is in these individuals that God's promise of a Spirit-wrought, renewed and restored Israel finds confirmation.

In this regard, it is of note that, in applying the divine filiation privilege of Israel to the gentiles, nowhere does Paul revoke the original designation as applying to Israel, as a whole. Rather, according to the apostle, God carries out his purposes regarding Israel, the gospel, and humanity, in general, by the present diminishment of Israel in a quantitative sense. That is, in the present new age, Israel is represented by the believing remnant. Unbelieving Jews are Israelites, being children of the promise, but they differ both from believing Israel and from non-Israelite persons, both believers and nonbelievers. This conception creates space for Paul to argue that, this liminal state is temporary, that unbelieving Israel, as an enemy of the gospel, nevertheless remains the beloved of God; and that, although unbelieving Jews are presently vessels made for destruction, they, unlike unbelieving gentiles, are the recipients of a past irrevocable divine calling and its accompanying gifts that makes them unique among the rest of currently unrepentant humanity.

Construction and utilization of these three groups of people as representative of the children of the promise is dependent on Paul's appeal to the fluid end of the identity spectrum. It is achieved by bringing to the fore the human response of faith to divine initiative as that which characterizes the present people of God. Having demonstrated that faith in the work of God, both as an attitude and as a pattern of conduct, is a characteristic of his people both in the past and the present, the apostle presents this element as simultaneously uniting believing gentiles with believing Israel and as differentiating this group from unbelieving Jews. Moreover, unlike unbelieving humanity, Israel has a zeal for God. The problem, according to Paul, is that Israel continues to use the law as its moral guide; thereby, stumbling on the stumbling stone of Christ and, consequently, missing out on the present, Spirit-wrought renewal and restoration promised to it in its Scriptures. However, by positing righteousness as the goal of both believing gentiles and unbelieving Jews, the apostle neutralizes the evaluative processes that lead to bias against the out-group. The liminal status of the latter as the people of God is due not to the fact that they are unrighteous, in the sense that unbelieving gentiles are, but rather to the fact that they continue to live as if the new age of the Spirit had not dawned. Because of God's past calling and promises, they remain Israel, children of the promise, neither superseded nor replaced by the gentile people of God. Yet, unlike their believing Jewish counterparts, they cannot participate in the present renewal and restoration of Israel, which now includes gentiles, due to their unbelief.

By shifting the focus between God's elective actions and the human response to these actions, that is, by foregrounding either divine promise or human faith in that promise as two sides of the same inter-group criterion coin, Paul skillfully brings to light the aspects of unbelieving Israel's identity that show that God rejection is not permanent, once again dissipating bias against the out-group. First, God has preserved a remnant; hence, it cannot be said that Israel is characterized by abandonment by God. Second, its hardening is part of a larger divine purpose. Consequently, the respective identities of Jewish believers as the elect and their nonbelieving counterparts as the hardened, are the result of God's sovereign decision regarding each of the groups and the particular purpose God intends for them. Moreover, the scriptures foretell of Israel's eschatological renewal and restoration; a time when divided Israel, the apostate and the remnant, will once again be one; a time, which has yet to come. In addition, the scriptures attest to God's fidelity to his people, a fidelity that eventually overcomes their unfaithfulness, so that those whom God has rendered insensible are redeemed and restored. Thus, the Jewish believing remnant are to view themselves and their nonbelieving counterparts as part of a larger divine purpose and plan, within which each plays a unique and equally valid role.

The apostle's leveling of potential Jewish bias against Israel is suggestive, rather than explicit. This is in contrast to the direct warning against negative bias that he gives to gentile believers. Given that ethnoracial identities were frequently nested in antiquity, it is probable that there would be a higher degree of gentile in-group bias against the out-group. Believing Jews would likely consider themselves both Jews and believers, making it less likely that in-group favoritism toward the believing community would result in strong out-group antagonism. Rather, Jewish believers would most likely be capable of negotiating the tension between membership in the new movement and their continuing identity as Jews. Gentile believers, on the other hand, would be more likely to develop a stronger antagonism toward the out-group, given the lack of ethnoracial affiliation. Consequently, Paul defines the place and role of gentiles in the new age in relation to Israel.

Drawing on the metaphors of the first fruits and the olive tree, Paul explains the dynamic relationship between believing Jews, their unbelieving ethnic counterparts, and believing gentiles. These metaphors are powerful not only because they clarify the proper relationship between related groups, but also because they preserve the distinction between Israel and believing gentiles. None of the three identities are conflated, even as each of the three are seen to spring from a single root. With the first metaphor, Paul establishes that both the patriarchs of the past and the present remnant ensure the continuing holiness of unbelieving Israel, despite its current rejection by God, with the image of the olive tree further refining the relationship of gentiles to both believing and unbelieving Jews. All three groups are related via the patriarchs, and, especially, via Abraham. Both unbelieving and believing Israel are related in terms of physical descent, while believing gentiles share ascribed kinship with members of believing Israel via faith. What Paul makes absolutely clear is Israel's continuing priority and its continuing identity as God's elect, despite God's current (yet, temporary) rejection of the Jewish majority.

Central to this image is God as divine horticulturist. He is the one who breaks off the natural branches, unbelieving Jews, and grafts in the wild branches, believing gentiles, breaking off and regrafting existing branches according to his purposes. This underscores all Paul has said regarding the divine origin and foundation of the people of God, which, in effect, levels all forms of group pride stemming from self-identity as the elect. Moreover, Israel's continuing temporal and hierarchical priority is highlighted in two ways. First, gentile believers are portrayed as unnatural branches taken from a wild olive tree that have been grafted into a distinctly Jewish tree with distinct Jewish roots.

The tree existed prior to this divine act of grafting and without the tree, with its natural branches, there would be nothing to graft the unnatural branches into. This includes the root which symbolizes the blessings of the Jewish tradition, including its scriptures and promises, from which the new movement springs and from which it receives sustenance. It is this root that supports the unnatural branches.

Moreover, the contrast Paul makes between the natural and unnatural branches, between the cultivated tree and the wild tree, is noteworthy in light of the ascribed kinship between Jewish and gentile believers. Although this kinship is no less real than physical kinship and although, believing Jews and gentiles are brothers and sisters, within the historical, eschatological framework of God's salvific plans for humanity, the people of Israel, as an ethnoracial entity, retain priority. God's choice of Israel in the past is firm, since he can and will with ease regraft the hardened members of Israel back into the tree, of which they were once a part, both now and in the future, if these members should return to faith. By way of contrast, formerly grafted-in gentiles can and will be broken off, with relative ease, if they should fail to continue in God's kindness. That is, gentiles remain members of God's people by remembering and by actively engaging in attitudes and behavior that reflect the fact that their membership in the in-group, and their possession of all the resultant benefits that formerly belonged only to Israel, is a gift, in the fullest sense of the term.

Thus, the nesting of identities and the fluidity of kinship constructs makes it possible to envision a single family (the people of God) composed of diverse ethnoracial people groups without dilution or supersession of any of the groups involved. The pressing question, particularly in light of all that Paul has said regarding God's people in the present, is unbelieving Israel's relationship to this newly constituted people of God. What the apostle makes clear is that the hardening of the majority of Israel has as its aim the salvation of the gentiles, with the latter's salvation having as its objective the provoking of the former to jealousy. Accordingly, the purpose of gentile salvation is explained explicitly in relation to Israel. Moreover, its salvation is not simply for its own benefit but has occurred, specifically, for the sake of members of the out-group. Put differently, according to divine intent, it is because of the out-group that gentiles are members of the in-group and their identity with the in-group serves in the interest of the out-group. By phrasing it in this way, Paul defines the place and role of gentiles in relation to Israel, which stands as the reference point. In other words, Israel's liminal position is depicted as a nexus between the new age, in which it does not yet directly participate, and the fullness of the new age to come, where its participation is divinely guaranteed. Thus, by placing Israel's liminal status within the divine salvific-purpose framework that spans past, present, and future, Paul demonstrates Israel's continuing and pivotal place in the unfolding eschatological present. Its stubborn persistence in remaining in the old age serves as the point where God's present blessings flow out to wider humanity. Moreover, it will stand there for as long as God wants it to and its eventual restoration will not only usher in the end but will bring even greater benefits. Israel, by its rejection of the new age, ultimately serves it, and will serve it until the end.

Having addressed both Jewish and gentile bias against the out-group, Paul brings his argument for Israel's priority to a climax by providing a concluding elaboration of the foundation account that he has already related that explicitly accounts for Israel's ultimate place among the people of God. In-group bias against the out-group is dealt a final blow by means of an extended consideration of the paradoxical operation of God's mercy that works to place both the believing community and Israel on the same level, in relation to God, while preserving the latter's priority in relation to the former. The prophetic revelation, the mystery, the apostle conveys represents the final chapter of the foundation account he has already related, accounting, as it does, for the ultimate fate of hardened Israel. This mystery, like the account of origins previously related, was foretold in the scriptures, specifically, in the sense that, the foundation of Israel as the people of God would ultimately involve the removal of its sin by God in fulfillment of his covenant with them. What is revealed to Paul and what, in turn, he relays to his audience is the sequence of events involved in this fulfillment: rejection by the majority of Israel; acceptance by the full number of gentiles; followed by the salvation of all Israel. Because of God's faithfulness, all of Israel, the remnant and the presently hardened, will eventually count among the people of God. Its divine founder has guaranteed this and has provided an account of origins for Israel that maintains its priority over the nations. Moreover, the positive identity Paul has constructed for the new movement rests on the premise that God's election of Israel was for the purpose of the eventual inclusion of the nations among the people of God as foretold by Israel's own scriptures.

Accordingly, Paul rounds off his argument by reminding his audience that despite Israel's priority with respect to the gentiles, all are equal recipients of God's grace and mercy, given that God has imprisoned each group in disobedience, for the purpose of showing each his mercy. Present gentile experience of God's mercy is premised on Israel's disobedience. The new age is juxtaposed with the old in a way that underscores the new movement's rootedness in and dependence on God's people of the past. Although Israel's current disobedience works to the advantage of the in-group, God's final word on the matter is that his recalcitrant people will once again experience his mercy because that has been the divine intention all along. Underlying everything Paul has said regarding the historical legitimacy of the believing community, its identity as the people of God, and the place and role of Israel in the new age is a divine founder whose inscrutable ways and judgments work to bring mercy and grace to all people.

Having constructed a worldview for his audience designed to work against the leveling forces of group disintegration and/or assimilation, Paul carries his ethnographic purposes forward by providing his audience with an ethos that coheres with its symbolic universe in order to fortify his audience's resolve to remain faithful to the gospel within an environment that continually exerts pressures toward social and cultural conformity. He accomplishes this both by establishing a causal link between the community's ethos and its account of origins and by providing viable boundary markers that work to maintain both group cohesion and group differentiation, while simultaneously allowing for the incorporation of the other.

In terms of ancient ethnography, a common way of life testified not only to the legitimacy of a given community but also to the achieved and ascribed bonds of kinship that knit together the individuals comprising it into an ethnoracial entity. A people who claimed such ties were expected to live in a way that was an observable manifestation of them. Consequently, having established the lawful character of the believing community, albeit apart from the written law, Paul delineates the basic contours of the allocentric or other-centered manner of communal living that characterizes the people of God in the new age. This Spirit-wrought allocentric identity not only entails the ability to resist normal, negative out-group evaluative processes but also empowers the believing community to express both in-group and out-group love. As such, it transcends the existing, traditional ethnoracial categories of Jew-gentile, incorporating diverse peoples under a common identity. For this ethnically diverse community, the living into and living out of its identity has as its beginning point the proper worship of God.

In keeping with the community's symbolic universe, it is the Spirit who enables members of the in-group to live sacrificially to God; that is, in a manner consistent with his will. This constitutes the proper of worship of God. Thus, possession of the Spirit, which occurs in tandem with faith in Christ/the gospel, evidenced in a transformed mind capable of discerning what is pleasing to God, is the primary identifying mark of those who belong to the believing community. Accordingly, the worship that characterizes and defines this singular people is similarly Spirit based, mirroring the community's account of origins. In other words, it is the type of worship reflective of a Spirit-infused and transformed people living in the in-breaking new age of the Spirit and entails the offering of the entire self, mind and body, to God, as a living sacrifice. Thus, ceremonial traditions, rites, and rituals are no longer necessary and, if they exist at all, are, at best, penultimate markers of the people of God. God's present people, who exist in unity with Christ, live according to Christ's sacrificial pattern of obedience, who himself lives for God. Thus, the new movement's social identity, as characterized by its worship, is at its core allocentric, since the Spirit-derived impetus that guides its thinking and actions is focused on God, the divine other, rather than on its own will or that of the world. Moreover, in line with Paul's larger ethnographic aims, the community's sacrificial worship/life includes its remaining faithful to the gospel in the face of social pressures to do otherwise.

Thus, it is God, through Christ and the Spirit, who unites the ethnically diverse members of the community into a singular people with a singular purpose. For this kinship bond to be viable there must necessarily be concern for the human other expressed specifically by the willingness to subordinate privileged identity, in this case, ethnoracial identity, for the sake of individuals not of one's ethnicity. Consequently, an other-focused social identity and communal life are viable only if members of the group see themselves in relation to the other and, as a consequence, live for each other. This allocentric stance has as its beginning point the proper assessment of self. According to Paul, who one is within the ethnoracially diverse community of believers is primarily defined by the spiritual gift that each member has been given. Moreover, these gifts are given expressly for the benefit of the community as a whole. Thus, identity and role are integrally linked and Spirit-determined. As such, no individual can claim special privilege, since each individual spiritual gift is freely bestowed, apart from human merit, achieved, ascribed, or otherwise. However, since these gifts are diverse, uniformity of social identity and purpose is manifested in a plurality of roles or functions, each organically linked to the other in a way that defies human derived standards of ranking and status. Thus, one is first and foremost a member of the body of Christ with a specific, divinely mandated function within that body that derives from one Spirit. All other social identities are subsumed and transformed by this reality and, as such, penultimate. The ontological reality of being in Christ has the effect of not only leveling all forms of self-promotion or self-glorification based on such things as genealogy, gender, place of birth, or any other humanly determined criteria, but also mandates an other-focused ethos.

The faith that unites a person to Christ also unites him or her to other believers. As slaves of God in Christ, believers become slaves of one another, each member serving the body by serving others. Unity in diversity is maintained by the active choice on the part of believers to view themselves not only in terms of their specific function within the body as determined by their gifts(s) but, more importantly, to see this identity and role as one that is organically linked to that of every other member in the community, such that one's gift(s) and its/their exercise is realized expressly within the context of the body as a whole. Moreover, the community worships God, in the sense Paul has already described, by embracing its gifts, in all their diverse forms, and using them in the manner intended by God. Accordingly, the Spirit-wrought allocentric social identity that characterizes this people group is manifested when each individual member sees him or herself as living/belonging not only to Christ but also to his or her siblings in Christ, such that each uses his or her gift(s) in service to the other. Moreover, it is the Spirit who directs the intragroup relationships between the ethnoracial other comprising the membership of the body of Christ, such that each exercises his or her gift for the benefit of the other, regardless of ethnoracial affiliation, gender, socioeconomic standing, or any other humanly conceived ranking. Apart from the Spirit, ethnoracial boundaries tend to be particularly unyielding. Yet, by virtue of a renewed mind, able to yield to the will of God, believers are enjoined to do just that, in addition to breaking other common boundaries that work to categorically separate humans, one from another; hence, the injunction to love one another.

CONCLUSION

Paul sets forth the basic principle of love for the other as that which is to guide the life of the community. This principle flows directly from the community's Spirit-wrought, allocentric self-identity and is in line with the apostle's conception of the community's terminal social identity as the Spirit-transformed children of God. As God's children each is to view the other as the closest of kin, eschewing competitiveness in favor of actively seeking to show respect for and hospitality to the other. Moreover, for the apostle, the renewal of the mind by the Spirit includes the ability to look beyond the interests of the in-group and to extend in-group benefits to all manner of outsider. The tight link Paul draws between intragroup relations and intergroup interaction points to an identity that is allocentric in the fullest sense of the term, maintaining in-group love and privilege while simultaneously extending those benefits to outsiders. Like the love that characterizes God's action in and through Christ, this love embraces the outsider and the enemy, as believers accept God's way of dealing with sinful, hostile humanity, living in a way that demonstrates God's love as revealed in and through the gospel.

Thus, it is this Spirit-wrought, allocentric identity, manifested in an other-focused disposition that fulfills the intent of the law, which is summed-up as love for the neighbor, broadly defined. Paul's recapitulation of this major theme serves to underscore the ultimacy of the identity that he has thus far constructed. The notion that love fulfills the law harkens back to the written law's provisional nature and the culmination of God's intent for it in the circumcision of believers' hearts by the Spirit. The law that first, in its written form, acted to divide Jews from all manner of non-Jewish people groups, now under the aegis of the Spirit, acts as the inner, creative agent of unity, uniting all manner of people groups into the one body of Christ by means of radical love of the other made possible by the empowering presence of that same Spirit, who views everyone as the neighbor to whom the benefits of the community apply. In the present, unfolding new age, the Spirit replaces the old, written law by transcending it, while at the same time bringing it to its fulfillment, all in accord with Scripture. The Spirit (faith) marks and maintains the boundaries of community, making them permeable, so that all are invited to enter in and to be transformed.

Accordingly, Paul reminds his audience of the gravity of the choice to embrace or not to embrace their identity and live accordingly, including their identity as a community that invites all manner of other to enter in and experience the transformative power of the gospel. Calling attention to the time, the time of the overlap of the old age and the new, Paul underscores the necessity for believers to take direct, decisive action in discerning the reality of the Spirit's transformation of the community's relationship with God and fellow human beings and to pattern their lives according to God's will. As a people who know that they live in the dawn of the new age of the Spirit, they are to eschew the type of conduct that is focused on the self and the gratification of its desires, including the desire to impose one's own view of what constitutes proper worship practices, in relation to food, drink, and the keeping of days, upon a trans-ethnic community.

As a trans-ethnic group, the community must be able to embrace diverse ethnicities, Jew and all manner of gentile, in a way that preserves the terminal identity of the group, without leveling ethnic differences into a generic whole. This means that no one ethnoracial criterion or set of criteria can be allowed to attain to a level where it functions as the primary marker of identity. Rather, lesser identities must be embraced and integrated, or nested, in a way that maintains the primacy of the terminal identity. For members of the new movement, the believing community, understood as the family of God, constituted in and by Christ and the Spirit, is the source of their terminal identity and, as such, circumscribes how ethnic differences are both preserved and lived out in a ethnoracially diverse social group claiming unity and cohesion on the basis of Spirit-wrought kinship. Thus, while the believing community remains, at one level, composed of Jews and all manner of gentiles, the group functions properly only when the ethnically diverse subgroups comprising it relate as interdependent members of a community that exists in Christ by the Spirit. The Spirit (faith) marks a new identity that relegates ethnic identity to a penultimate level. Paul provides a clear picture of how this works and what its operation looks like as he negotiates the vicissitudes associated with the worship of the one God by all manner of people groups. The theme of welcome/acceptance of the other runs throughout this portrait, against the backdrop of mutual tolerance on the basis of the principle of Spirit-wrought allocentricism. This concern for the other works to bind all subgroups into a unified worshipping community, such that the worshipping community as a whole worships God according to the pattern of Christ. Throughout all of this, the apostle maintains a delicate balance between the primacy of worship in/by the Spirit, in faith, that marks the new, ethnoracially diverse people of God and the continuing salience, at the penultimate level, of particular ethnic expressions of worship, including those defined by the Jewish written code.

In terms of Paul's larger ethnographic purposes, unity in worship is important for several reasons. Since group-identity and patterns of worship are interlinked and mutually constituting, the integrity of the community's identity is dependent on the group's acceptance of an understanding of worship that is group-identity constructing. In dealing with a trans-ethnic community it is essential for Paul to delineate a primary mode of worship that is commensurate with the group's worldview and that allows for the incorporation of diverse penultimate expressions. In addition, in more practical terms, factious attitudes and behaviors associated with subgroups advocating for unilateral adoption of their own specific customs and traditions destroys intragroup cohesion, making the group less appealing to both members and outsiders. Finally, the allocentricism that lies at the heart of the group's self-identity is expressed not only in the stance its members take toward one another, but also in the group's relations with outsiders. Suspicious, hostile, and/or unbelieving others would find little reason to join a group that displays a lack of tolerance among its members for each other. The lack of cohesion between what the community professes and what it actually does would seriously compromise the community's mission of reflecting the power of the gospel, which it professes to be at work among it, to the outside world. Thus, intragroup acrimony and disunity has serious repercussions for both the group's self-identity and its legitimacy as a valid subgroup among the variety of subgroups comprising the larger sociocultural context. Moreover, as the divinely constituted subgroup that uniquely reflects the one God's intent for all of humankind, in all of its diversity, its legitimacy has import on a scale unequaled by any other group.

Once again, in keeping with the community's symbolic universe, Paul maintains that the diversity of opinion regarding the place and manner of food and drink and the significance of keeping one or more days as markers of both ethnoracial identity and the group-identity of the new movement have validity if they are based on faith and if they are viewed as being penultimate in regard to the group's social identity. Consequently, he articulates the principle of "living to the Lord" that allows for diversity in unity by establishing worship by the Spirit (in faith) as the primary marker/practice that defines the allocentric, believing community. It is Spirit-wrought allocentricism that not only establishes the order of nesting of self-identities, placing ethnoracial identity at the penultimate level, but also empowers both the weak and the strong to mutual acceptance of each other, in all of the other's diversity. Particular worship customs are acceptable as long as their adherents do not try to impose their practices onto the community by judging and/or disdaining those who disagree.

The basis for diversity within unity is God, who has welcomed all into his household as his house slaves/servants. This powerful metaphor draws together several strands of the community's identity that Paul has already developed, grounding the exhortation to accept the other in the ontological reality of the group's divine origins. In effect, although every believer enters the community with his or her own particularity in terms of both identity, ethnoracial identity included, and spiritual gifts, all stand equally before God, whose purpose is to serve him and the interests of his household. Thus, believers' identity as members of the household of God, through the Spirit, who worship him by the Spirit, is primary. Since the master's affairs are paramount and the household, as a unit, is obliged to function in tandem to meet these interests, any specific acts of service/worship, including those governed by ethnically determined custom, are penultimate. In terms of believers' identity they are nested under the primary marker of identity, the Spirit (faith).

Moreover, varying opinions regarding the keeping of days, and implicitly the eating of meat and drinking of wine, are the result of equally valid judgments concerning these matters, since they stem from a conviction of the mind of each individual involved. That is, all believers, whether weak or strong have the Spirit-wrought ability to discern what are acceptable worship customs in light of their own past practices and ethnic affiliations, giving the community the charismatic freedom to allow varying opinions about such practices. Although each individual sacrificial life may look different due to differing spiritual gifts, convictions regarding worship, and ethnicities, all these ways of living are equally valid in so far as they have as their source the power and leading of the Spirit.

Thus, in keeping with the community's allocentric identity, although Paul acknowledges the claim of the strong that all forms of food and drink may be consumed by the present people of God on the grounds that they are all now clean, he does not ask the weak to give-up their ascetic practices. Rather, the crux of the matter, according to the apostle, is the wrong committed when one's freedom to eat and drink causes the other to stumble. The decision to eat and drink; that is, to live according to one's strongly held convictions, irrespective of the effect this decision might have on the other, is a decision not to walk according to the Spirit. It is a decision to deny one's primary identity by making the penultimate, the ultimate. According to Paul, allocentric concern for the other is denied when one's actions, irrespective of their objective truth, serve to entice or pressure an individual holding religious prescriptions to act in a way that goes against his or her own conscience. If the strong should insist on the presence of certain food items at communal worship, the choice to please the human-other over God becomes a viable reality for the weak; thus, creating the potential for sin, on the part of the latter should they choose to act against what they believe is acceptable to God. The potential for this kind of choice springing into existence for the strong simply does not exist, since, for them, food and drink are nonissues. Consequently, allocentric concern for the other means that believers' legitimate freedom must be subsumed under the more important responsibility of ensuring that the other is not enticed to act in a way that destroys his or her integrity.

The actions of the strong not only have consequences for the spiritual well being and ultimate fate of individual, weak members of the community, but also have important ramifications for the spiritual health and, thus, legitimacy of the group as a whole. That is, the community's validity as the signpost of God's kingdom resides, to a great degree, in the extent to which it embodies the transformative work of the Spirit in the relations of is members to each other. If the strong should choose to exercise their freedom indiscriminately the result would, in all likelihood, either be greater acrimony and group discord, or an increase in sinful choices among the weak, or both. In either case, this would destroy both the work of the Spirit and any appeal or good standing the community might have in the eyes of outsiders. However, if the strong should choose to take an allocentric stance and implement the higher principle of pursuing what makes for peace and for mutual upbuilding over their rightful exercise of freedom, then they would not only serve Christ but also gain the approval of watchful, often suspicious, outsiders. In sum, love of the weak neighbor fulfills the law and, thus, establishes the community's legitimacy, maintains its spiritual robustness, and actualizes its mandate to welcome all persons with the good news that God has welcomed all into his kingdom.

CONCLUSION

Drawing all these strands together, Paul rounds out his ethnography by linking the group's identity and its legitimacy, which is manifested in its Spirit-crafted unity in diversity, to Christ. As at every key juncture of his ethnography, the apostle presents Christ as the nexus between past and present. Welcome of the other is associated with Christ's act of welcoming sinful humanity for the express purpose of bringing glory to God. As Christ humbled himself on behalf of both the Jewish and non-Jewish other in order to bring glory to God, forming Jews and all manner of non-Jews into the one, present people of God, believers are to humble themselves on behalf of the other in order to bring glory to God by worshipping God as one, unified people. According to Paul, the unity of all people groups as the people of God is something promised and foretold in the scriptures. It is in and through Christ that God confirms the promises given to Israel and brings them to fruition. Moreover, it is the community in Christ that stands as a witness to what God has done.

In sum, continuing ethnoracial subgroup salience is a good that Paul sees as necessary in light of the new eschatological situation in Christ for two reasons. First, when the present people of God, composed of Jews and all manner of non-Jews, worships the one God and Lord of all the world, in one Spirit-wrought, trans-ethnic voice this serves as a confirmation that the promises given to Israel have been brought to fruition in and through Christ. This is because Christ has welcomed all people groups, in all of their diversity, into the family of God through his death and resurrection. Second, since Christ's teaching and example have replaced the Jewish law as that which circumscribes the worship of the people of God, with worship broadly defined as living one's life entirely to God, believers are to welcome the ethnic other, as the ethnic other, just as Christ has. This suggests that the reason that Paul never uses the term "γενός" in relation to the new or present people of God is because the scriptures envision the eschatological people of God as ethnically diverse. Paul pictures entrance into the believing community as becoming a member of an ethnically diverse family. Moreover, it is a family whose members are united by the Spirit who empowers believers to preserve particularity without allowing any of the basic categories of human difference to assume a primary place in the group's self-identity. Thus, although Jews and Greeks, slaves and free, and male and female continue to exist within the people of God, this identity is secondary to that which defines the children of God, who are one in Christ, who has presently welcomed all humanity, in all of its diversity.

The allocentric love of God/Christ that stands at the heart of these promises foretold in the scriptures is reflected in the allocentric love that stands at the heart of a trans-ethnic community that is empowered to embrace and incorporate the other. It is precisely when the believing community in all its ethnoracial diversity is able to glorify God with one voice that it stands as a faithful witness to the gospel. By seeking to please the neighbor, rather than the self, both the weak and the strong ensure that opinions regarding food and drink will not destroy the unity of their trans-ethnic community—a solidarity that lies at the heart of its witness to a hostile world, manifested in its unified worship of the one God.

7.2 Implications for Further Study

This reading of Romans, which focuses on its ethnographic characteristics, raises several possibilities for further research on Paul's use of the law-faith and Jew-gentile dichotomies in his construction of in-Christ identity. In light of the long, tortured history of scholarship on Paul's attitude toward the law and Judaism and the related principle of salvation by faith alone, a fresh approach to these dichotomies provides a natural entry point for such work. Paul's letter to the Galatians is a case in point. This epistle is a veritable treasure trove of important information regarding the apostle himself; his controversies with Peter and the Jerusalem apostles; the Christian communities he founded; and the nature of gentile-Jewish relations within the church.[1] However, like Romans, interpretation of it has tended to focus on soteriological categories, and how these relate to the viability and vitality of Judaism and Christianity as routes to securing eternal salvation. Moreover, like Romans, despite the inclusion of sociological categories by some exegetes, the focus remains largely on Paul's attitude toward the law.

An accurate assessment of the apostle's view of the law, particularly its effect on distinguishing and distancing Jews from gentiles within the Christian community, is undoubtably crucial for the exegesis of this letter. Nevertheless, Paul is not simply interested in ensuring that the believers in Galatia have a correct understanding of the law and its function. He is also seeking to ensure that they have a proper understanding of who they are in Christ. In other words, the question of the position of gentiles and Jews within the new movement is ultimately a question of identity. Accordingly, both sociological analysis, utilizing aspects of social identity theory, and an examination of how the apostle utilizes the law-faith dichotomy in answering the question of whether gentile believers are required to observe certain or all aspects of the law, particularly circumcision, would be fruitful. Moreover, an analysis of the role of the Spirit in constructing, establishing, and defining the community's identity might provide a means of further clarifying the role of both the law and faith in the present, unfolding eschatological age. With respect to both of these analyses, Paul's use of traditional, Jewish narratives and their chief characters, particularly the story of Abraham, affords another avenue of research regarding the issue of the degree of continuity/discontinuity between Judaism and the in-Christ movement. If it is found that application of this methodological approach to Galatians provides a viable, explanatory link between the so-called theological section of the epistle (Gal 3:1—5:12) and its paraenetic portion (Gal 5:13—6:10), this will then provide further evidence that Paul's understanding

---

1. Barclay, *Obeying the Truth*, 1.

of the relationship between law and faith, Judaism and Christianity, is more nuanced and more Spirit-centered than traditional scholarship implies. That is, broadening the interpretational lens from a narrow focus on soteriological categories would afford a more robust view of Pauline ethnoracial diversity in in-Christ unity.

In addition to comparative work within the Pauline and Deutero-Pauline corpus, comparison between Paul and both his Greco-Roman contemporaries and the early Christians apologists would yield fruitful avenues of study with respect to the mechanisms of ethnoracial inclusivity, whereby diverse people groups are subsumed within a trans-ethnic social group. With regard to the former, my relatively broad, motif-based analysis of ancient ethnography did not leave space for a detailed examination and explanation of how, for example, Rome, achieved incorporation of diverse people groups into a viable hegemony, while retaining ethnoracial diversity. Evidence that they successfully did just that abounds, as I have demonstrated. However, the proof I presented was of the more general kind, since my focus was specifically on Paul's mechanisms of identity construction in Romans. In other words, a more comprehensive and thorough investigation of the socially constructive discourse involved in this process, as it is found in contemporary, extra-biblical sources, might provide helpful points of comparison between the exact mechanisms of group-identity construction within the early Pauline communities and those employed by non-Christian groups. Such a comparison would serve to pinpoint points of divergence between the mechanisms Paul ascribes, that is, unity with Christ and transformation by the Spirit, to group self-identity construction, shedding further light on his distinct method. The points of convergence would likewise provide further clarity by giving additional insight into precisely how ancients went about constructing trans-ethnic group identity.

With regard to the early Christian apologists, it is noteworthy that Paul never refers to the believing community as a new race or γένος as the former writers do. Rather, the apostle places the emphasis on continuing ethnoracial identity after incorporation into the community, with unity premised on the ontological reality of existence in Christ, marked by possession of and transformation by the Spirit. In other words, Jews and all manner of gentiles may be members of the one family of God, but this family is composed of a diversity of people groups, whose penultimate identities differ. By way of contrast, the early apologists emphasize the universalizing effect of membership within the believing community.[2] For example, Clement maintains that those who accept faith are gathered into one γένος of the saved people, whose common ground is the one Lord (*Strom.* 5.14.133.8). Thus, there appears to be a shift in emphasis from viewing the believing community as an ethnically diverse family to seeing it as an ethnoracial entity in its own right. That is, membership in the new movement is

---

2. Buell, "Race and Universalism," 430, 467, and "Rethinking the Relevance of Race," 459–60. Kuecker makes a similar observation regarding the difference between the Lukan author and the early apologists. He notes the markedly different approach found in the *Epistle to Diognetus*, which affords Christians some ethnic continuity (Kuecker, *Spirit and the 'Other,'* 225–26).

depicted as an ethnic alternative to both Jewish and all non-Jewish ethnoracial identities. Continuing ethnic diversity on the penultimate level of self-identity is not even mentioned, much less emphasized. This raises a host of questions concerning the reasons for such a marked difference between Paul's and his successors' approach to the continuing validity of ethnoracial identity within the believing community. Moreover, it raises the issue of whether the identity described by the apologists is in actuality a third kind of identity; that is, one that is neither Jew nor Greek. In other words, given the predominantly Greek character of the church during that period, it is conceivable that this third type of identity might have taken on a distinctly Greek flavor, despite assertions to the contrary. Thus, a study of Christian identity and its formation in the post-apostolic period would shed light on both Paul's conception of believer self-identity and to what degree this identity was shaped and refashioned by a community composed of predominantly ethnoracially Greek leaders and members.

Finally, given my goal to provide a completely fresh approach to reading Romans, by making a foundational shift in understanding both its primary purpose and its genre, this study is limited in the sense that it can only afford a panoramic view of its ethnographic features. More detailed attention to each of the ethnographic motifs present in the epistle would be fruitful. For example, one could trace the theme of divine causation throughout the epistle in order to analyze if and how this motif is held in tension with human causation. If it should prove that Paul, like his Greco-Roman and Jewish contemporaries, is able to maintain this tension, this would have important ramifications for modern theological explanations regarding God's sovereignty and human responsibility and the related, theological construct of predestination.

7.3 Suggestions for Contemporary Application

Reading Romans in light of ancient ethnography brings attention to its pastoral character, which tends to be obscured by readings that begin with the premise that Paul's main concern is with soteriology. That is, unlike the latter, which focuses on the relationship between law/works and eternal salvation, the reading presented here brings to the forefront the pressing, present-day issues that the believing community faces as it seeks to live faithfully in a world hostile to the gospel. With one eye on the eschatological horizon, Paul's attention throughout is on the need for daily perseverance on the part of believers as they strive to be the people of God amidst the myriad of social groups vying to provide them with a primary source of identity and thereby, become the group to which they give their first allegiance. Romans is not a lesson about justification by faith and the place of the law in this theological scheme. Paul seems to assume that his audience is familiar with both this gospel theme and the traditional teaching that judgment will be according to deeds.[3] Rather, it is a message

---

3. It is noteworthy that Paul does not explain the exact mechanism of this, neither the exact mechanism of God's accounting of them, nor the precise relationship between them and the results of

of encouragement aimed at providing the people of God with a foundational narrative and a corresponding ethos that constitutes and defines them as a people. In this sense, Romans is for today. It is for the people of God of this century, who still live in the unfolding eschatological age of the Spirit and who continue to define themselves according to the gospel and the greater scriptural context from which it draws its full significance and meaning.

Thus, at the most fundamental level, Romans is a powerful reminder for Christian groups, facing government sanctioned persecution, suffering at the hands of terrorist or other, fringe groups, or experiencing general social hostility and/or pressures to assimilate, of both who it is that sustains them and who they are as a result. As such, it serves as a buttress against the societal, political, and cultural forces that seek to level the community's unique identity as the people of God. The fact that this is not primarily how Romans is read in the West, especially in the United States and in the more affluent, and often more secular, societies in Europe, may not be due solely to the soteriological-focused scholarship that predominates interpretation in this part of the world. That the communities in these regions are not facing persecution or general, societal hostility of any real kind raises the question of whether the Church is living out its mission. Apart from the stance that some Christians, churches, and/or denominations may take on hot-button, political issues, such as abortion and gay marriage, the Church, as a whole, appears to have blended quite well, perhaps, too well, with the surrounding culture. Rather than drawing its primary identity from the reality that all believers are united with Christ, as his body, and that the Church, as a whole, represents the Spirit renewed people of God, its members tend to align themselves with denominational and/or political groups. It is these groups that then provide Christians with their primary identity. Similarly, the group-specific ideologies associated with these sociopolitical entities define the ethos that governs their relations with and actions toward fellow members, other Christians, and the outside world. Irrespective of the merit these groups may have in terms of advancing the gospel and the mission of the Church, these entities are human-derived and constituted and dependent on human mechanisms of sustenance. In addition, these groups tend toward tribalism, since their boundaries are maintained by the normal social mechanism of negative appraisal of the other, whether this is defined as other denominations or other political parties, and/or groups. At best, they are penultimate with regard to providing both a primary identity for the Church and a viable ethos that reflects God's intent for humanity in all of its diversity.

In the fragmented sociopolitical context of the twenty-first century, Romans stands as a powerful reminder to the Church of who it is and of how it is to define itself in relation to all of its members, in all of their diversity, and to the outside world, in all of its heterogeneity. As Paul reminds us, the primary allegiance of Christians is

---

judgment. The lack of explanation suggests both that this subject is not his main concern and that his audience is familiar with this teaching.

not to a particular nation, political group, or denominational entity. It is to Christ, the risen Lord, through whom God constitutes his people and through whom he sustains them as a Spirit transformed community that reflects his intent for all of humanity. In cases where affiliation with a given denominational and/or political entity conflicts with in-Christ identity and ethos, Paul reminds Christians that the penultimate must, in all cases, be subsumed under the ultimate. The fragmentation of the Church into denominations was, in all likelihood, not something foreseen by Paul, nor was/is it always due to serious doctrinal differences that go to the heart of orthodox, Christian belief. More often than not, the bone of contention is disagreements related to worship practices, governance, the participation and role of certain members in the Church, and theological issues that are not central to the Christian faith. Romans reminds us that these are places where Christians may differ. However, regardless of such differences, all believers are one people in-Christ. We would do well to remember that as brothers and sisters in the family of God, it is our common foundational narrative and the power of the Spirit that constitutes our primary identity. Moreover, the Church would do well to heed Paul exhortation to be mindful of the watchful eye of the outside world, which is all to ready to find any reason to condemn Christianity as no better than the fragmented, divisive world that it professes to serve.

Finally, for the contemporary Church, Romans speaks not only to ethnoracial diversity within the believing community, but also to diversity in terms of spiritual gifts, raising the issue of power over the other. Ethno-racial superiority is but one example of this common social dynamic of self-definition that is premised on the polar categories of us versus them. For instance, in antiquity, Jews saw themselves as better than gentiles, while Romans and Greeks saw themselves as the best. Similarly, native ethnographers commonly posited their own group as the source and supreme expression of humanity. Accordingly, ethnoracial difference was often conceived and understood as superiority over the ethnoracial other. However, Paul deconstructs this particular definition of ethnoracial difference, understood as power over the other, by casting believers' primary identity in terms of spiritual gifting and the exercise of these gifts within the community. In essence, he levels the traditional binary opposites of Jew-gentile, male-female, slave-free, which form the basis of dichotomous us versus them thinking, without dissolving ethnic, gender, and other social differences. Within the believing community, these differences continue at the penultimate level, suggesting that the us versus them line of thought, which is normally expressed in terms of power over the other, no longer has a place within the body of Christ.

This in turn suggests that Paul is envisioning a transformed society where gender relationships are transfigured in such a way that men and women, male and female, are empowered to relate in unity without dissolving difference.[4] The idea that

---

4. That this is the case is evidenced by the fact that Rom 16:3–16 praises more women than men for their distinctive ministry in/to the believing communities. A notable example is Junia, who is commended for being an outstanding apostle (v. 7) (Lampe, "Roman Christians of Romans 16," 222–23;

the exercise of women's spiritual gifts must be limited on the grounds that gender differences can be preserved only if men have power over women (women must always be submissive to men) necessarily entails raising gender to the ultimate level. According to Paul, spiritual authority is not invested in an essentialist way. That is, the Spirit neither grants authority or power just to Jews, nor, for that matter, just to men. Rather, the Spirit distributes gifts and the authority inherent in them as he chooses. Moreover, given that these gifts are given for the benefit of the community, some members will necessarily have power over others in certain, limited situations, depending on the particular gift and its exercise. For example, Christians are to submit to the teaching authority of their teachers, who are gifted by the Spirit to be such, regardless of whether they are Jews or gentiles, male or female, slave or free. Thus, at a time when the Church remains divided over the role of women in the worshipping community, Romans opens the door to rethinking gender difference and in-Christ unity. Gender, like ethnicity, inheres and is good, but human constructions that understand gender or racial difference in terms of one group having power over another are transformed by the Spirit. Accordingly, definitions of gender and ethnoracial difference that depend on positing one group as inherently and inevitably subordinate to the other are invalid, since in Christ all are one. The penultimate characteristic of gender must be subsumed under the Spirit who marks all believers as members of transformed humanity. It is this identity that unites men and women in Christ as they submit to each other according to the principle of love of one's neighbor that is central to the community's ethos.

7.4 Conclusion

For Paul, the new movement is new in the sense that it is deeply rooted in a venerable, Jewish past, yet discontinuous with it in that it reflects the eschatological reality of Christ's coming and the concomitant events of gentile inclusion and the empowerment and transformation by the Spirit of all peoples, who respond to the good news of the gospel. The retention of ethnic diversity within in-Christ unity is the vision of the present people of God that Paul presents to his Roman audience. The unity of all humankind, Jew and gentile, male and female, in Christ forms the cornerstone of the ethnographic account that he offers the Roman believers in his attempt to provide them with an account of origins that will help them meet the challenges of a new age marked equally by a divinely conceived and orchestrated, unfolding, eschatological reality and by the mundane workings of a world suspicious of and often hostile to the community within which this reality is being made manifest. Like the believers in Rome, the present-day Church stands at the nexus between past and present. With one eye on the eschatological horizon, its members

---

see also, Witherington and Hyatt, *Paul's Letter to the Romans*, 383–94.

strive to live faithfully according to the foundational narrative and its corresponding ethos that define all believers as the people of God. Empowered by the Spirit we are a community able to demonstrate both in-group and out-group love as we seek to bring God's good news to all of humanity, in all of its diversity.

Bibliography

Adams, Edward. "Abraham's Faith and Gentile Disobedience: Textual Links between Romans 1 and 4." *Journal for the Study of the New Testament* 65 (1997) 47–66.

Anderson, Bernhard W. "The Apocalyptic Rendering of the Isaiah Tradition." In *The Social World of Formative Christianity and Judaism: Essays in Tribute to Howard Clark Fee*, edited by Jacob Neusner et al., 17–38. Philadelphia: Fortress, 1988.

Asano, Atsuhiro. *Community-Identity Construction in Galatians: Exegetical, Social-Anthropological and Socio-Historical Studies*. New York: T. & T. Clark, 2005.

Athanassiadi, Polymnia, and Michael Frede, eds. *Pagan Monotheism in Late Antiquity*. Oxford: Oxford University Press, 1999.

Aune, David E. "Romans as a *Logos Protreptikos* in the Context of Ancient Religious and Philosophical Propoganda." In *Paulus und das antike Judentum*, edited by Martin Hengel and Ulrich Heckel, 91–121. Tübingen: Mohr, 1991.

Barclay, John M. G. *Obeying the Truth: Paul's Ethics in Galatians*. Vancouver: Regent College, 1988.

———. *Paul & the Gift*. Grand Rapids: Eerdmans, 2015.

Barclay, William B. *"Christ in You": A Study in Paul's Theology and Ethics*. New York: University Press, 1999.

Bar-Kochva, Bezalel. *The Image of the Jews in Greek Literature: The Hellenistic Period*. Berkeley: University of California Press, 2010.

Barrett, C. K. *The Epistle to the Romans*. 2nd ed. London: Hendrickson, 1991.

———. *The First Epistle to the Corinthians*. Black's New Testament Commentaries 7. Reprint, Peabody, MA: Hendrickson, 2006.

Barth, Karl. *The Epistle to the Romans*. Translated by Edwyn C. Hoskyns. 6th ed. New York: Oxford, 1968.

Bloch, René. "Posidonian Thoughts—Ancient and Modern." *Journal for the Study of Judaism in the Persian, Hellenistic, and Roman Period* 35.3 (2004) 284–94.

Brawley, Robert L. "Identity and Metaethics: Being Justified and Ethics in Galatians." In *Character Ethics and the New Testament: Moral Dimensions of Scripture*, edited by Robert L. Brawely, 107–23. Louisville: Westminster John Knox, 2007.

Brillante, Carlo. "History and the Historical Interpretation of Myth." In *Approaches to Greek Myth*, edited by Lowell Edmunds, 91–138. Baltimore: Johns Hopkins University Press, 1990.

Brown, Rupert J., and Gordon F. Ross. "The Battle for Acceptance: An Investigation into the Dynamics of Intergroup Behavior." In *Social Identity and Intergroup Relations*, edited by Henri Tajfel, 155–78. Cambridge: Cambridge University Press, 1982.

Buell, Denise Kimber. "Race and Universalism in Early Christianity." *Journal of Early Christian Studies* 10.4 (2002) 429–68.

———. "Rethinking the Relevance of Race for Early Christian Self-Definition." *Harvard Theological Review* 94.4 (2001) 449–76.

———. *Why This New Race: Ethnic Reasoning in Early Christianity.* New York: Columbia University Press, 2005.

Byrne, Brendan. *Romans.* Sacra Pagina 6. Collegeville, MN: Liturgical, 1996.

Campbell, William S. *Paul and the Creation of Christian Identity.* The Library of New Testament Studies 322. New York: T. & T. Clark, 2006.

Carson, D. A. *Divine Sovereignty & Human Responsibility: Biblical Perspectives in Tension.* Eugene, OR: Wipf & Stock, 1994.

Carter, Timothy L. "Looking at the Metaphor of Christ's Body in 1 Corinthians 12." In *Paul: Jew, Greek, and Roman*, edited by Stanley E. Porter, 93–115. Leiden: Brill, 2008.

Clarke, Katherine. *Between Geography and History: Hellenistic Constructions of the Roman World.* Oxford: Oxford University Press, 1999.

Cohen, Shaye J. D. *The Beginnings of Jewishness: Boundaries, Varieties, Uncertainties.* Berkeley: University of California Press, 1999.

Conzelmann, Hans. *A Commentary on the First Epistle to the Corinthians.* Translated by James W. Leitch. Philadelphia: Fortress, 1975.

Cousar, Charles B. *A Theology of the Cross: The Death of Jesus in the Pauline Letters.* Minneapolis: Fortress, 1990.

Cranfield, C. E. B. *The Epistle to the Romans.* 2 vols. Reprint. London: Bookcraft, 2001.

———. "'The Works of the Law' in the Epistle to the Romans." *Journal for the Study of the New Testament* 43 (1991) 89–101.

Cranford, Michael. "Abraham in Romans 4: The Father of All Who Believe." *New Testament Studies* 41.1 (1995) 71–88.

Creach, Jerome F. D. *Violence in Scripture: Interpretation: Resources for the Use of Scripture in the Church.* Louisville: Westminster John Knox, 2013.

Das, A. Andrew. "The Gentile-Encoded Audience of Romans: The Church Outside the Synagogue." In *Reading Paul's Letter to the Romans*, edited by Jerry L. Sumney, 29–46. Atlanta: SBL, 2012.

———. "Paul and Works of Obedience in Second Temple Judaism: Romans 4:4–5 as a New Perspective Case Study." *Catholic Biblical Quarterly* 71.4 (2009) 795–812.

Davies, Glenn N. *Faith and Obedience in Romans: A Study in Romans 1–4.* Journal for the Study of the New Testament Series 39. Sheffield, UK: Sheffield Academic, 1990.

Dillery, John. "Greek Sacred History." *American Journal of Philology* 126.4 (2005) 505–26.

Dionysius of Halicarnassus. *The Roman Antiquities.* Translated by Earnest Cary. 7 vols. LCL. Cambridge, MA: Harvard University Press, 1937.

Dodson, Joseph R. *The 'Powers' of Personification: Rhetorical Purpose in the Book of Wisdom and the Letter to the Romans.* Berlin: de Gruyter, 2008.

Dohrmann, Natalie B. "Manumission and Transformation in Jewish and Roman Law." In *Jewish Biblical Interpretation and Cultural Exchange: Comparative Exegesis in Context*, edited by Natalie B. Dohrmann and David Stern, 51–65. Philadelphia: University of Pennsylvania Press, 2008.

Donfried, Karl P. "Introduction 1991: The Romans Debate Since 1977." In *The Romans Debate*, edited by Karl P. Donfried, xlix–lxxii. 2nd ed. Peabody, MA: Hendrickson, 1995.

———. "A Short Note on Romans 16." In *The Romans Debate*, edited by Karl P. Donfried, 44–52. 2nd ed. Peabody, MA: Hendrickson, 1995.

Donlan, Walter. "The Foundation Legends of Rome: An Example of Dynamic Process." *Classical World* 64.4 (1970) 109–114.

Doty, William G. *Mythography: The Study of Myths and Rituals*. Tuscaloosa: University of Alabama Press, 1986.

Dunn, James D. G. *The New Perspective on Paul*. Rev. ed. Grand Rapids: Eerdmans, 2008.

———. *Romans*. 2 vols. Word Biblical Commentary 38. Nashville: Nelson Reference & Electronic, 1988.

———. "Romans, Letter to the." In *DPL* 838–50.

———. *The Theology of Paul the Apostle*. Grand Rapids: Eerdmans, 1998.

Edmunds, Lowell. "Introduction." In *Approaches to Greek Myth*, edited by Lowell Edmunds, 1–40. Baltimore: Johns Hopkins University Press, 1990.

Elsner, John. "Hagiographic Geography: Travel and Allegory in the *Life of Apollonius of Tyana*." *Journal of Hellenic Studies* 117 (1997) 22–37.

Eskola, Timo. *Theodicy and Predestination in Pauline Soteriology*. WUNT 2/100. Tübingen: Mohr Siebeck, 1998.

Esler, Philip F. *Conflict and Identity in Romans: The Social Setting of Paul's Letter*. Minneapolis: Fortress, 2003.

Fee, Gordon D. *God's Empowering Presence: The Holy Spirit in the Letters of Paul*. Peabody, MA: Hendrickson, 1995.

Feldman, Louis H. *Studies in Josephus' Rewritten Bible*. Journal for the Study of Judaism in the Persian, Hellenistic and Roman Period Supplement Series 58. Leiden: Brill, 1998.

Field, Barbara. "The Discourses behind the Metaphor 'the Church is the Body of Christ' as Used by St. Paul and the Post-Paulines." *Asia Journal of Theology* 6 (1992) 88–107.

Fitzer, Gottfried. "σφραγίς κτλ." In *TDNT* 7:939–53.

Fitzmyer, Joseph A. *Romans*. Anchor Bible 33. New York: Doubleday, 1992.

Forman, Mark. "The Politics of Promise: Echoes of Isaiah 54 in Romans 4:19–21." *Journal for the Study of the New Testament* 31.3 (2009) 301–24.

Fornara, Charles William. *The Nature of History in Ancient Greece and Rome*. Berkeley: University of California Press, 1983.

Furnish, Victor Paul. *Theology and Ethics in Paul*. Nashville: Abingdon, 1968.

Gäckle, Volker. *Die Starken und die Schwachen in Korinth und in Rom Zu Herkunft und Funktion der Antitheses in 1 Kor 8, 1–11,1 und in Rom 14,1–15,13*. WUNT 200. Tübingen: Mohr Siebeck, 2004.

Galinsky, Karl. "Virgil's *Aeneid* and Ovid's *Metamorphoses* as World Literature." In *The Cambridge Companion to the Age of Augustus*, edited by Karl Galinsky, 340–58. Cambridge: Cambridge University Press, 2005.

Garroway, Joshua D. *Paul's Gentile-Jews: Neither Jew nor Gentile, but Both*. New York: Palgrave Macmillan, 2012.

Gathercole, Simon J. *Where Is Boasting? Early Jewish Soteriology and Paul's Response in Romans 1–5*. Grand Rapids: Eerdmans, 2002.

Gruen, Erich S. *Rethinking the Other in Antiquity*. Princeton: Princeton University Press, 2011.

Guerra, Anthony J. *Romans and the Apologetic Tradition: The Purpose, Genre and Audience of Paul's Letter*. Society for New Testament Studies Monograph Studies 81. Cambridge: Cambridge University Press, 1995.

Gupta, Nijay K. "Which 'Body' Is a Temple (1 Corinthians 6:19)? Paul Beyond the Individual/Communal Divide." *Catholic Biblical Quarterly* 72.3 (2010) 518–36.

Hall, Jonathan. *Ethnic Identity in Greek Antiquity*. Cambridge: Cambridge University Press, 1997.

Harland, Philip A. "The Declining *Polis*? Religious Rivalries in Ancient Civic Context." In *Religious Rivalries in the Early Roman Empire and the Rise of Christianity*, edited by Leif E. Vaage, 21–49. Waterloo, ON: Laurier University Press, 2006.

Hays, Richard B. "Have We Found Abraham to Be Our Forefather According to the Flesh?: A Reconsideration of Rom 4:1." *Novum Testamentum* 27.1 (1985) 76–98.

Heil, John Paul. *Romans-Paul's Letter of Hope*. Analecta Biblica 112. Rome: Rome Biblical Institute Press, 1987.

Herodotus. *Histories*. Translated by A. D. Godley. 4 vols. LCL. Cambridge: Harvard University Press, 1920.

Hodge, Caroline Johnson. *If Sons, Then Heirs: A Study of Kinship and Ethnicity in the Letters of Paul*. Oxford: Oxford University Press, 2007.

Homer. *Iliad*. Translated by A. T. Murray. Revised by William F. Wyatt. 2 vols. LCL. Cambridge, MA: Harvard University Press, 1999.

———. *Odyssey*. Translated by A. T. Murray. Revised by George E. Dimock. 2 vols. LCL. Cambridge, MA: Harvard University Press, 1995.

Hooker, Morna D. *From Adam to Christ: Essays on Paul*. Cambridge: Cambridge University Press, 1990.

Horrell, David G. *Solidarity and Difference: A Contemporary Reading of Paul's Ethics*. New York: T. & T. Clark, 2005.

Hultgren, Arland J. *Paul's Letter to the Romans: A Commentary*. Grand Rapids: Eerdmans, 2011.

Hurtado, Larry W. *Lord Jesus Christ: Devotion to Jesus in Earliest Christianity*. Grand Rapids: Eerdmans, 2003.

Jervis, L. Ann. *At the Heart of the Gospel: Suffering in the Earliest Christian Message*. Grand Rapids: Eerdmans, 2007.

Jewett, Robert. "The Corruption and Redemption of Creation: Reading Rom 8:18–23 within the Imperial Context." In *Paul and the Roman Imperial Order*, edited by Richard A. Horsley, 25–46. Harrisburg, PA: Trinity, 2004.

———. *Romans: A Commentary*. Edited by Eldon Jay Epp. Hermeneia 59. Minneapolis: Fortress, 2007.

Jipp, Joshua W. "Rereading the Story of Abraham, Isaac, and Us in Romans 4." *Journal for the Study of the New Testament* 32 (2009) 217–42.

Josephus. *Against Apion*. Translated by H. St. J. Thackeray. LCL. Cambridge: Harvard University Press, 1926.

———. *Jewish Antiquities*. Translated by H. St. J. Thackeray, et al. 9 vols. LCL. Cambridge: Harvard University Press, 1998.

———. *The Life*. Translated by H. St. Thackeray. LCL. Cambridge: Harvard University Press, 1926.

Kaminsky, Joel S. "Israel's Election and the Other in Biblical, Second Temple, and Rabbinic Thought." In *The "Other" in Second Temple Judaism: Essays in Honor of John J. Collins*, edited by Daniel C. Harlow et al., 17–30. Grand Rapids: Eerdmans, 2011.

Kamtekar, Rachana. "Distinction Without a Difference? Race and *Genos* in Plato." In *Philosophers on Race: Critical Essays,* edited by Julie K. Ward and Tommy L. Lott, 1–13. Oxford: Blackwell, 2002.

Karris, Robert J. "Romans 14:1—15:13 and the Occasion of Romans." In *The Romans Debate,* edited by Karl P. Donfried, 65–84. 2nd ed. Peabody, MA: Hendrickson, 1995.

Käsemann, Ernst. *Commentary on Romans.* Translated and edited by Geoffrey W. Bromiley. Grand Rapids: Eerdmans, 1980.

Keener, Craig S. *Romans.* New Covenant Commentary Series. Eugene, OR: Cascade, 2009.

Kim, Yung Suk. *Christ's Body in Corinth: The Politics of a Metaphor.* Minneapolis: Fortress, 2008.

Kuecker, Aaron J. *The Spirit and the 'Other': Social Identity, Ethnicity and Intergroup Reconciliation in Luke-Acts.* New York: T. & T. Clark, 2011.

Laato, Timo. *Paul and Judaism: An Anthropological Approach.* Translated by T. McElwain. Atlanta: Scholars, 1995.

Lampe, Peter. "The Roman Christians of Romans 16." In *The Romans Debate*, edited by Karl P. Donfried, 216–30. 2nd ed. Peabody, MA: Hendrickson, 1995.

Laurence, Ray. "Territory, Ethnonyms and Geography: The Construction of Identity in Roman Italy." In *Cultural Identity in the Roman Empire,* edited by Ray Laurence and Joanne Berry, 95–110. New York: Routledge, 2001.

Lee, Jae Won. "Paul and Ethnic Difference in Romans." In *They were All Together in One Place?: Toward Minority Biblical Criticism*, edited by Randall C. Bailey et al., 141–57. Semeia Studies 57. Atlanta: SBL, 2009.

Lee, Michelle V. *Paul, the Stoics, and the Body of Christ.* Society for New Testament Studies Monograph Series 137. Cambridge: Cambridge University Press, 2006.

Levison, John R. *Portraits of Adam in Early Judaism: From Sirach to 2 Baruch.* Journal for the Study of the Pseudepigrapha Supplement Series 1. Sheffield, UK: JSOT, 1988.

Lieu, Judith M. *Christian Identity in the Jewish and Graeco-Roman World.* Oxford: Oxford University Press, 2004.

Lightstone, Jack N. "Roman Diaspora Judaism." In *A Companion to Roman Religion*, edited by Jörg Rüpke, 345–77. Oxford: Blackwell, 2007.

Lowe, Bruce A. "Oh dia! How Is Romans 4:25 to be Understood?" *Journal of Theological Studies* 57 (2006) 149–57.

Lucas, Alec J. "Reorienting the Structural Paradigm and Social Significance of Romans 1:18–32." *Journal of Biblical Literature* 131.1 (2012) 121–41.

Marshall, Eireann. "Constructing the Self and Other in Cyrenaica." In *Cultural Identity in the Roman Empire*, edited by Ray Laurence and Joanne Berry, 49–63. New York: Routledge, 2001.

McVay, John K. "The Human Body as Social and Political Metaphor in Stoic Literature and Early Christian Writers." *Bulletin of the American Society of Papyrologists* 37.1 (2000) 135–47.

Meeks, Wayne A. *The First Urban Christians: The Social World of the Apostle Paul.* 2nd ed. New Haven: Yale University Press, 2003.

Mengestu, Abera M. *God as Father in Paul: Kinship Language and Identity Formation in Early Christianity.* Eugene, OR: Pickwick, 2013.

Metzger, Bruce M. *A Textual Commentary on the Greek New Testament.* 2nd ed. Stuttgart: German Bible Society, 1994.

Minear, Paul S. *Images of the Church in the New Testament*. Louisville: Westminster John Knox, 2004.

Moo, Douglas. *The Epistle to the Romans*. New International Commentary on the New Testament. Grand Rapids: Eerdmans, 1996.

Nanos, Mark D. *The Mystery of Romans: The Jewish Context of Paul's Letter*. Minneapolis: Fortress, 1996.

Niskanen, Paul. *The Human and the Divine in History: Herodotus and the Book of Daniel*. Journal for the Study of the Old Testament Supplement Series 396. New York: T. & T. Clark, 2004.

O'Brien, P. T. "Letters, Letter Form." In *DPL*, 550–53.

Ochsenmeier, Erwin. *Mal, souffrance et justice de Dieu selon Romains 1–3 Étude exégétique et théologique*. Beihefte zur Zeitschrift für die neutestamentliche Wissenschaft 155. Berlin: de Gruyter, 2007.

———. "Romans 1:11–12 A Clue to the Purpose of Romans?" *Ephemerides theologicae lovanienses* 83 (2007) 395–406.

Olster, David M. "Classical Ethnography and Early Christianity." In *The Formulation of Christianity by Conflict through the Ages*, edited by Katherine B. Free, 9–31. Symposium Series 34. Lewiston, NY: Edwin Mellen, 1993.

Orlin, Eric. "Urban Religion in the Middle and Late Republic." In *A Companion to Roman Religion*, edited by Jörg Rüpke, 58–70. Oxford: Blackwell, 2007.

Osiek, Carolyn. "Romans 'Down the Pike': Glimpses from Later Years." In *Celebrating Romans: Template for Pauline Theology: Essays in Honor of Robert Jewett*, edited by Sheila E. McGinn, 149–61. Grand Rapids: Eerdmans, 2004.

Pate, Marvin C. *The Reverse of the Curse: Paul, Wisdom, and the Law*. Tübingen: Mohr Siebeck, 2000.

Pelser, G. M. M. "Once More the Body of Christ in Paul." *Neotestamentica* 32.2 (1998) 525–45.

Plutarch. *Numa*. Translated by Bernadotte Perrin. LCL. Cambridge: Harvard University Press, 1914.

Preston, Rebecca. "Roman Questions, Greek Answers: Plutarch and the Construction of Identity." In *Being Greek under Rome: Cultural Identity, the Second Sophistic and the Development of Empire*, edited by Simon Goldhill, 86–119. Cambridge: Cambridge University Press, 2001.

Rabens, Volker. "'Von Jerusalem und rings umher . . . ' (Römer 15:19). Die paulinische Missionsstrategie im Dickicht der Städte." In *Das frühe Christentum und die Stadt*, edited by Reinhard von Bendemann and Markus Tiwald, 219–37. Stuttgart: Kohlhammer, 2012.

Rengstorf, Karl Heinrich. "σημεῖον." In *TDNT* 7:200–69.

Richardson, Peter. "Augustan-Era Synagogues in Rome." In *Judaism and Christianity in First-Century Rome*, edited by Karl P. Donfried and Peter Richardson, 17–29. Grand Rapids: Eerdmans, 1998.

Ricoeur, Paul. *The Conflict of Interpretations: Essays in Hermeneutics*. Edited by Don Ihde. Evanston, IL: Northwestern University Press, 1974.

Ridderbos, Herman. *Paul: An Outline of His Theology*. Translated by John Richard De Witt. Grand Rapids: Eerdmans, 1975.

Rutgers, Leonard Victor. "Roman Policy towards the Jews: Expulsions from the City of Rome during the First Century C.E." In *Judaism and Christianity in First-Century Rome*, edited by Karl P. Donfried and Peter Richardson, 93–116. Grand Rapids: Eerdmans, 1998.

Sanday, William and Arthur C. Headlam. *Romans*. International Critical Commentary. 5th ed. Edinburgh: Clark, 1902.

Sanders, E. P. *Paul and Palestinian Judaism: A Comparison of Patterns of Religion*. Minneapolis: Fortress, 1977.

Sandnes, Karl Olav. "Abraham, the Friend of God, in Rom 5." *Zeitschrift für die neutestamentliche Wissenschaft und die Kunde der älteren Kirche* 99 (2008) 124–28.

―――. *Belly and Body in the Pauline Epistles*. Society for New Testament Studies Monograph Series 120. New York: Cambridge University Press, 2002.

Schliesser, Benjamin. *Abraham's Faith in Romans 4: Paul's Concept of Faith in Light of the History of Reception in Genesis* 15:6. WUNT 224. Tübingen: Mohr Siebeck, 2007.

Schwartz, Seth. "Language, Power and Identity in Ancient Palestine." *Past & Present* 148 (1995) 3–47.

Seyoon, Kim. *Christ and Caesar: The Gospel and the Roman Empire in the Writings of Paul and Luke*. Grand Rapids: Eerdmans, 2008.

Skinner, Joseph E. *The Invention of Greek Ethnography: From Homer to Herodotus*. Oxford: Oxford University Press, 2012.

Stanley, Christopher D. "The Ethnic Context of Paul's Letters." In *Christian Origins and Hellenistic Judaism*, vol. 2, edited by Stanley E. Porter and Andrew W. Pitts, 177–201. Leiden: Brill, 2012.

Sterling, Gregory E. *Historiography: Josephos, Luke-Acts & Apologetic Historiography*. Supplements to Novum Testamentum 64. Leiden: Brill, 1992.

Stowers, Stanley K. *Letter Writing in Greco-Roman Antiquity*. Philadelphia: Westminster, 1986.

―――. *A Rereading of Romans: Justice, Jews, & Gentiles*. New Haven: Yale University Press, 1994.

Strabo. *Geography*. Translated by Horace Leonard Jones. 7 vols. LCL. Cambridge: Harvard University Press, 1926–1965.

Stumpff, Albrecht. "ἱκανός." In *TDNT* 3:402–406.

Tajfel, Henri. *Human Groups and Social Categories: Studies in Social Psychology*. Cambridge: Cambridge University Press, 1981.

―――. "Introduction." In *Social Identity and Intergroup Relations*, edited by Henri Tajfel, 1–11. Cambridge: Cambridge University Press, 1982.

Talbert, Charles H. *Romans*. Smyth & Helwys Bible Commentary 24. Macon, GA: Smyth & Helwys, 2002.

Tellbe, Mikael. *Paul between Synagogue and State: Christians, Jews, and Civic Authorities in 1 Thessalonians, Romans, and Philippians*. Stockholm: Almquist & Wiksell, 2001.

Tobin, Thomas H. *Paul's Rhetoric in Its Contexts: The Argument of Romans*. Peabody, MA: Hendrickson, 2004.

Tucker, J. Brian. *"Remain in Your Calling": Paul and the Continuation of Social Identities in 1 Corinthians*. Eugene, OR: Pickwick, 2011.

Turner, John C. "Towards a Cognitive Redefinition of the Social Group." In *Social Identity and Intergroup Relations*, edited by Henri Tajfel, 15–40. Cambridge: Cambridge University Press, 1982.

Ukwuegbu, Bernard O. *The Emergence of Christian Identity in Paul's Letter to the Galatians: A Social-Scientific Investigation into the Root Causes for the Parting of the Way between Christianity and Judaism.* Arbeiten zur Interkulturalität 4. Bonn: Borengässer, 2003.

Van Kooten, George H. *Paul's Anthropology in Context: The Image of God, Assimilation to God, and Tripartite Man in Ancient Judaism, Ancient Philosophy and Early Christianity.* Tübingen: Mohr Siebeck, 2008.

Virgil. *Aeneid.* Translated by H. Rushton Fairclough. 2 vols. LCL. Cambridge: Harvard University Press, 1916.

Visscher, Gerhard H. *Romans 4 and the New Perspective on Paul: Faith Embraces the Promise.* New York: Peter Lang, 2009.

Wagner, J. Ross. *Heralds of the Good News: Isaiah and Paul in Concert in the Letter to the Romans.* Leiden: Brill, 2002.

Walters, James C. "Romans, Jews, and Christians: The Impact of the Romans on Jewish/Christian Relations in First-Century Rome." In *Judaism and Christianity in First-Century Rome,* edited by Karl P. Donfried and Peter Richardson, 175–95. Grand Rapids: Eerdmans, 1998.

Watson, Francis. "The Law in Romans." In *Reading Paul's Letter to the Romans,* edited by Jerry L. Sumney, 93–108. Atlanta: SBL, 2012.

———. *Paul, Judaism, and the Gentiles: Beyond the New Perspective.* Revised and enlarged edition. Grand Rapids: Eerdmans, 2007.

White, L. Michael. "Epilogue as Prologue: Herod and the Jewish Experience of Augustan Rule." In *The Cambridge Companion to the Age of Augustus,* edited by Karl Galinsky, 361–88. Cambridge: Cambridge University Press, 2005.

Wilson, Stephen G. "Rivalry and Defection." In *Religious Rivalries in the Early Roman Empire and the Rise of Christianity,* edited by Leif E. Vaage, 51–71. Waterloo, ON: Laurier University Press, 2006.

Wilson, Walter T. "Urban Legends: Acts 10:1—11:18 and the Strategies of Greco-Roman Foundation Narratives." *Journal of Biblical Literature* 120.1 (2001) 77–99.

Witherington III, Ben. *Conflict and Community in Corinth: A Socio-Rhetorical Commentary on 1 and 2 Corinthians.* Grand Rapids: Eerdmans, 1995.

———. *The Paul Quest: The Renewed Search for the Jew of Tarsus.* Downers Grove, IL: InterVarsity, 1998.

Witherington III, Ben, and Darlene Hyatt. *Paul's Letter to the Romans: A Socio-Rhetorical Commentary.* Grand Rapids: Eerdmans, 2004.

Wright, N. T. *The New Testament and the People of God.* Minneapolis: Fortress, 1992.

———. *Paul and the Faithfulness of God.* 2 vols. Minneapolis: Fortress, 2013.

———. *Romans.* New Interpreter's Bible 10. Nashville: Abingdon, 2002.

www.ingramcontent.com/pod-product-compliance
Lightning Source LLC
Chambersburg PA
CBHW060508300426
44112CB00017B/2588